Ideas of monarchical reform

MANCHESTER
1824

Manchester University Press

STUDIES IN EARLY MODERN EUROPEAN HISTORY

This series aims to publish
challenging and innovative research in all areas
of early modern continental history.
The editors are committed to encouraging work
that engages with current historiographical
debates, adopts an interdisciplinary
approach, or makes an original contribution
to our understanding of the period.

SERIES EDITORS

Joseph Bergin, William G. Naphy, Penny Roberts and Paolo Rossi

Also available in the series

Full details of the series are available
at www.manchesteruniversitypress.com

Ideas of monarchical reform

Fénelon, Jacobitism and the political works of the Chevalier Ramsay

ANDREW MANSFIELD

Manchester University Press

Published by Manchester University Press
Altricham Street, Manchester M1 7JA, UK
www.manchesteruniversitypress.co.uk

British Library Cataloguing-in-Publication Data
A catalogue record for this book is available from the British Library

Library of Congress Cataloging-in-Publication Data applied for

ISBN 978 0 7190 8837 7 *hardback*

First published 2015

The publisher has no responsibility for the persistence or accuracy of URLs for any external or third-party internet websites referred to in this book, and does not guarantee that any content on such websites is, or will remain, accurate or appropriate.

Typeset in Perpetua with Albertus display
by Koinonia, Manchester
Printed in Great Britain
by TJ International Ltd, Padstow

For Samantha

Contents

Acknowledgements

This book developed from my D.Phil. thesis at the University of Sussex and has morphed into something much larger, and much improved. As a consequence I have accrued a number of debts of gratitude that are both professional and personal. On a professional level I would like to thank the editors at MUP for their support and help in the writing of this monograph, as well as the anonymous reviewer whose advice was perspicacious and most helpful. To those involved in the process of formulating ideas and writing the monograph I would particularly like to thank Cesare Cuttica for his invaluable advice and comradeship over the past few years. I would also like to single out Doohwan Ahn, Sophie Bisset, Nick Funke, Knud Haakonssen, Rob Iliffe, Jim Livesey, Amanda McKeever, Mia Saugman, Norman Vance, and Richard Whatmore for their support. I am grateful to the Sussex Centre for Intellectual History, plus my colleagues in the Department of History, and former students. For other assistance and answering repeated email queries Eveline Cruickshanks, Peter van den Dungen, Miriam Eliav-Feldon, Anna Lazzarino Del Grosso, Colin Kidd, Enrico Pasini, Murray Pittock, Paul Schuurman, Christoph Schmitt-Maaß, Koen Stapelbroek, Daniel Szechi, Paul Wood, as well as Richard Bourke, Quentin Skinner, and those who participated in the Popular Sovereignty Project.

Most of all I would like to thank my family and friends, some of whom have lived the book and Ramsay with me, especially Kay and Lee who allowed me to invade their house to write sections of the monograph. I wish to dedicate the book to my daughters Charlotte and Lana who have endured my obsessive hours working, but principally I dedicate this to my wife Samantha (Sam). She has managed the highs and lows as I worked on the project with great toleration, and taken on the lion's share of duties at home to make it possible, while supporting me throughout.

Note on the text

The spelling, punctuation, italicisation and use of capital letters in quotations has followed the original in both English and French. All translations are my own unless stated.

Introduction

The political ideology that emerged during the seventeenth century in Britain and France had a powerful effect on the theory of the eighteenth century. Following the Restoration of Charles II in 1660, the Stuart monarchy's efforts to centralise government triggered an abundance of hostile publications. Such works propounded principles of liberty, religious toleration, and the existence of a mixed constitution that retained an important role for Parliament. The successful defence of these tenets in the Glorious Revolution (1688) saw other problems come to the fore. Deeply entrenched opposing perspectives continued to shape ideology over issues like the revolutionary settlement, religion, the growing importance of political economy, as well as governmental and civic corruption. The first three decades of the eighteenth century therefore witnessed a perpetuation of issues from the seventeenth century and the reliance on its ideology to tackle similar or persistent uncertainties. In France this active public sphere of discussion was often inhibited by the censorship of Louis XIV's government. Yet from the end of the seventeenth century concerns were raised in France over the state's aggressive foreign policy and the ineffectiveness of the king's form of (absolute) sovereignty. After Louis XIV's death in 1715 these questions were raised far more openly, as some French political theorists looked to British ideology and its model of government for answers to its ills. The transference of ideas between the two states during this period, not greatly investigated in historiography, witnessed the development of several shared perspectives by the 1720s. Moreover, a number of theorists specifically acted as conduits or channels for these political ideas aiding their transference between the two states.

Andrew Michael Ramsay (1686–1743) was a Scottish émigré who spent most of his adult life in France after leaving Scotland on a journey of spiritual and intellectual enlightenment. He was a Jacobite, a deist, a leading European freemason, a biographer, and pedagogue. Ramsay also briefly acted as tutor to the young Bonnie Prince Charlie at the exiled Jacobite court, until a duel forced him to leave Rome in disgrace. A man of letters, his work *Les Voyages de Cyrus*

(1727) was one of the publishing successes of the eighteenth century. He was very well connected and knew the Archbishop Fénelon, Pierre Poiret, Cardinal Fleury, Viscount Bolingbroke, Jonathan Swift, Baron de Montesquieu, Voltaire (who despised Ramsay), and David Hume among others. Despite these accomplishments, Ramsay remains a largely shadowy figure of whom little is really known, and his political works have been frequently misunderstood. His initial resistance to the development of popular government provides an insightful view of early Enlightenment political theory, when the seventeenth-century preoccupation with monarchical supremacy was called into question by the British model of mixed government.

During the period between 1719 and 1732 Ramsay wrote five works that contained his political thought. These were the *Essay de Politique* (1719), *Essay philosophique sur le gouvernement civil* (1721), *L'Histoire de la Vie de Fénelon* (1723), *Les Voyages de Cyrus* (1727), and *A Plan of Education for a Young Prince* (1732). With the exception of the last, all of his political works were written in French before being published in English.[1] Two important points arise from this. First, Ramsay's decision to write in French accentuates his association with that country and the influence it held over his ideas. In spite of moving away from his native Scotland, his connections and Jacobitism also firmly rooted him in British thought and traditions. Ramsay thereby provides a fascinating example of an intellectual firmly embedded in the culture and philosophy of Britain and France who integrated with both, blending their political thought.[2] Second, regardless of the short span of time that these works cover, they reveal two phases of thought. The first, which includes the two editions of the *Essay* and the *Vie* were designed to promote a Jacobite restoration to the British throne. The theory contained within them not only grappled with the consequences of the Glorious Revolution (1688), it also used ideology prevalent from the seventeenth century to oppose the removal of James II. In the second phase Ramsay's focus broadened beyond political considerations to encompass an enduring interest in religion, mysticism, education, science, and political economy. This greater representation of his eclectic interests not only witnessed a shift in emphasis and the inspirations that affected his ideas, it enabled Ramsay in the *Plan* to perform a volte face on his earlier political views.

This monograph is therefore not a biography of Ramsay, although it does include a biographical account of his life (in Chapter 6) pertaining to his political works. Rather, it critiques his political output as seen across the five works during a thirteen year period within a much wider political and ideological context. They chart the impact of Jacobitism on his work, his part as a propagandist for the cause of James Stuart, and his place in the history of political thought as a theorist. His work moved beyond simple refutations of the Hanoverian succession under George I, to the creation of a system that explained the origins of government stressing the illegality of 1688. The engagement in such a discourse saw an ambitious attempt to develop a universal 'plan of government' that would combat the ills of modern governments and society. Ramsay's background and intellectual debts invite a re-examination of British and French political thought regarding monarchical reform during the early eighteenth century. In extensive contextual chapters, therefore, this monograph underlines the importance of seventeenth-century ideology and history on the eighteenth century. A time when both nations were confronting the legacies of the seventeenth century: the rule of Charles II and James II in Britain, and Louis XIV in France. This theory was attached to a persistent application of classical political and religious wisdom, as Ramsay, like others, searched history and mythology to combat modern corruption with reason and civic virtue. The two aims of this work will be: first, to survey currents of political thought in Britain and France within their historical context from the 1660s into the 1730s, while exploring the transference of ideas between them; and, second, to situate Ramsay's work into this context while assessing his role as a conduit for the two states.

A time of transformation

Ramsay's application of French and British thought from both the seventeenth and eighteenth centuries occurred in an environment of great change. During the seventeenth century many European states began to embrace the idea of absolute monarchy, as bureaucracies were centralised to cope with a continuous theatre of war.[3] France and Britain shared many similar experiences at this time. Both had undergone strong religious and political upheavals from the sixteenth century that had led to bloodshed, violence, and persecution. From the early seventeenth century, James I of England and Louis XIII of France had endeavoured to gain independence from the elective institutions of the state. By the middle of the century both nations had suffered civil wars driven by a reaction against state centralisation and the bid to dominate government, exacerbated by religious turmoil. The undeveloped and infrequent nature of the elective institutions of France proved a much easier obstacle for Louis XIV to overcome than for the Stuarts in England. Yet as revisionists have shown, Louis XIV did not truly succeed in becoming absolute.[4] A great deal of cooperation with the various institutions and orders of the state in fact took place, although the king did possess an aura of supremacy rarely matched in European history. Louis XIV's conscious personification of the French state engendered a belief both internally and abroad that France was absolute. The consequences of this absolutism spread beyond the borders of France, drawing Europe into recurrent conflict and greater competition.

Simultaneously, his first-cousin Charles II had been restored to the throne of England. Charles's restoration had been a somewhat botched affair. The nation hastily embraced monarchy after the death of Oliver Cromwell and his son Richard Cromwell's weak leadership in preference to renewed uncertainty and potential civil war. Problematically, the Restoration settlement returned the king with much of the powers of his executed father, leaving key political and religious issues that instigated the Civil Wars unresolved.[5] While Charles initially followed a concessionary path, by the 1670s (new) fears emerged within the aristocracy that the king was striving to emulate his absolutist father or Catholic French cousin.[6] Throughout the Exclusion Crisis (1679–81), when the Whigs attempted to exclude the king's Catholic brother and heir James Duke of York from the succession, ideology arose to resist arbitrary government (tyranny). Charles's defeat of the Bill of Exclusion with the assistance of a pension from Louis XIV placed him in a position close to independence from Parliament. After his death, Whig concerns regarding James (II) came to fruition through his hasty struggle to consolidate absolute ascendance over government, leading to the 1688 Revolution. James was removed from power by a combination of leading British aristocrats, the people and William of Orange's Dutch-led invasionary fleet. The brief moment of predominant national unity enjoyed quickly dissipated, as disagreement emerged surrounding the Convention government's declaration that James II had abdicated. Division, faction, party (in-)fighting and opposition followed the revolutionary settlement, as some disputed the legality of removing a king and his legitimate heir from the monarchical succession, spawning the Jacobites in the process.

As Britain responded to the removal of another Stuart king and confronted the consequences of electing their monarchs in 1688, the early eighteenth century continued to be divisive. Not only did Britain experience problems with the High-Anglican Church as it battled to sustain its supremacy in an era of religious plurality and toleration, political parties guided by religious affiliations fought over the inheritance of 1688. In a process that witnessed the growing prominence of the Commons to the British constitution, antipathy between the Whig and Tory parties fed by older ideology shaped modern political behaviour. Reaching back to ideas that opposed Charles II's tyranny in the 1670s and Exclusion Crisis, the Whigs and Tories continued to rely on the principles that gave rise to their party doctrines. In the eighteenth century the Tories' strict reliance on the tenets of indefeasible hereditary right, passive obedience and non-resistance reinforced a firm commitment to the notion that James II had vacated his throne by fleeing to France. To forge the revolutionary settlement, differences of opinion over 1688 as an act of resistance against tyranny were initially set aside, but over time a growing number of Whigs propounded a view of resistance to James II. Added into this crucible of enmity and faction were groups opposed to

1688, particularly the Jacobites. Initially supported by Louis XIV, from 1708 a period of intensive Jacobite activity ensued under James Stuart (the 'Pretender'): James II's Catholic son and heir. Encouraged by Queen Anne's poor health, the outpouring of vituperation in the political literature between 1708 and 1714 reflected the hostility and fears of a Jacobite restoration. While Jacobite hopes were ended by a trifecta of the Treaty of Utrecht (1713), George I's accession (1714), and the failed Jacobite rising (1715–16), opposition remained. A new commercial society from the 1710s produced a rising perception that the effects of the Financial Revolution were corrupting government. Attempts by the executive (the crown and Whig ministry) to assert its superiority stimulated cries against the erosion of political liberty, the balanced constitution, and traditional society in a degenerated age of politics. In the process, wider public debate and Parliament's pre-eminence underlined the shift away from later Stuart absolutism as both sides utilised seventeenth-century doctrines to oppose or support such an event.

The context in which Ramsay wrote therefore saw a continued confrontation and adaptation in both countries with the legacy of the seventeenth century. Louis XIV's death in 1715 after a seventy-two-year reign meant that the regency period (1715–23) for the child Louis XV under the duc d'Orléans, originally offered hope of reform for the French state. After years of Louis XIV's dominance over European geopolitics through a bellicose foreign policy of aggrandisement, a fresh perspective on government policy was desired. Ideas for such reform had begun in the 1690s when France's foreign and economic policies began to reveal administrative deficiencies. Its inadequacy and reliance on the will of the king no longer suited the demands of a newer commercial age that had witnessed the rise of Britain, now allied with the Dutch. Some members of the high aristocracy – notably the Burgundy Circle around the future Dauphin, the duc de Bourgogne (1683–1712) – began drafting reform plans that would transform France after the death of Louis XIV. Bourgogne's premature death ended many of the group's aspirations to ease the burden of rule under one man (king). While Orléans briefly implemented a limited version of the Burgundy Circle's initiative for expanded government (the polysynody), by 1718 the regent had returned to Louis XIV's method of sovereignty.[7] Yet such notions of extended administration galvanised visions of a potentially mixed constitution that would step away from domination by a single will. The impact of the Circle's leading member, the Archbishop Fénelon, and his attack on absolutism in favour of public liberty in *Télémaque* (1699) was potent. In the 1720s influenced by Fénelon and British ideas of governance, political theorists such as Montesquieu and Voltaire looked across the Channel for possible solutions to escape despotism and generate public liberty under a balanced government.

Ramsay offers an important bridge between the thought of France and Britain for two particular reasons. First, as stated, Ramsay's position as a Scots-born naturalised Frenchman saw him engage a confluence of ideas in his work when assaulting the repercussions of 1688 as a Jacobite. Ramsay grappled with theory from both nations in both centuries (and beyond), to tackle the shift towards the growing role of Parliament in contemporary politics. He blamed popular government as the progenitor of revolution and disharmony. Relying on a juxtaposition of classical and English history, Ramsay set out to confirm that Britain's current problems had been generated by the gradual inclusion of Parliament in the legislation, a process accelerated under the Tudors. The internecine turmoil experienced in the seventeenth century had been a consequence of this development. As history had revealed, the rampant egotism of the multitude always overturned the social order and established government for its own anarchic ends. Second, when Ramsay settled in France he initially lived at Cambrai with the Archbishop Fénelon. After the prelate's death, Ramsay was employed by the Marquis de Fénelon to edit his uncle's work – Ramsay published a comprehensive edition of *Télémaque* in 1717 – and composed the first biography. Ramsay's position proved to be alluring to the Jacobites, who pursued him in order to exploit his connection with Fénelon in order to portray the Catholic James Stuart in a light favourable to the British people.[8] This association with the legacy of Fénelon saw Ramsay's admittance into the famous *Club de l'Entresol*, which included Montesquieu and Bolingbroke. Alongside the club's determination to discuss modern government was a genuine desire to grapple with the ideas of Fénelon.[9] It was here that Ramsay read out drafts of his *Les Voyages de Cyrus* prior to publication sharing his opinions on government and religion, outlooks that were potentially influential on Bolingbroke in particular. Bolingbroke's reputation as a conduit for French thought into Britain and vice versa through Montesquieu, Voltaire, and members of the *Entresol* has recently been reappraised.[10] Yet a number of ideas and especially Bolingbroke's reliance on a natural law system to underpin his view of (ranked) society are very similar to Ramsay's. It is therefore argued here that Ramsay was an important channel in his own right, who relied on a number of innovations in political thought that were of later value to Bolingbroke and others.

Ramsay's endeavours

The historiography on Ramsay is not extensive, particularly in English. While Ramsay is a name known to historians of political thought, a detailed review of his political works in English has not been carried out. Much of the earlier references to Ramsay can be found in the biographers of Fénelon often pointing to and using Ramsay's *Vie de Fénelon* as a blueprint for their own works. The knowledge that Ramsay stayed with Fénelon at his Archdiocese of Cambrai for a period of over two years, led to an assumed intimacy between the two men. It also generated the sustained opinion that Ramsay's *Essay* provided a continuation of Fénelon's political principles as expressed to him privately. Critically, many such as Cardinal Bausset, Paul Janet, and Chanoine Moïse Cagnac claimed that Ramsay's ideas related to a conversation between Fénelon and James Stuart when the prince visited Cambrai in 1709.[11] The difficulty with this claim, unknown to many commentators, was that he did not arrive in Cambrai until 1710 so could not have been present. Ramsay's duplicitous cultivation of his presence at the meeting and the wider conviction he possessed an intimate private knowledge of the Archbishop's thought,[12] meant that into the 1960s the *Essay* was supposed an accurate depiction of Fénelon's political values.[13]

In the early twentieth century scepticism began to emerge regarding the veracity of this view. Albert Cherel made two important breakthroughs in relation to Ramsay's political thought. The first was that it did not strictly match Fénelon's own philosophy; rather, it appeared to represent a version of the Archbishop that Ramsay preferred.[14] For Cherel, Ramsay deviated at times in depicting Fénelon's character as a man in the *Vie* and also strayed away from his exact political principles, although they were essentially accurate. Second, the reason for this was that Ramsay had used his *Essay* to promote Jacobitism. Both of these opinions were followed by G.D. Henderson, Ramsay's only English-speaking biographer. He moved further than Cherel to argue that it had become necessary to shape the legacy of Fénelon to fit a perception that would chime with Jacobite endeavours to promote James Stuart's cause.[15] A growing involvement in the Parisian Jacobite movement had provoked Ramsay to use the high opinion of Fénelon for his own propaganda. It has recently been stated by Gabriel Glickman, that the Jacobites did in fact deliberately seek out Ramsay due to his association with Fénelon.[16] This reputation and James Stuart's regard for the Archbishop were to be exploited to soften British Protestant hearts towards a Catholic Stuart monarch aided by the industrious Ramsay.

Beginning in the twentieth century, doubts began to surface concerning Ramsay's claim to be appropriating the principles of Fénelon. It was noted that while Fénelon's *Télémaque* strongly rebuffed despotism, Ramsay's *Essay* contained natural law elements that looked remarkably like absolutism.[17] Commentators from this point have subsequently proposed a number of influences, the most prevalent of which are Hobbes and Filmer included by Ramsay to undermine Locke's justification of 1688.[18] The *Essay* was thereby a Jacobite denunciation of the Whiggish principles embodied in Locke's *Two Treatises* that vindicated the Revolution. Jean Molino advanced beyond this to state indefatigably that the *Essay*'s proclivities for absolute monarchy did not reflect the ideas of Fénelon at all. The Archbishop's concerns with public misery had been stripped away,[19] and Molino perceived an absence of Fénelon in the *Essay*, because he could not discern his religious sentimentality.[20] Recent scholarship frequently underlines Ramsay's connection to Fénelon through a shared reliance on religion in their political thought. Yet this assertion has been tempered by some who have noted other influences beyond the Archbishop on Ramsay's political thought. Contemporaries noted that *Cyrus* in particular, plagiarised the work of Bossuet in describing ancient civilisations and theology, an observation recently shared by Doohwan Ahn which I here extend to the *Essay*.[21] *Cyrus* was a vehicle Ramsay harnessed to promulgate a mélange of ancient and modern mythology, theology, and historical observation to generate modern virtue, unity, and order.[22] Problematically, commentators believe his religion and Catholicism were the primary motivation for Ramsay's works, dominating his political considerations and informing his Jacobite sensibilities.[23] This reflects a general underestimation of Ramsay's focus, ability and ambition as a political theorist, whose inspiration was far more diverse than credited. As is shown in Chapters 7 and 8, not only were religion and politics frequently entwined for Ramsay but his 'plan of government' drew on an assorted range of sources.

Chapters

With this historiography in mind, it is vital to extrapolate the perceived truths of Ramsay's political works and the elements that are not accurate. This monograph unpacks these interpretations and provides an outline of Ramsay's political works and the motivations behind them. To achieve this it is essential to pay close attention to Ramsay's thought within its British and French contexts, and a large portion of this monograph is given to discussing them. Not only does this place Ramsay's works into these contexts while elucidating his motivations, theory, and impact; it delineates and considers important contributions to ideas on monarchical reform in the early eighteenth century. For this consideration to be realised, it is necessary to chart the developments in both countries from 1660 into the 1730s. The work comprises three parts: the British contextual Chapters (1 and 2), the French contextual Chapters (3–5), and the chapters on Ramsay (6–8). This allows the monograph to accomplish its aims of examining both this period of political thought in the two states while placing Ramsay into this history.

Chapters 1 and 2 entitled 'Division and unity' chart the progress of British thought from 1660 through to the late 1730s, and should essentially be viewed as one continuous chapter separated into two parts. Despite the book's claim to delineate early eighteenth-century political theory, it would not be possible to examine this period without analysing the late seventeenth century. Both the Exclusion Crisis and Glorious Revolution shaped historical events and the accompanying ideology that many, including Ramsay, were attempting to engage with in the 1720s and early 1730s. The response to potential absolute government in the 1670s and 1680s formed ideas for and against public liberty, the monarch's rule through Parliament, republicanism, toleration, and the corruption of the constitution. These chapters are applied to examine some of the ideology in this period as Britain moved from the Restoration through the Revolution to the growing ascendancy of Parliament. The reaction to parliamentary (popular) Whiggish power covers the *Answer* debate between Benjamin Hoadly and Charles Leslie. In Chapter 7 this discussion is revealed to have been used belatedly by Ramsay to undermine Whig justifications for 1688. Rather than reacting directly to Filmer and Locke he followed Leslie (a Jacobite) to condemn the Whig firebrand Hoadly, whom he mocked in the *Essay*. Chapter 2 ends with a description of the country platform that provided oppositional ideology to the Whig Oligarchy and the perceived corruption on government and society in the 1720s. The country methodology employed by both *Cato's Letters* and Bolingbroke to challenge government corruption had been utilised earlier by Ramsay.

Following British dialogues on liberty and the rejection of absolute monarchy, Chapter 3 looks at the 'political principles of Fénelon'. Independently of British thought but contemporaneously with it, from the 1690s the French began to wrestle with alternatives to Louis XIV's absolute rule. Louis's circumventing of the high aristocracy from their traditional role as the king's servants in government, led Fénelon to deplore the ineffective observation of the public good as the people suffered and moral degeneracy permeated society. *Télémaque* used Prince Telemachus's education for rule through virtue, justice, liberty, and frugality to infamously critique the ravages of luxury and war on France. The incredible success of *Télémaque* meant that Fénelon's political legacy has been predominantly secured in a work written for the duc de Bourgogne when a child and published without his consent. Chapter 3 argues that it is in the later reform works for the adult Bourgogne that the Archbishop's pragmatic political mind was truly evident. It was this Fénelon that Ramsay chose to ignore as editor and author, deciding to trade off the fame of *Télémaque* to promote Jacobitism. The chapter serves to outline the differences between the two men's thought, as well as revealing a desire to reform France which may have been actuated had Bourgogne lived to be king. In terms of the monograph's structure, it has been placed after a discussion of Britain and before that of France to emphasise the unusual qualities of the work. Its appeal to republicanism reveals commonality with British ideas of liberty and the public good through a shared heritage of classical political thought. Positioning the chapter before an examination of the French context accentuates its distinctiveness, and lays the foundation for oppositional thought to Louis XIV's form of monarchy during and after his reign.

Linking with Chapters 4 and 5 ('The reign of Louis XIV' and 'Confronting the legacy of Louis XIV'), Fénelon's ideas are highlighted in relation to the development of Louis XIV's sovereignty from 1661. Again two chapters that can be regarded as one chapter, part one deals with the reign of Louis XIV, and part two, works following his death. Louis's perception of his role as king are outlined through an examination of his *Mémoires* then linked to Bishop Bossuet's scriptural defence of his rule. Connecting with the Fénelon chapter, the differing ideas of members of the Burgundy Circle are explored to disclose the potential direction of France after the death of Louis XIV. Despite much variation in their ideas they shared a collective aspiration to enlarge government beyond the focus on a single man. These notions bled into the *Régence* regardless of Bourgogne's premature death, and through discussion of Montesquieu and Voltaire's early political ideas the embrace of British political notions are also assessed. These British and French contextual chapters emphasise a shared aspiration to escape absolute sovereignty, and move towards a more expansive government via a mixed constitution. While both states faced their own internal issues, certain commonalities of experience plus shared ideology in the seventeenth century and 1720s provoked exchanges of ideas. This provides a comparison of the two states unusual to the history of political thought for this time period, revealing a number of parallels among the more obvious variances. It also stresses Ramsay's initial attempt to return to seventeenth-century values, before acknowledging the eighteenth-century determination for public liberty.

Following a biographical chapter on Ramsay's life and important associations (Chapter 6), Chapter 7 ('A mythical conversation') and Chapter 8 ('A mythical education') separate Ramsay's political works into their two periods. Chapter 7 discusses Ramsay's promotion in both editions of the *Essay* and the *Vie* of Jacobitism and absolutism in relation to Fénelon's ostensive conversation with James Stuart. Chapter 8 moves on to *Cyrus* and the continued themes from the *Essay* as Ramsay investigated his deistic beliefs to provide an education for a prince furthered in the *Plan of Education*. The overriding aims of the final two chapters are to reveal a number of important observations regarding Ramsay's political thought. The separation of his works into two periods (and chapters) stresses the importance of Ramsay's involvement with the Jacobites. His departure from Rome in 1725 designates a dividing line between a time when he actively engaged in Jacobite propaganda, and the time after when his Jacobitism became secondary to other intellectual interests. It is here demonstrated how Jacobitism made politics Ramsay's primary consideration as he responded to the consequences of 1688. Furthermore, while religious concerns informed

Ramsay's politics, politics was not secondary but always interwoven. This drives to the heart of the primary influences on Ramsay's political works. In Fénelon, politics (especially in his reform works) made spiritual power subservient to temporal political concerns. Desiring to anchor the origins of civil government in natural law through God, Ramsay turned to Bossuet in the *Essay* to provide a system of government that exalted (absolute) monarchy and excluded the possibility for popular revolution. Ramsay was able to confront the legitimacy of 1688 by portraying it as a treasonable attack on the laws of nature. His key engagement of Fénelon in the *Essay* was a bastardised application of his aristocratic-led reform.[24] Ramsay inverted the Burgundy Circle's desire to expand government by promoting the extirpation of the British Parliament, favouring a robust monarchy supported by a hereditary aristocratic senate akin to Charles II's example in 1680s Scotland.

This assault continued in *Cyrus*, as Ramsay decried the development of popular government for its corruption of modern society. In this work the influence of Fénelon was far more prevalent, but the use of Bossuet continued. Following Bossuet and Fénelon, *Cyrus* reveals that Ramsay's Catholicism had little bearing on his political thought. Rather, he remained a deist, determined to promote human knowledge and to understand the place of humanity in the world through education and truths lost to man in a corrupted age. The mixture of classical religion and mythology with contemporary knowledge will be highlighted to expose a keen (deistic) mind, resolute in its use of a multiplicity of sources to educate a modern king. This would preferably see a Stuart monarch ruling an economically strong Britain that had positioned itself as the 'Capital of the Universe' working cooperatively with its European neighbours, including France. These chapters affirm that Ramsay harnessed a range of sources to provide solutions for perceived problems. This included English country ideology, absolutism, Bossuet's natural law, Fénelonian pedagogy, French views on aristocratic-led reform, plus classical and religious conceptions of virtue. In the end, this search for understanding and answers led him to perform a reversal regarding his principles on popular politics. Like Montesquieu and Voltaire, his visit to England in the late 1720s revealed the importance of Parliament in a mixed constitution as an institution capable of serving the public good and potentially combating corruption. The juxtaposition of the *Plan* with his earlier natural law philosophy underpinning his views of ordered society reveals a theory that anticipated the work of Bolingbroke. Ramsay therefore offers an excellent example of a thinker who had a foot in each country, using ideology from each and each century to produce ideas that found an audience in both kingdoms. The monograph assesses Ramsay's importance to the history of political thought, as it considers the early Enlightenment ideological context in which he worked.

Notes

1 While the *Essay de Politique* was not translated into English, its second expanded and revised edition of the *Essay philosophique sur le government civil* was, much of which contains the same content. See Chapter 7.

2 For the purpose of this monograph I have not differentiated between England and Scotland unless necessary. Given that Ramsay wrote his political works after the Act of Union (1707) and his desire to effect a restoration of James Stuart to the British throne, Ramsay appealed to the British, which would also have included Ireland. In fact, the history that he employed in the editions of the *Essay* was predominantly English with some seventeenth-century Scottish history. Much of the British thought used by Ramsay and (British) contemporaries comprised political theorists from the three kingdoms of England, Ireland, and Scotland.

3 James Tully, *An Approach to Political Philosophy: Locke in Contexts* (Cambridge, 1993), 9–10.

4 See Roger Mettam, *Power and Faction in Louis XIV's France* (Oxford, 1998); Nicholas Henshall, *The Myth of Absolutism: Change and Continuity in Early Modern European Monarchy* (London, 1996); Peter R. Campbell, *Power and Politics in Old Regime France 1720–1745* (London, 1996). For those supporting a view of an absolute France, see Guy Chaussinand-Nogaret, *La noblesse au XVIIIe siècle. De la Féodalité aux Lumières* (Paris, 1976); Yves-Marie Bercé, *La naissance dramatique de l'absolutisme, 1598–1661* (Paris, 1992); Emmanuel Le Roy Ladurie, *L'Ancien Régime* (Paris, 1991).

5 See Jonathan Scott, 'Radicalism and Restoration', *Historical Journal*, 31, 2 (1988), pp. 453–67 (458–9); Jonathan Scott, *Algernon Sidney and the English Republic, 1623–1677* (Cambridge, 1988); Mark Knights, *Politics and Opinion in Crisis, 1678–81* (Cambridge, 1994), 10–15; Tim Harris, *Politics under the Later Stuarts: Party Conflict in a Divided Society 1660–1715* (London, 1993), 8. Knights claims, however, that Scott perhaps focuses too much on the past in shaping these events and ideologies as 'consecutive events', rather than considering contemporary issues.

6 See [Andrew Marvell], *An Account of the Growth of Popery, and Arbitrary Government in England* (Amsterdam, 1677), 14–15, 28, 153–4; J.G.A. Pocock, 'Machiavelli, Harrington, and English Political Ideologies in the Eighteenth Century', *William and Mary Quarterly*, 3rd series, 22, 4 (Oct. 1965), pp. 549–83 (565).

7 See J.H. Shennan, *Philippe, Duke of Orléans: Regent of France 1715–1723* (London, 1979), 35; Colin Jones, *The Great Nation: France from Louis XV to Napoleon* (London, 2002), 42.

8 Gabriel Glickman, *The English Catholic Community 1688–1745: Politics, Culture and Ideology* (Woodbridge, 2009), 230–4, 251.

9 Nick Childs, *A Political Academy in Paris 1724–1731: The Entresol and Its Members* (Oxford, 2000), 147–8.

10 On Bolingbroke's role as a conduit, see Rachel Hammersley, *The English Republican Tradition and Eighteenth-century France: Between the Ancients and the Moderns* (Manchester, 2010), 54–5, 83, 82 n.

11 See Cardinal Louis François de Bausset, *Histoire de Fénelon, Tome Troisième* (Paris, 1850), 616; Chanoine Moïse Cagnac, *Fénelon: Politique tirée de l'Evangile* (Paris, 1912), 29; Paul Janet, *Fénelon: His Life and Works*, trans. Victor Leuliette (London, 1914), 280. This view is not restricted to older biographers, as recent scholarship has also claimed that the model for Ramsay's *Essay* was Fénelon (see Marialuisa Baldi, *Philosophie et politique chez Andrew Michael Ramsay* (Paris, 2008), 30–42).

12 The preface to both editions of the *Essay* and the *Vie de Fénelon* make this claim (see Chapter 6 in this book for a discussion of this behaviour).

13 See Françoise Gallouédec-Genuys, *Le Prince selon Fénelon* (Paris, 1963), the work infuses Fénelon's political philosophy with ideas taken from Ramsay's *Essay*.

14 Albert Cherel, *Fénelon au XVIIIe siècle en France (1715–1820): Son prestige – son influence* (Paris, 1917), 31. The chapters in this work were extracted to create a biography of Ramsay that contained an additional introduction and conclusion (see Albert Cherel, *Un aventurier religieux au XVIIIe siècle: André-Michel Ramsay* (Paris, 1926)).

15 See Cherel, *Fénelon au XVIIIe Siècle en France (1715–1820)*, 98; G.D. Henderson, *Chevalier*

Ramsay (Edinburgh, 1952), 79, 82. Henderson's work is a biography that at times lacks a rigid application of scholarship. While including views on his political thought and activities, the work is predominantly a description of his life. Georg Eckert's recent biography of Fénelon provides a broad investigation of his works and life (*'True, Noble, Christian Freethinking': Leben und Werk Andrew Michael Ramsay (1686–1743)* (Münster, 2009)).

16 Glickman, *English Catholic Community 1688–1745*, 227–8.

17 Henderson, *Chevalier Ramsay*, 175; Jean Molino, *'L'"Essai philosophique sur le gouvernement civil"*: *Ramsay ou Fénelon?'*, *La Régence*, ed. Henri Coulet (Paris, 1970), 285; Baldi, *Philosophie et politique chez Andrew Michael Ramsay*, 42–67; Georges Lamoine, 'Introduction', *Essais de Politique*, ed. Georges Lamoine (Paris, 2009), 40–1.

18 See Cherel, *Fénelon au XVIIIe Siècle en France*, 94; Molino, *'L'"Essai philosophique sur le gouvernement civil"'*, 282; Baldi, *Philosophie et politique chez Andrew Michael Ramsay*, 68–9, 76–8; Lamoine, 'Introduction', 42–3.

19 Molino, *'L'"Essai philosophique sur le gouvernement civil"'*, 289.

20 *Ibid.*, 292.

21 See Doohwan Ahn, 'From Greece to Babylon: The Political Thought of Andrew Michael Ramsay (1686–1743)', *History of European Ideas*, 37, 4 (2011), pp. 421–37 (425–6). Baldi sees similarities in the *Essay's* discussion of absolute power and hereditary monarchy, but believes that the inspiration for Ramsay's natural law system was Richard Cumberland (*Philosophie et politique chez Andrew Michael Ramsay*, 70).

22 Ahn, 'From Greece to Babylon', 437.

23 See Baldi, *Philosophie et politique chez Andrew Michael Ramsay*, 86; Glickman, *English Catholic Community 1688–1745*, 240–3.

24 The outcome of Ramsay's political legacy is investigated in Chapters 7 and 8. It is argued that as Fénelon's editor and first biographer the impact of Ramsay's use of Fénelon for Jacobitism had a profound effect on public conceptions of the Archbishop's thought.

1

Division and unity I:
revolution and party

In a brief moment of unity, the 1688 Revolution triumphed as opponents coalesced to preserve their religious and civil liberties threatened by a Catholic absolute monarch. Despite this cessation of enmities antagonism quickly returned, and produced divisions that lasted for decades. These discords were the result of a nation made insecure by disagreements over religion, and the conflict between successive Stuart monarchs determined to rule independently of Parliament which sought to restrain the monarch's power. Following the Restoration, the issues of the Civil War that had led to much bloodshed and regicide still cast a shadow. This chapter will discuss the potential for absolute sovereignty after the Restoration, assessing the political and ideological consequences of Charles II and James II's reigns. Charles's reign empowered his brother James II to continue upon a course of absolute royal prerogative that instigated a lasting opposition against the crown's behaviour. The endeavour cost James II his throne, as his subjects rebelled during the Dutch-led invasion of Britain that was to become known as the Glorious Revolution. While the settlement and Declaration of Rights addressed the perceived injustices of the two reigns, the transient unison of the Convention quickly dissipated into acrimony and recrimination. Ideological disputes of church and state concerning the legality of the Revolution recycled earlier country protest that continually reappeared beyond the Hanoverian succession over the next five decades. Confrontation with the modifications wrought by 1688 drove political party divisions and factious disputes as parliamentary power augmented.

Approaching absolutism[1]

In 1660 the Stuart monarchy was restored to the thrones of its three kingdoms of England, Ireland, and Scotland under Charles II (1630–85). The death of Oliver Cromwell in 1658 followed by the precipitate resignation from the office of Lord Protector by his ill-suited son and heir, Richard Cromwell, created anxieties over the resultant power vacuum and fears of another civil war. The Commonwealth General and Governor of Scotland George Monck, who had been in clandestine correspondence with Charles, used the prince's Declaration of Breda (4 April 1660) to effect his restoration to the throne. In the Declaration, Charles promised to pardon sins committed during the Civil War and Inter-regnum if he was returned as king. After the election of an evenly split royalist and parliamentarian Commons, many were keen to reconcile with the prince for the sake of stability. Problematically, the Restoration settlement did not address the issues that had led to the Civil War in 1642. Uncertainties concerning the state's religious and political boundaries were not resolved, so 'there was little consensus over what sort of monarchy should be restored'.[2] The monarchy was reinstated with possession of Charles I's powers after the reforms passed by the Long Parliament. These reforms had attempted to prevent a repeat of Charles I's experiment with 'personal rule' during the 1630s, but in the main Charles II escaped many limitations and possessed considerable control.[3] Wrangles over the political and religious settlements meant that the tensions of the 1640s and 1650s endured beyond 1660.[4] Yet a determination to rely on the familiar model of monarchy to circumvent anarchic regime change, particularly among members of the aristocracy, effected the Stuarts' restoration.[5] This resulted in what Tim Harris has termed 'constitutional' and 'religious' problems, which shaped the Restoration's political climate and prevailed into the eighteenth century. In other words, the uncertainty over the balance of power between the crown and Parliament, the extent of the royal prerogative, and levels of parliamentary corruption led to 'constitutional' difficulties; while ('religious') disagreements over dissent and toleration centred on the Anglican Church.[6]

The ambiguity over the power and authority of Charles II's rule began to crystallise during the 1670s. Under the Lord High Treasurer Lord Danby (1632–1712), the executive power was strengthened via a strategy that under-lined the pre-eminence of the Anglican Church. Often skirting the wishes of Charles II, Danby began to enact policies that undermined the 1672 Declaration of Indulgence, which had provided some toleration for Protestant Dissenters. In 1673 he helped to introduce the Test Act, which although targeted at Catholics essentially prevented non-Anglicans from attaining office because of the neces-sity to take Anglican Communion. Danby also initiated the organisation of the parliamentary backbenchers into some semblance of a court party that could be bribed via 'patronage, places, and pensions' to ensure the passage of the king's legislation through Parliament. Principally, the crown was attempting to master the 'arts of parliamentary management' which had not been accomplished by either James I (r. 1603–25) or Charles I (r. 1625–49).[7] By controlling Parliament and appeasing the Anglican Church, the government reforms under Charles II bolstered the crown as it pursued a path towards absolutism. Charles II's court was able to use its extensive authority granted by the Restoration settlement to expand his sovereignty beyond that of his father and grandfather.[8] Control of Parliament and a propitiated Church granted the monarch a prospect for independence of action freed from the impediment of other elements of the state. During the 1670s and 1680s both Charles and James saw Parliament as an 'opponent rather than an ally or resource, and strove to rule without it', and from 1679 to 1688 Parliament met five times for a total of 171 days.[9]

This behaviour began to raise the suspicions of a number of prominent figures, notably the Earl of Shaftesbury (1621–83). Shaftesbury had formerly been a member of the Cabal Ministry under Charles II: a group of five privy councillors who assisted the king in directing internal and foreign policy.[10] Danby effectively replaced the Cabal, which had simultaneously been viewed as either a danger to crown power or a danger to Parliament. Shaftesbury understood that Danby's innovations and creation of a court party subverted the independence of MPs through crown bribery. On 20 October 1675 Shaftesbury gave a speech in the House of Lords drawing attention to the hazard faced by Parliament and the nation. This criticism was broadened to include the augmentation of the standing army by the crown, which was viewed as a further attempt to under-mine the two Houses. Applying James Harrington's belief that a standing army could be employed by the crown as a '*pouvoir intermédiarie*' between the king and the people, Shaftesbury argued that Charles II was using his to enfeeble the nobility.[11] In so doing, Shaftesbury repeated Harrington's opinion that England possessed a (Gothic or Germanic) mixed constitution which provided a balanced system that relied on bicameral government.[12]

Andrew Marvell's *Account of the Growth of Popery* (1677) paralleled Shaftes-bury's warning, claiming to expose a design in the crown to change the lawful government to an absolute form which would convert England to Catholi-cism. Bribery and placemen would allow Charles's pro-French Catholic-leaning court to emasculate Parliament by emulating Louis XIV's attack on his state's representative organs.[13] These 'neo-Harringtonian' admonitions by Shaftesbury and Marvell emphasised the courts' ambition to shift the constitution towards absolute monarchy.[14] Neo-Harringtonian or commonwealth ideology encour-aged antipathy in the country against the crown by highlighting a risk to liberty, property, and the king's undertaking to sterilise Parliament. As their name would suggest, the Commonwealthmen exhibited republican ideals such as liberty, civic virtue, and the importance of government assembly found in the parlia-mentarians during the Commonwealth.[15] For the Commonwealthmen, good government possessed a representative (republican) element which permitted those who were members of the body politic (freeholders) to participate equally in determining the laws they were subject to, thereby certifying their political rights.[16] They embraced ideology extant in the Roman Republic and Renaissance city states of Italy, in which the liberty of the citizen was promoted by the balance offered through the interaction and cooperation between the people and the nobility. This relationship, often fractious, was viewed as vital to the state's effectiveness, virtue, and maintenance of the public good. Transposed into a seventeenth-century English context, the development of Parliament over successive centuries meant that the Stuart monarchy's behaviour threatened this legislative role. The clash throughout the century between the (Stuart) monarchy and Parliament undermined a role the aristocracy – who filled both Houses – had become accustomed to. The recourse to classical liberty not only endeavoured to protect the rights, religion, and property of the people under a mixed constitution, it sought to protect the position of the aristocracy too.

Shaftesbury's opposition to Danby and the behaviour of the crown reached its zenith during the Exclusion Crisis (1679–81). The Exclusion Crisis was an attempt by the burgeoning Whig party – a diverse grouping of those opposed to the crown symbolised by Shaftesbury – to exclude the openly Catholic heir James the Duke of York, from the succession. Following the fantastical revelations of Titus Oates and Israel Tonge, who implicated the Duke of York in a conspiracy to kill the king, the Popish Plot tapped into a widespread fear of Catholicism in England leading to public disturbances. Anti-popery had been prevalent since the Reformation, and drew from a very real sense that Counter-Reformation European powers were determined to return England to its Catholic past, as verified by the Armada (1588) and the Gunpowder Plot (1605) for example.[17] The strength of Catholic, absolutist France was also an acute stimulus in the paranoia regarding the crown's behaviour and the reaction to the Popish Plot. Louis XIV was a colossus in European geopolitics during this period, shaping the political landscape and British foreign policy through his numerous wars. As the first cousin of Charles and James, the connection was not lost on many contemporaries, who foresaw a Stuart emulation of France and feared a move towards Catholicism and absolutism as suggested by Marvell.[18] Indeed, there were parallels in the behaviour of the two states in the seventeenth century and particularly from the 1660s. Over the century France had been able to consolidate a graduation towards absolute sovereignty after the internecine fighting of the Wars of Religion (1562–98). Following further divisions in the seventeenth century, when his personal rule began in 1661 Louis XIV made a determined bid to establish the king's supremacy. To achieve concord under the crown he undermined the power of the aristocracy, the state's representative institutions, and religious toleration at times utilising brutal physical force.[19] English anti-Catholic rioting in 1679 was therefore not only fuelled by internal tensions and paranoia, but a wider geopolitical context that feared French intervention. The Bill of Exclusion drafted to alter the succession as if 'the said James, Duke of York, were naturally dead', reflected a concerted effort to eschew Franco-Catholic absolutism under a pro-French James.[20]

The political ideology that was promulgated during the Exclusion Crisis formed an important connection between the early Stuarts of the seventeenth century and the late Stuarts into the eighteenth century. A number of works were republished from the era of Charles I by both sides to scorn the other's position. Notably the Court (or Tory) party published Sir Robert Filmer's *Patriarcha*, a work written in the late 1620s which reasserted the authority of the king by using patriarchalism to undermine republican proclivities in a time of 'crisis'.[21] In *Patriarcha*, Filmer claimed that men were born subject to their parents and the king, thereby never experiencing liberty.[22] As the first father of the nation, kings enjoyed a political authority over their people inherited from Adam and granted directly by God.[23] This guaranteed that all subjects were entirely subordinate and obedient to the monarch and could therefore be directed at the king's pleasure. Filmer discounted any belief that the basis of sovereign power was found in the populace, insisting that even if the people had granted this gift to kings it could not be returned. The king was bound only by his obligation to God, so was not answerable to the people, the law, or the parliaments which derived their authority from the monarch.[24] Influenced by the theory of Jean Bodin (1530–96) and King James VI of Scotland and I of England (1566–1625), Filmer's kingship was absolute. Patriarchy was applied by Filmer amongst other principles to strengthen claims for absolute monarchy. They were: divine right theory, indefeasible hereditary succession, non-resistance, and passive obedience. These theologically inspired political tenets were intended to create unconditionally subordinate subjects, possessing no inalienable rights as they were born dependent upon and subject to their king and parents. In such a state the king retained the sole authority which directed the government, its laws, and the people. *Patriarcha* is an interesting text, because it joins divine right theory and patriarchy when they 'were frequently advanced independently of one another, into one uniformed argument for the king's absolute authority'. This 'striking' approach was easily assimilated into the Royalist position of the 1680s, which sought to enhance the king's power over the nation.[25]

The publication of *Patriarcha* tied the objectives of the crown neatly with the doctrines of the Anglican Church and predominant social attitudes of seventeenth-century English society. Despite the regicide and upheavals of the Civil War, England remained patriarchal as men continued to dominate the family and wider society. The doctrine of patriarchalism located its origins in the theology of the antediluvian biblical patriarchs such as Abraham, Isaac, and Jacob. Patriarchy also possessed an economic basis, and from classical times it had denoted the absolute authority of the male landowner over a household (*oikos*) or family unit.[26] This worked on two levels. The first was the obedience due to the father of the family. It signified that a wife and children were subordinate to the father (husband) who led the family and any servants the family may employ. In a society where up to 95 per cent of the population were common people and could not afford servants, a second level of patriarchal authority came into being warranting commoners to obey their social superiors and employers.[27] People were therefore bound by the principle of patriarchal subordination: subservience to their social superiors, to their employers, to their fathers, and to men. Ultimately, subordination was due to the king as the foremost man of the kingdom and the pinnacle of the social strata. An attitude underpinned by the Anglican Church and scriptural authority was exploited from the pulpit to ensure the effective obedience of the masses. In an age when political ordinances and news were often spread via the Anglican pulpit – as well as a thriving print industry – collaboration between church and state made it relatively easy to create 'positive attitudes toward the political order' as these established relations were unquestioned.[28] Society was thus rigid, and subordination was universally accepted by people at all levels.[29] It was understood to be derived from ancient ideas centred in the authority of the king, and essential for the preservation of social order and the privileges of men of property.[30] Filmer's originality in patriarchal doctrine stemmed from his joining together social and political patriarchalism. Through an Adamite succession, sovereign power was passed to mankind from God via kingship, creating order and subordination for society under the monarch.[31]

Filmer's central premise that kingship was underpinned by an Adamite patriarchal inheritance, however, was rejected by James Tyrrell's *Patriarcha non Monarcha* (1681), John Locke's *Two Treatises of Government* (pub. 1689), and Algeron Sidney's *Discourses Concerning Government* (pub. 1698).[32] For the three, all men were born into liberty not subjugation and were not dependent on their parents throughout their entire life. Sidney, a neo-Harringtonian, and Locke vociferously attacked the absolutist pretensions extant in Filmer and by implication, Charles II. Such government was tyrannical and led to the arbitrary use of power by the monarch as he extirpated the people's liberty in quest for his own ends. Sidney and Locke claimed that the king's pursuit of personal objectives over the public good of the nation was tyranny and could be resisted by the people.[33] For the two proto-Whigs, sovereignty found its origin in the body of the people who legitimated the political community through consent.[34] If the executive acted in an illegitimate manner it broke its (original) contract with the people, whose consent could be withdrawn and the government resisted.[35] Reaction to *Patriarcha* fed into a larger opposition to the crown's apparent augmentation of its powers. Works such as Henry Neville's *Plato Redivivus* (1680) reiterated Shaftesbury and Marvell's contention that the (ancient) constitution, the nobility and the liberty of the people were being destabilised by the behaviour of the crown.[36] The

Whig agenda during the Exclusion Crisis was designed to prevent absolutism, remove the threat of a standing army, save Protestantism from a popish king, and defend the 'lives, liberties and property' of the people.

Two key issues dominated the widening division between the country (Whig) and court (Tory) parties during the Crisis, and both reflect the problematic Restoration settlement. Religion was the first question, specifically whether dissenters should be granted toleration. For the Tories, who were loyal to the supremacy of the Anglican Church this was out of the question, as the High-Church opposed toleration for non-Anglicans Protestants and Catholics. By contrast, the Whigs believed that toleration should be granted to the Dissenters. The pro-Anglican politico-religious reforms of Danby were therefore attacked by men such as Shaftesbury who championed the Dissenters. The dispute over toleration enabled the Whigs to besmirch Danby and the pretension of High-Church bishops, whom they opposed.[37] High-Anglicanism was treated with some suspicion and seen to retain pro-papist leanings, as evident in certain Catholic practices such as high communion. The perceived Catholicity of the court conjured images of an unholy alliance between the Anglican High Church and the court which could reintegrate Catholicism into England.[38]

The second issue was the source of the highest legal authority in the land. According to the Whigs it was the law which dictated the ability of the king to act, but for the Tories the crown was superior. The Tory conception of the law – which was the more pervasive view in England – saw the king as proprietor of the law, which he could use according to his will so long as it did not conflict with the rights of his subjects. Fundamentally both sides believed the crown's prerogative (emergency powers) was essential for maintaining liberty, property, and the public good. The Tories, however, were more open to the monarch possessing such unlimited authority on a more permanent basis, as power originated and descended from the crown in their interpretation. The key point of divergence between the two parties on the law was the Whig rejection of the king as 'proprietor' of the laws and father of the state. Instead they believed the king to be a 'trustee'.[39] This necessitated the king to rule through the law and Parliament, making it simpler to bridle the crown's ability to act arbitrarily or tyrannically. Furthermore, it asserted that England existed through a mixed constitution which contained the king, lords, and parliament rather than a sole monarch ruling independently. According to Whig propaganda a mixed constitution signalled the ancient customs of the Gothic (or pre-Conquest Germanic) origins of the state. In which the king ruled in cooperation with his nobles and a parliament (or witan) to represent the realm and its people. The historical veracity of a (Whig) ancient constitution was successfully attacked by a number of writers, notably Robert Brady (1626–1700),[40] who had been employed by the Tories. They used the Norman Conquest to undermine the Whig depiction of an ancient constitution – which incorporated an active role for the Commons in the legislation – that had remained unbroken from time immemorial.[41] Yet a belief in the Germanic origins of a mixed constitution that contained representative elements continued beyond 1688.[42]

The failed attempt to exclude James from the succession over three successive parliaments (1679, 1680, and 1681) revealed the constitutional weakness of Parliament. Despite popular support for the Whigs' bill to exclude James from the succession, Charles was able to prorogue and dissolve Parliament in order to buy himself time. The crux of the reciprocal relationship between the king and Parliament was the exchange of revenue by the Commons in return for a role in the legislative process. By the third (Oxford) Parliament Charles had managed to negotiate a pension with Louis XIV that empowered him to disperse Parliament. In accepting a pension from Louis XIV, Charles managed to subvert this relationship because he no longer required Parliament for financial assistance. He gained the independence he craved to pursue his political (and religious) ambitions. The king's ability to dissolve Parliament at will, revealed the supremacy of the king's prerogative over the legislative body. Despite the early public popularity of the Whig cause for exclusion and the impeachment of Danby in 1678 for secret dealings with the French, all accounted for naught when compared with the royal prerogative. They failed in their enterprises to bridle the king's ambitions for the crown, remove the Catholic heir from the succession, or eliminate the threat of the standing army.[43]

The Oxford Parliament was exploited by the crown to decimate the Whig opposition. In truth, the Whigs also made the Tory task of disseminating anti-Whig propaganda easier through the discovery of the Rye House Plot in 1683. The plot aimed to assassinate the king and the Duke of York upon their return from the Newmarket races, but its discovery led to the execution of men such as Lord Russell and Sidney.[44] Throughout the 1680s an ascendant court managed to suppress the Whig opposition as some, such as Shaftesbury and Locke, fled to Holland, or many simply maintained a low profile. The depletion of the Whigs as an oppositional force during the 1680s and the financial independence of the crown generated by Louis XIV's pension and a number of tax innovations, provided Charles II with the opportunity to intensify his position as monarch. Growing liberation for the crown as finance and law were used with greater sophistication, witnessed England's move 'inexorably towards absolutism'.[45] It placed the king in a stronger position than his father, as he was able to dispense with Parliament while emboldened by the support of a loyal army. Charles used the final years of his reign to strengthen the position of the crown for his brother's succession, facilitated by his brother's organisation of the state purse and administration.[46]

After the Exclusion Crisis, James enjoyed a return to public favour, especially after the Rye House Plot. He had spent the period between October 1679 and

March 1682 as the king's high commissioner in exile in Scotland. Rather portentously, the Duke of York ruled Scotland as a 'virtual viceroy', continuing the Duke of Lauderdale's practice of upholding the Episcopalians in Scotland, while intensifying the position of the crown and suppressing extreme Presbyterian antagonism. James embedded absolutism into Scottish law through a number of acts. He made it high treason to attempt to alter the succession to the crown, and created an oath to 'renounce resistance, to defend all the king's prerogatives, and to repudiate attempts to alter the government in church or state'.[47] The significance of his sojourn to Scotland was the revelation of James's determination to take further steps towards an absolute form of sovereignty. Charles perhaps lacked the inclination or determination to move closer to imposing absolutism upon England, although his reign had provided the scaffolding for it. The defeat of the Whig opposition and the financial independence of the crown offered it the prospect of government with either a compliant weakened Parliament or its redundancy. The final ingredient was the rule of a king who was determined to reign unencumbered by such an impediment.

Thwarted absolutism

The death of Charles II in 1685 and the accession of the Duke of York as James II of England and VII of Scotland, placed the king in a very strong position. His frugality and ability as an administrator had improved his brother's finances, while his advocacy of commerce had shown signs of greater reward at the beginning of his reign. The Monmouth and Argyll Rebellions in 1685 further increased his popularity among a public roused by the threat to the king's life and title. His acclaim from defeating the rebellions, the declarations of loyalty, his parliamentary pension for life, and his ability to expand the size of the standing army made James overly confident that the nation's feelings were 'unconditional'.[48] What ensued was a rapid state expansionist programme that alarmed the Anglican Church, aristocracy, and general public. Within three years of ascending to the throne James had managed to undo the gains made by his brother, as his premature centralisation of the bureaucracy galvanised an array of disparate opponents to correct his rule with the assistance of the Dutch.

There were essentially four key problematic lines of state modification that led to the Glorious Revolution. The first was the quadrupling of the standing army to 40,000 men and the construction of garrisons across England. As previously recognised by Shaftesbury and the country (Whig) opposition, such manoeuvres to control a people if they possessed the men and arms made it much easier for a ruler's authority if spread throughout the kingdom. In geopolitical terms, the mid 1680s were a relatively more peaceful time between the

English, Dutch, and French. So this increase, rather redolent of the French military system reliant upon domestic force of arms, was not a necessary development for foreign policy. This behaviour emphasised the king's power over his people throughout the country and realised a desire for 'absolute obedience'.[49] Such obedience would enable the king to place himself above the law, a feat made simpler through the domination of Parliament. The subversion of the role of Parliament provided the second concern involving James's rule: a planned subordination of the Commons. From the beginning of his reign, James stated to the French ambassador Barillon, marquis de Branges (1630–91) his intention to call Parliament in order to obtain a pension before dismissing it. After receiving his sizeable pension following his victory over Monmouth, James eventually dissolved his first parliament in 1687 over disagreements concerning the inclusion of Catholic officers in the army. This pension was boosted by another from Louis XIV, after the French king had given James permission to pursue his plan so that he could subdue Parliament and follow a Catholic path.[50]

Thirdly the inclusion of Catholic officers undermined the penal laws in England that prohibited non-Anglicans from filling civic positions. Ignoring Anglican sensibilities James embarked upon a programme of religious toleration for non-Anglicans, allying himself with dissenting groups (such as the Quakers) to weaken the Church. Religious toleration was both a point of principle for the king as well as a political expedient.[51] The subsequent divisions permitted him to widen the rift between his Protestant enemies while safeguarding the protection of fellow Catholics. Determined to repeal the Test Act, James introduced a Second Act of Indulgence in 1687, which suspended the penal laws. This was juxtaposed with the replacement of Protestant heads of colleges with Catholics at Oxford and Cambridge, and the removal of unsympathetic members of the judiciary. Moreover, after the dismissal of Parliament, James conducted a survey in the country to locate pliable future MPs who would be willing to alter the Test Act and penal laws.[52] The king's purpose was to form a packed future Parliament filled with sympathetic MPs that would enable the creation of an Act of Toleration which included Catholics, as well as two Houses ready to obey his will. The reissuing of the Declaration of Indulgence 27 April 1688 was rejected by William Sancroft, the Archbishop of Canterbury (installed 1677–90), and six other leading bishops. Their refusal to read the Declaration from the pulpit led to their trial for seditious libel, and they were subsequently acquitted on 30 June 1688.

The fourth issue drew together some of the above problems when galvanising opposition towards James's authority, though making economic considerations paramount. This argument has been recently renewed by Steve Pincus, who has argued that the 1688 Revolution was the result of a choice for the English between two particular models of government: a French model or a Dutch.[53] Following the Restoration of Charles II the English had begun to concentrate on commercial expansion as the national interest, and their rivals in this enterprise were the Dutch who frequently impinged on their activities.[54] While some contemporaries believed that the English should ally with the Dutch, for others their neighbours were a problematic threat competing aggressively for the same markets; hence the Anglo-Dutch wars (1665–67 and 1672–74). In both states, from the middle of the seventeenth-century political economy became 'vital' to the object of governance, principally as they feared a French universal monarchy of commerce.[55] Despite this competition and wars many in England still favoured ties with the Dutch, especially since they had a shared reliance on a mixed constitution (although very different), were Protestant, and held similar views on commerce.[56] For some this desire became more acute when a number of leading aristocrats suspected the English court of favouring a Gallican model of government that was centralised and Catholic. Pincus claims that James II was committed to a project of Catholic modernisation that would centralise the state and 're-Catholise England along Gallican lines'.[57] In terms of political economy, a Gallican model would continue to favour 'finite' land wealth and territory over the precarious 'infinite' wealth generated by Dutch commercial endeavour.[58] The 1688 Revolution therefore rebuffed James II's Gallican intentions towards government, the economy and England's territorial expansion. It declined closer ties with the French, or the possibility of falling under the influence of Louis XIV's aggrandising economic and political plans in Europe.[59] Instead the English (British) embraced a commercial model brought by the Dutch that helped to instigate the Financial Revolution in the 1690s, while securing Protestantism and a mixed constitution.[60] This template, keenly supported by the Whigs, signalled a modern appreciation that wealth would be required for war: at a time of great concern regarding future French expansion and hostility.

While this is a somewhat simplified version of the troubles concerning James II's reign and other issues could be considered, these four were the most important. The dual issues over the religious and political settlement unresolved from the restoration became pertinent due to the behaviour of the king. While Charles's gradual assumption of power and ability to dissemble had left him personally unchallenged, this was not the case for his brother. James's brusque personality and determination to forge swiftly ahead with centralising reforms quickly alienated his support. The combination of a move towards an absolute form of sovereignty with a direct assault on the Anglican Church through toleration and the prominent placement of Catholics threatened the 'lives, liberties and property' of the nation. This manifest shift towards Catholicism and absolutism was untenable, and indicative of Louis XIV's French state. Indeed, James and his court appeared to be 'committed to a Catholic project' that shadowed the

French model of government.[61] While perhaps not disdainful of English Protestantism, James was certainly in pursuit of a Gallican-style rule and religion that suited his own tastes; tastes that did not match the nations. The birth of his son James Francis Edward Stuart (10 June 1688) made the issue exigent. On the day that the seven bishops were acquitted, the 'Immortal Seven' invited the Dutch Prince William of Orange to use military intervention to force James II to make his eldest (Protestant) daughter Mary his heir.[62] Claims that the new Prince of Wales was illegitimate highlighted the deep concern over the perpetuation of a Catholic Stuart line. While many Tories had been willing to obey (passively) the dictates of James, the birth of a Catholic heir raised the prospect of permanence for his political and religious reforms. In effect, the trepidations over (Catholic) arbitrary rule raised by the Whigs during the Exclusion Crisis came to pass under James and made it impossible for some not to act.

The collective action taken from 5 November 1688 by the Dutch invasionary force and British opponents to James II was indeed a revolution.[63] Despite forewarning from the French regarding the preparations of a Dutch fleet, James was slow to digest the likelihood that his kingdom would be invaded. Notwithstanding James's numerical advantage of troops, the important abandonments of his daughters (Mary and Anne), his advisers (such as Churchill and Ormond), his soldiers, and the rioting wider populace led James to believe he was being rejected by his subjects.[64] The invitation of a foreign power that arrived with a massive expeditionary force exposes the intent to counteract James's standing army. Following the initial instigation of a small number of aristocrats, upon landing the opposition towards the king from people all spectrums of society indicates a revolution and the king's untenable position. His impetuous attempt to create civil anarchy before fleeing the country by burning the parliamentary writs and tossing the Great Seal into the Thames (11 December 1688) were designed to disrupt the business of government. Yet his capture and the ease with which he was allowed to leave London (17 December) before William's arrival (18 December), show an encouragement for him to depart. With diminishing support, the king fled to France (22 December) believing that this would save his life and avoid greater bloodshed. To avert public and political chaos members of the Lords spiritual and temporal unified to form some semblance of a government. After initially refusing the crown, William called another assembly of the peers, and on 26 December they were joined by members of Charles II's Oxford Parliament. Claims of an abdication for the king plus his son and heir, are therefore difficult to justify for two reasons. The first was the reaction of the king's subjects upon the arrival of William's fleet, which reveal proactive opposition against the king. Second, a proposal of a conditional restoration of James II from the Earl of Nottingham (1647–1730) and supported by the Archbishop of Canterbury was rejected by William in favour of the calling of a convention assembly. Both factors and the refusal of a bid to reconcile the monarch with his subjects expose a desire to remove the king from his office.

The parliamentary Convention that met on 22 January 1689 was not a legal assembly, as it flouted the constitution. In the immediate aftermath of James II's departure to France, the Whigs and Tories unified to stave off potential social and political anarchy. Much of the Convention's business was defined by a need for both parties to compromise on their differing political philosophies to engender unity within the nation. A Tory-dominated Lords and a Whig-dominated Commons struggled to interpret the ramifications of the vacant throne. It became evident that James's daughter Mary would not rule without her husband, William, so to protect some semblance of a hereditary succession it was eventually agreed that the king had abdicated his throne. William and Mary were offered the throne jointly on condition that they accepted the Declaration of Rights, to confirm protection 'from all other attempts upon their religion, rights and liberties'.[65] The acceptance of the Declaration by the two saw William III and Mary II jointly crowned on 13 February 1689.

A number of problems were apparent before the Prince and Princess of Orange filled the crown vacancy. It was clear to contemporaries that James II had been resisted in some capacity by his subjects, and this had ultimately led him to flee his kingdom. Despite his departure from Britain's shores, James did not formally resign his crown. While this *ipso facto* alteration sat comfortably with elements of Whig doctrine favouring resistance to tyrannical rulers, it contradicted the firmly held Tory and Anglican beliefs of non-resistance and passive obedience. It also subverted the Tory and Anglican allegiance to indefeasible hereditary right as the throne should have subsequently passed to James's son in place of the father. In essence the entire edifice of divine right theory (and patriarchy) was challenged by the subjects' repulsion of their king. The insistence that the king had relinquished his rights to the throne and that of his Catholic heir, the infant Prince of Wales, by fleeing to France was deployed to assuage the consciences of many Tories and Anglicans. The absence of the king and the requirement for effective leadership at a time of crisis to prevent a civil war glossed over the fundamental destruction of many Anglican and Tory tenets. It concealed the desire to avert the crown's move towards absolutism and potentially permanent Catholicism. Despite this, it has been argued that the Tory 'Ideology of Order' survived the Revolution and actually dominated the settlement.[66] Whig notions of resistance and original contract which made the king's behaviour accountable to his people were dismissed by the Tories and did not appear in the settlement. James II's flight had prevented resistance and made it necessary to adjust the succession – which although not ideal due to William's pre-eminent role – was now Anglican and determined to rule through Parliament and law. The king's perceived abdication and removal of the Prince of Wales as the de facto heir meant that Mary became heir. For Tory sentiments this succession to James's daughter allowed indefeasible hereditary right to remain intact; as well as non-resistance, passive obedience, patriarchy, and divine right.

Undeniably, the Convention and the Declaration of Rights should be recognised as acts of conciliation in which there was a 'broad degree of consensus'.[67] Compromise was achieved not only between the Tories and the Whigs, but also within the parties, between the Lords and Commons, and within the Church. While 1688–89 did not create a new type of monarchy – as William III and Mary II possessed the powers of James II – the extension of the role of Parliament was highly significant. The Declaration ensured that certain limitations were placed on the monarchy in light of the behaviour of Charles II and James II; for example, the inability to suspend laws without the consent of Parliament and the power to raise or keep a standing army in peace time.[68] The monarch now ruled through a Parliament that monitored the king's behaviour and prevented an increase in the crown's authority. The Revolution has been interpreted in a number of ways by historians. For some it was an act of resistance which essentially entailed the election of a new limited monarchy; yet for others very little altered as the old (aristocratic) order of church and state were retained.[69] What remains clear is that it began a process by which Parliament rapidly attained power within government, leading to its ascendancy within the space of two decades.

A divisive revolution

This schismatic approach reflects contemporaneous reaction to the Revolution. Much of the wider population accepted the monarchical alteration and quickly acclimatised to James II's removal.[70] However, two important groups did not assent to the revolutionary settlement, believing that the Convention did not possess the right or authority to crown the new monarchs in place of James II. The first of these groups was the Nonjurors: those who would 'not swear' the oath of allegiance to the new monarchs. This relatively small number of nine English bishops, over 400 Anglican clergy, a much larger proportion of Scots Episcopalian bishops and an Irish bishop believed that their previous oath of allegiance to James II was still extant. This included the Archbishop of Canterbury, William Sancroft (1617–93), and four of the seven bishops who had been tried for seditious libel in petitioning the Second Act of Indulgence. Sancroft and the other bishops were deposed from their offices in 1690 but the group became very vocal opponents of the Glorious Revolution into the second decade of the eighteenth century. The Nonjurors retained an unshakable belief in religious ideals of kingship as well as a desire to protect and expand the interests of the Church. Nonjurors 'were unflinching adherents of divine right' and the belief that 'the authority of kings derived from God and that they were consequently not to be resisted', although this 'did not entail support for the freedom of monarchs to do as they pleased'.[71] For Nonjurors 'not only Scripture, but English law, natural law, and history designated who was the true king. The Revolution was an offence against nature and the constitution as well as against God'.[72] The Nonjurors furnished much of the early ideology of opposition against the Revolution, harnessing the tenets of divine right theory to rebuff the intervention by the populace against the king's position.

An example of this theory is provided by George Hickes (1642–1715), a polemicist and bishop of the Nonjuring church. Over a decade after the Revolution Hickes sustained his rigid opposition to the altered monarchical succession on theological grounds. So 'Sacred and Inviolable does our Religion make the Ties of Duty and Civil Obedience, to our *Rightful King*', that to 'cast off our *Sovereign*, that we may keep our *Religion*, is but a weak Plea, and will certainly be over-rul'd before the Tribunal of Heaven'.[73] Such a course of action had seen a: 'Violation of the Hereditary Title (which will hover over all Usurpations) [that] may yet cost this already near ruin'd Nation'.[74] The 'Christian Foundation of Loyalty' made it a duty incumbent on the people to obey passively God's will and the laws of nature. It was illegal for the people to select their monarch, as the crown's hereditary succession had been determined by God's will. The Revolution spurned the will of God, and the people of England faced a terrible future price for such action. Furthermore, it could not be argued that the crown had respected the royal hereditary line by passing to the daughter of James Queen Mary II (1662–94), as the rightful claimant was the Prince of Wales. The omission of the prince from the succession was another mark of the Revolution's illicitness. The rightful heir had been excluded from the throne when it was to him that the English people were obligated: for if there was 'any Person of the *Royal Line*, to whom by the Course of *Succession* the *Crown* does of Right belong', it was to them that they were 'bound in Conscience to be in Subjection'.[75] After the usurpation or decease of James II his son James Francis Edward Stuart (1688–1766) was owed allegiance; in not following this dictate the people had acted against God's will and natural law.

Such sympathies connected the Nonjurors closely to the second important group of opposition to the Revolution: the Jacobites. Indeed, the Nonjuring schism has been described as 'the clerical counterpart of Jacobitism'.[76] Jacobitism, taken from 'Jacobus' the Latin for James, was born as a consequence of the Revolution's Scottish settlement. Amidst a distinctly Presbyterian settlement and the abolishment of the Episcopacy, religious divisions in Scotland and loyalty to the Stuart king gave rise to Jacobitism. After the Scots recognised William and Mary as monarchs in April 1689 – declaring that James II had 'forfaulted' his throne – James's commander-in-chief of the Scottish forces Lord Claverhouse (1648–89), set up a rival convention at Stirling. Despite defeating a Williamite force at Killiecrankie (27 July 1689), Claverhouse's Jacobite armed defiance led to their eventual defeat and slaughter at Dunkeld (21 August) and Glencoe (16 January 1691). The Massacre at Glencoe stained the memory for a large number of Scots who contested the new settlement. This bloody suppression of Jacobite resistance was mirrored by the experiences in Ireland. Persuaded by his cousin and host Louis XIV to engage his usurpers in Ireland, James II landed in Kinsale on 12 March 1689.[77] After initial successes under the Lord Deputy of Ireland, Richard Talbot the Earl of Tyrconnell (1630–91), this large Catholic army besieged the Protestants at Derry. King William was forced to undertake an expeditionary force in Ireland to meet his father-in-law in battle. Despite logistical advantages, the poor leadership of James II led to the Irish Jacobites defeat in a number of battles, notably at the Battles of the Boyne (1 July 1690) and Limerick (3 October 1691). A stout Jacobite defence in both kingdoms led to massacres that have left a lasting legacy on these countries relationships with England. The immediate result of the Williamite victories, were settlements that favoured the English that provided them with economic, religious, and political hegemony.

Jacobitism continued to provide a key focal point for hostility to the Revolution. As William's reign began to establish itself in the 1690s opposition evolved beyond the revolutionary settlements to a reaction against William's qualities as a monarch and his style of rule. The old religious and political divisions remained. Anglican feathers were ruffled by the introduction of the Act of Toleration on 24 May 1689, which was granted to all Protestants except for Quakers and Unitarians. The Act had been introduced by William as a means for healing rifts between Protestants.[78] It was designed to engender unity at home as the English and her allies fought against (Catholic) France's aggrandisement on the continent in what was to become the Nine Years' War. Whig antipathies meant the Act was viewed by them as a means to undermine the established church. This animosity was symptomatic of a rapid resumption of hostilities between the Whigs and Tories in spite of the conciliatory unity of the Convention during the settlement. William had initially attempted to employ ministers in his government from both parties as another gesture of reconciliation. But the Whigs' pursuit of vengeance against those (Tories) who had persecuted them during the 1680s, led to such rancour that the king prorogued Parliament as early as January 1690 because party behaviour was proving to be so divisive.

After the Revolution, Britain was a muddle of parties and affiliations, many of which were frequently in conflict with one another. While parties had existed from the time of the Exclusion Crisis, it was following 1688 that a fully-fledged party system began to emerge into one of government and opposition.[79] Prior to this time the key distinction was that of the court, those who supported or were under the influence of the crown, and the country, those who claimed independence from the crown when making political decisions and could hold the court to account.[80] During the 1690s party politics defined opposition with greater acuteness than court and country, although these loyalties remained.[81] The Whigs for example, split into court and country after the compromise reached with the Tories over the Declaration of Rights was perceived to have 'emasculated' true Whig philosophies like resistance.[82] Such 'true' or 'real Whig' principles expressed many of the country values held by the Commonwealthmen that condemned the corruption of Parliament (through court bribery), the growth of centralised power, and standing armies. The use of the Whigs by William in his governments after 1692 led to further divisions within the party. From this time the Earl of Sunderland (1641–1702) persuaded the king that coalitions with Tory ministers would be 'inadequate', so the king relied predominantly on the Whigs.[83] The death of the Queen in 1694 meant that William could no longer rely on Mary to rule in his stead during his absences on the continent. The king's engagement in the Nine Years' War meant that he was frequently abroad, and from 1694 the Whig Junto began to take effective control of the operations of government. This group of privy councillors were predominantly Whig with some Tories, and included Lords Somers, Halifax, Wharton, Russell, Orford, and Sunderland. The Junto essentially formed the first cabinet and shifted the process of government from the monarch overseeing day-to-day operations towards a state run by ministers.

The development of the Junto highlighted a number of political problems during the 1690s. By 1695 the Junto's control of government had come to be viewed by Tories and Whigs as 'oligarchic, commercialist and committed to extensive executive power'.[84] Many country supporters felt threatened by the expanding state, high taxes, and meddling ministerial officials. An interpretation of William's government as autocratic therefore emerged, plus a belief that the court needed to be restrained. For the Whigs their infiltration of the court was viewed by some as a further rejection of the country principles which had originally founded the party. It led to a decisive split from the Commonwealthmen who believed the Revolution had been a failure. A few Whigs like Charlwood Lawton (1660–1721) turned to Jacobitism, arguing that James II or a Protestant-converted Prince of Wales should be restored.[85] These 'Whiggish Jacobites' wanted James II to govern by the laws, settle the liberty of conscience and limits to dispensing power in a free parliament, to refuse aid from France, and to disband his army.[86] William was perceived as a foreigner trampling upon the laws of the kingdom. Jacobitism provided an outlet for opposition, and Whig Jacobitism utilised country sentiments to contradict the behaviour of the court. The association of country ideology with the Whigs was also loosened as many

Tories moved towards its position through antagonism to the reign of William III. For the Tories, Jacobitism under William became a 'murky issue', as all had sworn an oath of allegiance to the new king although many held an attachment for James II.[87] During the Tory opposition some backbenchers fell into the arms of Jacobitism and a country ideology that rejected William's rule, the mounting cost of a foreign war, and the standing army. Jacobitism provided a focal point for varying opposition to the behaviour of government, the revolutionary settlement, or the king.

Notwithstanding its fall from power in 1700 following its attack on William's authority, the Junto's new method of governing highlighted the extension of parliamentary power as it had been required to take the lead in policy due to the king's absences. The extent of this power was underlined by the Disbanding Bill (February 1699) which forced William to reduce the numbers in his standing army after the Treaty of Ryswick (1697). The fallout from this dispute between the king and the Whigs – who disagreed with the size of the standing army on old principle – led to their replacement in government by the Tories.[88] Yet although William 'ruled through "parliamentary title", his "kingship" was "by no means as "limited" as that of George I'.[89] His authoritarian style of kingship made it necessary for Parliament to introduce legislation to restrict his power. Two key pieces of legislation were the Triennial Act (1694) and the Act of Settlement (1701). The Triennial Act invaded the king's prerogative to dissolve Parliament, and it was a bid to weaken the king's use of patronage by keeping Parliament open indefinitely freshened by frequent elections. The Act of Settlement reiterated Parliament's independence from the crown in the same manner as the Declaration of Rights. It directly addressed both the perceived problems of William's autocratic style and the issue of a foreign monarch. Following the death of Princess Anne's son the Duke of Gloucester (30 July 1700) it had become necessary to ensure the Protestant succession. Bypassing dozens of Catholic heirs, Sophia of Hanover (1630–1714) who was fifty-forth in line to the throne was named as heir to the throne.[90] The Act further restrained the king's facility to wage war, to employ foreign ministers or privy councillors, and ability to leave the country. Importantly, this was a piece of Tory legislation supported by all parties in another show of unity. Anxieties over Catholicism and a need to protect the revolutionary settlement, revealed an acceptance of 1688–89 irrespective of the manifest differences in how the Revolution's origins were perceived. Despite the lack of enthusiasm for William as a king, before his death on the 8 March 1702, he had ensured that Protestantism was secure in the kingdom and that the throne under Anne would pursue a hereditary succession.

A Tory *Answer* to the Whigs

During the first decade of the eighteenth century the contrasting Whig and Tory perceptions of the Revolution once more became salient. Supported by a more widely accepted ideology of patriarchal order, the Tories were able to portray themselves as saviours of the Revolution. Their principles of divine right, obedience, and hereditary right had restrained the potential chaos offered by the resistance theory of the Whigs.[91] For their part, a healthy number of Whigs had become emboldened by the emergent authority of Parliament. To their eyes 1688 had seen the deposition of James II by Parliament, and the Act of Settlement had certified that Princess Anne's title as heir was fully 'parliamentary'.[92] These acts by Parliament had extinguished any claim the Prince of Wales or 'Pretender' may have held, regardless of legitimacy or a conversion to Protestantism. According to this view, the rights and authority of Parliament were in harmony with the dictates of reason and God's will. The English mixed constitution that contained a representative element reflected its rationality. It also connoted that its freeholders possessed a power in, and over, government through election and the original contract that held the state to account.

In *Anglia Libera* (1701), the Irish freethinker John Toland (1670–1722) with country Whig and Lockean sympathies, confronted the Tory view of a government created through kingship by God. Toland's 'intimate' connections with the Whigs led him to defend 'Protestant liberty' and the Act of Succession (1701).[93] His earlier advocacy of republicanism was redirected towards a defence of limited monarchy. Invoking a Harringtonian analysis, Toland argued that the conflict between kings, clergy, nobility, and commons had been caused by an overbalance of power and property. The Act of Settlement preserved the balanced constitution and liberty through limited monarchy, preventing the rule of absolutism which placed government in a condition worse than the state of nature.[94] Toland's justification for English liberty began with an analysis of the foundation of government. He argued the people had formed society through a beneficial and natural interdependent relationship that provided security and assistance. For, 'every Individual Member thereof, that Men enter into Society, they agree among themselves (or by such as they authorize to represent them) on certain Rules and Laws'.[95] What this meant for government in England, was that while the legislative power held supreme authority in society and the executive was 'styled' the government, both were accountable to the people. As such, law could not be abused by the executive and must pursue its original mandate as the government must be 'order'd for the common good of Society'.[96] English history was filled with examples of contests between the king, the nobility, and the Commons as they jostled for power, and crucially over time the power of the Commons had grown and become 'fixt'. By the time of James II's reign the Commons had acquired the power and right to act in accordance with the original compact of government as:

> King James the Second having forfeited his Rights to the regal Government of these Nations by a Notorious Neglect of his Declaration when he ascended the Throne, by an open Breach of his Coronation Oath and of the natural Relation or original Compact between all Kings and their Subjects; but more particularly by endeavouring to extirpate the *Protestant* Religion, to subvert our Laws and Liberties, and actually being guilty of several arbitrary and tyrannical Proceedings, the free People of this Kingdom invited over the Prince of *Orange*, under whom they put themselves in a Posture of Defence, and successfully recover'd the Just Rights of themselves and their Posterity.[97]

According to Toland's view the people (which included the nobility), had acted for the security of their rights against a monarch who had shown his unsuitability to rule England. Toland accused him of being a perfidious, Catholic sympathiser who endangered Protestantism and above all held pretensions towards absolutism. Such sovereignty was worse than a Hobbesian state of nature as it generated an environment of chaos. A perilous place where the 'Rule of Men's Actions [was] inconstant, dubious, or altogether unknown', as the king 'without being accountable to any' could 'abolish tomorrow' what been established that day. An absolute monarch's power and will was such, that if he desired he could 'dispense with the very Laws of God, and oppose the clearest Dictats of Nature'.[98] The immensity of this power potentially enabled one man to beggar the entirety of society through his personal will over the common good. Under an 'Arbitrary' government most of the inhabitants were forever 'excluded from all Hopes of changing the Condition of their Birth by any certain or regular Steps', whereas 'one of the noblest Effects of free Governments' was that a 'Man may ascend from the Meanest to the Highest Degree according to his Merit'.[99] Accountability and a mandate for the public good, guaranteed that in popular government no King would 'ever be so good as one of their own making' for 'the Voice of the People is the Voice of God'.[100]

The Revolution was therefore a necessity for Toland. It not only implemented the divine basis of popular government, it also ensured the liberties of the English people while preserving the Protestant faith from James II's Catholic proclivities. The Act of Settlement in the mind of Toland was nothing more than a 'zealous' attempt by William III to ensure acts such as Magna Carta and the Declaration of Rights for a Protestant England. William had hoped '*in a little Time our infamous Distinctions and Partys, but particularly* Jacobitism, *should be wholly abolish[ed] and extirpated*'.[101] The 1689 Revolution and Act of Settlement were a reflection of the need for the government to represent the people's ability to 'dispose of themselves in the Manner they shall think most likely to secure their Liberty of Wealth, and to procure their Happiness'.[102]

This view of the Revolution was trenchantly rejected by numerous Tory and High Church grandees. One of the more prominent refutations of Toland's Whiggish interpretation of the evolution of Parliament was provided by Ofspring Blackall, the Bishop of Exeter (c.1655–1716). In a sermon preached before Queen Anne on 8 March 1709 to mark her accession, Blackall unwittingly instigated a controversy surrounding the connotation of obedience as expressed in Romans 13:4.[103] The sermon was published under the title *The Divine Institution of Magistracy* (1709). In it, Blackall asserted Filmerian claims that all men were born subject to their parents and to their governors.[104] There was no possibility that sovereignty could originate in the people as authority had descended from God to kings via Adam. The people were therefore born obligated to patriarchal government. Not only did this mean that both magistrates and the people were subject to the power of God, it enshrined the importance of the church within the state, and insisted on the absolute obedience of subjects. According to St Paul, the duty of subjects was their 'Submission to the Authority of their Governours, and Obedience to their Laws'.[105] Attainment of the public good was secured through the obedience of the people to their ruler; to do otherwise was treason.[106] While God had not sanctioned one particular form of government, the office of magistrate had been instituted by God for the public good. The office of the magistrate thus possessed the authority of God and shared a 'Portion of the Divine Authority and Power'.[107] This permitted the magistrate to rule through an absolute authority that could not be corrected or punished by any upon earth.[108] The divine source of the power invested in the magistrate – who was frequently a king – meant that he did not embody the people but rather he was accountable to God alone. Moreover, as the representative of God the magistrate could not be resisted by the people no matter how tyrannical their behaviour. Any resistance against the magistrate resulted in the eternal damnation of those subjects as sinners against God for rejecting his will.[109]

This Tory royalist or Filmerian explanation for the origin of government and the role of the people relegated all freeholders to subjugation under the monarch. Resistance was discounted under any circumstances, as the prescribed behaviour of the subject was absolute obedience. Such a view diametrically opposed the position held by many Whigs and it provoked Benjamin Hoadly (1676–1761), then the Rector of St Peter-le-Poer, into responding to the Bishop in spite of his inferiority of rank. In *Some Considerations Humbly Offered* (1709), Hoadly disputed Blackall's interpretation of Romans 13:4. He claimed that God granted his power to the commonality of man to make whatever form of government they desired, imbuing the sovereign with their power.[110] Government had not been instituted through patriarchy or Adam, as paternal right held no civil grounding in Hoadly's opinion.[111] Power did not reside in a single magistrate or king, but existed in the wider populace as revealed by the elective part of

England's constitution. Like Locke and Toland before him, Hoadly claimed that the people possessed the right to defend themselves if their rights were being assailed by a tyrannical monarch. Absolute obedience under such circumstances was foolish; for why would a people allow a ruler to destroy the public happiness and ruin the kingdom due to passive obedience? Such a notion subverted the rights of self-defence and the desire for preservation naturally inherent in the people.[112]

Importantly, Hoadly questioned Blackall's loyalty to the Queen and the revolutionary settlement. He asked the Bishop whether 'all *Resistance* in a whole Nation should be called *Rebellion*, and the Practicers and *Defenders* of it, in any *Case* whatsoever, be so often doomed to eternal Damnation'.[113] In Hoadly's opinion, the 1688 Revolution was an act of resistance against James II that comprised the entire nation to secure the church and kingdom from papism, including the then Princess Anne. Hoadly's larger question to Blackall, was whether the nation and the queen should face a 'Sentence of *Condemnation*'. If so, the Queen illegally possessed her title of monarch as a usurper. This suggestion was strongly rebuffed by Blackall in *The Lord Bishop of Exeter's Answer to Mr. Hoadly's Letter* (1709). In his response Blackall assured the world that he did not question Anne's title or claim it was held through usurpation.[114] Such a suggestion was precluded by the fact that James II had 'withdrawn himself, and abdicated the Government', making it necessary for government to fill the vacancy with the heir: Princess Mary.[115] Blackall reiterated his condemnation regarding populist views on the origins of government being located in the people. Stating that an original contract did not physically exist that proved the monarch was subject to the people.[116] He dismissed the notion that the governed could govern their governors as absurd, again echoing his view that the authority of magistrates was granted directly by God.[117] Patriarchy ensured the succession of authority between rulers and excluded the people from sovereign power. The inequality inherent in patriarchy further undermined a belief in an original contract as such a contract could not be made between inferiors and superiors. Sovereign authority was retained by the magistrates even when elected, as they acted with God's authority not in the people's name.[118] Hoadly's assault on obedience and his penchant for rebellion – like Harrington before him – was a dangerous advocacy of rights for liberty that undermined the Gospels and the state.[119]

Rather disingenuously Hoadly's second response further assailed Blackall's loyalty to the Queen. He repeated his point that a denunciation of resistance was to condemn her and the nation to usurpation and eternal punishment.[120] Ignoring Blackall's appeal to James II's abdication, Hoadly contended that it was not possible to express allegiance to the Revolution if promulgating the view of absolute passive obedience.[121] It precluded resistance and when juxtaposed with patriarchy it restricted the people to subjection forever, regardless of the tyranny of a ruler.[122] Hoadly's enterprise in his dispute with Blackall was to render the Tories hostile to the Revolution. Underlining the belief that 1688 was an indispensable act of resistance highlighted Tory uneasiness over certain truths regarding the revolutionary settlement.[123] The wider implication of a non-resistance outlook was a Tory party that was an enemy of government, which did not oppose the Pretender, either as natural heir or conqueror.[124] Hoadly's rebuttals of a divinely decreed government and non-resistance allowed his Whiggism to boil over as he attacked the Tories, High Church, and Nonjuror positions.

This exchange happened against a backdrop of the controversy following the publication of a sermon by another High Church Tory Henry Sacheverell (1674–1724). *The Perils of False Brethren* (1709) concurred with Blackall's adherence to non-resistance and belief that the Revolution had been the consequence of James II's abdication of the throne.[125] Sacheverall argued that such Whig falsehoods placed the queen under the power of the people and removed her hereditary right as a usurper.[126] The Whigs were portrayed as republican papists who thrived on producing faction as they endeavoured to undermine the Church and state.[127] Depicted as an attack on the Revolution, the ensuing trial against Sacheverell manufactured by the Whigs was to serve as anti-Tory, anti-High-Church propaganda. Instead the trial in 1710 made Sacheverell a martyr (despite his conviction) as his sentiments reflected a wider public sentiment regarding the Revolution. The prosecution proved to be a spectacular failure for the Whigs who were soundly beaten in the 1710 general election and replaced by the Tories in government.[128] The controversy underlined the level of division between the two parties and the relentless separation of their views over the Revolution.

Filmer and Locke revisited: Leslie and Hoadly

Into this mêlée entered Hoadly's great opponent, the Nonjuring controversialist and Jacobite Charles Leslie (1650–1722). In *The Best Answer Ever Was Made. And to which no Answer Ever Will Be Made* (1709), Leslie stated that his work would venture to lift the reader from Hoadly's 'Pit of Whiggism'.[129] He claimed that as a minister of the Church, Hoadly's attack upon the doctrine of non-resistance made him a hypocrite. Leslie disputed Hoadly's interpretation of scripture and supported Blackall's view that a people could not disobey the commands of a magistrate as God did not provide legal recourse to self-defence.[130] Absolute obedience to the magistrate was a duty beholden on the people from God. Political power did not lie in the people, as the last resort was always the province of God and the sovereign on earth. No original contract existed therefore between the people and government because God had given power directly to the sovereign, and God was the sole '*Fountain of Authority*'.[131] This obviated

Hoadly's use of a Lockean, or in Leslie's opinion, Hobbesian state of nature.[132] Government had always existed from the creation of Adam and had descended through patriarchy. Leslie's Filmerian claim that government had sprung from the family via Adamite patriarchy and primogeniture, precluded the possibility of a state of nature.[133] Such a state would be an anarchic and ungodly creation. The divine right of the magistrate therefore made it impossible for the people to judge an authority above themselves, and following the example of Christ and the Apostles they must submit to the civic ordinances of governors.[134] Passive obedience was essential for the peace and happiness of the people and kingdom, and submission to one's rulers was designated by God.

This more prevalent patriarchal view of an ordered society ensured that Hoadly's promulgation of resistance theory came under pressure from a variety of angles: High Church, Low Church, Tories, and Whigs. His steadfast advocacy of resistance was held to be a threat to society and government regardless of party affiliation. *Obedience to Civil Government Clearly Stated* (1711) bluntly attacked Hoadly's theory, stating that the acceptance of papist resistance theory undermined all state's security and ordered society.[135] It placed political authority with the anarchic multitude and would provoke a chaos that held the government to ransom by the 'People or Demagogues' when 'they pleas'd'.[136] Hoadly's resistance was also rejected by some with Whiggish leanings, such as Jonathan Smedley (1671–1729), the Dean of Clogher. In *The Doctrine of Passive Obedience and Non-Resistance Stated* (1710) Smedley contended that unity, peace, and love would be destroyed by resistance.[137] Resistance meant the 'taking Arms to fight or coerce the Prince, the taking the Sword and smiting with it',[138] causing an internecine destruction of the virtues and society they coveted.

Leslie's *The Best Answer Ever Was Made* further defended Blackall against Hoadly's charge that the Bishop of Exeter believed Queen Anne to be a usurper. He approached this vindication from two angles. The first was the standard interpretation of the Revolution as an act of abdication by James II. As 1688 was not an act of resistance, Anne did not possess her title through usurpation, particularly as resistance was both illegal and treasonous.[139] His second point of defence for Blackall and the Queen was slightly more tenuous. It argued that as Anne had received her title after the settlement had been altered by the Revolution, she was therefore not responsible for the beneficial changes made to the succession thus protecting her from the title of usurper. These points were reiterated in a second pamphlet *Best of All* (1709), which again dismissed the notion that the Revolution had been an act of resistance. Instead, Leslie cunningly turned Hoadly's claim that it was '*Impossible* [for] *a Woman*' to possess paternal right into a treasonous question over his own loyalty to the queen and her ability to succeed her father.[140] Additionally, Leslie probed the Whig requirement to label 1688 as an act of resistance. Such a claim betrayed the Revolution by implying it could 'not stand upon former *Principles*, but must have a *Set of Principles* for it self, which they call *Revolution Principles*'.[141] This compulsion present in some Whigs to rely on resistance was born from the republican origins of the party, and its inclusion of the people. From the '*Grecian Commonwealths* (the first in the World)', republics had always thrived on '*Mutiny* and *Rebellion*', because they listened to the wider populace.[142] The people were all 'agog' in civil society and their voice was like 'the Roaring of the Sea', uncontrollable and capable of subsuming all before it. Leslie asserted that the unpredictability of the people had ensured that the last resort of government could not lie with such a destructive force. Popular power was equated to selfish individuality, for the people was nothing more than a collection of egoistical individuals desiring to obtain more for their own ends, destroying society and order in the process.[143]

This attack on the republican or commonwealth origins of the Whigs did not express a new methodological approach for Leslie. From *An Answer to a Book, Entitled the State of the Protestants of Ireland* (1692), Leslie had propounded the principles of passive obedience and non-resistance, while excluding the people from political power. These assertions continued into the eighteenth century and were allied to a strong reliance upon Filmer's promulgation of Adamite patriarchy and divine right theory. His biweekly newspaper *The Rehearsal* (1704–9) espoused a Tory-cum-Jacobite position, which 'reminded his readers that it was [the] Whigs and Dissenters who had destroyed episcopacy and monarchy during the civil war'.[144] In Leslie's opinion a new association had emerged between 'moderate' Churchmen and Whigs. This fanatical 'association' had actively sought to indoctrinate the masses with commonwealth ideas that attacked the Church of England's '*Priest-Craft*', which was depicted as 'inconsistent with *Religion* and *Government*'.[145] *The New Association* (1703) described the division of the Anglican Church into two sorts of churchmen: the 'Violent Men', who were High Churchmen dedicated to the liturgy and opposed toleration; and the 'Moderate Men', who promoted toleration as well as holding latitudinarian views of religious doctrine and practice. Toleration was a weapon with which to assault the High Church by claiming that those who opposed it were 'anti-Christian'.[146] This current Whig tactic exposed an intelligence lacking in their forefathers (the Commonwealthmen), as they now knowingly used division to injure the Tories and the High Church.[147]

To Leslie's mind, toleration and a proliferation of religious sects had always been a source of schism within a church and state. Queen Anne's first speech to Parliament had declared her loyalty to the Anglican Church. The Whigs used this potential threat to their pre-eminence under William as a pretext to claim that Queen, the Tory party, and the High Church were '*Popishly* affected'.[148] Actually it was another political manoeuvre by the Whigs and moderate churchmen as they endeavoured to undermine the recent Tory ascendancy under the new Queen.

This divisive strategy was symptomatic of the Whigs and the genesis of their birth according to Leslie. They possessed a desire to extirpate the monarchy and the church because their principles were of 'the Presbyterian Government' and were 'Republican in the State as well as the Church'.[149] These republicans had instigated the Civil War in 1642 and had murdered Charles I in their struggle for religious toleration. The proof of this Presbyterian divisiveness was now evident in Scotland, where its synod had declared a Presbyterian form of government that had abolished the Episcopacy.[150] This conduct had troubled Scotland since the seventeenth century and now threatened to infect England too.

Such schismatic behaviour stemmed from the Presbyterians' commitment to its foundational doctrine of resistance, an ideology designed to engender division.[151] This divisive yearning was generated by the commonwealth belief in public liberty against monarchy. It had been witnessed during the Exclusion Crisis when the Whig party had hypocritically claimed allegiance to Charles II while systematically endeavouring to overthrow the church and state.[152] Liberty was the 'Word and Cry' of the Whigs, whose republicanism attempted to harness the power of the whole people which was impossible.[153] According to Leslie, the voice of the people was not the voice of God, and it was absurd to believe that God would not have ordained a form of government from the beginning of time. Discounting the idea of the original contract, Leslie belittled the suggestion of a state of nature which have made the formation of government among men necessary. God would not have left men like *Brute Beasts*, to *Range* about in the *Wide World*' until by their own wisdom and the plurality of their own voices they framed government for themselves. If such an arrangement had occurred it meant that God had been 'oblig'd to concur' and make government divine, so that the *'Voice of the People*, from that Time forth, was the *Voice of God*'.[154] As scripture had decreed that government had been handed down to man through Adam, the Whig view was a nonsense that subverted the natural order. God's wisdom had ordained that the people were necessarily excluded from the law and government to eschew the confusion and chaos of their schemes. The Whig promotion of the 'Liberty of the People' was paradoxical, as the arbitrary power of the people that threatened society.[155]

Leslie's need to refute the distinctly Lockean claims of resistance and original contract expressed by the Whigs and Hoadly during the first decade of the eighteenth century bolstered his use of the patriarchalism of Filmer.[156] Leslie allied Filmer's Adamite patriarchy to a Tory concept of an ordered patriarchal society and the staple doctrines of divine right theory as expressed by the Nonjurors. He rejected schismatic religious toleration and called for the Dissenters to be dismissed from office to prevent another civil war.[157] In an assault on Whig doctrine he rebuffed the notion of public liberty, and therefore popular involvement in government. Patriarchy decreed that men were not born

free, as sovereignty had been passed by Adam to his heirs through primogeniture and all children were subject to their parents and king.[158] The generality of
mankind were not owed natural freedoms and did not possess a 'Birth-Right'
because they were born under subjection. This was proven by English law, in
which men did not own 'Liberty or Property'. Such legislation did not exist
because the vast majority of men were not involved in government or election as
it would be chaotic.[159] Indeed, the truth concerning England's mixed constitution was that no government was truly mixed. There was always a 'fountain', in
England's case a monarch, which was the spring of all government and this truly
exercised supreme authority within the state.[160] As Leslie's Jacobitism became
fiercer his use of Filmer not only undermined Whig doctrine but took a broader
swipe at the Revolution itself. In *The Finishing Stroke* (1709) Leslie reiterated the
primacy of the king within government and the inability to resist the sovereign
under any circumstances. According to St Paul's teachings, obedience was due
at all times, even when ruled by a tyrant. In an absolute rejection of the popular
element in Whig doctrine Leslie stated that a tyrant was preferable to the rule of
the people, for unlike the latter the former would not 'destroy' his own subjects
and state and would still do good.[161]

Hoadly's two major works during this period specifically responded to
Leslie's patriarchalist attack upon the Whig interpretation of 1688 and his belief
in resistance. In an echo of the Exclusion Crisis the ideas of Locke were used
to oppose the Filmerian patriarchalism and divine right theory expounded by
Leslie.[162] Hoadly not only sought to undermine Leslie's Nonjuror ideology from
the foundations up, but also the Tory view of government and society. In *The
Measures of Submission to the Civil Magistrate Consider'd* (1706), Hoadly argued that
no particular form of government had been favoured by God in scripture.[163]
God had ordained that government should exist for the peace and happiness
for human society but its institution as a form of government had been left to
humanity.[164] The role of government was to pursue the public good, and magistrates who did not follow this dictum could not be said to act according to God's
will or authority.[165] Rejecting the Tory and Anglican belief in passive obedience,
Hoadly claimed that the people were exempted from their normal bond of obedience if the ruler no longer followed God's decree, as submission was not 'unlimited'. Resistance and rebellion were permissible as the magistrate had lost their
authority to uphold the public good which made it beholden on the people to
defend their rights. Civil government did not function for the benefit of a Prince,
but for the sake of the public, so no man was 'under the least obligation to submit
to any signal instance of *Oppression*'.[166] Submission to such governors helped '*to
destroy and raise the Public Interest, and to betray the Public Happiness*'. Leslie's patriarchal standpoint favoured the interest of one over the many, when it was clear
to Hoadly's proto-liberalism that human society had been constituted for the

benefit of all. Blind submission to oppression meant the destruction of society and the general interest as the magistrate followed 'their own private *Interest*'.[167]

Hoadly clarified his earlier discussion on resistance in *The Original and Institutions of Civil Government, Discussed* (1709), claiming that the public's right to self-defence required a safety mechanism within the state against tyranny. In such circumstances when the public good was threatened by the magistrate, the people could either choose to ignore the government through 'passive submission' or directly resist it to protect the public good.[168] Moreover, as God had not chosen a particular form of government it was perfectly logical to suggest that He had allowed His authority to be used in the creation of a compact between men when they decided on society. A '*Humane Compact*' to found government would provide the whole of society with the right to take care of itself, 'superior to the *particular Right* of any Man to govern, which was given only for the good of the whole'.[169] The involvement of a compact in the institution of government reflected the 'Equality' and 'Independency' that existed before the original contract, as well as the need for the 'Dependency' that brought the people together. It also imitated the people's ability and power to change and restructure government, as the 'Right of preserving [society] ... and its Privileges against those who [had] no right to invade, or destroy them'.[170] Popular authority was the source of government, as it defended liberty and focused the state on the public good at all times.

In his rebuttal of Leslie, Hoadly was able to link the institution of government to the absolutist leanings of the Nonjuror's theory. He contended that God had not favoured any particular form of government, and was able to reject the notion that God had sanctioned patriarchy or primogeniture to support lineages that could not be proved. Over time (absolute) monarchies and governments had relied on such concepts as 'obedience', 'subjection', 'rule', and passive obedience to enforce their power and authority.[171] The primary argument for the defence of absolute power and unlimited obedience was the need to counteract the wickedness of their subjects through the 'last resort' (in law and justice). The doctrine of '*Passive Submission*' (obedience), however, removed the people's ability to defend themselves against the '*Desolation*' of government, placing them 'under an *Absolute Monarch*' without any 'possibility of *Redressing* the greatest *Universal Misery* that can be conceived'. Such a situation would equate to 'the miserable Condition of the whole of the *People of France*, which hath proceeded from the *King's* being *Absolute*'.[172] A nation that embodied patriarchy and absolutism in the person of Louis XIV who claimed to reign by divine right, yet who would not be able to trace back his ancestors to Noah or Adam, as no other king could.

Hoadly boldly linked Leslie's Nonjuror, Tory, Anglican predilection for submission and passive obedience to the absolutism of France. This tactic played on the very real fears extant at this time regarding the intentions of the French towards Europe and Britain. Now engaged in the War of the Spanish Succession (1702–14),[173] France's accommodation of the exiled Jacobite court at Saint-Germain-en-Laye offered a dual threat of a Jacobite-led French invasion of Britain. This trepidation had been present throughout the decade, and the Whigs frequently linked a rejection of contract and resistance to the slavery of absolute France. Toland for example, claimed that the connection between the French and the Pretender – James II died in 1701 – created a real threat to Britain's 'happiness' and 'liberty'. The importation of absolutism and Catholicism by both parties would plunge the nation into 'the most dismal and lasting Scene of Violence and Blood' as the people fought for their religion and liberties against the tyranny and superstition of a foreign prince.[174] If the French were successful in their aggrandising attempts at hegemony, Europe would collapse into Catholic absolutist 'slavery'.[175] A fear echoed by Daniel Defoe, who asseverated that England's political and religious divisions had weakened the state.[176] Defoe attacked the Nonjurors such as Leslie for focusing their energies upon the altered succession rather than preserving the nation from the French. Protestant Jacobites were also condemned for feeding information to their Catholic counterparts in France. His answer to the French menace was an end of division in England as the consequence of not healing such divisions was a French dominance of Europe.[177] While these divisions continued apace throughout the reign of Queen Anne, his call for an alliance with the Dutch and the Austrians took shape during the War of the Spanish Succession. The wider significance of this relationship was its ability to generate great psychological fear from two enemies of the state and the Revolution: the French and the Jacobites. Anxiety over French territorial expansion in Europe under Louis XIV proved a heady mixture when mixed with the threat of arbitrary government and Catholicism. France was not only the traditional enemy of the English it symbolised the assault on the political and religious freedoms they had fought to save throughout the seventeenth century. Louis's support for the Jacobites aggravated memories of a past rejected, and threatened further peril to the state and its people.

The polemic surrounding the *Answer* reveals the remaining divisions between the Whigs and Tories over the nature of the Revolution. While both had recognised the necessity to act after the birth of the Catholic Pretender in 1688, neither side could agree on the genesis of James II's removal from the throne. The belief that the king had abdicated his throne was widespread among the establishment, and thus passed to the wider populace. It reflected a patriarchal order of society that was inherently Tory or court in nature and acted as a social bond. Ideas of resistance were less popular, and despite their Whiggish origins in the seventeenth century it was not supported by all Whigs and was an unpalatable reality for many. The ramifications of James's forced removal by William III's expeditionary force and the prince's predominant reliance on the Whigs in his government energised tensions between the two parties into the eighteenth century. The favour shown to the Tories under Queen Anne provided an opportunity to revel in the survival of Tory and High Church doctrines that had remained intact as they had taken the lead in the Convention of 1688 to prevent anarchy. Yet the uncomfortable truth that would not dissipate was the premature end of James II's divinely instituted tenure in office. It not only stimulated divisions between two parties seeking political dominance, it fuelled the activity and ideology of groups opposed to 1688 and the altered monarchical succession. These issues had their roots in the reigns of the early Stuarts. Unanswered questions over the political and religious settlements at Charles II's restoration ensured future divisions. Old loyalties, ideology, and traditions regarding an ordered society were threatened by new ideas concerning the origin of power in a mixed constitution. As will be discussed in the next chapter, this opposition was extremely vocal and influential as the parliamentary power increased in a modernising Britain. Antagonisms over the Revolution were later surmounted, but they were replaced by new threats of corruption to government and society.

Notes

1 The term absolutism is here defined as possessing the ability to act with freedom from institutional checks or in an unrestrained autonomous manner, and the argument of this chapter will claim that the Stuarts attempted to achieve this form of rule. As Durand and Bonney have made clear no European constitution became truly absolute, but a number of monarchs were able to free themselves from the constraints of parliaments and legal opposition while ruling along traditional lines (see G. Durand, 'What Is Absolutism?', *Louis XIV and Absolutism*, ed. Ragnhild Hatton (London, 1976), 18; Richard Bonney, *Society and Government in France under Richelieu and Mazarin, 1624–61* (Basingstoke, 1988), xiii). More recently Sommerville has qualified this point by claiming that absolutism was frequently a 'façade' of omnipotent political power (Johann P. Sommerville, 'Early Modern Absolutism in Practice and Theory', *Monarchism and Absolutism in Early Modern Europe*, eds Cesare Cuttica and Glenn Burgess (London, 2012), 117).

2 Tim Harris, *Politics under the Later Stuarts: Party Conflict in a Divided Society 1660–1715* (London, 1993), 7.

3 J.H. Plumb, *The Growth of Political Stability in England 1675–1725* (London, 1967), 32–4.

4 See Jonathan Scott, 'Radicalism and Restoration', *Historical Journal*, 31, 2 (1988), pp. 453–67 (458–61); Mark Knights, *Politics and Opinion in Crisis, 1678–81* (Cambridge, 1994); Jonathan Scott, *England's Troubles. Seventeenth-Century English Political Instability in European Context* (Cambridge, 2000); G.S. De Krey, *Restoration and Revolution in Britain: A Political History of Charles II and the Glorious Revolution* (Basingstoke, 2007).

5 Bruce Lenman, *The Jacobite Risings in Britain 1689–1746* (London, 1980), 12.

6 Harris, *Politics under the Later Stuarts*, 8.

7 J.G.A. Pocock, *The Machiavellian Moment: Florentine Political Thought and the Atlantic Republican Tradition* (Princeton, 1975), 406.

8 For a discussion on the potential for absolute sovereignty under the early Stuarts see the exchange between Johann P. Sommerville and Glenn Burgess (Sommerville, *Politics and Ideology in England, 1603–1640* (London, 1986); 'Political Ideas in the Early Seventeenth Century: Revisionism and the Case of Absolutism', *Journal of British Studies*, 35, 2, Revisionisms (Apr., 1996), pp. 168–94; Burgess, *The Politics of the Ancient Constitution: An Introduction to English Political Thought, 1603–1642* (Basingstoke, 1992); *Absolute Monarchy and the Stuart Constitution* (Yale, 1996)).

9 Julian Hoppit, *A Land of Liberty? England 1689–1727* (Oxford, 2000), 7.

10 The term cabal conveyed two meanings. First, that of a group (of men) rather than an individual advising the king, and, second, it also served as an acronym of the members names: Baron Clifford (1630–73); the Earl of Arlington (1618–85); the Duke of Buckingham (1628–87); the First Baron Ashley (Shaftesbury); the Duke of Lauderdale (1616–82).

11 See J.G.A. Pocock, 'Machiavelli, Harrington, and English Political Ideologies in the Eighteenth Century', *William and Mary Quarterly*, 3rd series, 22, 4 (Oct. 1965), pp. 549–83 (558–64); Arihiro Fukuda, *Sovereignty and the Sword. Harrington, Hobbes and Mixed Government in the English Civil Wars* (Oxford, 1997), 79–81.

12 James Harrington, *The Commonwealth of Oceana*, ed. J.G.A. Pocock (Cambridge, 1992), 51, 174, 205.

13 See [Andrew Marvell], *An Account of the Growth of Popery, and Arbitrary Government in England* (Amsterdam, 1677), 14–15, 28, 153–4; J.G.A. Pocock, 'Machiavelli, Harrington, and English Political Ideologies in the Eighteenth Century', 565; Harris, *Politics under the Later Stuarts*, 54. Louis XIV's reforms of government will be outlined in Chapter 4.

14 See Pocock, 'Machiavelli, Harrington, and English Political Ideologies in the Eighteenth Century', 564–5; *Machiavellian Moment*, 406–17; Mark Goldie, 'John Locke and Anglican Royalism', *Political Studies* 31, (1983), pp. 61–85 (63).

15 See Caroline Robbins, *The Eighteenth-Century Commonwealthman. Studies in the Transmission, Development and Circumstance of English Liberal Thought from the Restoration of Charles II until the War with the Thirteen Colonies* (Harvard, 1961), 5, 22; in relation to 'classical republicanism', see Jonathan Scott, *Algernon Sidney and the English Republic, 1623–1677* (Cambridge, 1988), 14–18; Scott, 'What Were Commonwealth Principles?', *Historical Journal*, 47, 3 (2004), pp. 591–613 (603–16)

16 See M.M. Goldsmith, 'Liberty, Virtue and the Rule of Law, 1689–1700', *Republicanism, Liberty, and Commercial Society, 1649–1776*, ed. David Wootton (Stanford, 1994), 200; Quentin Skinner, *Liberty before Liberalism* (Cambridge, 1998), 74–5.

17 See Carol Z. Wiener, 'The Beleaguered Isle: A Study of Elizabethan and Early Jacobean Anti-Catholicism', *Past and Present*, 51 (May 1971), pp. 27–62 (29); John Miller, *Popery and Politics in England 1660–1688* (Cambridge, 1973), ch. 3; Alexandra Walsham, "The Fatall Vesper": Providentialism and Anti-Popery in Late Jacobean London', *Past & Present*, 144 (Aug. 1994), pp. 36–87.

18 For a corresponding view, see J.F. Bosher, 'The Franco-Catholic Danger, 1660–1715', *History*, 79, 255, pp. 5–30 (21); David Scott, *Leviathan: The Rise of Britain as a World Power* (London, 2013), 204–5. Scott astutely contends that Louis XIV dominated British history more than any other individual during this period, including the Stuart kings. A lack of focus on the impact of Louis XIV and France has been noted by Rachel Hammersley who has highlighted a perception among historians caused by the influence of J.G.A. Pocock, that England moved away from European ideas and instead focused on the republican or Commonwealthmen concern over government corruption (*The English Republican Tradition and Eighteenth-century France: Between the Ancients and the Moderns* (Manchester, 2010), 1–2, 17).

19 See Chapter 4.

20 The Exclusion Bill (November 1680), *The Stuart Constitution 1603–1688. Documents and commentary*, 2nd edn, ed. J.P. Kenyon (Cambridge, 1986), pp. 382–9.

21 See Cesare Cuttica, *Sir Robert Filmer (1588–1653) and the Patriotic Monarch: Patriarchalism in Seventeenth-century Political Thought* (Manchester, 2012), 219–20; Cuttica, 'Reputation versus Context in the Interpretation of Sir Robert Filmer's *Patriarcha*', *History of Political Thought*, 33 (summer 2012), pp. 231–57 (243–4). As will be discussed below Filmer's *Patriarcha* was a highly influential work, not only within the Exclusion Crisis but also into the eighteenth century through thinkers such as Charles Leslie. This echoes the opinion of J.P. Kenyon, 'The Revolution of 1688: Resistance and Contract', *Historical Perspectives: Studies in English Thought and Society, in Honour of J.H. Plumb*, ed. Neil McKendrick (London, 1974), 60–1; an opinion of Filmer opposed by Laurence Stone, 'The Results of the English Revolutions of the Seventeenth Century', *Three British Revolutions: 1641, 1688, 1776*, ed. J.G.A. Pocock (Princeton, 1980), 70–2.

22 Sir Robert Filmer, *Patriarcha*, ed. Johnann P. Sommerville (Cambridge, 1991), I, i (4).

23 *Ibid.*, I, ii (6–9).

24 *Ibid.*, III, xii (52).

25 See Peter Laslett, 'Introduction', *Patriarcha and Other Political Works of Sir Robert Filmer*, ed. Peter Laslett (Oxford, 1949), 34–6; Gordon J. Schochet, *Patriarchalism in Political Thought: The Authoritarian Family and Political Speculation and Attitudes Especially in Seventeenth-Century England* (Oxford, 1975), 193–4; Richard Ashcraft, *Revolutionary Politics & Locke's Two Treatises of Government* (Princeton, 1986), 187. In his work Ashcraft challenges James Daly's contention that Filmer's ideas 'were largely unknown and unused by Royalist writers' (187, 16 n.); see James Daly, *Sir Robert Filmer and English political thought* (Toronto, 1979), 9–10, 124, 151. J.N. Figgis points out that patriarchy is actually a 'symmetrical form' of divine right theory, but was not an essential component of divine right theory or universally employed as a concept (8); see *The Divine Right of Kings* (New York, 1965), 5–16.

26 Cuttica, *Sir Robert Filmer (1588–1653)*, 2–3.

27 Gordon J. Schochet, 'Politics and Mass Attitudes in Stuart England', *Historical Journal*, 12, 3 (1969), pp. 413–41 (414–15).

28 *Ibid.*, 441; H.T. Dickinson, 'The Eighteenth-Century Debate on the Sovereignty of Parliament', *Transactions of the Royal Historical Society*, 5th series, 26 (1976), pp. 189–210 (191); J.C.D. Clark, *English Society 1688–1832: Ideology, Social Structure and Political Practice during the Ancien Regime* (Cambridge, 1985), 43–4; David Wootton, 'Introduction', *Divine Right and Democracy: An Anthology of Political Writing in Stuart England*, ed. David Wootton (London, 1986), 27–8.

29 J.H. Plumb, *The First Four Georges* (London, 1956), 24.

30 See Schochet, *Patriarchalism in Political Thought*, 19; H.T. Dickinson, *Liberty and Property: Political Ideology in Eighteenth-Century Britain* (London, 1977), 14.

31 See Laslett, 'Introduction', 28; Schochet, *Patriarchalism in Political Thought*, 139; Wootton, 'Introduction', *Divine Right and Democracy*, 31–2; Sommerville, 'Introduction', ix–x, xvi. Wootton argues that Filmer's model that created subordination towards the grandfather or head of the family did not exist in seventeenth-century England. Rather, once an adult male had established his own household he only owed a duty to his father but was independent of him. James Daly actually questioned whether Filmer's model was patriarchal at all, because the system relegated patriarchalism to the status of a 'necessary hypothesis' in order to promote political sovereignty (*Sir Robert Filmer and English Political Thought*, 152).

32 See James Tyrrell's *Patriarcha non Monarcha* (London, 1681), 47; John Locke, *Two Treatises of Government*, ed. Peter Laslett (Cambridge, 1999), II, xiii (150); Algeron Sidney, *Discourses concerning Government*, ed. Thomas G. West (Indiana, 1990), I, vi (30). Locke's work was not published until 1689 (although dated 1690), and Sidney's work was published posthumously in 1698.

33 Sidney, *Discourses concerning Government*, II, xvii (173), xix (186), and Locke, *Two Treatises of Government*, II, xviii (199–210).

34 Jonathan Scott has argued that Sidney's politics were 'not Whiggish', instead offering a broader and more religiously inspired insight into political action than many early Whigs. Scott also states that Sidney acted against Whig interests for the French as a spy during the Exclusion Crisis (*Algernon Sidney and the English Republic, 1623–1677*, 3–4).

35 In addition, Locke placed an emphasis on inherent natural rights and property that enjoyed protection under the law, safeguarding them from any (tyrannical) encroachment by the polity (*Two Treatises of Government*, II, xvi (393–4), xix (419)). While it has been argued that Locke's influence on his contemporaries and the early eighteenth century was not as entrenched as once believed, as will be shown below his views on rights and resistance were applied by a number of prominent Whigs in their attacks on the Tories. For a discussion of Locke's influence, see Peter Laslett, 'Introduction', *Two Treatises of Government*, ed. Laslett (Cambridge, 1988), 14–15; John Dunn, *The Political Thought of John Locke: An Historical Account of the Argument of the 'Two Treatises of Government'* (Cambridge, 1969), 6–9; Goldie, 'John Locke and Anglican Royalism' (61–2); James Tully, *An Approach to Political Philosophy: Locke in Contexts* (Cambridge, 1993), 96.

36 See Henry Neville, *Plato Redivivus, or Dialogues concerning Government*, 3rd edn (London, 1745), 22–6; Gaby Mahlberg, *Henry Neville and English Republican Culture in the Seventeenth Century: Dreaming of Another Game* (Manchester, 2009).

37 Harris, *Politics under the Later Stuarts*, 66.

38 See George H. Tavard, *The Quest for Catholicity: A Study in Anglicanism* (London, 1963), 70; Bernard and Margaret Pawley, *Rome and Canterbury through Four Centuries* (London, 1974), 49.

39 J.R. Western, *Monarchy and Revolution: The English State in the 1680s* (London, 1972), 31–2.

40 Jacqueline Rose, 'Robert Brady's Intellectual History and Royalist Antipopery in Restoration England', *English Historical Review*, 122 (2007), pp. 1287–1317 (1292).

41 For the Tory attack on the ancient constitution, see J.G.A. Pocock, *The Ancient Constitution and the Feudal Law: A Study of English Historical Thought in the Seventeenth Century, A Reissue with a Retrospect* (Cambridge, 1987), 40–5, 96–102, 110–23, 198–208; R.J. Smith, *The Gothic Bequest: Medieval Institutions in British Thought, 1688–1863* (Cambridge, 1987), 8, 12.

42 See Chapter 2. These two issues were reflected in the names of the burgeoning parties: Whig was derived from a Scottish Whiggamore, or a Presbyterian who rebelled against Charles I; Tory originated from a pejorative term relating to Irish Catholics (as supporters of the Catholic Duke of York).

43 See J.R. Jones, *The First Whigs: The Politics of the Exclusion Crisis 1678–1683* (London, 1963), 160–1; Harris, *Politics under the Later Stuarts*, ch. 4; Edward Vallance, *The Glorious Revolution. 1688: Britain's Fight for Liberty* (London, 2007), 32–48.

44 In the case of Sidney's execution, Judge Jeffries allowed the manuscript of the *Discourses concerning Government* to be used as the second witness in the trial.

45 James Daly, 'The Idea of Absolute Monarchy in Seventeenth-Century England', *Historical Journal*, 21, 2 (Jun. 1978), pp. 227–50 (248). This view of a move towards absolutism is supported by John Miller, 'The Potential for Absolutism in Later Stuart England', *History*, 69, 226 (Jan. 1984), pp. 187–207 (187); Howard Nenner, 'The later Stuart Age', *The Varieties of Political Thought, 1500–1800*, eds J.G.A. Pocock with Gordon J. Schochet and Lois G. Schwoerer (Cambridge, 1993), 181.

46 Western, *Monarchy and Revolution*, 46–7.

47 W.A. Speck, 'James II and VII (1633–1701)', *Oxford Dictionary of National Biography*, online: www.oxforddnb.com.ezproxy.sussex.ac.uk/view/article/14593?docPos=2

48 Vallance, *Glorious Revolution. 1688*, 74.

49 Steve Pincus, *1688: The First Modern Revolution* (Yale, 2009), 134–5.

50 See Western, *Monarchy and Revolution*, 105–7; H.G. Koenigsberger, 'Monarchies and Parliaments in Early Modern Europe Dominium Regale or Dominium Politicum et Regale', *Theory and Society*, 5, 2 (Mar. 1978), pp. 191–217 (204).

51 Vallance, *Glorious Revolution. 1688*, 80–4.

52 *Ibid.*, 93–4.

53 See Steve Pincus, 'From Holy Cause to Economic Interest: The Study of Population and the Invention of the State', *A Nation Transformed. England after the Restoration*, eds Alan Houston and Steve Pincus (Cambridge, 2001), 290–3, 297; Pincus, *1688*, 87, 134–5. This suggestion had been raised earlier by Christopher Hill, *The Century of Revolution 1603–1714* (Walton-on-Thames, 1980), 1–4.

54 Pincus, 'From Holy Cause to Economic Interest', 287.

55 *Ibid.*, 293, 297.

56 Pincus, *1688*, 87.

57 *Ibid.*, 178.

58 *Ibid.*, 372–4. Pincus claims that James II wanted to frame an alliance with the French that would divide the world between the English (seas and colonies and the French (the land and Europe) in terms of territory (319).

59 Sophus Reinert claims that both Charles II and James II were unconcerned by French expansion, while William III obsessively fought against it. Reinert points to a number of texts, notably John Cary's *Essay on the State of England* (1695) which reflect a contemporary concern with Louis XIV's endeavour to achieve a universal monarchy (*Translating Empire: Emulation and*

the Origins of Political Economy (Harvard, 2011), 78, 79).

60 See Chapter 2.

61 See Pincus, *1688*, 178; J.R. Jones, *The Revolution of 1688 in England* (London, 1972), 82.

62 The 'Immortal Seven' were composed of five Whigs (the Earl of Shrewsbury, Earl of Devonshire, Viscount Lumley, Lord Russell, and Lord Sidney) and two Tories (the Earl of Danby and Henry Compton, the Bishop of London). Sidney, the brother of Algernon Sidney, drafted the letter.

63 This view concurs with: Vallance, *The Glorious Revolution. 1688*, 307–11; Tim Harris, *Revolution: The Great Crisis of British Monarchy, 1685–1720* (London, 2007), 308; Pincus, *1688*, 8, 474–6.

64 For the importance of mob rioting during the Revolution, see Harris, *Revolution*, 308; for a counter view, William L. Sachse, 'The Mob and the Revolution of 1688', *Journal of British Studies*, 4, 1 (Nov. 1964), pp. 23–40 (23–4, 39–40).

65 *An Act Declaring the Rights and Liberties of the Subject and Settling the Succession of the Crown*, Avalon Project (Yale Law School): http://avalon.law.yale.edu/17th_century/england.asp

66 H.T. Dickinson, 'The Eighteenth-Century Debate on the "Glorious Revolution"', *History*, 61, 201 (Feb. 1976), pp. 28–45 (28); Dickinson, *Liberty and Property*, 42.

67 Harris, *Revolution*, 321–2.

68 Lois G. Schwoerer, 'The Bill of Rights: Epitome of the Revolution of 1688–89', *Three British Revolutions*, ed. Pocock, 228–31.

69 For the belief that the Revolution resulted in substantial change, see B.W. Hill, 'Executive Monarchy and the Challenge of Parties, 1689–1832: Two Concepts of Government and two Historiographical Interpretations', *Historical Journal*, xiii, 3 (1970), pp. 379–401 (380); Dickinson, 'The Eighteenth-Century Debate on the "Glorious Revolutionn"', 32; Hoppit, *A Land of Liberty?*, 22–3. For the belief that the old order survived, see John Cannon, *Aristocratic Century: The Peerage of Eighteenth-Century England* (Cambridge, 1984), 150–1; J.C.D. Clark, *English Society 1688–1832*, 6–7; Clark, *Revolution and Rebellion: State and Society in England in the Seventeenth and Eighteenth Centuries* (Cambridge, 1986), 73–5.

70 Mark Goldie, 'The English System Of Liberty', *Cambridge History of Eighteenth-Century Political Thought*, eds Mark Goldie and Robert Wokler (Cambridge, 2006), 40.

71 Paul Kleber Monod, *Jacobitism and the English People, 1688–1788* (Cambridge, 1989), 17.

72 *Ibid.*, 22.

73 George Hickes, *The Pretences of the Prince of Wales Examin'd, and Rejected* (London, 1701), 4.

74 *Ibid.*, 12.

75 *Ibid.*, 15.

76 Mark Goldie, 'The Nonjurors, Episcopacy, and the Origins of the Convocation Controversy', *Ideology and Conspiracy: Aspects of Jacobitism 1689 -1759*, ed. Eveline Cruickshanks (Edinburgh, 1982), 15.

77 Louis XIV supported the campaign in Ireland to open a second front in the Nine Years' War (1688–97) against his key adversary William. As the Dutch Stadtholder, William was the pivotal figure in the Grand Alliance that also comprised the Holy Roman Empire, Spain, and Savoy in a war against French aggrandisement in Europe, as well as revulsion towards the apparent mistreatment of Protestants following the French Revocation of the Edict of Nantes (1685). Louis used the support of his cousin James in Ireland as a means to distract William from war on the continent.

78 James E. Bradley, 'The Religious Origins of Radical politics in England, Scotland, and Ireland, 1662–1800', *Religion and Politics in Enlightenment Europe*, eds James E. Bradley and Dale K. Van Kley (Indiana, 2001), 187.

79 J.C.D. Clark, 'A General Theory of Party, Opposition and Government, 1688–1832', *Historical Journal*, 23, 2 (1980), pp. 295–325 (296).

80 Hill, 'Executive Monarchy and the Challenge of Parties, 1689–1832', 382.

81 Clark, 'A General Theory of Party, Opposition and Government, 1688–1832', 299.

82 Mark Goldie, 'The Roots of True Whiggism 1688–94', *History of Political Thought*, 1, 2 (Jun. 1980), 220.

83 *Ibid.*, 235.

84 *Ibid.*, 195, 235.

85 Charlwood Lawton, *The Jacobite Principles Vindicated: In Answer to a Letter Sent to the Author* (London, 1693), 10.

86 Paul Monod, 'Jacobitism and Country Principles in the Reign of William III', *Historical Journal*, 30, 2 (Jun., 1987), pp. 289–310 (298).

87 *Ibid.*, 290.

88 See John Trenchard, *An argument, shewing that a standing army is inconsistent with a free government and absolutely destructive to the constitution of the English monarchy* (London, 1697); Walter Moyle, *The second part of an argument shewing that a standing army is inconsistent with a free government, and absolutely destructive to the constitution of the English monarchy with remarks on the late published list of King James's Irish forces in France* (London, 1697); Andrew Fletcher, *A Discourse of Government with relation to Militias: The Political Works of Andrew Fletcher, Esq* (London, 1732).

89 Geoffrey Holmes, *The Making of a Great Power: Late Stuart and Early Georgian Britain 1660–1722* (London, 1993), 222.

90 See Ragnhild Hatton, *George I: Elector and King* (London, 1978), 72–5; Jeremy Black, *The Hanoverians: The History of a Dynasty* (London, 2004), 58.

91 Dickinson, 'The Eighteenth-Century Debate on the "Glorious Revolution"', 34.

92 J.P. Kenyon, *Revolution Principles: The Politics of Party, 1689–1720* (Cambridge, 1977), 104–5.

93 Justin Champion, *Republican Learning: John Toland and the Crisis of Christian culture, 1696–1722* (Manchester, 2003), 121.

94 *Ibid.*, 121–2.

95 John Toland, *Anglia Libera* (London, 1701), 2.

96 *Ibid.*, 16.

97 *Ibid.*, 22–3.

98 *Ibid.*, 6–7.

99 *Ibid.*, 12.

100 *Ibid.*, 26.

101 *Ibid.*, 50–1.

102 *Ibid.*, 107.

103 Andrew Starkie, 'Blackall, Ofspring (bap. 1655, d.1716)', *Oxford Dictionary of National Biography* online: www.oxforddnb.com.ezproxy.sussex.ac.uk/view/article/2507. In the King James Bible Romans 13:4 reads: 'For he is the minister of God to thee for good. But if thou do that which is evil, be afraid; for he beareth not the sword in vain: for he is the minister of God, a revenger to *execute* wrath upon him that doeth evil.'

104 Ofspring Blackall, *The Divine Institution of Magistracy, and the Gracious Design of Its Institution* (London, 1709), 10.

105 *Ibid.*, 3.

106 *Ibid.*, 24.

107 *Ibid.*, 6.

108 *Ibid.*, 16.

109 *Ibid.*, 8.

110 Benjamin Hoadly, *Some Considerations Humbly offered to the Right Reverend the Lord Bishop of Exeter* (London, 1709), 8.

111 *Ibid.*, 9.

112 *Ibid.*, 13–14. This connection between inherent natural rights and happiness within the generality of the people highlights Hoadly's Lockean influence rather than a neo-Harrington debt in discussing resistance and contract theory. Hoadly argued that it was the role of civil government to ensure people's happiness because of their individual natural rights as 'inculcated' by scripture (*An Humble Reply to the Right Reverend the Lord Bishop of Exeter's Answer* (London, 1709), 8–9). On Locke's view of rights, see Jeremy Waldron, *God, Locke, and Equality: Christian Foundations of John Locke's Political Thought* (Cambridge, 2002).

113 *Ibid.*, 15.

114 Ofspring Blackall, *The Lord Bishop of Exeter's Answer to Mr. Hoadly's Letter* (London, 1709), 51–2.

115 *Ibid.*, 27.

116 *Ibid.*, 26–7.

117 *Ibid.*, 12–13.

118 *Ibid.*, 45–6.

119 *Ibid.*, 55.

120 Hoadly, *An Humble Reply to the Right Reverend the Lord Bishop of Exeter's Answer*, 66.

121 *Ibid.*, 58–9.

122 *Ibid.*, 36, 47.

123 *Ibid.*, 63.

124 *Ibid.*, 61–2.

125 Henry Sacheverell, *The Perils of False Brethren, both in Church, and State* (London, 1709), 12.

126 *Ibid.*, 18–19.

127 *Ibid.*, 13–14, 16.

128 See Robbins, *The Eighteenth-Century Commonwealthman*, 86; Kenyon, 'The Revolution of 1688: Resistance and Contract', 65–8; Champion, *Republican Learning*, 142.

129 Charles Leslie, *The Best Answer Ever Was Made. And to which no Answer Ever Will Be Made* (London, 1709), 28.

130 *Ibid.*, 11.

131 *Ibid.*, 8.

132 For a discussion on the relationship between Hobbes and Locke's approach to natural law and religion, see Timothy Stanton, 'Hobbes and Locke on Natural Law and Jesus Christ', *History of Political Thought*, 29, 1 (spring 2008), pp. 65–88.

133 *Ibid.*, 10, 15–16.

134 *Ibid.*, 18, 20–1.

135 [anonymous], *Obedience to Civil Government clearly stated* (London, 1711), 81. For the detailed rebuttal of Hoadly, see 52–3, 64–5, 70–9, 81.

136 *Ibid.*, 18.

137 Jonathan Smedley, *The Doctrine of Passive Obedience and Non-Resistance Stated* (London, 1710), 3.

138 *Ibid.*, 6.

139 Leslie, *The Best Answer Ever Was Made*, 2, 4.

140 Charles Leslie, *Best of All: Being the Student's Thanks to Mr. Hoadly* (London, 1709), 7. Leslie's (devious) condemnation of the Whig Hoadly contains elements found in Mary Astell's attack on the Presbyterian Whig belief in resistance. Astell (like Leslie), claimed that Queen Anne enjoyed the full powers of a king (*An Impartial Enquiry into the Causes of Rebellion in this Kingdom: In an Examination of Dr Kennett's Sermon, Jan. 31. 1704, Astell: Political Writings*, ed. Patricia Springborg (Cambridge, 1996), 136, 170–1).

141 Leslie, *Best of All*, 19.

142 *Ibid.*, 27.

143 *Ibid.*, 29, 30. This analogy of the multitude and the sea is taken from Filmer, although the meaning is different. While Leslie used the analogy to show the multitude's unpredictable nature and propensity for all-consuming chaos, in Filmer it revealed that equality and freedom stifled decision-making through a proliferation of the faceless masses. Filmer wrote: 'Mankind is like the sea, ever ebbing and flowing, every minute one is born another dies. Those that are the people this minute, are not the people the next' (*The Anarchy of a Limited or Mixed Monarchy, Patriarcha and Other Writings*, ed. Sommerville, 142).

144 Robert D. Cornwall, 'Leslie, Charles (1650–1722)', *Oxford Dictionary of National Biography*, online: www.oxforddnb.com.ezproxy.sussex.ac.uk/view/article/16484?docPos=1

145 Charles Leslie, *The New Association* (Dublin, 1714), 3.

146 *Ibid.*, 11.

147 *Ibid.*, 28. Simone Zurbuchen has argued that religious toleration was employed by commonwealth Whigs such as Toland, to disguise a full liberty of conscience that would legitimise '"free thinking" in matters of religion and politics' ('Republicanism and Toleration', *Republicanism: A Shared European Heritage. Volume II: The Values of Republicanism in Early Modern Europe*, eds Martin van Gelderen and Quentin Skinner (Cambridge, 2002), 48).

148 Leslie, *New Association*, 27.
149 *Ibid.*, 55.
150 Leslie, *New Association II* (London, 1703), 2.
151 *Ibid.*, 13, 32.
152 *Ibid.*, 23.
153 *Ibid.*, 27.
154 *Ibid.*, 5.
155 *Ibid.*, 6–7.
156 Rather than being viewed as a direct engagement with Filmer, Leslie's patriarchalism has frequently been seen as a response to Locke's *First Treatise* and the group of Whigs – such as Hoadly – who employed Lockean ideas of resistance and contract theory. See John Dunn, 'The Politics of Locke in England and America in the Eighteenth Century' (*John Locke: Problems and Perspectives: A Collection of New Essays*, ed. John W. Yolton (Cambridge, 1969), 63–5); Clark, *English Society 1688–1832*, 47, 84.
157 Leslie, *New Association*, 7, 13.
158 See Leslie, *New Association II*, 5; Leslie, *The Finishing Stroke* (London, 1711), 6–7, 13, 27.
159 Leslie, *New Association*, 16–17.
160 Leslie, *Finishing Stroke*, 71–2.
161 *Ibid.*, 103–4.
162 For Hoadly's employment of Locke, see Robbins, *Eighteenth-Century Commonwealthman*, 84; Reed Browning, *Political and Constitutional Ideas of the Court Whigs* (Baton Rouge, 1982), 83; Goldie, 'The English System of Liberty', 52; William Gibson, *Enlightenment Prelate: Benjamin Hoadly, 1676–1761* (Cambridge, 2004), 100.
163 Benjamin Hoadly, *The Measures of Submission to the Civil Magistrate Consider'd* (London, 1706), 2.
164 *Ibid.*, 3.
165 *Ibid.*, 4; see Locke, *Two Treatises*, II, I (268), xix (411).
166 Hoadly, *Measures of Submission to the Civil Magistrate Consider'd*, 28; Locke, *Two Treatises*, II, I (268), xix (419, 427).
167 Hoadly, *Measures of Submission to the Civil Magistrate Consider'd*, 39; Locke, *Two Treatises*, II, I (268), xix (407, 417).
168 Benjamin Hoadly, *The Original and Institutions of Civil Government, Discussed: The Works of Benjamin Hoadly, D. D.*, vol. II, ed. John Hoadly (London, 1773), 203; Locke, *Two Treatises*, I, ix (205).
169 *Ibid.*, 256; see Locke, *Two Treatises*, II, iv (283), vii (324), viii (330–1).
170 *Ibid.*, 204; Locke, *Two Treatises*, II, xviii (199–210)
171 *Ibid.*, 189.
172 *Ibid.*, 187.
173 The war was instigated by the death of King Carlos II of Spain and who possessed the right to succeed him. Both the Austrian Habsburgs and the French Bourbons claimed this right, and in the will of Carlos II it was Louis XIV's grandson the duc d'Anjou (1683–1746) who inherited the throne. France effectively stood alone against the Grand Alliance who supported the Habsburg Archduke Charles (1685–1740), in what was essentially a continuation of the Nine Years' War.
174 Toland, *Anglia Libera*, 32.
175 *Ibid.*, 170.
176 Daniel Defoe, *The Two Great Questions Consider'd* (London, 1701), 356.
177 *Ibid.*, 364.

2

Division and unity II:
fear and corruption

The divisions present throughout the Stuart seventeenth century continued to dominate the opening two decades of the eighteenth century. Perceptions of the revolutionary settlement and suspicions of absolutism drove the behaviour of government and propagandists. The rising fear of Jacobitism before the accession of George I in 1714 witnessed a proliferation of propaganda and manifest disagreements regarding 1688 over twenty-five years after the Revolution. Paranoia concerning the power of French absolutism and Catholicism were reignited in antipathy towards Louis XIV's support for the Jacobites. Yet a trifecta of events between 1714 and 1716 quickly ended these concerns allowing new worries to take precedence. Innovations following 1688, notably the Financial Revolution, generated great changes in a new commercial age which were invaluable to the ambitions of an ascendant Parliament. Juxtaposed with the expedience of modern finance were attendant issues concerning the moral fabric of the nation. From the 1690s a Reformation of Manners railed against a corruption extant in government and wider society as civil virtue and Christian living were ostensibly thrown over for Mammon. Overcoming political divisions, country ideology once more emerged as a form of opposition to the Whig Oligarchy and economic degeneracy that was seen to have engulfed wider society. Important Whig and Tory publications from the 1720s began to call for a unity of purpose and parties to accommodate the modernising regime under the Hanoverians.

The fear of Jacobitism

Jacobitism became extremely active in the latter part of the first decade of the eighteenth century as James Francis Edward Stuart, or the Pretender as he was deemed by many in Britain, became a young man.[1] After the unsuccessful challenges to retrieve the throne for James II following the Revolution and the 1696 Assassination Plot, Jacobitism had been largely inert.[2] The claimed accession to his father's titles as James III of England and VIII of Scotland saw a renewed vigour in the activities of the Jacobites. Several attempted invasions, numerous intrigues, and a full-scale rebellion on British soil did have 'an impact on British society', although much of this impact 'was almost uniformly negative'.[3] Jacobitism often provided a focal point for opposition, not only to the revolutionary settlement but to subsequent governments and also the Hanoverian regime. This was one of its two strengths, the other being its relationship with the French.

Following the 1688 Revolution, hostility to James II's removal from power created two ideologically committed groups: the Jacobites and the Nonjurors. While they were not necessarily Jacobites, Nonjuror theory was often used by the Jacobites to voice their ideological hostility to 1688. Frequently this entailed reliance upon divine right theory, indefeasible hereditary right, non-resistance, passive obedience, a belief in providential justice, and patriarchy. The Jacobites effectively employed this ideological apparatus as propaganda to undermine the foundations of the revolutionary settlement. It was guileless to argue that all of the above religious doctrines and political tenets had been overthrown with the king, as these divine ordinances proved the illegality of the Revolution for the Jacobites and Nonjurors. While William III may have held the throne by de facto usurpation, according to the doctrines mentioned plus English law, natural law, and scripture, James remained de jure king.[4]

During the 1690s the symbolism of an oath of loyalty to the King (James II) was sacrosanct to most who had sworn it. While abdication assuaged concerns over breaking a covenant under God, for some 1688 was an act of usurpation and to reject the oath previously sworn was illegal and treasonous to God. Such opinion ensured that the Jacobite court contained a core of ideologically committed followers who remained loyal to the person of the king. Under his son this inner core endured although somewhat diminished, surrounded by a thicker layer of 'politically embittered' antagonists to the new regime, and a very thin outer layer of 'adventurers'.[5] The Jacobites' ideological outlook was affected by the make-up and etiquette of the court, which remained 'absolute' in nature. In some ways this had been a necessity to create cohesiveness in an 'extremely loose organisation' of disparate members. Problematically, it meant that such an outlook permeated the predominantly Catholic aristocratic court at a time when such values caused revulsion in Britain; a consideration quite often lost on the Jacobite hierarchy.[6] Core Jacobite (philosophical) beliefs often relied on Bodinian absolutist theory and Filmerian patriarchalism as a rebuttal to the overthrow of James, and Leslie was an exemplar of this approach.[7]

Philosophical support for the Jacobite cause after the Revolution was small, and in England and Ireland effective backing was non-existent.[8] In Scotland, however, there was a stronger footing for support. Not only was Scotland the ancestral homeland of the Stuarts, it was rife with religious, political, and economic tensions. The revolutionary settlement in Scotland had seen the abolition of the Episcopacy and the supremacy of Presbyterianism in Church and state through an alliance with William III.[9] Economic deprivation and decline crippled a Scottish Parliament weakened by stultified commercial development.[10] The failed Darien Scheme (1698–1700), which sought to create a Scottish trading empire, manifested the economic and financial weakness of Scotland. Despite protests against unification with England for fear of Scotland's subsumption from notable politicians such as Andrew Fletcher of Saltoun, union occurred on 1 May 1707.[11] Indubitably the union favoured English interests. It was a method of tying the Scottish kingdom to the shared monarchy due to the uncertainty of the Hanoverians.[12] Union prevented the restoration of the Stuarts in Scotland or the accession of a Protestant king who could make alliances unfavourable to England. For the Scots' part, while union had numerous supporters it was disliked in many quarters, and antipathy towards the Act provided an opportunity for the Jacobites.[13] In 1708, with the assistance of the French navy and 6,000 French troops, James Stuart set sail to invade Scotland by landing at the Forth of Firth. Much to the chagrin of the Jacobites, the landing was abandoned because of Admiral Byng's pursuit of the invasionary force around Scotland.[14]

This undertaking by the Jacobites to invade Britain was significant for three reasons. First, it witnessed a concerted effort on the part of James Stuart to retain some semblance of his titles through the active engagement of arms. Unlike his father who had resigned himself to exile after Jacobite failures in Scotland and Ireland in 1691, his son was determined to exert his claims physically. Second, an invasion of Scotland revealed a new focus on that former kingdom as realising the best prospect of retrieving former Stuart dominions. While James did not relinquish his hopes of an English restoration, the sizeable portion of Jacobite support amongst the disaffected population made Scotland a more realistic target. A goal supported by the French tactically and logistically.[15] The deployment of French forces was symbolic of the 'auld alliance' between the two nations over several centuries in their allegiance against the English.[16] This association leads to a final point, one that acquires a degree of hindsight. The support delivered in 1708 drives at the heart of the relationship between the Jacobites and the French. Louis XIV had opened his arms to his cousin James II when he provided a court for him at Saint Germain-en-Laye in 1688. Part of his motivation was an abhorrence of the king's overthrow by (popular) rebellion, yet much of his support was political expediency. The installation of the king of Britain in France was a constant reminder to Louis's great opponent William III, that France held a significant ace through a rival (legal) claimant. The persistent support for his son continued this policy as it benefited France to distract or aggravate the British.[17] As with military aid in Ireland (1689), the invasion fleet of 1708 allowed the French to open up a second front in another European war. The relationship was hugely important to any hopes the Jacobites may have held for success in an invasion, and it provided the Jacobites with strength by creating a genuine fear of them in Britain. The realisation of this unequal association engendered a monomaniacal concentration on French assistance by the Jacobites. Yet, as will be discussed, it was the connection that generated a palpable fear of Jacobitism in England, especially its connotations of absolute Catholic rule.[18] Once the association was terminated the Jacobites lost most of this power, and in retrospect 1708 offered their only meaningful chance of triumph (if they had landed) due to French backing.

Regardless of the failure of the 1708 invasion, the attempt proved to be a major psychological success for the Jacobites. Between 1708 and 1716 the fear and suspicion over a French-led Jacobite invasion escalated. It was matched by questions and doubts regarding the alteration of the monarchical succession and Queen Anne's lack of an heir. While Anne's Jacobite leanings have been disproved,[19] uncertainties over the Pretender's ability to regain the throne upon her death, coupled with a lack of enthusiasm for the Hanoverians inflamed growing anxieties. Added to this apprehension was further ambiguity over the intentions of the Tory party. Since the Revolution the Whigs had laboured to taint the Tories with charges of Jacobitism because of their faith in doctrines such as indefeasible hereditary right, non-resistance, and passive obedience.[20] Undoubtedly a good number of Tories did support the Jacobites at times from 1688, but a much larger percentage of Tories were loyal to the revolutionary settlement even when in opposition. Despite this loyalty accusations of a Tory plot to reinstall James Stuart abounded. Rumours not eased by the disputes between the two leading Tories, Harley the Earl of Oxford (1661–1724) and Viscount Bolingbroke (1678–1751), over the latter's prospective contact with the 'Pretender' in France.[21] Potential complicity from the current Tory government therefore added to the general firmament over the succession. This anxiety was promulgated in a large number of political pamphlets published during this period, many written by anti-Jacobites expressing their trepidations.

Anti-Jacobite propaganda followed two paths during this eight-year period. The first emphasised the ramifications of a French-led Jacobite invasion of Britain. For a number of authors a major point of concern was the potential endeavour to 'introduce Popery and Tyranny' into Britain.[22] After its former struggles against Catholicism and absolutism Joseph Cannell believed that if successful there would be 'no Peace', no 'Security, or 'Common Comfort of Life' simply a 'meer Arbitrary Lawless Sway'.[23] The (illegitimate) prince's upbringing in France would have immersed him in French lessons of kingship that endowed him with a taste for absolute rule. This view was repeatedly echoed, and focused on the double terror of Catholicism and absolute government offered by France.

The two were inextricably linked in the British psyche, as a proselytising religion Catholicism would arbitrarily force the conversion of the British nation under a papist king.[24] Parliament and Protestantism would necessarily be extinguished to enforce these precepts on an unwilling people, as James II had endeavoured to do.[25] Recent French history provided a foretaste of what would happen due to the Revocation of the Edict of Nantes (1685). Louis XIV's desire to create religious uniformity had led to the elimination of religious toleration for Protestants (Huguenots), compelling many of them to flee persecution and forced conversion. According to some, this brutal religious oppression was the Pretender's model for a ruler. One bent on religious unity coupled with an obsession for territorial aggrandisement that had engaged Europe in numerous conflicts, including the current War of the Spanish Succession. Such instructions would necessitate slavery for the English, and Louis XIV's hospitality would mean indebtedness to the French on the part of the Pretender.[26]

At the height of this period, circa 1713 to 1714, the Queen's poor health appears to have augmented such concerns. John Shute Barrington (1678–1734), claimed that the influence of France on the Pretender would present a number of ramifications if he was to be restored. First, a natural desire for vengeance in the Pretender would lead to 'Rivers of Blood' for the English. The treatment of his father, the handling of his religion, the public mocking of his legitimacy as a '*Warming-Pan Imposture*', and his disinheritance would create a natural craving for revenge fuelled by his supporters.[27] Second, Barrington argued that French backing had left the Pretender in Louis XIV's (financial) debt. While the Dutch were frequently regarded as Britain's great trading rivals, for Barrington the French were of weightier concern. France's extortion of commercial gain from the Pretender as repayment for his debt would prove disastrous to Britain. It would become a 'Province' of France while persecuted for its Protestantism.[28] In Barrington's opinion, the British must repel Catholicism and absolutism by preserving its commercial prosperity, allowing liberty and prosperity to thrive.[29] This could only be achieved if the divisions that dogged the Anglican Church and state were set aside through a unified support for liberty. Such support required the abandonment of absolute principles like divine right theory, patriarchy, providence, absolute submission and obedience, and hereditary right. These were the principles of the Jacobites and opponents of 1688, and many of them (particularly hereditary right) could never be proven.[30] The Lords and Commons had legally deposed James II and lawfully modified the succession in a Hanoverian settlement because the English tripartite constitution empowered two estates to oppose the third to defend the people's 'Laws, Liberties and Religion'.[31] Barrington therefore dismissed the belief that James II had vacated his throne. It undermined the authority of the legislative and implied that the Revolution was not 'Worthy'.[32] High Church Tories such as Francis Atterbury, the Bishop of Bangor and eventual Jacobite (1663–1732), should desist from their reliance on non-resistance, because resistance in 1688 had justly rejected James and his Catholic successors for ever.[33] The removal of James II had meant that 'Passive Obedience, and Non-Resistance, and Indefeasible Right in one particular Branch of the Royal family, after a Sea of Bloodshed' were 'at last destroyed'.[34] The extirpation of these tenets in practice meant that those who continued to rely on them were perpetuating a defunct papist Stuart agenda.

This reiteration of (Hoadly's) Whig resistance theory sat within the debate surrounding the second pathway of rejection for the Pretender. While popular pamphlets like *Vox populi, vox dei* stoutly defended 1688 as an act of popular resistance, its application was largely rebutted during this period even by opponents of the Pretender.[35] Barrington's plea to the justification of resistance was unusual as many pamphlets asserted the tenet of non-resistance until the accession of George I in 1714. Up to that point, the ability to retain the precept was made possible by the notion that James II had vacated the throne. Declarations advocating non-resistance were a method for undermining Jacobite attacks on the legitimacy of Queen Anne or incitement for people to rebel. Just as Blackall, Sacheverell and many other High Church Tories had rejected resistance, thus it continued because a 'prosperous Rebellion' would be impossible and chaotic.[36] As with Leslie and the Nonjurors, non-resistance and passive obedience were divinely stipulated ordinances decreed for the preservation and equanimity of society.[37] The separation between the two groups over non-resistance stemmed from the diverging viewpoints of the Revolution's legitimacy. No matter how convenient it may have been, many Tories believed that James had abdicated the throne, but for the Nonjurors and Jacobites this was an erroneous notion.

The subversion of the religious doctrines expounded by the Nonjurors after 1689 was therefore utilised by the Jacobites to attack the Revolution, the Act of Settlement, and James Stuart's loss of his inheritance. Hereditary right proved to be a fertile hunting ground in this regard. George Hickes questioned how it was legitimate that James II had abdicated his crown for himself and his heir, when no legal authority could remove the inheritance under such a circumstance.[38] George Harbin's highly provocative *The Hereditary Right of the Crown of England Asserted* (1713) defended the Nonjuror's refusal to swear an oath of allegiance, by stressing the importance of hereditary right for the succession of the crown.[39] While it was permissible to fill an empty throne, James II had not legally resigned or declared his abdication of the throne. This voided any discussion of an abdication; first, because he had been driven from his kingdom, and, second, he had not shown any intent to resign.[40] The consequence of the illegitimate revolutionary settlement was the creation of two claimants to the throne. Yet the existence of a de jure claimant concurrently with a de facto usurper always undermined the latter's (illegal) position, as the historical precedent of Henry IV's tainted reign revealed following the usurpation of Richard II's crown revealed.[41] The solution to this conundrum was the resignation of Queen Anne, which was supported by the precedent of Edward Duke of York's resignation (1470) in favour of Henry VI. Anne's replacement by James Stuart would restore legality to the throne, allowing Britain to flourish under its rightful inheritance.[42]

From 1714, the Treaty of Utrecht (1713) and the accession of George I (1714) began to calm some of the horror surrounding a Jacobite invasion. The treaty which formally concluded the war between Britain and France ensured the recognition of the Act of Settlement was acknowledged by Louis XIV and all formal support for the Jacobites ended. While recognising the increased fear of the Jacobites in recent years, Daniel Defoe alleged the treaty eradicated the real threat to Britain: France. Jacobite strength had been generated by French assistance, and now it had been eliminated so 'the Fears and Apprehensions of Honest and Well-minded People [should] abate also'.[43] While suspicion of the French remained despite peace,[44] the strongest antidote to the issue of the succession was the accession of George I (and the Hanoverians) on 20 October 1714. In spite of rioting, the immediate aftermath appears to have seen a general sense of relief that the succession was 'secured' through a 'Protestant King'.[45] One who was experienced and would uphold the power of the law, parliamentary authority, the toleration of Dissenters, plus the maintenance of liberty and property.

A tangible sense of release from the terror of a Jacobite invasion did not occur until after the Jacobite rising in 1715. The rising was inspired by the Hanoverian succession, the ambitions of the former Secretary of State John Erskine, the Earl of Mar (1675–1732), and the poor economy in Scotland.[46] Despite initial gains in Scotland and an attempt on Preston, without effective support from a foreign backer – i.e. the French – the Jacobites were defeated. Dogged by poor tactics and indecisive leadership under men like Mar and James Stuart (for the five weeks he spent in Scotland), once the British government had galvanised its forces, the Jacobites did not possess the capacity to mount a sustained invasion.[47] Regardless of a good response from Scottish fighters for the cause, an absence of Jacobite military cohesion and English support connoted failure for the rising. The consequence of its failure was the solidification of the Act of Settlement and George I's accession, plus the longer term preclusion of a further invasion under James Stuart. Moreover, the Whigs emerged stronger than ever as Jacobite supporters became deeply disillusioned, as many in Britain and Europe comprehended the weakness of the Jacobites.[48] In Britain, the Jacobites were transformed from a terrifying spectre of brutal absolute oppression to a group of self-interested papists who had unnecessarily engaged in a pointless and costly rebellion.[49] From this point onwards, regardless of sustained successes by the Jacobites under James Stuart to achieve foreign funding for potential rebellions and invasions – in 1717, 1719, and 1722 – the Jacobites once more became a voice of opposition. The Treaty of Utrecht, the accession of George I and the failure of the '15 ended twenty-six years of Jacobitism as a serious alternative to the adjusted monarchical succession. Along with the demise of the Stuart claim in 1716, the successful accession of George I in 1714 made irrelevant the Nonjuror ideology that underpinned many of the Jacobite claims as hereditary right and divine right theory had clearly been dispensed with.

A number of prominent Tories joined the Jacobites at this time due to the ascendancy of the Whigs, including the Earl of Mar, Viscount Bolingbroke briefly, and Francis Atterbury. The impact of the firebrand Atterbury on the Jacobites is important. His antipathy towards the Whigs' assaults on the High Church and Tories led to his central involvement in the failed Atterbury Plot (1722). The scheme intended to spark a general uprising in London during the 1722 general election, harnessing the aversion felt at the moral turpitude and political corruption manifested in the South Sea Bubble (1720). Unknown to the Jacobites, the plot had been stillborn for some time, as the French government had informed the ministry of the conspiracy which had been subsequently monitored.[50] Its failure allowed the Jacobites to be portrayed as dangerous challengers to the state and Hanoverian succession, empowering Walpole's government to apply stronger censorship and prohibitive controls to inhibit wider opposition.[51] While the Jacobites became a phantom used by the Walpolian Oligarchy to augment its own powers and galvanise the public, Atterbury was partially responsible for Jacobite complicity in its own demise as an ideological force. As one of James Stuart's closest advisers, Atterbury persuaded the prince not to allow the Jacobite court to engage in printed propaganda from the 1720s (to 1743) to avoid hostility from the British government.[52] It led to the cessation of the Jacobite court under the 'Pretender' as a viable alternative to Hanoverian government, or even delivering a salient focal point of opposition.

Notwithstanding this extremely myopic manoeuvre, a number of independent supporters did retain Jacobite sympathies in their continued opposition to the Whig government. This moved beyond the application of religious tenets that argued against the illegality of the Revolution, such as seen in Leslie's approach, to a new contemporary rejection of the regime.[53] In which the re-emerging (Whig) country opposition was employed by a number of Jacobites to denounce the maintenance of a standing army and parliamentary corruption.[54] Assaults on the Whig's duplicitous and divisive nature as revealed by resistance remained;[55] as did the insistence that the general populace had to be restrained from politics as they pursued 'specious' notions of liberty and happiness.[56] But these later Jacobites accepted the necessity of Parliament to restrain a king yet spurned the degeneracy of government and society at large, encapsulated by the South Sea Bubble.[57] It was principally the government's corruption of the balanced constitution in favour of George I that led them to reject both the Whigs and the new king. *Mist's* and *Fog's* call for a restored James Stuart proved to be incredibly popular, as they and other publications reflected an opposition to the new regime present in the public. Such discontent was rarely strong enough to encourage a rebellion, however, and after 1716 Jacobitism was little more than vocalised discontent.

Hostility to the Whig Oligarchy

The opposition provided by Jacobite publications like Mist's *Weekly Journal* was part of a wider adjustment to a new political and social era dominated by the Whigs. The Treaty of Utrecht, the accession of the George I and the '15 saw the removal of several old adversaries: the French, fears over the Protestant succession, and the Jacobites. Whig control of government following the accession of George I (1714) until the reign of George III (1760) did offer some semblance of unity. Through the creation of the Oligarchy and the efforts of Robert Walpole (1676–1745), by 1722 Walpole was able to separate 'Whiggery from radicalism' and fuse the 'interests of aristocracy, high finance, and executive government' in a process that embraced the 'bulk of the landed gentry'.[58] By doing so, Walpole embraced the leadership of the aristocracy and landed gentry melding the power of land and commerce. The eighteenth century saw an extension of the 'influence of the peerage' as both houses of Parliament exerted greater power and took charge of the day-to-day running of the state.[59]

This transference of power from the monarchy to both houses of Parliament and the aristocracy was made possible by the political innovations during the reigns of William III, Mary II, and Anne. While the revolutionary settlement left the monarchy with its previous powers, the inclusion of Parliament as a permanent part of government ensured that Britain now possessed a limited monarchy. The constitution and the executive, despite the monarch's prerogative, were subject to the laws of the state and penalties from Parliament; a role that provided it with the opportunity to evolve. The monarch's rule through Parliament after the death of Queen Mary II (1694) meant that William's frequent journeys abroad during the Nine Years' War necessitated the reliance on ministers to run the executive in his absence. The creation of the Junto offered the prospect for the king's ministers to take a large step towards independence in enacting government policy. Coupled with this advancement was a growing belief within the two parties that William's autocratic proclivities should be restrained through legislation. Regardless of the internecine ideological rivalry between the Whigs and Tories, the two parties at various times eroded the crown's own independence in government. In the reign of Anne, the queen preserved the prerogative to appoint, retain, and dismiss ministers at her pleasure, and formed a ministry from either House with differing party loyalties. Earlier in her reign Anne often overlooked the triennial elections to retain key ministers, but as each year passed it became more difficult to ignore the dominant party of each election.[60] By this point, the solidification of a two-party system with distinct ideologies had occurred through a 'party conflict' that increasingly permeated society.[61] Later it was not possible for Anne or her government to ignore the leading party after an election as they were required to secure the Commons' vote when creating legislation.[62] Added to this growth in parliamentary importance, was Anne's willingness to allow her ministers a freer role in the running of government on her behalf. This built upon the earlier function of the Junto and assured a greater autonomy for the ministry (cabinet) in managing British affairs.

The Hanoverian accession in 1714 under George I continued this process of parliamentary expansion. Notwithstanding the absolutist nature of their rule as Electors of Hanover, neither George I (r. 1714–27), or George II (r. 1727–60) could act autocratically in Britain.[63] The Act of Settlement plus the aforementioned developments provided limitations to the authority and power of the two kings. These restrictions were further consolidated by George I's long sojourns to Hanover which precluded his direct involvement in the day-to-day running of the state. The great innovation of George I's reign was the immediate reliance upon the Whigs and rejection of the Tories as the party of government. George's personal preference for loyalty drew him towards the Whigs whom he perceived to have been dedicated to the Hanoverian succession for many years, in contrast to the Tories.[64] His antipathy was exacerbated by the Tory involvement in the Treaty of Utrecht, which had damaged British relations with its European allies for settling a peace regardless of wider alliance benefits, and the potential endeavours of Oxford and Bolingbroke to seek a Jacobite restoration. The appointment of George's first Whig ministry led to rioting on coronation day (20 October 1714) lasting for several months across Britain. This has been seen as a demonstration 'directed at dissenters' by the High Church fuelled by its belief that it was under threat from the Low Church Whigs favoured by the Hanoverians.[65]

This High Church reaction to the Hanoverian succession and the impending general election was evident in Francis Atterbury's *English Advice to the Freeholder's of England* (1714). In the pamphlet, Atterbury protested against the Whig domination of the new king while propounding Tory loyalty to George. He claimed that the Whigs intended to pack Parliament through a bribed election that would enable them to control the king's 'Regal Power' by ruling him through a 'Junto'.[66] This would engender an 'Arbitrary and Tyrannical' government allowing the Whigs to complete their war upon the High Church and landed interest as highlighted by the Sacheverell trial.[67] Once this had been achieved, it would act as a mere prelude to the Whigs' larger ambitions over the state. These aspirations would include the engagement in further foreign wars, the development of a standing army, the removal of the liberty of the press to enforce their reforms, and the dismantling of the (Tory) limitations on the king's power as proscribed by the Act of Settlement.[68] The only means of preventing such behaviour was to vote Tory in the election to safeguard the freedoms secured under the 1688 settlement. As with Blackall and Sacheverell, the Tories were depicted by Atterbury as loyal defenders of 1688 who safeguarded the people and the crown. Contrary to Whig jibes regarding their disloyalty to the state (Utrecht), to the king and to the people, the Tories offered the only consistent party of fidelity as the Whigs frequently undermined and divided the nation.[69] The Tories would stoutly defend the kingdom in the interest of the freeholder and ensure that any Hanoverian pretensions to their native absolutism would be prevented.[70]

Despite Atterbury and the High Church's pleas, the Tories lost the election. The return of a Whig majority witnessed the pursuit of measures to safeguard the king's position on the throne. Bolingbroke, Oxford, and the Duke of Ormond were all impeached, while the 'Riot Act of 1715, the suspension of habeas corpus, the arrest of a trio of peers and of half a dozen MPs, and a strengthening of the army all made it clear that the Hanoverian and protestant succession would be defended with strength and vigour.'[71] However, the result of George's reliance on the Whigs saw the enactment of policies that actually limited the crown's power at a time when it was still 'central' to government.[72] This dependence and George's absences in Hanover meant that the Whigs were able to consolidate their position through the Septennial Act (1716), while asseverating a traditional Low Church form of Anglicanism that made concessions to Dissenters. Religious toleration was granted by the Religious Worship Act (1718), which placed all Protestants under the state's protection, although the Universities Bill (1716) was used to root out wider disloyalty through an attack on property and patronage.[73] The consequences of the disastrous South Sea Bubble, which will be discussed below, allowed Walpole to create an unassailable position for himself and the Whig Oligarchy from 1722 onwards.[74] As the Tories were relegated to a position of perpetual opposition, the superiority of parliamentary power continued and led to a belief that the 'absolute power of kings had merely been replaced by the absolute power of parliament'.[75]

Corruption and virtue

It has been argued that from the Financial Revolution of 1694 until the mid 1750s political economy dominated British thought.[76] Yet it was not until after the defeat of the Jacobites in 1716 and sustained peace with France that this sentiment exerted greater currency, when fears of the monarchical succession were obliterated. After the Treaty of Utrecht there was a noticeable shift from a preoccupation with war and invasion to economic possibilities. For some it meant an opportunity to trade with the French,[77] but for many there was a fear that rivalry with the French could damage British trade.[78] An increase in the discussion of commerce, however, had steadily taken place during the seventeenth century, and, as noted, economic considerations were a motivation for 1688.[79] The Financial Revolution helped to consolidate the events of 1688, as it developed the economy through 'the institutions of credit: banks, stocks, a stock-market and a public debt'.[80] The foundation of the Bank of England in 1694 had used subscription to raise capital to establish the bank. While other innovations such as shares, lotteries, and the creation of a national debt also helped to bank roll William III's wars against France. Financial modernisation brought about a brave new world in which the commercial economy was stimulated to generate much greater revenue for the beneficence of the state. In turn, this revenue not only allowed the economy to flourish: from the 1690s, it also provided the financial underpinning which enabled government and the state to expand. The 1688 Revolution and the subsequent Financial Revolution brought together political and commercial concerns in a manner not seen before, as the state began to intervene socially.[81]

An important consequence of the Financial Revolution was the shift from a focus on land wealth towards commercial wealth. Under the rule of Charles II and James II it was believed that economic prosperity was derived from territory and land. As such, the world contained only a finite amount of land. This territory frequently provoked a 'zero-sum' competition between nations, which endeavoured to take as large a share of land as possible for their gain at the expense of their rivals. Crucially, land ownership reflected the social hierarchy and bond that held the kingdom together: the monarch was chief proprietor; the status and privileges of the nobility and landed gentry reflected their ownership of much of the kingdom; the freeholder possessed a sufficient stake in the land to qualify as citizens that allowed them to vote; and the common man frequently worked the land but did not own it. Unfortunately, the emergent emphasis on commercial, liquid wealth generated fears within the elite that it subverted traditional values. The 1688 Revolution and the innovations of the Financial Revolution moved away from this finite view of wealth towards one which saw the possibility of infinite prosperity production through commercial enterprise. This model, already extant in the Dutch Republic, believed that ingenuity and labour created capital, so was not limited by restricted resources.[82] The new economic order created by the Financial Revolution undermined the traditional (Tory) order of a ranked society based upon land ownership (wealth), and the status it produced over many successive generations. Commercial innovations under the Whigs during the 1690s now made it possible for people at the bottom of the social order to generate vast amounts of wealth akin to or beyond the traditional elite. Linked with fears over the national debt, the creation of stock companies tied these new moneyed men to the government allowing non-aristocrats to become extremely powerful as London committed itself to liberalism.[83] The Whig ascendancy after the 1714 election entwined economics and politics, as the interests of moneyed men and government concatenated. From this time the rural gentry were slowly squeezed as taxation levels rose and those squires who held no other interests beyond their annuities struggled to survive.[84] The established social order was therefore endangered by a growing fluidity of movement for some, which heralded an unwelcome change to many in the elite who did not want transformation.[85]

Closely associated with this destabilisation of social rank was an accompanying threat offered to British morality by allegations of a sinful pursuit of Mammon. As George Berkeley made clear, it was essential to 'recover a Sense of Public Spirit' through religion and traditional public works that employed the nation (such as building).[86] The rapacious pursuit of luxury and credit had so 'bewitched and debauched the Nation', the people had grown into 'vile corrupt Slaves' who were 'undone' by 'Vice and Irreligion'.[87] Such public outcry had begun in 1689 as a reaction to the profligacy of the Restoration, condemning the rise in 'blasphemy, swearing, perjury, drunkenness and profaning the Sabbath'.[88] The fall in church attendance following the Act of Toleration (1689) and the Financial Revolution provided momentum for what has become known as a Reformation of Manners. The development of numerous societies and associations to combat the perils of public vice proved to be popular and influential into the 1730s. This is perhaps emphasised by the furore and prosecution of Bernard Mandeville's *The Fable of the Bees: or, Private Vices, Public Benefits* (1714 and 1723). The materialist work criticised the hypocrisy of an artificial Christian morality that divorced humanity from its natural impulses by telling them certain natural behaviours were sinful and to be avoided.[89] Mandeville challenged such assumptions by claiming it was these natural passions – ambition, greed, envy, and competition – that acted as the incentive for humanity to achieve greatness and civilisation.[90] Developments in the arts and (international) commerce were driven by humanity's selfish desires, rather than stultifying Christian dictates that promoted moderation or inactive contemplation.[91] It was the darker, sinful nature of humanity that made it prosperous, not virtue, a realisation that should be embraced rather than lamented.[92]

Such sentiments and the mounting threat to civic virtue posed by modern egoistic political economy saw the re-emergence of republican ideology as a voice of opposition in the eighteenth century.[93] Advocates of the country perspective, such as Andrew Fletcher of Saltoun, had earlier pointed to the correlation between the loss of virtue with the growth of economic considerations (particularly luxury goods) during the 1690s. For the neo-Harringtonian

Fletcher, the rise of absolute monarchy from 1500 had been achieved through the replacement of militias with standing armies.[94] Driven by a desire for luxury and wealth, this development had subverted the ancient Gothic constitution as the crown replaced barons and vassals with a professional army to augment its power. Standing armies lacked the former military virtue extant in a militia while also removing the nobility as an important part of the balanced constitution.[95] Fletcher wanted to reinstitute a militia in Britain – which was internally secure enough not to warrant a standing army – to return to the classical discipline, public liberty and virtue that prevailed in Europe for over one millennium prior to 1500.[96] He bemoaned the preoccupation with luxury and a monarchy that corrupted the state and its people for its own ends.

Fletcher's reliance on classical or neo-classical thought was not uncommon after 1714. Opponents of the modern economic regime tried to advance 'an ideal of virtue practiced in antique Mediterranean republics, particularly Rome and the quasi-mythical Sparta'.[97] This new Augustan Age relied on a language that promoted virtue over corruption, a landed interest over mobile wealth, and public service over self-interest. The financial innovations that had followed the Revolution had provided the executive with another opportunity to subvert the constitution as witnessed under Charles II and James II. Financial prosperity sustained a standing army, and allowed the widespread corruption of Parliament through bribery and placemen. The resurgence of country ideology in opposition to the court blended classical republicanism, civic humanism, and puritan frugality. It defended English liberties and the constitution from the 'supposed intrusion' of private wealth and arbitrary (government) influence.[98] Exemplars such as Cato and Cicero who had attacked the invasion of liberties by the corrupt and tyrannical state symbolised by Caesar were often deployed to attack the Whig oligarchy. So was Machiavelli, frequently a conduit for this classical thought, whose dictum of the necessity to rejuvenate a corrupted government by returning to its first-principles drove much of this republican-inspired country ideology.[99]

A country Whig approach: *Cato's Letters*

Cato's Letters is perhaps the great country exemplar that assessed the corruption of government and the nation shot through with classical and Commonwealthmen imagery. Published in the *London Journal* and then the *British Journal* between 1720 and 1723, its authors John Trenchard (1668/9–1723) and Thomas Gordon (1691–1750) were both Whigs who possessed anti-clerical views. Trenchard was a Commonwealthman, his *An Argument Shewing that a Standing Army Is Inconsistent with a Free Government* (1697) after the treaty of

Ryswick, initiated an 'eventually successful paper war against William III's standing army'.[100] Gordon was a classical scholar and pamphleteer. The 'anti-clerical polemic' contained in his *Independent Whig* (1719 and 1720) so inflamed some members of the clergy they tried to suppress the work.[101] In 1720 Gordon and Trenchard originally began a weekly publication under the title *Independent Whig*, before producing *Cato's Letters* which moved beyond a focus on religious and clerical matters. *Cato's Letters* were used to analyse society in a broader sense, paying particular attention to the corruption of government and its invasion of the people's liberty in the new commercial age. The figure of Cato had proved popular in the early eighteenth century.[102] The politician and writer Joseph Addison's play *Cato* (1712) – which premiered on 14 April 1713 at Drury Lane – employed the Roman Republican figure of Cato of Uticensis as the bastion of liberty and virtue who opposed Caesar's tyranny. Both Whigs and Tories tussled to appropriate the popular figure of Cato for their cause, for each party believed the other threatened British liberty. Yet it was to be Trenchard and Gordon's (country) Whig Cato that was to prove so influential within its own time and beyond into the later eighteenth century.[103]

Cato's Letters expressed a number of concerns regarding the problems faced by British society in the modern economic age of finance and expanded (Whig) government. In an immediate sense the publication arose from the public disgust at the political corruption revealed by the South Sea Bubble and subse-quent lenient treatment of ministers caught in the scandal, particularly Lord Sunderland.[104] The South Sea Company was a joint-stock company that enjoyed a monopoly on South American trade. It had been created in 1711 to diminish the national debt, and despite the company's inability to return a profit, overin-vestment whipped up by insider-trading and government corruption ensured exaggerated returns. In 1720 share prices peaked before disastrously collapsing. This enriched some including those with insider knowledge of a potential collapse (such as ministers and royalty), but bankrupted more, including members of the traditional elite. The ensuing political scandal reflected the concerns expressed from 1688 regarding the poisonous economic behaviour which had now infected the government and society at large.[105] Stockjobbers, companies, and moneyed men had prospered while great estates had been 'ransacked'. The social fabric had been undermined as luxury and greed sanctioned traders to feed off the elite for their own benefit, inflicting 'ruin, devastation, and havoc' upon estates and 'public misery'.[106] Such social turmoil would potentially destabilise the British constitution as members of the elite were left with great political power but no wealth, while the newly rich lacked influence. Excessive wealth in private individuals was not desirable for they possessed the means to cause mischief, while the loss of wealth for some members of the elite could provoke a need to produce even greater injury.[107] Rather than fulfilling the modern mantra that stocks enabled private interest to produce public benefit, for Cato it mainly led to luxury, ruin, and corruption.

The current financial behaviour in Britain had allowed economic degeneracy to contaminate politics, as corruption had destroyed not only itself but 'everything else'.[108] Bribery was the means by which corruption had infected government. A good proportion of British MPs had sold themselves to 'leaders' who induced them through 'villainy and knavish designs' to follow their interests like 'calves and sheep'.[109] In undermining the normal process of impartial free government it enabled such leaders to sequester the king while framing government and its policy for their own interests.[110] These excessively influential ministers had a proclivity for promoting the king's power to enhance their own.[111] This undermined the balance of the mixed constitution and was redolent of the emperors of Rome or the modern French kings: who ostensibly ruled through a representative senate or *parlement* but were in fact absolute.[112] Such tyrannical behaviour was reinforced by excessive taxation and a standing army, a tactic evocative of Louis XIV's internal oppression of his people.[113] The concatenation between government corruption and its extraordinary thirst for Mammon evident in modern British society was therefore very suggestive of absolutism. The quest for wealth seen in the French, Spanish, and Turks had led to internal policies that used taxation to suppress and drain the people's capital, while a standing army was a further instrument of domestic oppression and foreign aggrandisement.[114] At a time when the Jacobites were no more than a 'huge train of half-starved beggars',[115] and no other internal or external threats to the nation existed, there was no requirement for a standing army. A standing army was nothing more than a tool with which to control the populace. Claims of a corruption in the people were rejected by Cato. Instead he proffered the argument that standing armies only appeared when the government itself was corrupt and desired to manage the state according to its own will, as seen under Cromwell, Charles II, and James II.[116]

Cato's condemnation of the standing army, parliamentary bribery, and excessive taxation repeated the Commonwealthmen fears expressed in the reigns of Charles II and William III. Trenchard and Gordon drew on republican country ideology to highlight the erosion of 'spirit of liberty', virtue, and the constitution under the new Whig Hanoverian regime. The use of absolutist tactics seen in recent English history and on the continent, threatened a new insidious endeavour to enslave the British people. Government was administered to maintain the good of society, and as all men were born equal before the law. Freedom was a gift they received 'from God himself'. Liberty provided the 'power which every man [had] over his own actions, and his right to enjoy the fruit of his labour, art and industry'. This Lockean promotion of rights preserved the freedom and property of the individual from external dangers signifying that this role of government should enshrine 'human happiness'.[117] A government that allowed financial society to impinge deliberately upon these rights for its own prosperity was patently corrupt, when it should protect them. Government should strive to guard the 'spirit of liberty' within the populace jealously, not jealously extinguish that liberty to augment its own power.[118] In menacing the liberty and property of the nation through a purchased Parliament and standing army, Britain not only faced a tyranny of government but a potential revolution from its people to overthrow this danger.[119] Under such illicit circumstances, Cato argued, it was lawful to kill tyrannical rulers (Caesar).[120]

Cato proffered a number of suggestions to combat the ills of government. Predominantly they referred to a check upon the power of the magistrates who were responsible for creating the issues. It was imperative that politicians were held accountable to the people as nations were free 'when their magistrates [were] their servants' and slaves 'when their magistrates [were] their masters'.[121] Civic virtue should provoke the nobility to vote alongside the freeholders against the corruption of money in Parliament. As the natural leaders of society the nobility should use their influence and leadership to petition Parliament and the king. Echoing the example set by Fénelon's *Télémaque* (1699), disinterested moral and heroic guidance provided by the nobility could act as a foil to the arbitrariness of the executive (Louis XIV).[122] Fénelon was seen as a kindred spirit by Cato; an independent foreign advocate of liberty and the public good struggling against (economic) corruption and an arbitrary executive.[123] Like Fénelon, Cato believed it was possible to defend the country through civic virtue, while understanding that self-interest dominated the considerations of all men. The problems and corruption experienced by Parliament had been driven by the need of some MPs and leaders to enrich themselves at the expense of the general public. According to Machiavelli, corrupted institutions must be repaired otherwise liberty would be lost as government in its entirety was subsumed.[124] Machiavelli's belief that no government could 'long subsist, but by recurring often to its first principles',[125] was accepted by Cato. It was essential that the British people assured Parliament's role as the keeper of liberty by defending their role as the source of its political power, to which they were allowed access.[126]

Cato's solution was to generate a political environment in which free speech and regular elections were sacrosanct. Frequent elections attacked parliamentary corruption by offering the people the opportunity to remove magistrates (MPs) who were venal or indolent.[127] This required two things. First, an active electorate that monitored the behaviour of Parliament and demanded virtuous magistrates like Cato the Younger; and, second, a cross-party harmony between the Whigs and Tories. Cato's dismissal of years of abuse and conflict between the two parties dismissed apparent differences to emphasise a unity of purpose and ideology. Both parties wanted to ensure the protection, plenty and happiness of the nation, and both parties were attached to the king, property, the nobility, the Church, clergy, trade and the people.[128] Despite separate founding ideologies, the 'grounds of distinction [were] now at an end', for depending on the issue Whig and Tory behaviour was interchangeable. The re-emergence of country ideology in opposition to the court, allowed the two parties to jointly restrain the 'hands of government' and consider what was 'best for the whole'.[129] Political virtue according to Cato, redefined an opposition by the wider country to the corrupt intentions and practices of the court. *Cato's Letters* therefore went beyond a neo-Harringtonian veneration of the Gothic past and a belief in a civic virtue that relied on an arms-bearing freeholder,[130] towards a sophisticated plea for political unity. It redefined the Machiavellian notion that the 'have-nots' faced potential peril at the hands of the 'haves', who would use corruption to deprive them of their freedom and their rights through tyrannical government.[131] Such concerns had been prevalent under the Stuarts and now returned under the expanse of the parliamentary court Oligarchy. Yet as the example of Fénelon revealed, the executive's attempt to overwhelm the public will and liberty of the people was not only a British problem.

Tory country opposition and unity: Bolingbroke

The call for a unification of the Whigs and Tories as a voice of opposition to the Whig oligarchy was notably sustained by the periodical the *Craftsman*. It was the brainchild of the disgraced former Tory minister Viscount Bolingbroke, and the Whig politician William Pulteney (1684–1764), publishing its first issue in 1726. The periodical was used to highlight an entrenched 'parliamentary corruption' in the Whig ministry led by an 'evil minister' (Robert Walpole) as hegemony was consolidated into the 1730s.[132] Like *Cato's Letters* before it, the *Craftsman* paid particular attention to the threat presented to British liberty posed by its standing army, taxation, and excessive national debt. It emphasised the dangers caused by the Financial Revolution to the established aristocratic-led social order, and the domination of the legislative by the executive (crown) which jeopardised Britain's balanced constitution.[133] Bolingbroke's personal contribution to the journal included the *Remarks on the History of England* (1730–31), *A Dissertation upon Parties* (1733–34), and other pieces. Within them he called for the Whigs and Tories to join under shared 'country' values, while reasserting a 'Spirit of Liberty' within Parliament inherited from Saxon ancestors that would engender the patriotism required to tackle the corruption of the state undermining liberty.[134]

The background to Bolingbroke's fierce antagonism against Walpole stemmed from a mutual personal enmity begun while they were both pupils at Eton. This antipathy was fuelled by Bolingbroke's attempt after 1710 as secretary of state under Queen Anne to break the Whigs, as Walpole's Oligarchy were then hounding the Tories.[135] Following the accession of George I, Bolingbroke's loss of his offices and the defeat of the Tories at the general election left him with an uncertain future. Fearful of imprisonment over his role in the Treaty of Utrecht, Bolingbroke fled to France on 27 March 1715. Insecurity led him to the Jacobites, which has been categorised as an 'enormous blunder' that caused his prolonged exile, plus the loss of his estates and titles.[136] As James Stuart's secretary of state he was charged with organising the preparations for the '15, but his counsel was often ignored by the Jacobite court. Failure of the '15 led to recrimination, as James Stuart blamed Bolingbroke for issuing poor supplies and reinforcements to Scotland. This tension was augmented by Bolingbroke's wish to impress upon the exiled prince the need to 'accept many of the major constitutional developments that had occurred in Britain since the revolution'. Bolingbroke 'desired to preserve a limited monarchy and a constitution balanced between crown and parliament'.[137] These issues witnessed the irretrievable breakdown of Bolingbroke's relationship with the Jacobites and in 1716 he began long negotiations with Lord Stair, Britain's ambassador to France, for a pardon as he fed information to the government. Recriminations continued, and Boling-broke referred to the 'Pretender' as a religious 'bigot' whose false espousals of toleration were undermined by a French upbringing that would lead to the extirpation of liberty and the Church of England.[138] He deemed the Jacobites shambolic and unrealistic regarding the need for French support to achieve a restoration.

Bolingbroke endeavoured for ten years to attain a pardon from the English government for his role as a Jacobite, which he vigorously tried to refute over the years. His time in France, however, proved to be extremely fruitful for his intellectual development, as much of it was spent studying history and philosophy. Bolingbroke moved in the 'highest social and intellectual circles' in France.[139] He was befriended by Montesquieu, Voltaire, Boulainvilliers, the abbé Alary, which as a consequence saw his invitation into the *Club de l'Entresol* where he became acquainted with Ramsay and the abbé de Saint-Pierre. This admittance into French intellectual society forged strong connections with a number of these thinkers, and made Bolingbroke an important conduit between French and British thought. Bolingbroke is perceived to have taken the Commonwealthmen ideology with him to France, influencing Montesquieu for example.[140] When he returned to Britain in 1726, he brought with him traces of French thought that expressed a *thèse nobilaire* perspective of aristocratic-led government reform within a (Gothic) balanced constitution.[141] These ideas sat well with the country ideology. It opposed the behaviour of an overbearing (Whig) executive and the threat to liberty, and comfortably accommodated his Tory propensity to defend the British ordered and ranked society with a proactive aristocracy.[142]

The central object of Bolingbroke's attentions in the *Craftsman* was Walpole. Walpole's usefulness to the king in dealing with the dual scandals of the South Sea Bubble and the Atterbury Plot surrounding Charles Spencer, the Earl of Sunderland (1675–1722),[143] led to his promotion as de facto prime minister. His adroitness at inflating the threat of Jacobitism created a phantom that enabled the greater assumption of power for himself and his ministry (Oligarchy). Matched by poor leadership in the Tory party undone by the accession, the Septennial Act and the king's antipathy towards them; Walpole's ministry was able to extend further its control of government throughout the late 1720s and into the 1730s. The ostensible frustration of meaningful opposition to the Whig ministry catalysed Bolingbroke and Pulteney's periodical. The *Craftsman* built on the concerns of *Cato's Letters* but vocalised a much stronger hostility towards Whig government, claiming that Cato's 'narrow principles' of virtue were too abstract, and not broad enough for the realities of contemporary Britain.[144] Significantly, the *Craftsman* concentrated personally on Walpole as the figurative embodiment of corruption. Bolingbroke attacked the deceptive mismanagement of government by Walpole, who had artificially manipulated crises to destroy the principles of 1688 for his own gain.[145] Walpole was a 'malicious' statesman who used the tools of a housebreaker on the nation to protect his own position and his allies while destroying opposition.[146]

The Whig consolidation of power during this period manifested the problematic alliance between political and economic corruption. An excessive focus on wealth within the nature both at a personal and national level had seen taxes and trade generate a 'general Spirit of Prodigality and Excess'.[147] Riches were leading to an obsession that could cause the state's ruination in two ways. First, the bribery of politicians by companies to do their bidding, and, second, the increase of the national debt as revenues decreased.[148] Bolingbroke saw a genuine threat to the legislation (Commons) through the executive's use of placemen and the interference in elections. Such behaviour adversely affected the 'architecture' of the constitution as the venality of Parliament undermined its capacity to fulfil its role within the constitution.[149] As neo-Harringtons such as Shaftesbury and Marvell had made clear fifty years earlier, such an encroachment by the executive was tyrannical. In the name of the crown, Walpole's ministry was able to use bribery and a standing army to enforce its will and protect itself from the 'Hatred of the People'.[150] The ministry further protected itself by employing tactics that were designed to suppress the vocalisation of opposition such as suppression, imprisonment, and deportation to the colonies. It was the intent of the *Craftsman* to challenge such 'Arbitrary Power, Oppression and Maladministration' by highlighting the tyrannical threat to liberty through the virtue of patriotism.[151]

While a patriotic defence of liberty may have been the *raison d'être* of the periodical, for court Whigs such as Baron John Hervey (1696–1743) this was not the ministry's perception. Hervey accused the *Craftsman* of hiding behind the freedom of the press to use the English law in preventing its prosecution. Press freedom allowed the *Craftsman* to publish libellous calumnies against a number of leading figures including George II and Queen Caroline. This was regarded by Hervey as 'guarded Treason': a new 'species of treason' which permitted the press to make slanderous allegations when they should be tried for treason.[152] Hervey rebuffed Bolingbroke's claims regarding standing armies, liberties, and the destruction of the coronation oath by stating that George II was restrained by the law and the Act of Settlement.[153] Rather than a 'Spirit of Liberty', the *Craftsman* revealed 'private Views', resentment and ambitions worn beneath 'the Mask of publick Good'.[154] Bolingbroke's implacable hatred of Walpole had ensured the 'Craftsman's Quiver' was levelled at 'one Mark' (Walpole), with the intent to destroy that 'Minister'. These proclamations exhibited nothing more than a papal behaviour that allowed Bolingbroke to proclaim dogmatically against the ministry by inaccurately representing English history.[155] After 1688 the constitution had become modernised and no longer stood on the degenerated (historical) original principles that Bolingbroke exalted. Court Whigs like Hervey now advocated a reformist age of pragmatic politics beyond ideological calls for 'political perfection'.[156] In reference to Bolingbroke's former Jacobite affiliation, Hervey stated that like *Fog's Weekly Journal* he was simply regurgitating Jacobite revolutionary propaganda.[157] Such misinformation not only exposed disloyalty to the king, but also aided the Pretender by using grievances with Parliament to 'Manufacture ... Jacobite-making'.[158]

Hervey's view was rejected by Bolingbroke, and he was personally attacked, notably by Pulteney (as leader of the opposition) in Parliament. In fact, Bolingbroke reiterated that it was tyrannical to prevent the people from voicing complaints against the state regarding its behaviour. The *Craftsman* had striven 'to persuade' its fellow citizens through argument, and by not forcing them to coalesce against their will.[159] The publication did not possess a 'seditious, rebellious spirit' that perpetuated Jacobitism or 'tumult and disorder'; rather, it was a 'true old English spirit' which had prevailed in the Revolution. It stood for the protection of liberty, the 'preservation of the community and good order' which defended it from the tyranny of princes and ministers.[160] Under the present British system the threat was located in the crown and court which was determined to use its prerogative to invade the liberties and constitution. A 'spirit of faction' was not enough to repel this threat. A 'national spirit' had to be evoked to create the strength of opposition to withstand the invasion of liberty now experienced.[161]

The *Craftsman* essentially demanded a 'middle point' to secure the mixed constitution that eschewed the extremes of despotism and 'Athenian anarchic and tyrannical democracy'. Traditional Whig country ideology served a number of Bolingbroke's purposes in shielding the 'spirit of liberty'. First, as recent British history revealed, country ideology lent itself to opposition of the court. From the neo-Harrington opposition in the 1670s to the first Whigs of the Exclusion Crisis and the blending of party ideology in the 1690s, concerns over the activity of the court manifested itself in a wider country opposition that was essentially precluded from power.[162] The accompanying republican ideology that protested against the executive's corruption of the constitution and the use of tools like bribery and a standing army, were as pertinent in the 1720s and 1730s as in the 1670s. Second, this country ideology married well with earlier Toryism that believed ordered society required mixed government and the moral leadership of monarchy to provide the public good. The *Craftsman* reflected the concerns of the landed gentry against the new moneyed interest and the Troy frustration with the development of paper credit and a national debt.[163] Finally, country ideology allowed Bolingbroke to remind Walpole and the nation that the Whig ministry had become so divorced from its foundational principles it had betrayed them as well as the revolutionary settlement.

Despite Hervey's attempt to strike at its use, historical lessons provided an invaluable method in the *Craftsman* for highlighting the present corruption of the British constitution. This approach echoed Machiavelli and evaluated the present through past history while revealing its continuity in the constitution.[164] Machiavelli's application of Livy enabled Bolingbroke to advocate a republican renewal of 'first principles' to refresh a government and restore what worked best for that nation.[165] Rome had declined because of the increasing excesses of liberty between the patricians and plebeians, as the interests of the commonwealth were subsumed by faction. As the opponent of liberty, faction controlled and destroyed liberty for its own ends and power. The corruption of the British Parliament revealed a similar emergence of faction as the executive crushed the independence of the legislative and the balanced constitution to augment the ministry and court's supremacy.[166] While Rome had only experienced 700 years of liberty, Bolingbroke expressed pride for living in a Britain that had lived under liberty for 1,700 years. Enhanced by the Saxon democratic or Gothic principles this ancient liberty had survived all invasions – including by the Romans – to perpetuate its internal spirit.[167] It had withstood William the Conqueror, the potential absolutism of Richard II, and the factious behaviour of Charles II and James II.[168] In the case of Charles II, his determination to extinguish liberty through absolutism had led to the emergence of parties to withstand the king and frighten compliance with Parliament. Bolingbroke blamed the reign of James I for this trenchant quest to instil absolutism into the English constitution. Queen Elizabeth was lauded as a patriotic queen who had been a moderate and peaceful mediator. Tolerant, prudent, economically rational, her pursuit of the public good ensured that she was loved by her people whose liberty she defended.[169] In contrast to her kingly behaviour, James I's 'foreign rule' had generated the problems for his heirs during the seventeenth century. The repeated grievances against the Stuart extension of prerogatives, wasteful expenditure of the crown, monopolies, and popery in government stemmed from this source.[170] Stuart self-interest struggled to embed absolutism in a manner that was alien to the limited monarchy of England. This bid to erode liberty instigated Parliament's war against Charles I who had pursued his father's style of government.[171] Any attempt to ostracise the British government from its preservation had therefore always been thwarted due to its foundation on liberty.[172] This 'spirit of liberty' sustained the people against tyranny and maintained the freedom of the Gothic balance.[173]

Parliament's historic opposition to the executive called it to account by reminding the crown that it had always been limited by a mixed constitution. Indeed, political parties had become necessary when the crown had endeavoured to leak into the legislative branch of government by influencing Parliament through Danby's court party. Regardless of the wider fears of revolution that Whig opposition caused during the Exclusion Crisis so near to the Restoration, its intervention was for public liberty.[174] Parties were one element of opposition that protected the people's liberty from invasion by the crown. Bolingbroke's desire for concord between the Whigs and Tories was a call for the unity of 1688, when the revolutionary settlement engendered a new Magna Carta.[175] Strict division between the parties no longer applied, rather there was a 'Court and a Country party in being'.[176] Britain required the power of a united Commons to preserve its liberty, and repulse the infiltration by the executive through its placemen and standing army.[177] Just as the people had been represented in early Britain's Gothic (Saxon) tribes, balanced free government remained, and frequent elections would subvert the ministry's plans.[178]

Unlike France, British liberty had retained distinct cooperative roles for the Commons, nobility, and the crown. In a criticism of Boulainvilliers's interpretation of the French Gothic balance, Bolingbroke stated that French history revealed the king and nobility's use of the Estates-General to control the people and exclude them from power.[179] Conversely, the British nobility had insured that balance between the crown and commons remained by acting as mediators, particularly by cooperating with the latter. Liberty and the public good required a mixed constitution that allowed Parliament to be free and independent to fight against corruption. If this were achieved, a popular king of Britain would not only be secure, he would be 'in effect absolute ... the absolute monarch of a free people'.[180] This meant that if the executive cooperated rather than fought to reach beyond its bounds within the mixed constitution, the support it would receive from the wider populace would greatly enhance its power. It would thereby harness the unity of purpose in a balanced government to preserve the public good, and possess the support to act in an unlimited manner if required.

Bolingbroke found the genesis of the troubles in the 1720s and 1730s in the court's corruption of the seventeenth century under the Stuarts. James I had been responsible for initiating the pretensions of absolute sovereignty alien to the English court. It had created a struggle with Parliament as he attempted to undermine the mixed constitution in favour of the crown. His son had paid for this endeavour with his life, while his grandson's actions had given birth to political parties: a vocal means of protest that provided a restraining opposition to the king's extension of power. Charles II was also held accountable for the later development of financial corruption which had entwined politics and economics. For, the Restoration court's obsession with luxury had turned Britain into a 'national prostitute' as private and public corruption merged in the state.[181] The long-standing consequence of this indecorous alliance was fifty years of disharmony, in a modernising financial state riven with political faction and an executive attempting to corrupt the constitution. Bolingbroke's employment of country ideology revealed the ability for elements beyond the court to withstand the power of the executive in the interest of the nation. Such action required the alliance of parties, Church and people, but as the ideology revealed the country's interest was frequently the same, it was the court that undermined this potential unity. In his longer-term defence of the nation's liberty and its balanced constitution Bolingbroke moved his appeal beyond the people and nobility to the monarchy itself.[182] He advocated the rule of a 'Patriot King' – Frederick the Prince of Wales (1707–51) – who could govern with 'ease, security, honour, dignity' and sufficient 'power and strength' to enjoy the absolute support of the nation.[183] Overcoming corruption (through education) in himself and government, the king would deliver a virtuous example of a patriarchal king to his people under public scrutiny. The king would enjoy a reign freed from revolution and public disquiet as he sacrificed himself to the public good.[184] Such a king was redolent of Archbishop Fénelon's prince in *Télémaque* (1699). A prince who attacked the encroachment on the people's liberty by overbearing absolutism (Louis XIV), and sacrificed himself to the public good for the benefit of his people while providing an example of virtue.[185] The two men shared a desire for unity, harmony and peace within kingdoms that were dominated by insecurity and a perceived threat to the public good. Liberty was essential in actuating a reversal of the domineering and haughty executive corrupted by self-interest.

While Bolingbroke's time in exile had forged connections with French thinkers, his theory was strongly representative of British traditions that existed from the seventeenth century. Nations such as France had experienced the extension of executive absolutism across Europe, while the aristocracy often tried to resist (or embrace) this trend ideologically. The attempt was successful in England in the seventeenth century, because its representative institutions and the aristocracy had become embedded in the business of government and did not wish to relinquish their role. Despite this the Stuarts strove throughout the seventeenth century to govern through absolute sovereignty. They employed theory that was prevalent across Europe and famously found influential expression in Bodin as well as James I. This theory applied scripture and defended a traditional patriarchal order in which the crown possessed a descending authority over all below it. Unfortunately for the Stuarts the growth of parliamentary power in the preceding centuries, notably under the Tudors, led to an inevitable collision with the monarchy's plan for independence. After the Restoration, the engagement of republican Commonwealth ideology against Charles II revealed a determination to protect the perceived role of Parliament in a mixed constitution by expounding liberty. The defeat of the Whigs in the Exclusion Crisis was a transient victory for the Stuarts, as James II's swift destabilisation of the Church and state led to the 1688 Revolution. Amidst a geopolitical context of French power, an absolute Catholic Stuart with empathy for Louis XIV was unpalatable to the British.

Yet regardless of this brief moment of unity, divisions in church and state continued to dominate British politics. This discord was reflected in the party behaviour of the 1690s and their ideology manifest in the Sacheverell and *Answer* controversies. More evidently it was reflected in the creation and persistence of the Jacobites, whose French backing reminded the British of its fears over Catholic absolutism prevalent from the 1660s to 1680s. While these divisions ended in the Treaty of Utrecht, George I's succession and the failure of the '15, other problems quickly replaced them. The concatenation of political and social degeneracy in the financial age led to an observed corruption of the executive, in which the ministry led the crown. Republican ideals guided by classical thought against Charles II were utilised once more at the end of this period to safeguard liberty and the independence of Parliament against the executive, its bribery, and a standing army. Country opposition drew on a much wider basis of support than the narrower definitions of Whig and Tory in its response to court corruption, and revealed a general unity extant in times of threat. The appeals of Cato and Bolingbroke provided valuable challenges, which especially highlighted the belief that Parliament's position within the constitution had been enshrined by 1688. However, Bolingbroke's attempt to retain the older traditional view of ordered (Tory) society in a (Whig) commercial age was less successful. Notwithstanding pleas for unity, Britain remained politically divided regardless of one party's domination of the ministry into the second half of the eighteenth century.

Notes

1 The fortuitous birth of James Francis Edward Stuart in June 1688 at a time of great trouble for James II immediately led to questions regarding his legitimacy. As a result of the 1688 Revolution, his Catholicism and extraction to France alongside his father meant that the Prince of Wales was removed from the succession in favour of Mary II and William III. Claims of his illegitimacy proved to be politically and religiously expedient to the revolutionary settlement. His repeated calls for the restoration of his birth right and titles earned him the title of 'Pretender' (claimant to the throne).

2 Steve Pincus has argued that Jacobitism was effectively ended after the Assassination Plot (of William III) in 1696, whereas Nenner has claimed that there was no way back for the Jacobites after 1689 (Pincus, *1688: The First Modern Revolution* (Yale, 2009), 454; Howard Nenner, 'The Later Stuart Age', *The Varieties of Political Thought, 1500–1800*, eds J.G.A. Pocock with Gordon J. Schochet and Lois G. Schwoerer (Cambridge, 1993), 206–7).

3 Daniel Szechi, *Jacobitism and Tory Politics, 1710–14* (Edinburgh, 1984), 2.

4 See J.N. Figgis, *The Divine Right of Kings* (New York, 1965), 166, 169–70; Lenman, *The Jacobite Risings in Britain 1689–1746*, 11–13, 16, 19; Howard Erskine-Hill, 'Literature and the Jacobite Cause: Was There a Rhetoric of Jacobitism?', *Ideology and Conspiracy: Aspects of Jacobitism 1689–1759*, ed. Eveline Cruickshanks (Edinburgh, 1982), 51; Clark, *English Society 1688–1832*, 46–50, 82, 130; Paul Kleber Monod, *Jacobitism and the English People, 1688–1788* (Cambridge, 1989), 17–19.

5 Daniel Szechi, *The Jacobites, Britain and Europe 1688–1788* (Manchester, 1994), 14. The national make-up of the court was: 60 per cent Irish, 35 per cent English, and 5 per cent Scots. Of the total, 40 per cent were of noble birth, at a time when the nobility comprised 1 per cent of the population (Nathalie Genet-Rouffiac, 'Jacobites in Paris and Saint-Germain-en-Laye', *The Stuart Court in Exile and the Jacobites*, eds Eveline Cruickshanks and Edward Corp (London, 1995), 18).

6 Szechi, *Jacobitism and Tory Politics, 1710–14*, 47–9. On the court's Catholicism and absolute proclivities, also see Gabriel Glickman, *The English Catholic Community 1688–1745: Politics, Culture and Ideology* (Woodbridge, 2009), 90, 100–3.

7 Mark Goldie, 'The English System of Liberty', *Cambridge History of Eighteenth-Century Political Thought*, eds Goldie and Wokler (Cambridge, 2006), 45–7.

8 On the weakness of the Irish Jacobite cause under the 'Pretender', see Éamonn Ó Ciardha, *Ireland and the Jacobite Cause, 1685–1766: A Fatal Attachment* (Dublin, 2004), 184.

9 Murray G.H. Pittock, *The Invention of Scotland. The Stuart Myth and the Scottish Identity, 1638 to the present* (London, 1991), 13–18, 30–1.

10 Andrew Fletcher of Saltoun, *Two Discourses concerning the Affairs of Scotland: The Political Works of Andrew Fletcher Esq* (London, 1732), 81–2, 88, 122–3; *An Account of a Conversation concerning a Right Regulation of Governments for the common Good of Mankind, Works*, 384.

11 Fletcher, *An Account of a Conversation*, 394.

12 Mark A. Thomson, 'Self-determination and Collective Security as Factors in English and French Foreign Policy, 1689–1718', *William III and Louis XIV: Essays 1680–1720 by and for Mark A. Thomson*, eds Ragnhild Hatton and J.S. Bromley (Liverpool, 1968), 281.

13 See Bruce Lenman, *The Jacobite Risings in Britain 1689–1746 (London, 1980)*, 106; T.M. Devine, *The Scottish Nation 1700–2000* (London, 1999), 17.

14 See Szechi, *The Jacobites, Britain and Europe 1688–1788*, 56–57, and Eveline Cruickshanks, *The Glorious Revolution* (London, 2000), 52–53.

15 Daniel Szechi, 'Jacobite Politics in the Age of Anne', *Parliamentary History*, 28, 1 (Feb. 2009), pp. 41–58 (43, 44, 50–2, 55–6).

16 Murray G.H. Pittock, *Jacobitism* (London, 1998), 1.

17 See J. H. Plumb, *The First Four Georges* (London, 1956), 29; Lenman, *Jacobite Risings in Britain 1689–1746*, 181–2; G.V. Bennett, 'English Jacobitism, 1710–1715: Myth and Reality', *Transactions of the Royal Historical Society*, 5th series, 32 (1982), pp. 137–51 (140); Jeremy Black, *Natural and Necessary Enemies. Anglo-French Relations in the Eighteenth Century* (London, 1986), 1–3; David Scott, *Leviathan: The Rise of Britain as a World Power* (London, 2013), 277–8.

18 See J.F. Bosher, 'The Franco-Catholic Danger, 1660–1715', *History*, 79, 255 (Feb. 1994), pp. 5–30 (21–24); Julian Hoppit, *A Land of Liberty? England 1689–1727* (Oxford, 2000), 214–22; Glickman, *English Catholic Community 1688–1745*, 40–3.

19 Edward Gregg, 'Was Queen Anne a Jacobite?', *History*, 57, 191 (Oct. 1972), pp. 358–75. Gregg reveals that Anne was actually rather fearful of the Jacobites and their Catholicism (369).

20 See Eveline Cruickshanks, 'The Tories and the Succession to the Crown in the 1714 Parliament', *Historical Research*, 46, 114 (Nov. 1973), pp. 176–85 (176–7); J.C.D. Clark, *English Society 1688–1832: Ideology, Social Structure and Political Practice during the Ancien Regime* (Cambridge, 1985), 46; Paul Kleber Monod, *Jacobitism and the English People, 1688–1788* (Cambridge, 1989), 2–3; Tim Harris, *Politics under the Later Stuarts: Party Conflict in a Divided Society 1660–1715* (London, 1993), 157–60, 210–12.

21 H.T. Dickinson, 'St. John, Henry (1678–1751)', *Oxford Dictionary of National Biography*, online: www.oxforddnb.com.ezproxy.sussex.ac.uk/view/article/24496?docPos=1. It is actually known that both men were in contact with the exiled prince regarding a potential restoration, but James's refusal to convert to Protestantism halted the correspondence. It is claimed that Bolingbroke stated that the 'sultan of Turkey would be more acceptable to the English people than a Catholic Stuart', and from March 1714 the Jacobites were discounted as an option by the Tory ministry (J.H. and Margaret Shennan, 'The Protestant Succession in English Politics, April 1713–September 1715', *William III and Louis XIV*, eds Hatton and Bromley (Liverpool, 1968), 257–9).

22 Joseph Cannell, *The Case of the Pretender Stated* (London, 1708), 3–4; Richard Steele, *The Crisis* (London, 1713), v.

23 *Ibid.*, 10.

24 [anonymous], *Reasons against Receiving the Pretender* (London, 1710), 3.

25 *Ibid.*, 4, 5.

26 *Ibid.*, 7.

27 John Shute Barrington, *A Dissuasive from Jacobitism* (London, 1713), 10–11.

28 *Ibid.*, 30–4.

29 John Shute Barrington, *The Revolution and Anti-Revolution*, 3rd edn (London, 1714), 38, 40.

30 *Ibid.*, 5–14, 80, 89.

31 *Ibid.*, 48, 89.

32 John Shute Barrington, *The Layman's Letter to the Bishop of Bangor* (London, 1716), 9–10.

33 *Ibid.*, 6; and Francis Atterbury, *English Advice to the Freeholders of England* (London, 1714), 8, 19–26.

34 Barrington, *Layman's Letter to the Bishop of Bangor*, 39.

35 See [anonymous], *Vox populi, vox dei: Being the True Maxims of Government* (London, 1709), 8, 26; [Viscount Robert] Molesworth, *The Principles of a Real Whig, Franco-Gallia* (London, 1775), 7–8; Thomas Bradbury, *The Lawfulness of Resisting Tyrants*, 3rd edn (London, 1714), 25.

36 Edward Matthews, *The Divine Original of Civil Government* (Dublin, 1714), 23.

37 See George Berkeley, *The Measure of Submission to Civil Government* (London, 1784), 38, 44; Luke Milbourne, *The Measures of Resistance to the Higher Powers*, 2nd edn (London, 1710), 2.

38 George Hickes, *Some Queries propos'd to Civil, Canon, and Common Lawyers* (London, 1712), 13.

39 [George Harbin], *The Hereditary Right of the Crown of England Asserted* (London, 1713), 13.

40 *Ibid.*, 278.

41 *Ibid.*, 94.

42 *Ibid.*, 100. For reaction to the work's claims, see [anonymous], *The British Liberty Asserted* (London, 1714), 43, 62; John Asgill, *The Succession of the House of Hannover Vindicated* (London, 1714), 54, 68.

43 Daniel Defoe, *A View of the Real Danger of the Protestant Succession* (London, 1714), 25.

44 Black, *Natural and Necessary Enemies: Anglo-French Relations in the Eighteenth Century*, 7–8, 12–14, 211.

45 Daniel Defoe, *Advice to the People of Great Britain* (London, 1714), 11–12. J.G.A. Pocock has pointed out that the 'Augustan age' following the accession of George I remained 'deeply divided' culturally and socially, and that the Hanoverian succession was at first extremely

precarious (*Barbarism and Religion Volume III: The First Decline and Fall* (Cambridge, 1999–), 313–14.

46 See Devine, *The Scottish Nation 1700–2000*, 36–7; Kieran German, 'Jacobite Politics in Aberdeen and the '15', *Loyalty and Identity. Jacobites at Home and Abroad*, eds Paul Monod, Murray Pittock and Daniel Szechi (Basingstoke, 2010), 88–9.

47 See Lenman: *The Jacobite Risings in Britain 1689–1746*, 107–8; *The Jacobite Cause* (Glasgow, 1986), 45–6; Pittock, *Jacobitism*, 40–9.

48 See Ragnhild Hatton, *George I* (London, 1978), 180; Daniel Szechi: '"Cam Ye O'er Frae France?" Exile and the Mind of Scottish Jacobitism, 1716–1727', *Journal of British Studies*, 37, 4 (Oct., 1998), pp. 357–90 (357–8); *1715: The Great Jacobite Rebellion* (Yale, 2006), 255–6.

49 See Matthew Tindal, *The Defection Consider'd* (London, 1717), 53; Whitelocke Bulstrode, *A Letter Touching the Late Rebellion* (London, 1717), 5; [anonymous], *The Present Exigencies of the Government Consider'd* (London, 1719), 29; Richard Arnett, *A Seasonable Hue and Cry after the Pretender* (London, 1719), 2–3

50 See, G.V. Bennett, *The Tory Crisis in Church and State: The Career of Francis Atterbury, Bishop of Rochester* (Oxford, 1975), 224–5, 251–2; Eveline Cruickshanks, 'Lord North, Christopher Layer and the Atterbury Plot: 1720–23', *The Jacobite Challenge*, eds Eveline Cruickshanks and Jeremy Black (Edinburgh, 1988), pp. 92–106; Eveline Cruickshanks and Howard Erskine-Hill, *The Atterbury Plot* (Basingstoke, 2004).

51 See J.H. Plumb, *The Growth of Political Stability in England 1675–1725* (London, 1967), 168–72; Paul S. Fritz, 'The Anti-Jacobite Intelligence System of the English Ministers, 1715–45', *Historical Journal*, 16, 2 (1973), pp. 265–89; G.V. Bennett, 'Jacobitism and the Rise of Walpole', *Historical Perspectives: Studies in English Thought and Society, in Honour of J.H. Plumb*, ed. Neil McKendrick (London, 1974), 91; Nicholas Rogers, 'Riot and Popular Jacobitism in Early Hanoverian England', *Ideology and Conspiracy: Aspects of Jacobitism 1689–1759*, ed. Eveline Cruickshanks (1982), 71.

52 See P.M. Chapman, 'Jacobite political argument in England, 1714–66', unpublished Ph.D. thesis (Cambridge, 1983), 58, 298; Andrew Hanham, '"So Few Facts:" Jacobites, Tories and the Pretender', *Parliamentary History*, 19, pt 2 (2000), pp. 233–57 (242).

53 Chapman, 'Jacobite political argument in England, 1714–66', 40, 47, 252–4.

54 Nathaniel Mist, *A Collection of Miscellany Letters, Selected out of Mist's Weekly Journal*, 2 vols (London, 1722), II, 160.

55 *Ibid.*, I, 235; II, 7–8.

56 *Ibid.*, II, 267–9.

57 *Ibid.*, II, 279.

58 See Plumb, *The Growth of Political Instability*, 187; H.T. Dickinson, *Liberty and Property. Political Ideology in Eighteenth-Century Britain* (London, 1977), 130–2.

59 John Cannon, *Aristocratic Century. The Peerage of Eighteenth-Century England* (Cambridge, 1984), 93–5.

60 Geoffrey Holmes, *British Politics in the Age of Anne*, rev. edn (London, 1987), 346

61 *Ibid.*, 108–9, 418.

62 *Ibid.*, 347; Geoffrey Holmes, *The Making of a Great Power: Late Stuart and Early Georgian Britain 1660–1722* (London, 1993), 257.

63 See Jeremy Black, *The Hanoverians: The History of a Dynasty* (London, 2004), 43–5. This view of Hanoverian sovereignty disputes J.C.D. Clark's belief they were autocratic (*Revolution and Rebellion: State and Society in England in the Seventeenth and Eighteenth Centuries* (Cambridge, 1986), 78).

64 G.C. Gibbs, 'George I (1660–1727)', *ODNB*: www.oxforddnb.com.ezproxy.sussex.ac.uk/view/article/10538/?back=,10539

65 *Ibid.*

66 Atterbury, *English Advice to the Freeholder's of England*, 3, 5–6.

67 *Ibid.*, 4, 19–21.

68 *Ibid.*, 18–29.

69 *Ibid.*, 6, 7, 8, 12–13, 14–15, 31.

70 *Ibid.*, 26.

71 Gibbs, 'George I (1660–1727)'.

72 Black, *Hanoverians*, 47.

73 Gibbs, 'George I (1660–1727)'.

74 See Plumb, *The Growth of Political Stability*, 187; Hatton, *George I*, 294–7; Holmes, *Making of a Great Power*, 227.

75 Goldie, 'English System of Liberty', 41.

76 J.G.A. Pocock: *The Machiavellian Moment: Florentine Political Thought and the Atlantic Republican Tradition* (Princeton, 1975), 426–7; 'The Varieties of Whiggism from Exclusion to Reform: A History of Ideology and Discourse', *Virtue, Commerce, and History* (Cambridge, 1985), 239.

77 [anonymous], *A General History of Trade, and Especially Consider'd as It Respects British Commerce* (London, 1713), 5.

78 See Steele, *The Crisis*, 31; Barrington, *A Dissuasive from Jacobitism*, 30–4; Daniel Defoe, *And What If the Pretender Should Come?* (London, 1713), 13, 19.

79 See Jürgen Habermas, *The Structural Transformation of the Public Sphere: An Inquiry into a Category of Bourgeois Society*, trans. Thomas Burger and Frederick Lawrence (Cambridge, 2002), 27; Steven Pincus, 'The State and Civil Society in Early Modern England: Capitalism, Causation and Habermas's Bourgeois Public Sphere', *The Politics of the Public Sphere in Early Modern England*, eds Peter Lake and Steven Pincus (Manchester, 2007), 217.

80 M.M. Goldsmith, *Private Vices, Public Benefits: Bernard Mandeville's Social and Political Thought* (Cambridge, 1985), 128.

81 See Habermas, *Structural Transformation of the Public Sphere*, 57–8; Pincus, 'State and Civil Society in Early Modern England', 220–1.

82 See Christopher Hill, *The Century of Revolution 1603–1714* (Walton-on-Thames, 1980), 1–4; Pincus: 'State and Civil Society in Early Modern England', 223; *1688*, 87, 372–4.

83 Isaac Kramnick, *Bolingbroke and His Circle: The Politics of Nostalgia in the Age of Walpole* (Harvard, 1968), 41.

84 *Ibid.*, 56–7, 60–1.

85 Plumb, *First Four Georges*, 27–8.

86 George Berkeley, *An Essay towards Preventing the Ruine of Great Britain* (London, 1721), 20.

87 *Ibid.*, 1, 5.

88 Goldsmith, *Private Vices, Public Benefits*, 21.

89 Bernard Mandeville, *The Fable of the Bees: Or, Private Vices, Publick Benefits*, ed. F.B. Kaye (Oxford, 1924), 42–3; Remark O (149–51). Mandeville's (negative) delineation of human motivations for behaviour was influenced by Hobbes. Its connection with trade followed French discussions from the 1670s – by Pierre Nicole, Pierre le Boisguilbert, etc. – that were quickly followed in Britain by Nicholas Barbon, for example, in *A Discourse on Trade* (1690). Hobbesian state competition was seen as generating a positive effect for state revenues while also embracing the interdependence between nations that could benefit trade (see Chapter 3 in this book). According to Istvan Hont, Mandeville followed Hobbes's view in *De Cive* by rejecting the idea that man was by nature political (*zoōn politikon*). Yet from this foundation he deviated from Hobbes by arguing that a 'dexterous politician' – a legislator rather than a politico – could create peace by manipulating the passions, thereby overcoming negative impulses without prohibitive force ('The Early Enlightenment Debate on Commerce and Luxury', *Cambridge History of Eighteenth-Century Political Thought, Volume I*, eds Mark Goldie and Robert Wokler (Cambridge, 2006), 390).

90 Mandeville, Remarks I (101), M (133), N (134–5, 146).

91 *Ibid.*, Remarks L (119), Q (184–5, 197), Y (250).

92 *Ibid.*, Remark T (226, 234–5); Mandeville, *A Vindication of the Book* (394–5, 405).

93 Iain Hampsher-Monk, 'From Virtue to Politeness', *Republicanism: A Shared European Heritage. Volume II: The Values of Republicanism in Early Modern Europe*, eds Martin van Gelderen and Quentin Skinner (Cambridge, 2002), 85–6, 89.

94 Andrew Fletcher, *A Discourse of Government with relation to Militias: The Political Works of Andrew Fletcher, Esq* (London, 1732), 7–8, 14–16.

95 *Ibid.*, 8–9, 19–21, 39–40.

96 *Ibid.*, 47–8, 53–4, 67–8.

97 E.J. Hundert, *The Enlightenment's Fable: Bernard Mandeville and the Discovery of Society* (Cambridge, 1994), 9.

98 *Ibid.*, 12. See also Pocock, *Machiavellian Moment*, 424–5, 450; Goldsmith, *Private Vices, Public Benefits*, 26–7; Goldie, 'English System of Liberty', 64–70.

99 Niccolò Machiavelli, *The Discourses*, trans. Leslie J. Walker, ed. S.J. Bernard Crick (London, 1983), III, 1 (385–6).

100 Marie McMahon, 'Trenchard, John [*pseuds* Cato, Diogenes] (1668/9–1723)', *ODNB* online: www.oxforddnb.com.ezproxy.sussex.ac.uk/view/article/27706?docPos=2

101 Leslie Stephen, rev. Emma Major, 'Gordon, Thomas (d.1750)', *ODNB* online: www.oxforddnb. com.ezproxy.sussex.ac.uk/view/article/11083?docPos=1

102 According to Reed Browning, Cato of Uttica (95–46 BCE) should not be confused with Cato the Censor (234–149 BCE): a frequent occurrence in the eighteenth century. While both men were patriots and provided exemplars of traditional virtue, the former opposed the ambitions of Caesar 'at home', whereas the latter opposed the 'Carthaginian threats abroad' (*Political and Constitutional Ideas of the Court Whigs* (Baton Rouge, 1982), 2, 2n.).

103 *Ibid.*, 5–6; Goldsmith, *Private Vices, Public Benefits*, 20–1.

104 See John Carswell, *The South Sea Bubble* (Stroud, 2001), 200; Julian Hoppit, 'Myths of the South Sea Bubble', *Transactions of the Royal Historical Society*, 6th series, 12 (2002), pp. 141–65 (142–6); Ron Harris, 'Government and the Economy, 1688–1850', *The Cambridge Economic History of Modern Britain. Volume I: Industrialisation, 1700–1860*, eds Roderick Floud and Paul Johnson (Cambridge, 2004), 227–8.

105 John Trenchard and Thomas Gordon, *Cato's Letters or Essays on Liberty, Civil and Religious, and Other Important Subjects. Four Volumes in Two*, ed. Ronald Hamowy (Indianapolis, 1995), Vol. I, No. 2 (40–1).

106 *Ibid.*, II, 91 (650).

107 *Ibid.*, II, 91 (648–9).

108 *Ibid.*, II, 98 (702–4).

109 *Ibid.*, I, 16 (121).

110 *Ibid.*, I, 17 (124–7).

111 *Ibid.*, II, 76 (560).

112 *Ibid.*, II, 70 (505).

113 *Ibid.*, II, 73 (539).

114 *Ibid.*, II, 74 (546–7).

115 *Ibid.*, II, 82 (595), 94 (670).

116 *Ibid.*, II, 94 (671, 673–5).

117 *Ibid.*, I, 62 (429, 432). This reading of a Lockean infusion of justice regarding rights and property concurs with Ronald Hamowy. Hamowy disputes Pocock's view that *Cato's Letters* solely reflected republican ideology in the Commonwealthman tradition and that John Locke had no tangible influence on the period or *Cato's Letters* ('Cato's Letters, *John Locke, and the Republican Paradigm*', *John Locke's Two Treatises of Government. New Interpretations*, ed. Edward J. Harpham (Kansas, 1992), 154–6).

118 *Cato's Letters*, I, 33 (238–9).

119 *Ibid.*, I, 60 (412–13); II, 84 (607–8).

120 *Ibid.*, I, 55 (368–76).

121 *Ibid.*, II, 76 (557).

122 *Ibid.*, II, 93 (667–8). Cato was not calling for an aristocratic government, which would not be tenable within Britain's mixed constitution; see II, 85 (616). Blair Worden has stated that the work displays an 'anti-aristocratic sentiment' through its promotion of liberty and attack on Roman Republican senatorial oppression ('Republicanism and Restoration, 1660–1683', *Republicanism, Liberty, and Commercial Society, 1649–1776*, ed. David Wootton (Stanford, 1994), 184).

123 See Chapter 3.

124   Machiavelli, *Discourses*, I, 17–18 (158–9, 163–4).

125   See *Cato's Letters*, I, 16 (118–19); Machiavelli, *Discourses*, III, 1 (385–6).

126   *Cato's Letters*, I, 24 (178).

127   *Ibid*., I, 61 (422–3); II, 99 (711).

128   *Ibid*., II, 80 (583–5).

129   *Ibid*., II, 96 (693).

130   Annie Mitchell, 'Character of an Independent Whig – "Cato" and Bernard Mandeville', *History of European Ideas*, 29 (2003), 291–311 (308).

131   Machiavelli, *Discourses*, I, 5 (117–18).

132   Viscount Bolingbroke, *Contributions to the Craftsman*, ed. Simon Varey (Oxford, 1982), No. 123 (59–62)

133   See Bolingbroke, *Contributions to the Craftsman*, 123 (59); Quentin Skinner, 'The Principles and Practice of Opposition: The Case of Bolingbroke versus Walpole', *Historical Perspectives: Studies in English Thought and Society, in Honour of J.H. Plumb*, 125.

134   Viscount Bolingbroke, *A Dissertation upon Parties*, *Political Writings*, ed. David Armitage, 82–4, 123–5.

135   Kramnick, *Bolingbroke and His Circle*, vii–viii.

136   See H.T. Dickinson, *ODNB* online; Linda Colley, *In Defiance of Oligarchy: The Tory Party 1714–60* (Cambridge, 1982), 27.

137   Dickinson, *ODNB* online.

138   Viscount Bolingbroke, *A Letter to Sir William Windham: The Works of Lord Bolingbroke, Volume IV* (Philadelphia, 1841), 177.

139   See Kramnick, *Bolingbroke and His Circle*, 14; H.T. Dickinson, *Bolingbroke* (London, 1970), 155.

140   Rachel Hammersley, *The English Republican Tradition and Eighteenth-Century France: Between the Ancients and the Moderns* (Manchester, 2010), 54–5, 83 n. 82.

141   Kramnick, *Bolingbroke and His Circle*, 14–17. See Chapter 5 in the present book for a discussion of these ideas in their French context, and Chapter 8 for the influence of Ramsay upon Bolingbroke's thought.

142   See Chapter 8 for a discussion on the natural law system underpinning Bolingbroke's Tory view of civil society, and its connection to Ramsay.

143   For a (heated) discussion on the importance of Sunderland (and Jacobite historiography), see Clyve Jones, 'Whigs, Jacobites and Charles Spencer, Third Earl of Sunderland', *English Historical Review*, 109, 430 (Feb. 1994), pp. 52–73; Eveline Cruickshanks, 'Charles Spencer, Third Earl of Sunderland, and Jacobitism', *English Historical Review*, 113, 450 (Feb. 1999), pp. 65–76.

144   Viscount Bolingbroke, *The Occasional Writer I: The Works of Lord Bolingbroke, Volume I* (Philadelphia, 1841), 203.

145   *Ibid*., 205–8.

146   Bolingbroke: *Occasional Writer II, Works I*, 210–11; *Occasional Writer III, Works I*, 227.

147   Bolingbroke, *Contributions to the Craftsman*, No. 161 (96).

148   *Ibid*., 60 (10), 105 (47).

149   *Ibid*., 111 (49–51).

150   *Ibid*., 123 (62).

151   *Ibid*., 54 (18–19); 149 (90); 225 (119).

152   [John Hervey], *Farther Observations on the Writings of the Craftsman* (London, 1730), 10–12, 25, 30.

153   *Ibid*., 15–16.

154   [Hervey], *Observations on the Writings of the Craftsman* (London, 1730), 10.

155   *Ibid*., 7.

156   See Goldie, 'English System of Liberty', 76–7; Browning, *Political and Constitutional Ideas of the Court Whigs*, 65; J.G.A. Pocock, *The Ancient Constitution and the Feudal Law: A Study of English Historical Thought in the Seventeenth Century. A Reissue with a Retrospect* (Cambridge, 1987), 369–70.

157   *Ibid*., 16.

158   [Hervey], *Farther Observations on the Writings of the Craftsman*, 19.

159 Viscount Bolingbroke, *Remarks on the History of England: The Works of Lord Bolingbroke, Volume I* (Philadelphia, 1841), 293–4.
160 *Ibid.*, 295–6.
161 *Ibid.*, 297–8.
162 Pocock has discussed Bolingbroke's (neo-Harringtonian) use of country ideology against an aggrandising crown ('Machiavelli, Harrington and English Political Ideologies in the Eighteenth Century', *Politics, Language and Time: Essays on Political Thought and History* (London, 1972), 141).
163 See David Armitage, 'Introduction', *Bolingbroke's Political Writings*, ed. David Armitage (Cambridge, 1997), xi; Dickinson, *Bolingbroke*, 184, 188–9.
164 Machiavelli, *Discourses*, I, 18 (161); II, 1 (270); III, 49 (527–8). During this period, classical history and especially Rome, was probed to uncover lessons from the past which may be avoided in the present. This can be seen in Bossuet's *l'Histoire universelle* and French thought (see Chapter 4 in this book), but it was a methodology particularly popular in Augustan Britain and was used (by Ramsay and) in *Cato's Letters* for example (J.G.A. Pocock, *Barbarism and Religion, Volume Three: The First Decline and Fall*, 5 vols (Cambridge, 1999–), 313–24, 328–31).
165 Bolingbroke, *Remarks on the History of England*, 302.
166 *Ibid.*, 304–10.
167 *Ibid.*, 316.
168 *Ibid.*, 318–19, 326–8; Bolingbroke, *A Dissertation upon Parties*, *Political Writings*, ed. David Armitage (Cambridge, 1997), 36–7.
169 Bolingbroke, *Remarks on the History of England*, 363–93.
170 *Ibid.*, 424–5.
171 *Ibid.*, 445–6.
172 *Ibid.*, 449–50. Bolingbroke compares Walpole's detrimental ministry to the government of James I (452–5).
173 Bolingbroke, *A Dissertation upon Parties*, 82.
174 *Ibid.*, 39.
175 *Ibid.*, 9–11.
176 *Ibid.*, 7.
177 *Ibid.*, 92–5, 103–5, 156–7.
178 *Ibid.*, 114–15. It should be made clear that like most of his contemporaries, Bolingbroke was not advocating democracy in a modern sense. Just as it was 'unsafe to trust too much power to a prince', so was it 'unsafe to retain too much power in the people, as both led to 'tyranny and anarchy' (127). For Bolingbroke, the original contract between the people and their rulers was a renegotiable 'bargain' that allowed the ruling elite of crown, lords, and commons to rule the masses through an implied consent rather than a physical contract (123–5). In Boulainvilliers's opinion the French had originally been a free people because decisions on law and state had been made through assemblies which represented the people's interests. Kings needed the people and were in fact elected by them, but over time these rights and freedoms were usurped by the crown (*Histoire de l'ancien gouvernement de la France. Avec XIV. Lettres Historiques sur les Parlemens ou Etats-Generaux, Tome I* (The Hague and Amsterdam, 1727), Lettre II).
179 *Ibid.*, 144–7.
180 *Ibid.*, 162–4.
181 *Ibid.*, 182–3.
182 See Armitage, 'Introduction', *Bolingbroke's Political Writings*, xxi; Doohwan Ahn, 'British strategy, economic discourse, & the idea of a patriot king 1702–1738', unpublished Ph.D. thesis (Cambridge, 2012), 216.
183 Bolingbroke, *Idea of the Patriot King*, 234.
184 *Ibid.*, 263–4, 292–3.
185 Fénelon, *Télémaque*, Œuvres, *Tome II*, ed. Jacques Le Brun (Paris, 1997), 108, 214, 237–8, 317. See in the present book the following chapter for Fénelon's political thought, and the conclusion of this chapter for comparison.

3

The political principles of Fénelon

British concerns regarding the erosion of liberty by an overbearing absolute executive ran parallel to a central political concern of the Archbishop François Fénelon (1651–1715). During the reign of Louis XIV Fénelon produced a number of works that denounced Louis XIV's (absolutist) sovereignty, promoting a need to succour the public good over all other considerations. While his views were generated independently of British thought, an overlapping call for public liberty in expanded government chimed with thinkers on both sides of the Channel. Yet, between 1689 to 1696 Fénelon acted as the preceptor to Louis XIV's grandson the duc de Bourgogne and was a member of the French court. At that time he wrote *Télémaque* which brought him renown across Europe. Published in 1699 after it had been stolen by a copyist, its educational lessons on kingship for the young prince, were offered via entertaining mythological narratives representative of the 'mirror-for-princes' (*specula principum*) genre. *Télémaque* was perceived to be a condemnation of Louis XIV's government of France and proved to be a public sensation. Its criticism of issues such as France's continuous wars, mercantilism and an obsession with luxury struck an immediate chord with public and intellectuals alike, both in France and across Europe. His distinctive appraisal of political economy and demands for a king that observed the public good over his personal (absolute) will were to have influence on eighteenth-century thought. Yet *Télémaque* was not meant for public consumption. Fénelon considered its ideas to be unformed and continued to work upon the manuscript until his death in 1715. While its themes reflect Fénelon's pre-eminent concerns, this chapter will argue that the later plans produced for an adult Bourgogne actually contain Fénelon's cohesive aspirations for the transformation of France. The use of *Télémaque* as the de facto model for Fénelon's reforms of France lack accuracy therefore.[1] It is in his later *Mémoires* that his rejection of Louis XIV's absolutism can be truly located, where he proposed concrete aristocrat-led renewal of the apparatus of government that influenced French thought from the 1710s.

Preceptor to the duc de Bourgogne

François de Salignac de la Motte-Fénelon received his position as the young Bourgogne's preceptor on 17 August 1689.[2] Under the mentorship of a number of important benefactors attached to the French court including the Bishop of Meaux, Jacques-Bénigne Bossuet (1627–1704), Fénelon became a rising star of the Gallican Church. His *Traité de l'éducation des filles* (1687) had generated friendships with the duc de Beauvilliers (1648–1714) and his brother-in-law the duc de Chevreuse (1646–1712). Both men were high-ranking officials in the court of Louis XIV and had married the daughters of the king's former finance minister Jean-Baptiste Colbert (1619–83). Beauvilliers and Chevreuse were appointed as governors to Bourgogne, and they charged Fénelon with his education and that of his younger brothers the duc d'Anjou (1683–1746) and duc de Berry (1686–1714). It was during this period that Fénelon wrote the *Fables* (1689–91), *Dialogues des Morts* (1692–95) and *Télémaque* (1693–94) for the young princes. He eschewed the staid and didactic teachings that Bossuet had employed for their father, Prince Louis le Grand Dauphin (1661–1711), selecting a more entertaining but focused education reliant upon a mixture of scripture, mythology, (religious) morality, and classicism. These methods proved to be so effective in instructing Bourgogne that he was transformed from a recalcitrant, irascible child to a rather pliable perhaps even easily led adult. Throughout his life, Bourgogne continued to seek counsel and approval from his mentor Fénelon as the two men discussed the reorganisation of France, in which the Archbishop was the dominant voice.[3]

In these educational pieces Fénelon created a collection of children's allegories that comprised several principal themes repeated throughout all three works. Within the moral lessons on good kingship can be found censures on absolutism (identified with tyranny), poor counsel, the pursuit of glory, together with notable denigrations of war and luxury. The overarching theme is that to be a good ruler a king should labour for his subjects while remaining honest[4] and virtuous.[5] He must be moderate when dealing with his people, using the law to ensure that a king should be counted on at all times to offer justice, while protecting the poor as well as the honour and liberty of his people.[6] This was achieved by ruling disinterestedly: suppressing his personal desires to concentrate on policies that maximised the public good. Ultimately this would only be assured if a king were willing to sacrifice his own liberty – like a slave[7] – to focus on the requirements of his people over all other considerations.[8] Such behaviour was enshrined by three key lessons. The first was the practice of strong leadership. Not only should a king be altruistic in his administration: he must also avoid the temptation to arrogantly pursue excessive power.[9] Absolutism (or tyranny) confirmed a kingdom's misery,[10] as it detached the king from his people[11] when he should in fact be bound to them as a teacher or a shepherd.[12] Absolutism over his subjects manifested a corruption in the ruler as an individual, whose private ambition had subverted his public duty.[13] The will of the king no longer retained a 'bridle' for his passions and followed a path that rejected the people's needs.[14] Such unlimited power was undesirable,[15] and it led to a yearning within the people to overthrow or even assassinate the king who did not represent their welfare.[16] Absolutism was therefore never an attractive alternative. It exhibited poor leadership and revealed a weak king whose subjects were slaves to his will.[17]

The remedy for bad kingship was provided in a second moral strand of strong governance: law and good counsel. For Fénelon, the law was the foundation of all government. It existed above and independently of the king, and must be observed at all times to maintain the effective running of the kingdom. The law was a boon for the king. It curbed the people's behaviour,[18] and protected the public interest while acting as a restraint upon the king's own power.[19] This indispensable limitation on the king's authority was furthered by the king's application of good guidance from ministers.[20] Not only should a king seek out truthful ministers, men willing to offer contentious advice for the good of the state,[21] the king should be prepared to listen to that counsel even when it countered his own opinion.[22] A king could not govern his realm alone, and to create a 'perfect government' he must rely on able, virtuous men to provide assistance for the effective management of the state. Indeed, good administration allowed ministers to manage the kingdom independently while the king directed policy.[23] This form of government necessitated the existence of a parliament (or Estates-General) which interpreted the law for the monarch, utilising its experience and the virtue it enjoyed after long service.[24] Government not only required other branches and the assistance of ministers to achieve this, it was vitally important that a monarch did not rule surrounded by flatterers or deceivers. Such ministers were only interested in advancing their own welfare and possessed little regard for the people or their king.[25] Under such monarchies the public good was subsumed by the private interest of a handful of self-seeking ministers who divorced the king from his people. Instead, a healthy state would be sustained through the bond between the monarch and his subjects based on reciprocal need aided by able ministers.

The final lesson and central to this relationship was the observance of the public good. This was maintained by strong governance and policies that did not corrupt administration, or lead it into unnecessary difficulties. Fénelon underlined war and luxury as two problematic areas which should principally be abjured. His treatment of the issue of war was Erasmian in nature. War caused the slaughter of members of the human family in which men killed their brothers. It was a moral evil frequently transacted in the pursuit of empty glory that stained Christian Europe, and caused horrifying destruction to the countries involved.[26]

Kings obsessed with rivalry and aggrandisement were frequently never sated in their quest, so hubristic jingoism begat war upon war.[27] Fénelon thereby rejected war on two levels: the religious and the rational. His religious sensibility was repulsed at the unnecessary suffering of his fellow man as a Christian, exacerbated by a foreign policy of conquest that lacked pragmatism. The king who engaged in perpetual war faced the threat that others would unify against him, leading either to international isolation or a belligerent coalition that could attack.[28] Rather than pursuing a strategy of war a king should cultivate a reputation as a peaceful mediator.[29] Peace not only delivered security and stability at home, it engendered stronger international relations and curtailed pointless hostilities.[30] Such a king was admired for his ability to protect the people and his neighbours, augmenting prosperity and fostering the public good without the human and financial cost of war.

Fénelon's attack upon war found its genesis in an inability of rulers to restrain their ambition and avarice. The root of this issue linked with his noted attack upon luxury:

> The ambition and avarice of men are the only sources of their unhappiness. Men want it all, and they make themselves miserable because of their desire for superfluous things; if they would live simply and meet their real needs, we would see abundance, joy, peace, and unity.[31]

Like war, the quest for Mammon and luxurious goods distracted the attention of men and kings by filling their minds with superfluities and away from real needs.[32] His disgust with the effects of luxury led to the application of classical civic virtue as a means to control the rapacity and vice of modern man. It was deemed to weaken society and effeminate men, infusing the court with vice while enervating the rich by maintaining the poor who dealt in such goods. Luxury should be prohibited, and men were encouraged to live frugally through labour that harmonised with nature.[33] This would restore balance to the social order which had been overturned by luxury's ability to enrich the poor at the expense of the increasingly degraded nobility. Returning to simpler living and agricultural society would not only prevent this but also the exodus of poor to the cities in search of work in the trades of luxuries. A simpler alternative that garnered civic virtue was visualised by Fénelon's utopian land of Salente. Here, frugality was married to the industry of its people, who engaged in the continual activity of agriculture and trade (not luxury), in exchange for a dutiful king (Idomeneus) who sought the public good, enriching his people with liberty and education.[34]

Fénelon's vision of a return to agrarian commerce relied upon a fusion of a classical vision of duty with Christian morality. His engagement of history drew on lessons from the ancients not simply to emulate them but to improve them for the benefit of his contemporary Frenchman.[35] Fénelon's humanistic approach to politics and spirituality allowed him to seek the virtue and reason of the ancients, holding a mirror to modern society that reflected its corruption.[36] The application of classical civic virtue evident in Cicero for example, combated existing social problems, particularly luxury's destruction of 'frugal simplicity'.[37] Moreover, Fénelon's conviction that a king could act altruistically ('disinterestedly') towards his subjects was not only located in Christian teaching but also found in ancient thought.[38] Such love transcended egoistic considerations, practicing a simple life of humility and sacrifice to God. This interpretation was transposed to his political utopias to provide a corrective for contemporary France and the rule of Louis XIV. He anchored civic virtue (duty) to the state in an altruistic capacity to surrender oneself to God through selfless love. These earlier works applied ancient (political) thought, amalgamating it with Christian values in which the king and subjects are elevated through virtue and sacrifice.

After years of Louis XIV's egoistic policies a corrective was required that ensured the needs of the people were placed first. In contrast to Bossuet – who also embraced classical influences to promote the public good – Fénelon did not believe that its creation centred on the king's experience; rather, the care of the people should be pre-eminent.[39] What was unusual about Fénelon's (French) sovereignty was that he made the king secondary. The king's fostering of the public good was not for his own benefit but for his people's benefit. A king must therefore sacrifice his own selfish will and desires for the much larger consideration of the public good. In return, the virtue and love of the populace for their ruler ensured a mutually beneficial and harmonious relationship in which liberty was allowed to flourish. If a king sacrificed the public good to tyranny, he naturally exposed himself to the risk of rebellion or assassination by the people.[40] The development of seventeenth-century France saw a twofold assault on the people by the executive and political economy. In Fénelon's eyes both were riddled with corruption, as Louis XIV suppressed the people's liberty through absolutism (tyranny) while luxury celebrated greed and assaulted morality. Independently of British reaction to these issues, the use of similar classical sources elicited a response congruent with *Cato's Letters* and Bolingbroke. This celebration of the public good and liberty is why *Télémaque* and Fénelon have been viewed by some as promoting 'monarchical rule with republican virtues'.[41]

These classical utopian schemes for eradicating the problems of state were predominantly located in *Télémaque*, although they are scattered throughout the earlier works. Due to its popularity and influence many commentators have focused on *Télémaque* for an account of Fénelon's political and economic interpretation of Louis XIV's France.[42] However, while Fénelon claimed that *Télémaque* did contain lessons of kingship he rejected the idea that it was either a cohesive system or a satire on Louis XIV's kingdom:

It is true that I have put in these adventures all the truths necessary for government and any defects that may be in the sovereign power, but I have not labelled any with an allocation that tends to portrait of any character. The more you read this book, the more you will see that I meant everything without painting anyone, it's even a narration done in a hurry, detached pieces, written at different times, there would be much to correct; moreover, the print is not consistent with my original. I prefer it should appear formless and incoherent, than to give it away in the way that I did. All I ever wanted was to entertain the Duke of Burgundy, and to teach him by entertaining him with these tales, without ever intending for this piece to become public. Everyone knows that it has escaped me by the infidelity of a copyist. Finally, all the best servants of the king who I am acquainted with, know what are my principles of honour and religion of the King, on the state and the country, they know my gratitude for the blessings and tender gifts the King has loaded on me. Others are easily more capable than me, but no one has more sincere zeal.[43]

This plea of innocence is perhaps supported by his contention that it would be perfidious of him to satirise a king who had shown him favour. Moreover, Bossuet's reading and commentary on earlier drafts of the work would appear to undermine an attempt at satire due to the Bishop's loyalty to the king.[44] The pedagogical pieces were motivated by sincere moral and religious lessons on how a king should behave. Yet crucially these compositions were perceived to be 'formless' by Fénelon, and did not constitute a cohesive or pragmatic plan to tackle the maladies of state. Rather, they were theoretical truths on kingship wrapped in entertaining (utopian) diversions for a child that did not deliver practical reform. The immediate result of these diversions is well known, and this was the loss of favour shown to Fénelon by Louis XIV. His exile to his archbishopric of Cambrai was largely driven by the Quietist Affair and his doctrinal dispute with leading members of the Gallican Church, notably Bossuet.[45] But questionable theological orthodoxy and the publication of *Télémaque* were enough to separate him from his young royal pupil and induce permanent banishment from the court. The longer-term consequence was the great fame achieved by *Télémaque*. It appears to have ensured that most commentary on Fénelon centred on this work as the model for his political thought. This is perhaps not surprising as the work ran to multiple editions across Europe very quickly and from the first biographer the key focal point has been *Télémaque*.[46] Yet this preoccupation subsumes the clear demonstration in the later plans of a practical attempt to reorganise France under Bourgogne while rejecting Louis XIV's monarchy which is not present in the earlier works.

Censure of Louis XIV's reign: 1689–1715

The context in which Fénelon was writing for Bourgogne was one of almost continual war for France and Europe. From 1688 to 1713 France had been engaged in the Nine Years' War (1688–97) followed by the War of the Spanish Succession (1702–13) against the Grand Alliance. These wars were driven by French attempts to extend its authority beyond its borders, and the collective reaction of a number of European princes to Louis XIV's behaviour. Indeed Louis's entire reign had been dominated by war. Not long after he acceded to the throne, France was plunged into the Fronde (1648–53): an internecine civil war fought mainly between the king's supporters and disaffected nobility. Following the death of Cardinal Mazarin (1661), Louis began to administer the kingdom alone and a series of lesser wars ensued, which included the War of Devolution (1667–68) and the Dutch Wars (1672–78). Historians have debated the stimulus of France's engagement in war, questioning whether it was driven by Louis XIV's quest for *gloire* ('glory') or an attempt to become the universal monarch of Europe.[47] What is certain is that many of France's contemporary rivals were in no doubt that French aggrandisement was fed by a desire for hegemony.[48] The result was a Europe riven by conflict – as it had been for centuries – while states aligned to prevent French supremacy, making France increasingly unpopular internationally. Furthermore, in a government shaped by war, bellicose foreign conflict had dominated state policy while depleting resources at home.

The consequences of prolonged warfare were confronted in Fénelon's (unsent) *Lettre à Louis XIV* which expressed his unhappiness at the condition of France. The letter attacked the devastation wrought by war upon the French and European people citing Louis's pursuit of *gloire* as the cause. The king had surrounded himself with flatterers and advisers who magnified his authority and ego thereby ruining France.[49] His kingship had become lost through a mismanagement of the administration, poor government policy, and a monomaniacal obsession with war. Constant warfare had decimated the country. The land was uncultivated and had become depopulated, commerce had decreased, and taxation demands had impoverished the people.[50] The lost scrutiny of the public good meant that Louis had essentially turned his back upon his subjects and God, which had led to sedition and rioting. Such criticism was redolent of the Huguenot exile Pierre Jurieu's *Les soupirs de la France esclave, qui aspire après la liberté* (1689). Like Jurieu, Fénelon claimed that the king's severance from his people had been caused by his excessive elevation in status.[51] This power prevented him from ruling for the public good, an inability exacerbated by the prevalence of luxury within his court. Jurieu had asserted that these issues compounded by excessive taxation had fashioned a country oppressed by slavery and poverty, vitiating the public good under the rule of a tyrant.[52] While Fénelon did not refer to Louis XIV as a tyrant, the variance between the two critiques of the king's rule was negligible. Two interesting observations arise from their comparison. The first was Fénelon's aspiration to articulate his opinion to Louis on what he distinguished to be his major failings as king. As a Huguenot exile in Rotterdam following the Revocation of the Edict of Nantes (1685), Jurieu had an agenda, but Fénelon was a member of the court. His sense of duty to the people or to the king at the situation he perceived must have elicited the composition of such a letter. Realising his commitment to reform France, second, the *Lettre* does cast some doubt on the veracity of Fénelon's claims regarding the satirical nature of *Télémaque*, or rather its critical nature. The *Lettre* and *Télémaque* were written at the same time. It is clear that his perceptions of a failed kingship were present in both works, one as censure, the other as pedagogy. Even though he may have claimed not to have satirised Louis's governance, he sufficiently objected to instruct the young Bourgogne to rule differently from his grandfather.

The general lessons prevalent in the pedagogical works were a reaction against Louis XIV's method of leadership and the advancement of society in general. As will be discussed in the following chapter, after the death of Mazarin Louis was determined to extend the programme of centralised government witnessed under his father Louis XIII (r. 1610–43). This had seen the suspension of the Estates-General in 1614, by using tensions and acrimony between the estates to bypass it as an (vexing) instrument of government.[53] The crown utilised popular support following the assassination of Henri IV (1610) to augment its sovereignty and curb the influence of the nobility. What replaced it was a system of intendants directly responsible to the royal council, which from 1643 fell under the auspices of the *conseil d'en haut*, reliant on a handful of ministers and advisers. The state that Louis XIV inherited from Mazarin possessed finances, an army and bureaucracy that were centrally directed towards war. From 1661 and in an age of military glory, Louis's longing to actively rule alone without a chief minister was born from a yearning to dominate his state plus a suspicion of the high nobility after the Fronde.[54]

Louis was positioned at the pinnacle of government and society, divinely sanctioned by God to rule his people in a manner he supposed fitting for France.[55] The different parts of society which included the nobility were united in him, and he acted tirelessly (and gloriously) on their behalf. For many contemporaries including Fénelon, the ancient nobility or *noblesse d'épée* ('sword') were ostensibly excluded from the administration as its mechanism was realigned. While the king favoured the use of the (newer) *robe* nobility as his administrators, the *épée* still preserved some influence at court and at provincial level.[56] This shift away from the ancient structures and processes of government – alluded to in Fénelon's pedagogical works – was deemed problematic as the king now principally relied upon a limited group of *robe* nobles. They were perceived to be self-serving by the *épée* nobles who possessed an ancient responsibility to sacrifice themselves for the public good while the *robe* had purchased their titles for personal gain. The casting aside of the high nobility led to acrimony between the *épée* and *robe*, plus in Fénelon's (and others') opinion the former had been made redundant. Rather than serving the state, they were sitting idle at court often immured in vice and luxury.[57]

Fénelon's disapprobation regarding an indolent high nobility combined with a need to fuel a revised machinery of France through commercial development. Under the auspices of Colbert's brand of mercantilism, Colbertism focused on coinage and an attempt to control the flow of money into and out of France. Agriculture which only generated limited returns was not attributed much importance. Instead Colbertism fixated on the capacity to attract silver and gold coin into the realm, making the kingdom more prosperous as this wealth circulated throughout it; therefore, the better the commercial activity, the more coinage was in circulation, the greater the affluence and prestige of the state. This capital was controlled via direct and indirect taxation, and a belief that exports must exceed imports to ensure that capital was not leaving France. As it was assumed that Europe only possessed a limited amount of coinage this was particularly important, so protectionism attempted to maximise profit and prevent the loss of wealth to others. Colbertism was an aggressive doctrine based on a zero-sum economic perspective, which relied on tariffs rather than free trade to increase profit at the expense of others. Indeed, Colbert believed mercantilism was a weapon of war, and it was juxtaposed with France's territorial aggrandisement as a method of gaining pre-eminence in Europe. Colbert's 'imperfect understanding' of Dutch and English commercial success and his need to control policy rather than allowing merchants and manufacturing communities to develop freely, meant initiatives stalled.[58] As the aristocracy were precluded from engaging in commercial activity the burden was placed upon the bourgeoisie to create economic prosperity in a country whose wars consumed much taxation. Unfortunately French commercial activity was localised and fragmented, and regional competition stultified economic progress. Inertia within government was exacerbated by the sale of offices to create revenue – via venality and patronage – which saw a lack of initiative in terms of transformative reform of the economy. The restrictions placed on the aristocracy, especially when compared with the English aristocracy, were not advantageous for French success or venality inhibited government innovation.

Fénelon's utopian models in *Télémaque* became part of a long-standing discussion on commercial behaviour and French foreign policy. In 1615 Antoine de Montchrétien had promulgated a belligerent system of mercantilism in his *Traicté de l'oeconomie politique*. He argued that national wealth sufficient to subsidise the crown could be created through the development of trade and industry.[59]

Selfish individualism inherent in man could be fostered to offer social utility as avarice and ambition would maximise profit when people enriched themselves. Montchrétien employed Bodin's notion that God had ordered the world so that goods were found in different geographical locations to bind humanity interconnectedly to precipitate a necessity to exchange goods.[60] Bodin's outward-looking interpretation of trade was inverted by Montchrétien. He proposed harnessing the desires to compete and emulate others so that France could achieve mercantilist hegemony over other states and protect the welfare of its people.[61]

By the end of the seventeenth century after years of war, including the Thirty Years' War (1618–48), an advocacy of free trade can be seen to emerge. While there had been supporters of free trade and interstate commercial endeavour earlier in the century,[62] these later ideas were often a reaction to the policies of Louis XIV. Political economists desired to move beyond bellicose Colbertism and the aggrandising ambition of kings like Louis XIV entangled in an international state of war. Pierre Nicole's *Essais de morale* (1675) had argued that the interconnection among countries and individuals was driven by Hobbesian competition. This interdependency meant that the world was akin to a single city in Nicole's opinion which thrived on beneficial self-interested rivalry.[63] Nicole's view was engaged by Pierre le Boisguilbert in *Le détail de la France; la cause de la diminution de ses biens et la facilité du remède* (1696), to suggest a modification in Louis XIV's mercantilist policy. He believed France could eschew aggressive protectionism to produce affluence found wanting under Colbertism through free trade.[64] France's obstructive fiscal policies had limited growth due to an unhealthy fixation on antagonism with the Dutch and the English. Collaborative international trade would advance French interests farther than isolationist mercantile policies. Fénelon shared this sentiment, arguing for an openness and cooperation with other states that would allow for economic growth and prosperity.[65] His model of Tyre – based upon the Dutch Republic – reflected a free commercial society that was industrious, well-regulated, and frugal. Commercial endeavour was encouraged by Fénelon because it strengthened the kingdom, nurtured relations with others, and engaged its people in activity.[66]

Fénelon's hostility to mercantilism was conspicuously expressed through the pre-eminence he gave to agriculture. His promotion of rural simplicity possessed two strands of thought. The first was a practical view of French society as a predominantly rural country, which meant that most people worked on the land. His desire to advocate industriousness through agricultural labour was logical because this was French society. It was also reasonable to encourage a strategy that relied on the bountiful natural resources of France (Salente), while attacking a mercantilist policy that had embroiled France in injurious wars and economic torpor.[67] His attack on luxury was born from the same vantage point. Luxury was a boon for extending trade which could be taxed by the state. Unfortunately the consequence of this trade was its accompanying effeminacy and loss of civic interest as individuals were lost to this distraction. Such destruction to the natural industry of man found its unparalleled example in the French court. This environment provided an exaggerated depiction of the vice and laziness that had crept into modern society due to luxury. Louis XIV's restrictive policies towards the high nobility had artificially negated virtuous behaviour as the social order had become undermined. Nature had essentially been subverted by an erosion of France's ancient form of government, and a trading programme which tolerated superfluities to cause idleness.

Fénelon's reform plans

As a potential future chief minister of Bourgogne, the Archbishop's later plans offered practical advice on kingship and how to enact change. The important difference for these later studies (*Mémoires*) was that they proposed concrete designs on how to transform France. The utopian images contained within the pedagogical works ruminate (theoretically) on what was good or bad in the state. The *Mémoires* inculcate from an early stage a move beyond education to the priming of a prince for actual rule, particularly once Bourgogne became Dauphin in 1711. Yet the process began in 1701, when the adult Bourgogne re-established communication with Fénelon, now banished to his archdiocese of Cambrai.[68]

The first work to originate from this renewed contact was the *Examen de conscience sur les devoirs de la Royauté* (*c*.1702).[69] The work acted as a conduit between the educational works and the later plans, containing familiar elements and a pedagogical tone. Fénelon's opening supplications to Bourgogne ensured this link by emphasising the need for a prince to fear God and be well disposed to religion. He must understand the laws of God through the Gospel if he was to serve his people and God.[70] Such religiosity was not simply an expression of Fénelon's personal belief, it was an attempt to confirm that Bourgogne had remained a good Catholic. The prince would require religious faith as an antidote to the vice permeating Louis XIV's court. If a sovereign was to be an example to his people, he must begin by controlling his own vices, for a king's vices were never secret.[71] Vice was of immense consequence to a kingdom: a 'contagious poison' which easily infected men who were drawn to it. It was therefore the king's duty to prevent it, instead offering the people a paragon of virtue they could emulate. The most obvious illustration of this contamination was luxury which had become a 'growing evil' within France, corrupting the court and spreading out into the wider country.[72] Bourgogne must battle such iniquity by following the example of Saint Louis (Louis IX) and living in 'great plainness' – in his clothes, possessions, behaviour, etc. – to endow the people with a beacon of good. As in the work of his childhood, Bourgogne would be aided as a strong king through good counsel,[73] the avoidance of flatterers,[74] and averting war.[75]

While recognisable themes are unmistakable in the work, the pedagogical tone was transformed into instruction that possessed the appearance of a challenge to the prince's preparedness for leadership. Fénelon's guidance had moved beyond mythology and diverting literary entertainment to rather prosaic pithy aphorisms frequently delivered in short paragraphs. Fénelon appealed to Bourgogne as an adult, addressing the means at his disposal to combat France's tribulations. The mechanism of change was the law, which ensured the public good. Bourgogne must school himself in the 'laws, customs, and usages' of his kingdom and the law of nations if he were to administer justice for the kingdom.[76] A working knowledge of the law was essential, not only to govern France effectively but also to safeguard its harmonious relations with foreign powers. It fostered a comprehension of administration that was furthered by the study of history, morality, and the ancient workings of the government of France.

In Fénelon's opinion this was a duty incumbent upon the prince, who must understand the limitations on his sovereign authority. He was not an absolute monarch and could not govern arbitrarily. Indeed a king must reign through moderation, walking a line between '*les deux extrémités*' of tyrannical kingship and the anarchy of the people.[77] Understanding French history guaranteed that Bourgogne would be familiar with the tools that would aid him, such as the 'ancient *parlements*' and 'Estates-General'. In an oblique criticism of Bourgogne's grandfather, Fénelon claimed that the political difficulties now experienced in France had been caused by the pursuit of absolute power. The king had eroded the authority of these ancient bodies of government.[78] A ruler should make use of the institutions of government when drafting legislation searching for the opinion of wider, honest counsel that could be found in advisers. Such sensible use of guidance would remove the need to castrate the *parlements* because it disagreed with new legislation through veto. The demand of remonstrance against legislature would not be necessary if they were included in the process via wider government. This explained why sagacious kings sought out men of genius and integrity for their counsel and ministers. They would not only offer sound advice but could be trusted to carry out the business of state on the king's behalf.[79] Men such as these should be searched for to the 'ends of the earth'. Fénelon's more expansive approach to administration included a belief that too many employments should not be given to one man alone. This had been standard practice for many kings and was evident with Louis XIV. He had relied heavily – while rewarding in equal measure – a limited number of men such as

Colbert and the Marquis de Louvois (1641–91) the Secretary of State for War, as the king centralised government around himself.

Throughout the *Examen de conscience* Fénelon impressed upon Bourgogne the necessity of engaging in war for reasons other than *gloire*. Peace should always be sought as war harmed subjects and foreigners alike, and he should remember the dictum that 'your enemy is your brother'.[80] The work was written at the beginning of the War of the Spanish Succession as France (and Spain) fought an alliance of other European rivals over the right for the duc d'Anjou (Philippe V) to ascend the Spanish throne as the heir of Carlos II (d. 1700). Several of Fénelon's *Mémoires* written to Bourgogne between 1701 and 1710 discuss the consequences of the war. Before it had begun Fénelon argued the war would not be worth the trouble as victory contained no great benefit for France.[81] Rather than threatening the borders of the Spanish Netherlands, Louis XIV should assuage Dutch fears of French expansion by mollifying anxieties over the loss of independence. Eight years later the Archbishop's qualms about the perils of war had been borne out as the French army had become demoralised and the state was nearly bankrupt. After famous losses at Blenheim (1704), Ramillies (1706), Oudenarde (1708) the towns were depleted, people no longer lived like men, and had lost patience with war. The physical strains, the loss of farming and livestock, meant that people were starving and there was social disorder.[82]

Fénelon's province of Cambrai had witnessed the effects of the war first-hand, and he believed that the 'The nation [was] … falling into disgrace … becoming the object of public derision'.[83] Success was uncertain, Paris could be attacked and France was at the mercy of its enemies. The solution was for the French to sue for peace. Louis XIV should seize the initiative and place himself at the centre of peace negotiations to become an 'arbiter' and 'general mediator' for Europe, instead of a figure of antipathy. The destructive outcomes of the war – in which Bourgogne fought – realised two significant elements to Fénelon's political thought. The first was that his intense abhorrence of war expressed throughout his works, found its basis in the constant threat of war during the early modern period. The suffering and breakdown of social order provoked by the competition of kings was calamitous for many. Second, Fénelon's instructions for Bourgogne to abjure war were seriously intended. The *Supplément* located at the end of the *Examen de conscience* offered an intervention in the perpetual peace plan tradition, in which Fénelon posed a stratagem for preventing European war through the development of a league of peace. With France as the intended target, the league would offset any attempt by a larger state to undermine the balance of power in Europe as others could unite against the aggrandising power. The conflagra-tion of war and any attempt to achieve a 'universal monarchy' would therefore be neutralised by interdependent coalition. Europe could live in harmonious cooperation rather than the destruction Fénelon foresaw.[84]

The *Tables de Chaulnes*

The most salient of Fénelon's later political works is the *Tables de Chaulnes* (*Plans de Gouvernement*). It outlined in some detail designs for a future France after the death of Louis XIV. Perhaps unsurprisingly, the work, written in November 1711 as the war dragged on, looked at means for immediately ending hostilities. Despite the instigation of peace discussions as early as 1708, the conflict had continued as Louis XIV had sought greater concessions from a peace treaty. Fénelon pushed such considerations aside, and demanded an immediate cessation of aggression '*achetée sans mesure*', including the loss of Cambrai and Arras.[85] If peace could not be achieved, then France must pursue a defensive war which would be run by a 'council of war' that contained marshals and other aristocratic experts who would shape military policy. In opposition to the expansionist martial strategy of Louvois, the army would be reduced (from 400,000) to 150,000 men. This would make it difficult for France to wage war against Europe again, and it would instead have to seek alliances as the basis of foreign policy. The reduction of the army would see the beginning of a general assault against wasteful court expenditure. Beauvilliers and Fénelon had actually contacted all of the intendants of France prior to the Archbishop's exile to Cambrai, receiving statistical information regarding the state of the French economy and finances at a local level.[86] All but one of the intendants – who had died – responded, and this information was used in the *Tables* to provide a realistic assessment of the nation's problems and solutions. The surfeit of pensions, salaries, and possessions would be controlled by 'sumptuary laws' that would emulate the Romans in the regulation of excessive consumption, which included luxury.[87] To achieve this, the present state expenditure which included the king's debt, had to be calculated and contrasted with revenues. Agriculture, crafts, and trade would spearhead an economic recovery of the almost bankrupted France. Such growth relied upon the freedom of trade as the state stepped away from mercantilism, although sumptuary laws would prohibit luxury and financiers. To relieve the people's suffering tariff levels would be discussed, the unpopular *gabelle* (salt tax) would be abolished, and economic policy revitalised through deliberations in the re-established Estates-General.[88] Ultimately all economic policy should be settled by the council for trade (established in 1700). The burden of expenditure would be discussed cooperatively with the Estates rather than enacted arbitrarily as the provinces were granted autonomy for dealing with local revenue policy.

    The enhancement of the council for trade reflected an aspiration within the *Tables* towards the expansion and decentralisation of French government. Beginning with tax collection, there would be a shift from the intendant system to the use of an *assiette* in each province: a small diocese in which the bishop, local nobility and the third estate would settle taxation. The *assiette* would be subordinate to the reinstituted provincial Estates. These involved members from all three estates which would have the power to govern finance, the police, justice, trade, and agriculture. Fénelon pointed to the model of Languedoc as a working example which had survived Louis XIV's neglect of most of the provincial estates. Languedoc was seen to be a successful model of decentralised government. It had engaged in a number of independent public works – while supported by the crown – and had stimulated the local economy and raised taxes. Fénelon used the example of Languedoc to underline the possibility of a loyal province that could cooperate with the crown. One that worked with central government yet remained semi-autonomous through its utilisation of the local Estates to run its affairs.[89] This re-establishment of the Estates system would enable freely elected deputies to settle local issues. It would also develop an understanding for the needs of France as a whole as information filtered back to the crown. This move by Fénelon saw an assault on the absolutist pretentions of Louis XIV in favour of a more constitutional model when Bourgogne became king. The introduction of new assemblies below the king's council, the reinstitution of the Estates-General, the decentralisation of power to include local government, and the inclusion all members from all three estates represented a significant rejection of absolutism.

It is important to note that despite a wider involvement of the public in the governance of Languedoc, the region was dominated by the local elite. What is clear in the *Tables* is that while he was devolving government Fénelon was first of all endeavouring to re-establish the fortunes of the high nobility. In a section entitled '*Noblesse*' he called for an immediate catalogue of all nobles to be made in each province.[90] It was designed to prevent the sale of offices which diluted the prestige of the aristocracy, while elevating the interests of the ancient nobility which had been sidelined by venality. Additionally, ennoblement would be controlled to promote stricter rules of rank, guaranteeing that men were only rewarded for exceptional service to the state rather than buying their titles. This would see the gradual removal of the *paulette* by the *parlements* to re-establish the former prestige of office, by employing men with ability over the pecuniary needs of government. Furthermore, to confront the amalgamation of the financial and political problems, the nobility would be allowed to enter the magistrature and engage in trade.[91] The driving force of reorganisation, therefore, was a reassertion of the old social order and pre-eminence of the high nobility. Cataloguing the nobility, restricting ennoblement, abolishing venality from the army, and its gradual removal from government centrally placed the *épée* as ancient society was reconstituted.[92] Fénelon's extension and devolution of government meant that the *épée* would once more form an integral part of the administration of France under Bourgogne.

As the principal member of what has become known as Burgundy Circle

– a number of advisers to the prince – Fénelon's ideas of French reform were important because had Bourgogne lived they may well have been acted upon.[93] The truth of this group is that it was not a cohesive unit that promulgated a single philosophical standpoint. Rather it was a number of individuals representing two generations of advisers around Bourgogne who held competing views on the reconstitution of France. The one predominant element that was shared was an advocacy of aristocrat-led reform.[94] Yet despite the pre-eminence of the aristocracy, this reversion towards an ancient model of governance did not undermine Fénelon's attack on absolutism. It has been claimed that this promotion was simply a reactionary attempt to revitalise the aristocracy from within the absolutist system.[95] The restoration of these ancient parts of the state apparatus, however, shifted France back towards its constitutional past prior to absolutism. By sharing in the king's sovereignty and restraining his power the nobility were attempting to share the burden of government with the king because they believed the state was being mismanaged. Reinstatement of their ancient role would return France to a position prior to Louis XIV's absolutism, and gradually mitigate parts of the king's power.

Thwarted ambitions

In the end, Fénelon's reform plans for Bourgogne were stillborn as the prince died of measles on 18 February 1712. The Archbishop was genuinely grief-stricken at the loss of his former pupil, and part of his devastation was born from the loss of optimism over the future of France.[96] In a letter to the duc de Chevreuse, Fénelon stated that all hope was gone for France and lamented the difficulties of an impending regency under a young prince. Yet within the same letter Fénelon expeditiously pointed to the necessity of working with Louis XIV's wife Madame de Maintenon, to aid the young heir. A little over a week later in a second letter to Chevreuse he called for a plan of action to be created immediately. They owed it to Bourgogne to craft a 'council of regency' that would protect and educate his son.[97] The idea was crystallised in the *Mémoire sur les mesures à prendre après la mort du duc de Bourgogne* (15 March 1712). This work envisaged a means to provide the young prince with an effective education while ensuring that the plans under Bourgogne did not die. Its inception was taken so seriously by Fénelon that he persuaded Beauvilliers to use his influence over Madame de Maintenon in an attempt to convince the king to act upon the proposal. Louis XIV rejected the plan.

In the *Mémoire* Fénelon advocated the establishment of a 'regency council' that would work with Louis XIV while he remained alive.[98] The council would be selected from an 'assembly of notables'. Fénelon suggested Beauvilliers,

Chevreuse, Saint-Simon – all members of the Burgundy Circle – as well as the duc de Tallard (1652–1728), other ministers and secretaries of state, and headed by the Duc de Berry (1686–1714), Bourgogne's brother. The council would have two main functions. The first was to educate the young Dauphin using a curriculum that would be approved by the king until the prince's majority. The second function carried out with the king's authorisation saw the council's involvement in the administration of government.[99] The council would be attached to the *parlement* of Paris and would assemble at least six times a year. As with the *Tables*, further councils would replace the single secretaries of state as power was devolved from the king into the machinery of government, such as the Estates-General and the *assiettes*.[100]

While the council would operate under the king, it would immediately begin to address the issues of state such as the national debt and the war. Fénelon foresaw many complications but felt that the problems faced by France required an instant departure from Louis XIV's model of sovereignty. Louis's extraordinarily long reign had made government and his subjects accustomed to the absolute will of a single master.[101] Hence overcoming this situation would be hugely problematic for France. Yet if Louis died without making plans for the succession, government would have to frantically unify and organise itself in an attempt to stabilise France and fend off social 'confusion'. By creating these councils and using them to administer government while the king was alive, it would allow for a smooth transition of power.[102] They would assist in the reorganisation of France while consolidating their position to continue assisting the running of France when the Dauphin reached maturity. France would fundamentally evolve from absolutism by establishing wider government through the utilisation of councils, the Estates-General, and provincial assemblies comprising men from all three Estates.

As with the death of Bourgogne and the *Tables de Chaulnes*, Louis XIV's rejection of the 1712 *Mémoire* meant that a substantial transformation in France did not occur. The duc de Orléans, a friend and admirer of Fénelon, did begin the *Régence* by observing some of the Archbishop's later initiatives, but he had returned to Louis XIV's model by 1718. While peace was eventually established, Fénelon's reforms of state were shelved in favour of centralised bureaucracy as Orléans strengthened his position. As Fénelon's reorganisational plans were not published until later in the century, Bourgogne's death deprived these private memoirs from being acted upon. Their absence from public view, combined with the success of *Télémaque*, ensured that Fénelon's early utopias remained the public focus of his political theory. His influence on eighteenth-century thought, particularly political economy, stemmed from these earlier works. Yet while the central themes of his philosophy are apparent, they do not offer the concrete solutions to France's troubles as seen in the *Mémoires*.

These later works were designed for implementation under Bourgogne's rule and offered a reinterpretation of government based on the past. The termination of absolutism upon the death of Louis XIV would witness an aristocratic-led revolution of the administration. These plans were absent in the pedagogical works, and would have reinvigorated the contractual elements of the state while eschewing aggressive government policy. Fénelon was not alone in advocating such reforms, as will be shown in the following two chapters. As one member of the Burgundy Circle there were a number of competing views for the future direction of French government, and Fénelon's conservative view of economic society would have been abandoned by Bourgogne. But Fénelon's dismay at the erosion of liberty, virtue, and concern for the public good resonated with readers across Europe, including Britain. The expansion of state executives (often through absolutism) and commercial development challenged traditional views of ordered society. Despite Fénelon's predominantly conservative approach to these issues, his promotion of republican liberty and (a form of) representation can be seen as proto-contemporary application of classical history and moral virtue. Coincidentally, this approach had much more in common with Britain than it did with France. Yet it led to a wider appreciation in France of the Archbishop by opponents of absolutism, especially after when the decline of France was evaluated following Louis XIV's death.

Notes

1   See Françoise Gallouédec-Genuys, *Le Prince selon Fénelon* (Paris, 1963); Lionel Rothkrug, *Opposition to Louis XIV: The Political and Social Origins of the French Enlightenment* (Princeton, 1965); *Fénelon: Mystique et Politique* (1699–1999), eds F.-X. Cuche and J. Le Brun (Paris, 2004); Istvan Hont, 'The Early Enlightenment Debate on Commerce and Luxury', *Cambridge History of Eighteenth-Century Political Thought, Volume I*, eds Mark Goldie and Robert Wokler (Cambridge, 2006); Michael Sonenscher, *Before the Deluge: Public Debt, Inequality, and the Intellectual Origins of the French Revolution* (New Jersey, 2007). For an excellent appraisal of *Télémaque* which includes discussion of the later works, see Paul Schuurman, 'Fénelon on Luxury, War and Trade in the Telemachus', *History of European Ideas*, 38 (2012), pp. 179–99.

2   On Fénelon's life the salient works are: Andrew Michael Ramsay, *Histoire de la vie de Fénelon* (The Hague, 1723); Cardinal Louis François de Bausset, *Histoire de Fénelon*, 4 vols (Paris, 1850); Chanoine Moïse Cagnac, *Fénelon: Politique tirée de l'Evangile* (Paris, 1912); Ely Carcassone, *Fénelon: l'Homme et l'œuvre* (Paris, 1946); Jeanne-Lydie Goré, *L'itinéraire de Fénelon: humanisme et spiritualité*, 2 vols (Paris, 1957).

3   See E.K. Sanders, *Fénelon: His Friends and Enemies, 1651–1715* (London, 1901), 40; Paul Janet, *Fénelon: His Life and Works*, trans. Victor Leuliette (London, 1914), 51; Ely Carcassone, *Fénelon: l'Homme et l'œuvre* (Paris, 1946), 77; Sanford B. Kanter, 'Archbishop Fénelon's Political Activity: The Focal Point of Power in Dynasticism', *French Historical Studies*, 4, 3 (spring 1966), pp. 320–34 (322, 329, 333–4). For an example of their relationship when Bourgogne was an adult, see Fénelon au duc de Bourgogne (16 Sept. 1708), *Correspondance de Fénelon, Tome 14*, eds Jean Orcibal, Jacques Le Brun and Irénée Noye (Geneva, 1992), 66–8.

4   Fénelon, *Dialogues des Mort, Œuvres I*, 474. The *Dialogues* contain conversations on a range of subjects between ancient figures from history, followed by modern historical personages. Unless stated, all works by Fénelon are taken from *Œuvres I* (Paris, 1983) and *Œuvres II* (Paris, 1997), ed. Jacques Le Brun.

5   Fénelon, *Télémaque, Œuvres II*, 108.

6   *Ibid.*, 214.
7   *Ibid.*, 237–8, 317.
8   Fénelon, *Fables*, Œuvres *I*, 237.
9   Fénelon, *Dialogues*, 362.
10 *Ibid.*, 406.
11 *Ibid.*, 313.
12 Fénelon, *Télémaque*, 279–80.
13 Fénelon, *Dialogues*, 293.
14 Fénelon, *Télémaque*, 289–90.
15 Fénelon, *Dialogues*, 324.
16 *Ibid.*, 403; Fénelon, *Télémaque*, 290.
17 Fénelon, *Télémaque*, 168.
18 Fénelon, *Dialogues*, 315.
19 Fénelon, *Télémaque*, 59.
20 Fénelon, *Fables*, 237.
21 Fénelon, *Télémaque*, 149–52.
22 Fénelon, *Dialogues*, 475–6.
23 Fénelon, *Télémaque*, 293–6.
24 *Ibid.*, 65.
25 *Ibid.*, 25, 171–88.
26 Fénelon, *Dialogues*, 328–30. For Erasmus's view, see: *Praise of Folly*, trans. Betty Radice (London, 1971), 181; *The Complaint of Peace*, trans. Thomas Paynell (London, 1917), 44; *The Education of a Christian Prince*, trans. Neil M. Cheshire and Michael J. Heath (Cambridge, 1997), 66–73, 105–7.
27 Fénelon, *Dialogues*, 287.
28 Fénelon, *Télémaque*, 132–3.
29 *Ibid.*, 68–9.
30 *Ibid.*, 140–7.
31 *Ibid.*, 58: 'L'ambition et l'avarice des hommes sont les seules sources de leur malheur. Les hommes veulent tout avoir, et ils se rendent malheureux par le désir du superflu; s'ils voulaient vivre simplement et se contenter de satisfaire aux vrais besoins, on verrait partout l'abondance, la joie, la paix et l'union.'
32 Fénelon, *Fables*, 209.
33 Fénelon, *Télémaque*, 159–60.
34 *Ibid.*, 288–9.
35 Fénelon, *Lettre à l'Académie*, Œuvres *II*, 1217–18.
36 *Ibid.*, 1224–5.
37 *Ibid.*, 101. Cicero argued against the dissipation caused by excessive trade (and luxury) witnessed in Carthage and Corinth; see *On the Commonwealth*, ed. James E.G. Zetzel (Cambridge, 1999), II, 7 (35). For a discussion of Fénelon's approach to the ancients, see Patrick Riley: 'Rousseau, Fénelon, and the Quarrel between the Ancients and the Moderns', *The Cambridge Companion to Rousseau*, ed. Patrick Riley (Cambridge, 2001), 78–93 (82); 'Fénelon's "Republican" Monarchism in Telemachus', *Monarchisms in the Age of Enlightenment: Liberty, Patriotism and the Common Good*, eds Hans Blom, Christian Laursen, and Luisa Simonutti (Toronto, 2007), 78–91 (92–3).
38 See Fénelon, *The Maxims of the Saints Explained Concerning the Interior Life* (London, 1775), 153–8; *Christian Perfection*, ed. Charles F. Whiston and trans. Mildred Whitney Stillman (London, 1947), 178–80.
39 See the section on Bossuet in Chapter 4 of this book, for a discussion of Bossuet's political theory.
40 Fénelon, *Télémaque*, 290–1.
41 Riley, 'Rousseau, Fénelon, and the Quarrel between the Ancients and the Moderns', 82; Riley, 'Fénelon's "Republican" Monarchism in Telemachus', 78; Michael Sonenscher, *Sans-Culottes: An Eighteenth-Century Emblem in the French Revolution* (Princeton, 2008), 211. Jay M. Smith has astutely pointed out that while the French were familiar with late seventeenth-century

English republicanism, much of France's use of 'patriotic ideals' was taken directly from classical examples to confront the prospect of despotism. Classical republican models of politics and morality were 'critically important to the process of reimagining the nobility' at a time when the French saw themselves as the heirs of ancient Greece and Rome. Fénelon was a key exponent of ancient patriotism as a moral model, inspiring numerous intellectuals including the *Entresol* (*Nobility Reimagined: The Patriotic Nation in Eighteenth-Century France* (Cornell, 2005), 32–3, 34, 47).

42 See n. 2.

43 Fénelon, Œuvres de Fénelon, Tome III (Paris, 1835), 654: 'Il est vrai j'ai mis dans ces aventures toutes les ver/tiés nécessaires pour le gouvernement, et tous les défauts qu'on peut avoir dans la puissance souveraine; mais je n'en ai marqué aucun, avec une affectation qui tende à aucun portrait ni caractère. Plus on lira cet ouvrage, plus on verra que j'ai voulu dire tout, sans peindre personne de suite; c'est meme une narration faite à la hate, à morceaux détachés, et par diverses reprises; il y auroit beaucoup à corriger; de plus, l'imprimé n'est pas conforme à mon original. J'ai mieux aimé le laisser paroître informe et défiguré, que de le donner tel que je l'ai fait. Je n'ai jamais songé qu'a amuser M. le duc de Bourgogne, et qu'à l'instruire en l'amusant par ces aventures, sans jamais vouloir donner cet ouvrage au public. Tout le monde sait qu-il ne m'a échappé que par l'infidélité d'un copiste. Enfin, tous les meilleurs serviteurs du Roi qui me connoissent, savent quels sont mes principes d'honneur et de religion sur le Roi, sur l'État et sur la patrie; ils savent quelle est ma reconnaissance vive et tendre pour les bienfaits dont le Roi m'a comblé. D'autres peuvent facilement être plus capables que moi; mais personne n'a plus de zèle sincere.'

44 Cardinal Bausset, *Histoire de Fénelon, Tome Troisième*, 37.

45 Charlotte Haldane argues that the embarrassment caused to Madame de Maintenon by the Affair, and the rage she experienced from Louis XIV led her to blame Fénelon for the debacle as he had introduced her to Madame Guyon (*Madame de Maintenon: Uncrowned Queen of France* (London, 1970), 182–6).

46 The pattern began with Fénelon's first biographer Andrew Michael Ramsay in his *L'Histoire de la Vie de Fénelon* (The Hague, 1723), and until Paul Janet most biographers used Ramsay's work as their template (Janet, *Fénelon: His Life and Works*, trans. Victor Leuliette (London, 1914)). However, the emphasis on *Télémaque* continues: see n. 2.

47 John A. Lynn, *The Wars of Louis XIV 1667–1714* (Harlow, 1999), 28–9, 43.

48 For British contemporary views, see Chapter 2 in this book; also G. Zeller, 'French Diplomacy and Foreign Policy in Their European setting', *The New Cambridge Modern History Vol. V: The Ascendancy of France 1648–88*, ed. F.L. Carsten (Cambridge, 1961); J.F. Bosher, 'The Franco-Catholic Danger, 1660–1715', *History*, 79, 255, pp. 5–30; K.H.D. Haley, 'The Dutch, the Invasion of England, and the Alliance of 1689', *The Revolution of 1688–89: Changing perspectives*, ed. Louis G. Schwoerer (Cambridge, 1992), 25; Klaus Malettke, 'Fénelon, La France et le système des États Européens en 1699', *Fénelon: Mystique et Politique (1699–1999)*, eds F.-X. Cuche and J. Le Brun, 469–80.

49 Fénelon, *Lettre à Louis XIV*, Œuvres, *Tome I*, 543. According to Le Brun's notes (1409–10) the unsent letter to Louis XIV was drafted between December 1693 and early 1694, with some parts compatible with composition in 1695. The letter was first published by Jean d'Alembert in his *Histoire ...l'Académie Française* in 1787, although its authenticity was doubted until 1825 when the manuscript in Fénelon's handwriting was found by Renouard (*Selected Letters of Fénelon*, ed. John McEwen (London, 1964), 297).

50 Fénelon, *Lettre*, 546–7. Both François Bluche and Emmanuel Le Roy Ladurie have stated that Fénelon exaggerated France's suffering in the *Lettre* and created a deliberately bleak picture to evoke sympathy (Bluche, *Louis XIV*, trans. Mark Greengrass (Oxford, 1990), xiii, 453; Ladurie, *The Ancien Régime: A History of France 1610–1714*, trans. Mark Greengrass (Oxford, 1996), 210).

51 Fénelon, *Lettre*, 548–50. See Pierre Jurieu, *Les soupirs de la France esclave, qui aspire après la liberté* (S.l., 1689), 22–3.

52 Jurieu, *Les soupirs de la France*, 18–19.

53 Roland Mousnier, 'The Exponents and Critics of Absolutism', *The New Cambridge Modern History Vol. IV: The Decline of Spain and the Thirty Years War 1609–48/59*, ed. J.P. Cooper (Cambridge, 1970), 119–21.

54 Louis XIV, *Mémoires for the Instruction of the Dauphin*, trans. Paul Sonnino (New York, 1970), 23–6.

55 See Chapter 4 in this book, for a discussion of Louis XIV's reorganisation of the French state.

56 William Beik, *Louis XIV and Absolutism: A Brief Study with Documents* (Boston, 2000), 4.

57 Fénelon, *Télémaque*, 160–3, 291.

58 Beik, *Louis XIV and Absolutism*, 83–4.

59 Antoine de Montchrétien, *Traicté de l'oeconomie politique*, ed. Th. Funck-Brentano (Paris, 1889), 35–9.

60 Lionel Rothkrug, *Opposition to Louis XIV*, 22–6 and 61; Nannerl O. Keohane, *Philosophy and the State in France: The Renaissance to the Enlightenment* (Princeton, 1980), 160–1; Henry C. Clark, *Compass of Society: Commerce and Absolutism in Old Regime France* (Plymouth, 2007), 16–18.

61 See Rothkrug, *Opposition to Louis XIV*, 61; Keohane, *Philosophy and the State in France*, 164–7; Sophus A. Reinert, *Translating Empire: Emulation and the Origins of Political Economy* (Harvard, 2011), 4–5.

62 Andrew Mansfield, 'Émeric Crucé's *Nouveau Cynée* (1623), Universal Peace and Free Trade', *Journal of Interdisciplinary History of Ideas*, 2, 4 (2013), pp. 2–23 (15–17).

63 Keohane, *Philosophy and the State in France*, 294, 351–7.

64 Pierre le Boisguilbert, *Le détail de la France; la cause de la diminution de ses biens et la facilité du remède* (Paris, 1696), 21–2.

65 Fénelon, *Télémaque*, 36–8.

66 Hont has argued that Fénelon's attack on Colbertism was twofold. On the one hand he despised how luxury was used to maintain 'the poor at the expense of the rich', and on the other hand, he believed the pursuit of luxury was leading France the way of Rome. Such a path 'would lead to military defeat and [a] domestic revolution' in which the state would be overthrown ('The Early Enlightenment Debate on Commerce and Luxury', 383).

67 Fénelon, *Télémaque*, 288.

68 Bourgogne au Fénclon (22 Dec. 1701, Versailles), *Correspondance, Tome X*, ed. Jacques Le Brun (Genève, 1989), 214.

69 See Jacques Le Brun's notes in *Fénelon's Œuvres, Tome II*, 1664–7.

70 Fénelon, *Examen de conscience sur les devoirs de la Royauté*, Œuvres II, 973–4.

71 *Ibid.*, 979–80.

72 *Ibid.*, 981–3.

73 *Ibid.*, 983, 998–9.

74 *Ibid.*, 1001–2.

75 *Ibid.*, 989–91.

76 *Ibid.*, 976–8.

77 *Ibid.*, 977–8.

78 *Ibid.*, 984–5.

79 *Ibid.*, 996–8.

80 *Ibid.*, 990: '[v]otre ennemi est votre frère'.

81 Fénelon, *Mémoire sur les moyens de prévenir la guerre de la succession d'Espagne*, Œuvres, Tome II, 1013.

82 *Ibid.*, 1014.

83 Fénelon, *Mémoire sur la Situation Deplorable de la France en 1710*, Œuvres, Tome II, 1036: 'nation tombe dans l'opprobre. Elle devient l'objet de la dérision publique'.

84 Fénelon, *Supplément*, Œuvres, Tome II, 1005.

85 Fénelon, *Tables de Chaulnes*, Œuvres, Tome II, 1085: 'bought at any price'.

86 Rothkrug, *Opposition to Louis XIV*, 285–6.

87 Fénelon, *Tables*, 1088.

88 *Ibid.*, 1104. On several occasions the Romans enacted sumptuary laws (*sumptuariae leges*) to moderate excessive consumption of superfluities.

89 *Ibid.*, 1089. See William Beik, *Absolutism and Society in Seventeenth-Century France* (Cambridge, 1985), 335–9.

90 *Tables*, 1100.

91 *Ibid.*, 1101.

92 *Ibid.*, 1100–1.

93 See Chapter 4.

94 See Chapters 4 and 5 in this book; plus the duc de Saint-Simon, *Projets de Gouvernement du duc de Bourgogne*, ed. M.P. Mesnard (Paris, 1860), and abbé de Saint-Pierre, *Discours sur le Polysynodie* (Londres, 1718). These works contain the concept of the polysynody which was flirted with briefly during the *Régence* under the duc de Orléans, but later shunned as the regent began to embrace the sovereignty possessed by Louis XIV.

95 See Keohane, *Philosophy and the State in France*, 345; Harold A. Ellis, *Boulainvilliers and the French Monarchy: Aristocratic Politics in Early Eighteenth-Century France* (New York, 1988), 63–4.

96 Fénelon to Chevreuse (27 Feb. 1712), *Selected Letters of Fénelon*, ed. and trans. J. McEwen (London, 1964), 178.

97 Fénelon to Chevreuse (8 Mar. 1712), *Selected Letters of Fénelon*, 181–2.

98 Fénelon, *Mémoire sur les mesures à prendre après la mort du duc de Bourgogne*, Œuvres, Tome II, 1107.

99 *Ibid.*, 1112. This council was not the Regency council advocated in Louis XIV's will to restrain the power of Orléans by using the king's legitimised bastard the duc de Maine. Orléans persuaded the *parlement de Paris* to reject this will for subverting the fundamental laws of France, and it allowed him to act freely as regent (see next chapter).

100 *Mémoire sur les mesures*, 1111–12.

101 *Ibid.*, 1114.

102 *Ibid.*, 1115.

4

The reign of Louis XIV:
absolute monarchy

Fénelon's attempt to confront the practical and ideological consequences of Louis XIV's extraordinarily long rule (r. 1643–1715) was not an overly common occurrence during the king's reign.[1] Works did begin to emerge from the 1690s that addressed specific deficiencies within the bureaucracy questioning government policy, but censorship meant that their number was limited. Yet ideas were promulgated, frequently abroad, which desired to recover the health of a nation dogged by war and commercial under-achievement. Most accepted the system of government that had evolved throughout the seventeenth century, particularly under Louis XIV, so were not antagonistic in nature. Rather, they endeavoured to correct the system's inadequacies. During the century, France had witnessed a move towards a centralised state that was perceived to be absolute in authority. Indeed, Louis XIV's own conception of France was that it possessed absolute sovereignty through his God-given will. Building on the reforms of Cardinals Richelieu and Mazarin, Louis opted for a regime which positioned him centrally to command operations as the ancient structures of government were adapted for his personal rule. His policies and reliance on a handful of ministers to carry them out, however, meant that France began to suffer increasing financial difficulties worsened by an ineffective administration. The Burgundy Circle in which Fénelon was the renowned figure, offered a way to adjust the state's model of absolutism under the leadership of a new king: the duc de Bourgogne. This chapter will chart the development of seventeenth-century French absolutism and its ideological expression through Louis XIV and Bishop Bossuet, before examining Bourgogne's own vision of France as related by the duc de Saint-Simon. It will form the basis of later ideas for change that link with the following chapter which will analyse ideas of monarchical reform after the death of Louis XIV in 1715.

French absolutism and Louis XIV

The advancement of absolutism during the reign of Louis XIV reflected a gathering momentum in monarchical sovereignty during the seventeenth century. Over a process of several centuries, the French monarchy had struggled to contain the ambitions of the nobility and Catholic Church. As religious and political civil war tore France asunder from the sixteenth century, absolutism was propounded as an ideological weapon to combat division while creating peace. Into the seventeenth century European tensions and war endured, notably with Spain, and both Richelieu and Mazarin centralised the bureaucracy to augment the authority of the crown. In so doing, they took on the power of the aristocracy and provincial elites to provide France with stability. The erosion of the nobility's influence on government led to civil war – the Fronde (1648–53) – when members of the high nobility attempted to resist this encroachment on their power and privileges by the monarchy. Their subsequent defeat enabled the crown to advance a programme of reform that exploited the king's emergency powers, nullifying the nobility as a threat to produce order.

When embarking upon his personal rule in 1661 Louis began to write his *Mémoires*, which offered a manifesto of his views on government. This fascinating insight into the mind of the king reveals the profound impact that the Fronde left upon Louis XIV's psyche and future policy. In the eight years between the end of the Fronde and the death of Mazarin, Louis spent this time surveying the damage caused to France. According to the king, as he awaited his opportunity to rule alone he personally reviewed the problems in the courts, finances, the legal system, the Church, and the nobility.[2] After Mazarin's death, Louis resolved never to employ a prime minister again believing that they usurped the functions of a king. Instead he preferred to divide his counsel and the execution of his orders between a limited number of ministers, advisers, and councillors. This allowed the king to establish his mastery over government by controlling it alone. While a king should rely on the counsel and support of his ablest advisers, it was paramount for Louis that his position was beyond the reach of all others.

Lessons offered to him by both French and European history shaped Louis's desire for pre-eminence. Earlier examples and the Fronde had imbued him with a negative Hobbesian view of humanity.[3] He believed that people were naturally ambitious, and that the strongest possessed a desire to dominate. If a king did not deliver justice via absolute authority, neither security nor tranquillity would exist within a kingdom. Hence the need to be seen as a father to the state and its people, or a head that directed the body through law and authority while ensuring order. A king was able to neutralise the threat from his populace by elevating his authority beyond the rest, aided by personal merits and the paradigm he offered his subjects. His reputation and glory both home and abroad, would flourish if he worked assiduously to (im)prove himself for the benefit of his people. In return for this sacrifice and security, subjects submitted to his command and did not question his authority:

> It must assuredly be agreed that as bad as a prince may be, the revolt of his subjects is always infinitely criminal. He who has given kings to men has wanted them to be respected as His lieutenants, reserving to Himself alone the right to examine their conduct. His will is that whoever is born subject must obey without qualification, and this law, so explicit and universal, is not made in favour of princes alone, but is beneficial to the very people on whom it is imposed, who can never violate it without exposing themselves to much greater evils that those they claim to be guarding against.[4]

For Louis, the king unified the different elements, institutions, servants, and subjects, plus the relationships of exchange between them all. He bound them together and ultimately directed these relationships for the good of the state. Such power had to be guarded jealously by the sovereign to ensure that it was not undermined or divided.[5] The surest method to achieve this was to place the king so far above all his subjects none were able to challenge his authority:

> As important as it is for the public to be governed only by a single person, it is just as important for the one who performs the function to be raised so far above the others that no one else can be confused or compared with him, and one cannot deprive the head of state of the slightest marks of superiority without harming the entire body.[6]

Louis XIV's conception of himself as possessing absolute sovereignty dovetailed with an increasingly centralised France and the developing (theoretical) notion of the state as person. From the sixteenth century the monarchy had striven to exert more influence and power over a historically divided provincial France. The independence of these provinces and kingdoms had proved difficult to control from medieval times, as princes of the blood and the high nobility struggled to protect their autonomy and exert influence over the crown. The high nobility or ancient *noblesse d'épée* ('nobility of the sword') often provided a major obstacle to the extension of royal power. They had the capacity to utilise their land, private armies, plus economic and legal privileges to undermine the crown's sovereignty to gain concessions or to assert their own claims.[7] Over time and through continual war, however, the monarchy was gradually able to assert greater control over these provinces through the development of a professional army from the fifteenth century. Such advances were broadened by gaining independence from the papacy on appointments within the French Church's higher echelons, and an ability to undermine the role of the constitutional elements of government. By the reign of Louis XIII (r. 1610–43) the constitutional apparatus of state – the Estates-General, plus many provincial estates and *parlements* – had been progressively neglected. Due to the divisive nature of the Estates-General, emphasised in the reign of Henri III (r. 1574–89), Louis XIII had capitalised on its factional behaviour to cease calling it from 1614.[8] The initiatives from 1624 of Cardinal Richelieu as his chief minister, witnessed the attempt to fashion an absolute system within France. As a result of the religious, military, and economic pressures power was centralised under the unity offered by the monarch within a European theatre of war. Richelieu's efforts were continued by his (chosen) successor Cardinal Mazarin who was chief minister from 1642 to 1661. His sustained confrontation with the high nobility, led some to rebel against the monarchy in the Fronde in a failed bid to restore their prominence within the state.

As a reaction to centuries of division and internecine civil war, markedly the Wars of Religion (1562–98), the centralisation of the French state was accompanied by a theoretic promotion of absolute sovereignty. The sixteenth century saw a shift in thought from Claude de Seyssel's (c.1450–1520) promotion of three 'bridles' (of religion, justice, and the polity) to restrain the monarch's power to Jean Bodin's (c.1530–96) call for an absolute, unrestrained, and indivisible sovereignty to be placed into the hands of the king.[9] The cause of this shift was the Wars of Religion which undermined civil harmony and the monarchy.[10] During its political and religious civil turmoil, Huguenot publications such as François Hotman's *Franco-Gallia* (1573) plus the *Vindiciae contra tyrannos* (1579) employed anti-monarchical (*monarchomach*) juristic theory to expound notions of popular sovereignty and resistance to the tyrannical authority.[11] Such attempts at constitutionalism were rejected by Bodin (and others), who reacted to a background of continued belligerence by following Machiavelli's advancement of the state as a legal person.[12] Moving beyond the medieval imagining of the state as a ruler's territorial possession, the state evolved into a depersonalised 'public thing' (*res publica*). This view of the state had emerged in the thirteenth century, but found greater articulation during the intense conflicts and European competition of the sixteenth century. The single sovereign (body) best represented the territorial association of government and people unified as a sovereign person (state), when striving to achieve its aims in an interstate framework.[13]

According to the *Mémoires*, Louis XIV appeared to have thought it possible to personalise the state as a legal entity. While averring that the king belonged to the people, he was very firm in his belief that the people belonged to him: as did their lives, property, and money.[14] His role at the pinnacle of society ensured the relationships between the various aspects of state, its institutions and people; guaranteeing that French society operated as a specialised but unified whole directed and represented by him.[15] The advancement of absolutism under Louis XIV built on the progress of his predecessors, especially his father (Louis XIII) and the work of Richelieu and Mazarin. In many ways Louis XIV appears to have attempted to offer an embodiment of contemporary absolute theory. While it cannot be proved with any certainty, his desire for primacy to offset disunity and faction through an irresistible power greater than any other within the state, did echo the ideas of Bodin and Hobbes.[16] In Louis's opinion this supremacy was necessitated by a requirement to restrain the natural temptations of men, who were not 'angels' and possessed a lust for excessive power and dominion.[17] While such maxims on authority and obedience were directed at all of his citizens, there were three specific targets.

The first were those who participated in government, notably the *noblesse de robe* ('nobility of the robe'). After the death of Mazarin, Louis moved from the reliance upon a single chief minister to a limited number of ministers, councillors, and advisers when collating recommendations on the kingdom and policy. The king's authority and council were deemed indivisible, and from 1661 there were two types of royal council meetings: 'those of government at which the king himself presided and those concerned with judicial, financial and administrative matters mainly of a litigious nature'.[18] In the latter case, the chancellor or king's chief legal adviser presided over the latter council meetings on behalf of the king. Of the councils which the king presided over personally there were: the *conseil d'en haut* which dealt with the imperative domestic and foreign matters of state; the *conseil dépêches* that dealt with mundane matters from the provinces, and the *conseil royal des finances* managed the financial strategies of France.[19] The provinces were governed using a complicated system of jurisdictions that had to accommodate the distinct development over centuries of individual provincial institutions, laws, systems, customs, and language. This included a fiscal apparatus dominated by the use of intendants, which reported directly to the royal council and worked with the provinces in matters of taxation and finances. There was also the *parlements* and lesser courts that dealt with judicial matters, and the ecclesiastical dioceses.[20] In many ways the crown provided cohesion for these disparate parts and used the intermediary bodies to transmit its policies down to local level. Astride this convoluted system sat Louis XIV, directing it with an assiduous and scrupulous desire to be in control of his state and its government. These ministers, councillors, and courtiers – many ennobled by Louis – were used in place of the *noblesse de épée*, but they were also precluded from sharing in his authority.[21] The complicated evolution of the (provincial) French system allowed Louis to rely on the divisions of government to prevent threats to his authority, while centralising the state and amplifying his own power over them. His determination to sidestep the *épée's* involvement in government, however, meant that he depended heavily on the *robe* nobility. In so doing, he realised that any enticement their assistance may engender for a stake in his authority had to be controlled as he was unwilling to share power.

The second group and the principal target of Louis's enhanced sovereignty was the *noblesse d'épée*. The strife experienced by the crown from elements of the *épée* and princes of the blood over successive generations had left an indelible scar on the king, markedly in the shape of the Fronde. Due to the rebellion of members of the high nobility during the civil war it was essential that they knew their place within the state:

> [I]t was not in my interest to select individuals of a more eminent quality. It was, above all things, necessary to establish my own reputation and to make the public aware, by the rank I selected, that it was never my intention to share my authority with them. It was important that they [did] not conceive any greater hopes than I would be pleased to give them, which is difficult for people of high birth.[22]

After Mazarin's death, Louis pushed forward the policy of circumventing the high nobility's traditional supporting role within the apparatus of the state.[23] It has been persuasively demonstrated that the *épée* continued to wield influence at court and in the provinces;[24] yet it cannot be doubted that the *robe* nobility supplanted them at the top of government. While Louis XIV did not erode their ancient privileges and fundamental rights of property, the *épée* were essentially kept on a tight leash. This thwarted their involvement in state policy and government activity.

The final target of Louis XIV's elevated sovereignty were the representative elements of government, including the Estates-General and the *parlements*. Under the work of his Controller-General of Finances, Jean-Baptiste Colbert (1619–83), and the Secretary of State for War, Michel le Tellier (1603–85) followed by his son the Marquis de Louivois (1641–91), the king was able to gear French finances towards war. The desire for war and economic development drove government centralisation in order to improve the collection of taxation. Local intendants were given autonomy to pursue policy in order to raise taxation.[25] Due to the necessity to develop inadequate state bureaucracy the state did observe a conciliatory attitude when dealing with the nobility and provinces, although it compromised little with the general populace. A more flexible approach was adopted when the state and its intendants dealt with the provinces, and there was cooperation between them in terms of the collection of revenue and local government activity.[26]

As the state expanded, Louis decisively undermined the fundamentals of state that posed any restriction on his power, notably the *parlements* (which were primarily law courts). The *parlement* of Paris whose jurisdiction covered a third of France was the most important. It saw itself as the guardian of the law resisting anything, including the king that appeared to threaten law in order to save France. For Louis XIV the Wars of Religion and the Fronde had revealed a contractualist agenda among elements of the *parlements*. The *Mémoires* impressed the prerequisite to reform the courts and *parlements*, so that they acted in accordance with his will. Their behaviour had to be corrected as the *parlements* had over-extended their role as 'ancient bodies'. They had displayed a 'false notion that they were defending a supposed interest of the people' in opposition to him (the prince), and had not considered that the two interests were the same.[27] From 1666 Louis challenged the *parlements* (*Enquêtes*) who had delayed his legislation, and instructed them to verify his edicts without remonstrance. This was a clear demonstration for the king that royal authority had been perfectly restored.[28]

After 1673 the *parlements* were not allowed to remonstrate the king's legislation until after it had been registered, which effectively nullified their power. Louis XIV was able to achieve this through the use of prerogative under the auspices of emergency measures generated by the state's engagement in war with the Dutch (1672–78).[29] These emergency powers remained in place until after his death when war officially ended, and they allowed the king to subvert opposition to his power. His distrust of the *parlements* and other assemblies (central and provincial) appear to have been born from a fear of popular government. Councils and states that relied upon them were susceptible to their domination and a requisite to propitiate the many. While it was undesirable to require a prime minister, he would at least be grateful for his position. Popular assemblies expressed no such gratitude: 'the more you grant it, the more it demands; the more you caress it, the more it scorns you; and what it once has in its possessions is retained by so many hands that it cannot be torn away without extreme violence'.[30] It was far more effective for a king to rule the executive alone.[31] Such behaviour meant that Louis XIV's subjugation of the *parlements* to his will – albeit through emergency powers – was authoritarian and exhibited a capacity to act in an absolute manner.[32]

At this juncture it is perhaps sensible to clarify the importance of absolutism to Louis XIV's France. According to revisionist historiography the predominant view is that France did not possess absolute sovereignty. Instead, the king and his central bureaucracy worked through cooperation with the provinces, the various assemblies, the Church, and the nobility. The government did have the power to act arbitrarily at times – as seen in Louis's restrictions of the *parlements'* ability to remonstrate – but it did not rely on this approach continuously. Representative elements of the state endured during the reign of Louis XIV, although many were allowed to drift into disuse as they were not fit for the purposes of a remodelled state. Those provincial estates that did survive were important, and they were able to bargain with the crown.[33] In so doing, the crown allowed varying degrees of independence in certain provincial assemblies while bartering with the local elites. This involvement of the aristocracy has led historians to dismiss the wholesale removal of the high nobility from government. Accordingly, the *épée* still held great influence in the provinces and they had the ear of Louis XIV at court.[34] However, this drives to the heart of the issue for absolutism. While it is claimed that the *épée* were engaged in the state, many did not feel that they had enough say or influence over the direction of France. Their replacement by the *robe* nobility and the significant problems that were emphasised from the 1690s onwards, meant they were not in a position to assist the state or king. Due to the Fronde, Louis's insistence on surrounding himself with often newly ennobled *robe* ministers and advisers was an example of his ability to harness absolute power to control government. It has been claimed that Louis XIV's absolutism was theoretical rather than actual, and this is key.[35] While his sovereignty may not have been absolute in practice it was certainly perceived to be so at home by the nobility and abroad by neighbouring countries.[36] The façade of an absolute state supported effectively by royal propaganda, led to a persistent belief (in political theory) that the king possessed the ability to act in an absolute manner. This power frightened France's neighbours, alienated the high nobility, and appeared to oppress its own people.

In defence of absolutism: Bossuet

Perhaps the greatest ideological defence of Louis XIV's sovereignty was provided by Jacques-Bénigne Bossuet (1627–1704), Bishop of Meaux.[37] Bossuet was a favourite of the court and famed as a great orator of the Church. He was also a leading figure within the Counter-Reformation, taking an active part in the attempted conversion of Huguenots after the Revocation of the Edict of Nantes (1685). From 1670 to 1681 he acted as tutor to Louis *le Grand Dauphin*, which proved to be a difficult task as the prince exhibited little interest in education. Despite this, Bossuet wrote two pedagogical works that have possessed an enduring legacy: the *Discours sur l'histoire universelle* (published 1682), and the *Politique tirée des propres paroles de l'Écriture sainte* (published 1709).[38] In both works the former mentor-turned-nemesis of Fénelon portrayed France as a new Rome, and its absolute government as the expression of divine will. Bossuet embraced the centralisation of Louis XIV's France as a means for providing unity, controlling an excessive desire for liberty and rebellion within the people.[39] Bossuet's view of politics was firmly grounded in religion: religion and politics were the 'two things' on which humanity revolved.[40] In the *Discours* religious scripture offered historical truths for the Dauphin's lessons on kingship. History became an essential component of a prince's curriculum, for it revealed the motivations of men and state behaviour across time. The *Politique tirée des propres paroles de l'Écriture sainte* (*Politique*) created a picture of government that drew its conclusions on kingship from religion.

Bossuet began the *Politique* by stating that the basis of society was found in the unity and bonds of man. God, as the common father, engendered unity amongst men through their love of one another as 'brothers' which forged a bond between them as God's children.[41] This connection was augmented by a mutual interest unifying the whole as men consoled, assisted, and fortified each other as God had decreed for society to establish the 'well-being' of all. Interest ensured that men remained attached to one another, a curiosity that was further secured by the divergent 'talents' possessed by individuals through the division of labour. This made it essential that men acted together as one body, their union was strengthened by mutual desires and enshrined in law to profit the strong and weak alike.[42] The foundations of society were located in the same God, shared the same ends, common origin, the same blood, plus the same mutual wants and interests for the satisfactions of life.[43] Crucial to this concord was a 'love of country'. Society demanded that man should 'love the land' on which he dwelt with his fellows, for it was a common mother and nurse forming attachment and unity. While God obliged the individual to love all men, it was more reasonable to love his fellow citizens, and considered an 'execration of mankind' for a man not to love the country that sustained him and his family.[44] The love of country led to an observance of law and custom expressed via obedience. An example of which was to be found in Christ, who 'shed his blood with a particular regard for his nation'.

The Bishop relied upon a 'limited Hobbesianism' in describing a state of nature where each individual 'did what seemed right to himself' (Judges 17:6).[45] In order to prevent the corruption of the passions, legitimate authority and kingship were created through kingship which eschewed the state of nature in favour of the protection of government and the unity of the nation, creating an immortal state.[46] This genesis of civil government reflected the Christian interpretation of the birth of monarchy through Saul in the first Book of Samuel (13:1), and revealed a critical difference between Bossuet and Hobbes on the root of sovereignty. Despite a similar view of an all-embracing absolute sovereign, for Hobbes, government was created by leaving the state of nature to generate security and peace through a contract between the sovereign and its people.[47] Bossuet rejected the notion of any contract, believing that kingship had been divinely instituted by God. To claim that kingship was granted to Saul due to the demands of the people on God was erroneous and placed sovereignty in man. Precluding any possibility of an initial contract, Bossuet was attempting to propose a secular objection to the contractarianism that had been evident in France for over a century.[48] It was important that Bossuet reflected the divinely ordained nature of the rule of kings as a justification for the power of Louis XIV and his behaviour. The foundation of the king's authority could not be undermined or divided by the inclusion of the people.

Significantly Bossuet offered an alternative route for the development of the origin of sovereign authority: the family. Bossuet followed Christ's discussion of 'paternal power' (Matthew 12:25), and a belief that before the deluge the family formed the basis of society with fathers at their heads presenting a prototype for cities and then the kingdoms produced from those cities.[49] Fatherhood supplied the template for kingship, as several families united under the leadership of a common father before subjecting themselves to kings. Ancient custom revealed that obedience and subordination were generated from the will of the parents as expressed in law. Laws which were sacred and drawn from nature regulated 'all things human and divine, public and private', uniting people in society under the dominion of God.[50] Hereditary kingship was the most natural and robust form of government expressing the divine, paternal power while unifying the people under a single leader (father) who was required to make decisions to profit the public good. Kingship was therefore sacred. It invested the monarch – as God's lieutenants on earth – with the power and duty to furnish the public good, and in return, the people serve God by obeying the king no matter how he behaved.[51] A king was not born for himself but for a public that were frequently ungrateful. In detesting cruelty and acquiring mercy, a good king could reign mildly through love while listening to their people. While it was not for the people to disobey a tyrannical king, princes should rule to inspire love in their subjects, for if they were cruel and hated they could perish under God's divine justice.[52]

In order for a king to rule effectively and in the image of God his royal dominion must be absolute. Kings needed to exude strength in their rule for all government action flowed from them as the sovereign consolidated the state and its people.[53] Their behaviour was accountable to none but God; a king's decision was the only decision as no 'coercive' power could constrain his behaviour. A king was not free from the laws and subject to the equality of law like his subjects, especially those based in natural law, because royal authority was 'invincible'.[54] In asserting that a king's sovereignty was invincible, Bossuet distinguished between absolute and arbitrary. Bossuet dismissed arbitrary government as creating a nation filled with slaves, dispossessed of property, inheritance and rights as a king may do what he wished as there was no law but the king's will.[55] Yet for Bossuet's absolute sovereignty, the monarch's power could not be prevented or tempered in any manner as he must be supreme in his ability to represent the public. No flaw could prevent the king's capability to act or judge as the head of state. The king was the physical embodiment of majesty: God's greatness in the prince.[56] Bossuet's king was not an individual but a *personnage public* ('public personage') in whom the entire state was comprised, incorporating his own will and that of the people manifested in the person of the prince. Royal dominance acted simultaneously throughout the kingdom as God's dominion enlivened the universe. The king conducted his magistrates, captains, citizens, and soldiers in the provinces as his authority permeated the kingdom and united the people, 'enclosed in one head' that was sacred, paternal, and absolute.

Such absolute right and greatness required magnanimity, splendour and virtue in the king, but it also necessitated obedience in the people. In advocating such a sovereign Bossuet was clear that it was essential to restrict the multitude: 'so many humours, so many interests, so many tricks, so many passions'.[57] When one considers the contextual background of the *Politique* – over a century of religious turmoil, unrest, and war, ideological resistance to state centralisation, civil war, recurrent European war, and Counter-Reformation – Bossuet's need for an obedient populace was perhaps understandable. For their part, the people served the state by obeying and loving the prince, as the interests of the state and the king were the same. Disobedience to the sovereign meant that 'public order' was 'overthrown', and for that reason his decrees must be followed.[58] The only exception to this proscription was when a king ordered his subjects to break the commandments of God. In such an instance they should not obey, but even if the subject was suffering violence their only recourse was to passive obedience, or the possibility of respectful remonstrance to the king through his magistrates and other legitimate means. There could be no prospect of rebellion as the king must be served whether they were good or bad, to disobey was unchristian: a treason against God. The state fell into peril and the public peace was insecure when the people were permitted to rise up against their sovereign for any reason.[59] Differing from the view of Machiavelli (and the Commonwealthmen), the example of Rome had proved to Bossuet a state must be wary of granting the populace excessive liberty, for it led to the faction and internal war that produced the downfall of the Republic. While the love of liberty equated to a love of country under a king, extreme liberty in the people created jealousy and discord.[60] Revolution and the collapse of the Republic had occurred due to the perpetual divisions that existed between the patricians and the plebeians, as the latter thirsted for liberty and were envious of the power of the senate.[61] Bossuet's political system emphasised the necessity of absolute power in the king robust enough to withstand faction, liberty, and resistance towards the monarch.

This absolute model of kingship was enhanced by its relationship to religion and the Church. The Romans and other great barbarian empires had exploited religion when shaping their power as weapons of providence.[62] The happiness of princes was dependent upon providence, so piety and serious obligation to God were required for a king in the form of protection for his subjects and the avoidance of arbitrary power.[63] As God's representative on earth the king possessed an obligation to protect the Church, and in return God's lieutenant must be obeyed by his subjects. The Church was subservient to the state in the temporal realm, yet its position underwrote the absolutism of the state and ensured the king was a champion of the Church and a proselytising agent for religion.[64] While the two powers of state and Church were independent in terms of internal administration, for Bossuet there could be no secularisation as religion and politics existed co-dependently. Religion enhanced the authority of the king as it formed the basis of the constitution and provided stability for government.[65] Bossuet's view did overlap to a large extent with Louis XIV's own opinion in this regard. While Louis was suspicious of the Church and believed it should be subordinated to the demands of the state (including the use of its property), ultimately he believed religion was a tool for unity. Although claiming to understand the just complaints that arose during the Reformation the king was opposed to the schism that developed as unity was essential for a state. Those who subverted religion such as the Jansenists or Huguenots undermined the nation with their doctrine.[66] This strongly held conviction was part of the inspiration for the Revocation of the Edict of Nantes, which declared Protestantism to be illegal in France. In many ways this policy proved to be disastrous as it led to the mass exodus of Huguenots to Britain and the Dutch Republic, many of whom were leaders in commerce and trade. The persecution of Huguenots also undermined the standing of France abroad, adding to European geopolitical tensions, and perceived as a stain on Louis's reign.[67]

It has been stated that the inheritance of Louis XIV's reign shaped French behaviour during the eighteenth century.[68] His legacy was something Louis was acutely aware of during his lifetime and many of his actions, particularly his wars were driven by a thirst for recognition or *gloire* ('glory'). In essence success was ensured by distinguishing oneself as a king, which was achieved by behaving as an active and knowledgeable ruler. *Gloire* was ultimately attainable through military glory, an assertion of state power that was recognised abroad by other states.[69] Such an assertion was juxtaposed with the manifestation of greatness present in symbolism and grandeur, and to this end magnificent palaces and ostentatious wealth and luxury were methods of conveying power to one's neighbours and subjects.[70] Unlike Fénelon, Bossuet shared these views with the king, not only advocating luxury as a necessity for emphasising state power, but also believed that God had made kings warriors.[71] Although peace was to be preferred over war and war must possess just motivations, God had used His chosen people (Israelites) as weapons to destroy His enemies. Warrior kings were to be celebrated by their subjects and their acts of glory animated the people, supplementing unity under the king. The eminence of Rome had been built upon its military prowess, and contemporary France echoed this renown according to Bossuet.[72] Louis XIV therefore embodied Bossuet's vision of a new Caesar, who had fashioned the instruments of power to forge a new empire.

Bourgogne and Saint-Simon's *Projects of Government*

While Bossuet's endorsement of absolutism under Louis XIV was not without some moral censure, from the 1690s criticism of government behaviour began to emerge in public and private. A very interesting source of this criticism arises from Louis de Rouvroy, the duc de Saint-Simon (1675–1755). Saint-Simon was a peer of the realm who served under the king as a *Mousquetaire de la garde* ('musketeer of the guard') and was an active member of the court. From the 1690s until the end of the *Régence* Saint-Simon catalogued the behaviour and intrigues of the court, including waspish observations of its members and Louis XIV. More importantly, the *Mémoires* also disclose the duc's relationship with Bourgogne as Dauphin and the preparations the two men considered for the reorganisation of France under him as king. These plans were not published until the nineteenth century under the title of the *Projets de Gouvernement*, but they convey an alternative view of the administration of Bourgogne's France to that of Fénelon.

Saint-Simon's *Mémoires* are famous for providing a compelling insight into the life of the court, its intrigues, factions, and the quarrels between its members. Saint-Simon's often acerbic delineation of the leading figures of the court expose a man of strong opinion and a sense of frustration towards the later reign of Louis XIV. His proximity to the king at court over a twenty-year period left him with a picture of the monarch that was less than flattering. Much of his chagrin was directed at the ineffective running of the king's administration and the damage that had been caused to France. Saint-Simon laid the blame for this at the king's feet, whom he described as 'vainglorious', dominated by ambition, glory, and a love of war. Louis's upbringing had left him with below average intelligence plus a suspicion and jealousy of those with 'intellect, education, nobility of sentiment, and high principles'.[73] According to Saint-Simon this had significant consequences, as it shaped the course of government through the choice of ministers and advisers surrounding the king. As Louis desired to rule alone not sharing the burden of his authority, he selected ministers less intelligent and capable who would not threaten or overwhelm him. Unfortunately his ministers, generals, courtiers, and mistresses soon perceived his love of admiration and were able to achieve their ambitions by flattering the king.[74] If a minister could appeal to Louis's prejudices or explain matters in a manner conducive to his understanding, he would accept its premise often stubbornly sticking to that opinion at times to the detriment of a favourable alternative.[75] This enabled 'flatterers' to influence the king for their own benefit rather than the advantage of the state, much to the dismay of Saint-Simon.

To Saint-Simon's mind the ineffectual management of the state was caused by the limited group of frequently self-serving ministers, that had crippled

France. Its finances were in an appalling condition during the War of the Spanish Succession, made worse by a bad winter (1708/9) and poor fiscal organisation. This calamity had been passed on to the people, who were not only suffering through consequences of the war, but bore the financial burden for funding the war too.[76] In discussing these difficulties Saint-Simon pointed to the rebuffed financial remedies provided by Pierre le Boisguilbert (1646–1714) and Sébastien Le Prestre (1633–1707), Marquis de Vauban and Maréchal of France. He stated that after the publication of Boisguilbert's *Le détail de la France; la cause de la diminution de ses biens et la facilité du remède* (1695), which highlighted the abuses within the system and advocated its reform, the duc attempted to protect him from prosecution. Likewise, he commended the endeavour of Vauban – the great general and fort builder of France – who had collected information from across the kingdom at his own expense to proffer changes to the system in the *Dixme royale* (1707). Due to his extensive travels across France over many years in campaigns, Vauban had decided to appraise the financial hardship and suffering of the people in order to improve the government.[77] In Saint-Simon's opinion both schemes were commendable remedies to address the dire financial situation faced by France that had fallen foul to the ministry's censorship. He believed the works had prompted a knee-jerk reaction from the ministry, which created harsher 'imposts' after their publication to dissuade others from ideas of reform.

The treatment of Boisguilbert and Vauban's ideas for fiscal reform in France accentuate the essentially clandestine nature of the Burgundy Circle's reform plans.[78] In the *Dixme royale* Vauban did not set out to undermine the government or leadership of Louis XIV. Instead, he believed that his project would benefit both the welfare of the people plus the glory and revenue of the king.[79] The project involved the simplification and purification of the taxation system under a royal tithe, which would collect revenue from the 'fruits of the earth' and a percentage of the yearly income from all produces.[80] Use of the tithe would increase state revenues considerably by cutting out the corruption embedded within the system, which was ineffective and suffered from inaction. The current problems experienced in France were the result of mismanagement and the dishonesty of 'harpies' (officials), who took from the state at the expense of the poor.[81] As a result, this impoverished system relied on a taxation policy that was frequently arbitrary and placed unfair burdens upon the poorest members of society, who could barely afford to pay.[82] For Vauban this did not have to be the case. France possessed such an abundance of natural riches, desired by its neighbours, the country could be made exceptionally wealthy through commerce and enjoy a surplus in revenue.[83] The most controversial elements of the work was its discussion on the vitiating effects of poor administration and war on total revenue, plus the belief that all subjects from every order and rank should contribute or face punishment. A tithe would enable

France to flourish and the king to pay off his debts.[84] Vauban submitted the project to the king in the belief that the king had been ill-informed by his ministers regarding the condition of the kingdom. He felt that Louis would believe it was his duty to aid the suffering of the poor and seize the opportunity to enrich the coffers of the treasury.[85] Vauban was wrong. Louis rejected the proposal and ignored his ideas. The work was refused a licence, provoking Vauban to publish the work privately and anonymously for a limited number of friends to share his ideas on the importance of reform. Subsequently, the work was condemned, and although Vauban 'was not named personally', those who published the work were 'hunted down and punished'.[86]

Such a strong reaction by the state censors to potential reproach of Louis XIV's government explains some of the secrecy surrounding ideas of change and the Burgundy Circle's plans. As Saint-Simon made clear to the duc de Bourgogne during their clandestine meetings, while the prince may feel the disfavour of his grandfather the duc faced severe ramifications if they were discovered.[87] Despite this concern however, the two men began to meet regularly in the prince's private rooms at Versailles once he became Dauphin. Saint-Simon declared that Bourgogne's confidence had grown considerably after the death of his father in April 1711 from smallpox. The Grand Dauphin allegedly despised his son, and the cabal around him were opposed to the young prince. Evidence of this antagonism was offered by Saint-Simon who claimed that during the War of the Spanish Succession, the duc de Vendôme attempted to blame Bourgogne for his own military failures as marshal.[88] Vendôme, a close friend and ally of Bourgogne's father, resented the prince's deficiencies as a soldier and played on the Dauphin's implacable hatred of his son. At root, the cause of the hostilities towards Bourgogne arose from rival cabals within the court surrounding the two princes.[89] Once the Grand Dauphin had died this rivalry ended and Bourgogne's increased confidence saw a dramatic shift in his popularity at court and with the wider populace. Upon becoming Dauphin, Bourgogne's meetings on the reform of France as king with Saint-Simon began relatively quickly.

According to Saint-Simon, both men were of a similar view on the necessity to alter the monarchy and administration of France.[90] The plans of government drawn up by the two men for the future of France were an attempt to overthrow the structure spawned by Richelieu and Mazarin. For Saint-Simon, 'the most important thing to be done was to overthrow entirely the system of government in which Cardinal Mazarin had imprisoned the kingdom and the realm'.[91] Mazarin had cared only for his own power, so had systematically attacked the laws and traditions of the state – its 'rules and forms' – in order to subjugate it. The central target of the two cardinals had been the *épée*, who had been 'annihilated' within the state. By promoting the 'pen and the robe people' the great nobles of France had been left without power as government was placed into the hands of the 'meanest plebeian'. Saint-Simon and Bourgogne's design was to introduce the *épée* back into the ministry in accordance with the fundamental laws and customs of the kingdom. With the exception of the judiciary, by degrees the *robe* nobility would be dismissed from the administration. This would leave the administration of public affairs in the hands of the aristocracy, purging an unruly government of self-interested officials to succour the public good while removing their inadequate policy.

This agenda was made very clear in the *Projets de Gouvernement*, a plan from Saint-Simon based upon his discussions with Bourgogne. Saint-Simon made it clear that the new Dauphin was ready to rule France, and had spent much time studying kingship and what was required for France. Bourgogne alleged that he would be guided by truth and justice, and that paramount among his principles was the dictum that he was there for his people, they were not there for him.[92] These values eschew the narcissism of Louis XIV's authority and mirrored the education he received from Fénelon as a young prince. Under his grandfather the state had been shaped for the king's interests, especially his attraction to war, which had proved to be very wasteful and damaging for the nation.[93] Following again in the footsteps of Fénelon, Bourgogne's first actions as king would be to alleviate the suffering of his people through the modification of the state, particularly its dire financial abuses. To cleanse government of its imperfections and mismanagement, France would be divided into twelve provinces each containing its own estate comprising members from the three orders. The provincial estates were to filter information to the Estates-General that would meet every four years and contain a limited number of members from the provincial estates. The purpose of this administrative network was to collect and filter information on the whole kingdom back to the king while acting in an advisory capacity. Decisions taken centrally would then return to the provincial estates through the deputies that had taken part in the Estates-General, a process aided by a general audit of the state every five years.[94] The *parlements* and other superior courts would both be employed in this process, although there was an emphasis on the need to reform the courts (justice) and to reduce the excessive size of the *parlement de Paris*. Saint-Simon saw a need to break the factions that dominated the *parlement de Paris*, which would be assisted by creating two new *parlements* in Moulins and Poitiers.[95]

Overall, the *Projets* exhibited a desire to trim the government bureaucracy which had plagued Louis XIV's reign, propounding a streamlined government that would free up much needed revenue. Juxtaposed with an immediate introduction of free trade there would be a reduction of taxation levies to ease the burden on the people. It was the Dauphin's priority to address the debts accumulated over Louis's seventy-two-year reign. In order to achieve this, the Estates-General would be called to deliberate how to address the fiscal difficulties, and whether to raise taxes or declare a state bankruptcy.[96] Through a reorganisation of government its ancient apparatus would be rejuvenated, giving France a wider structure of administration. Louis XIV had limited the number of people he relied upon at the top of government to a small group of approximately five men. In the opinion of Saint-Simon and Bourgogne this was not good for France, as a king had to depend on a broader range of opinion when making policy, while also using more officials to share the workload of state. This burden would be lightened by the introduction of seven main councils – of the Church, of foreign affairs, of war, of the marine, of finances, of dispatches, and of order – plus a number of subsidiary councils.[97] These councils led by, and filled with, members of the *épée*, would help to reinvigorate France by addressing its disorders and restoring 'order, decency, honour' and dignity back to a kingdom.[98] Crucially, the king would remain firmly in command of the state. He would control the finances, make all of the important decisions aided by the *conseil d'état* plus a few chosen ministers. Bourgogne's modified aristocrat-led government would be more inclusive than his grandfather's, but its ultimate function was to deliver a detailed picture of the kingdom upon which he could act on the people's behalf.[99]

Bourgogne and Saint-Simon's restructuring of France therefore differed from Fénelon's reform plans in its scope and intent. As a concept the two sets of ideas have much in common. They both advocated the use of an aristocratic-led reform that relied upon the use of councils to decentralise government. This created a more accurate representation of France while trusting on a larger selection of administrators to relieve the burden of office in order to promote the public good. Yet for Fénelon there was a much stronger emphasis on the expansion of government to restrain the king's abuse of his subjects via excessive power. In Saint-Simon's *Projets* the councils were less ambitious in their objectives. There was a desire, presumably in Bourgogne, to retain the authority of his grandfather but to use the councils as an expedient for intelligence and the running of the administration.[100] Much of the *Projets* suggests a more realistic approach to reactivate the traditional apparatus of France than Fénelon's *Tables*. While both works reject Colbert's mercantilism in their advocacy of free trade to augment revenue, the *Projets* did not engage with the idea of abolishing luxury; in fact luxury was not mentioned. What can be inferred is that the engagement of a Board of Commerce that employed merchants from all the main commercial centres to assist domestic and foreign trade is that it would not have supported sumptuary laws on luxury goods.[101] Furthermore, the aspiration to expand the navy to increase commercial activity following a path set by the English and Dutch would also appear to undermine Fénelon's anti-luxury moral stance. Both states had profited greatly in terms of wealth and power from the development of their navies, which had benefited their trade in peace and the state in war.[102]

This highlights the other great absence in Bourgogne's reordered France, the cessation of war. While Louis XIV's excessive wars injured his finances and reputation of the nation, the main objective of the Council of War was to place the business of war into the hands of professionals.[103] As in other areas, the blame for Louis XIV's mismanagement of the state was laid at the feet of excessively powerful ministers who had deceived the king to further their own ambitions. In the case of Louvois, the *Projets* identified his ability to manipulate the king so that he could control the army and isolate the king for his own personal gain.[104] As a witness to this behaviour, Bourgogne placed less emphasis on the poor decisions of his grandfather than Fénelon, and more on the Machiavellian schemes of a limited number of ministers. Bourgogne and Saint-Simon viewed the reliance on a newer form of (*robe*) administrator as the general cause of France's ills. Conversely and perhaps more accurately, Fénelon saw a king who had not governed wisely and had damaged his kingdom as a result. Despite different end games, the solution for both groups' schemes within the Burgundy Circle was similar: the advancement of a range of councils filled with the aristocracy. This would return the *épée* to a more traditional inclusion in government before the grandiose wars, financial issues, and wider state problems experienced under Louis XIV.

At the heart of the division between these two arms of the Burgundy Circle there may have been two issues: one generational, the other relating to the potential proximity to power in the new reign. Fénelon, Chevreuse, and Beauvilliers were old men by the time that Bourgogne became Dauphin, and all died within a three-year period after the prince's death. Once their works are inspected beyond the general similarities for reform with the *Projets*, an air of conservatism and idealism emerges regarding the desire to eradicate luxury and war.[105] They rejected the modern commercial world that began to emerge during the seventeenth century, witnessing the rise of moneyed men and financial wealth. These concerns were avoided by Saint-Simon and Bourgogne who understood the necessity of generating wealth (beyond moral scruples) to sustain the state and advance its power. Aggressive war was not to be rejected either by Bourgogne, because war was part of a state's armoury if required by its ruler and people. The generational issue perhaps comes into being at this juncture. It has been claimed that Fénelon would have been Bourgogne's chief minister; however, this cannot be certain.[106] The Archbishop's banishment to Cambrai and utopian views on certain aspects of a modern state may have precluded him from that office. The *Tables* may well have influenced the prince's thought, but his own work with Saint-Simon shared little in its policy with Fénelon. As younger men of a similar age, figures such as Saint-Simon, Orléans, and others of that generation who were included in the *Régence* were far more likely to have been used in Bourgogne's government. Fénelon and the other men who tutored the prince may well have been ready to offer advice to him, but the *Projets* demonstrate that he did not necessarily listen to it. As a consequence, France would have marginally decentralised under Bourgogne but it would have remained more absolute in nature than Fénelon had hoped for.

The death of Bourgogne in 1712 ended the optimism of both groups within the Circle for the future of France under a new reforming king. Like Fénelon, Saint-Simon did not rest upon his laurels and once it became clear that his childhood friend the duc de Orléans (1674–1723) would become regent he immediately began to impress on him the necessity of following Bourgogne's designs. Saint-Simon, who had reconciled Bourgogne and Orléans just prior to the prince's death,[107] urged the Regent to move away from the use of ministers in favour of councils within his regency administration. Orléans bought into the idea according to Saint-Simon, and desired to make him the President of the Council of Finance. He declined the offer because of the invidious responsibility of overseeing French finances as it charted a course between the two evils of raising taxes or declaring a bankruptcy. Saint-Simon personally favoured a bankruptcy as he believed the people could not stand further financial hardship, likening it to the amputation of a sick man's leg in order for him to be well again.[108] Accepting a position in the Supreme Council during the *Régence* his optimism quickly faded. While he revelled in the subjugation of the *parlements*,[109] he was suspicious of John Law's schemes, and lost faith in Orléans shortly before his death when he had abandoned the polysynody in favour of making Cardinal Dubois prime minister.[110] This short-lived move – Dubois died swiftly after the appointment – and the abolition of the councils, revealed Orléans move towards a type of absolute government that accentuated his inadequacies as a ruler. Saddened by the abandonment of the plans for greater aristocratic inclusion and dismayed by Orléans poor comparison with Bourgogne, Saint-Simon withdrew from public life.[111] Under the regency of Orléans, France had swiftly embraced the form of monarchy shaped by Louis XIV.

While revisionists have rightfully concluded that absolutism did not technically exist in France (or elsewhere), in a psychological and theoretical sense contemporaries did consider Louis XIV to be an absolute monarch.[112] This was particularly true of the high nobility, who believed they had been excluded from the processes of power, marginalised particularly in their ability to aid the king in running the state. The impact of the sixteenth century followed by the Fronde, led Louis XIV to fashion a sovereignty that removed any potential threat to his authority. His desire not to share authority utilised contemporary strands of European absolute theory, notably Bodin but also the ideas of James I of England and Hobbes. British theory did therefore have an impact on French thought and its government. For within the republic-of-letters network, intellectual currents flowed between states and British and French theory interchanged: both regarding absolutism and contractualism. Problematically from the 1680s, Louis XIV's form of sovereignty caused great difficulties for the state and the apparatus of government limited by recent alterations. Juxtaposed with the king's personal desire for *gloire* through aggrandisement and military (and economic) conquest, the French economy had become grossly inefficient. So by the end of Louis's reign, France not only faced political uncertainty but also financial disaster. Such issues were to be tackled by Bourgogne, who would have maintained a similar form of monarchy to his grandfather but widened it beyond a limited group of advisers to invigorate government and alleviate French suffering. Bourgogne's premature demise meant the *Régence* that followed the king's death was a time of great insecurity. Yet it was also a period of optimism regarding potential reform. While this sanguinity was eventually disappointed by Orléans's embrace of Louis XIV's sovereignty, the hope of change seen in Fénelon and others prompted a number of theorists to explore new paths for French monarchical reform.

Notes

1   E. Carcassone, *Montesquieu et le Problème de la constitution française au XVIIIe siècle* (Geneva, 1970), 61–3.

2   Louis XIV, *Mémoires for the Instruction of the Dauphin*, trans. Paul Sonnino (New York, 1970), 23–6. The *Mémoires* were written for Louis the Grand Dauphin, and Paul W. Fox has claimed that the work was influenced by James VI of Scotland's *Basilikon Doron* (Edinburgh, 1599), written for his heir Henry, the Duke of Rothesay. Both works comprise an interesting intervention into the 'mirror-for-princes' genre, as they were written by kings for princes. See Fox, 'Louis XIV and the Theories of Absolutism', *The Canadian Journal of Economic and Political Science*, 26, 1 (Feb. 1960), pp. 128–42.

3   Andrew Lossky, 'The Intellectual Development of Louis XIV from 1661 to 1715', *Louis XIV and Absolutism*, ed. Ragnhild Hatton (London, 1976), 107–9. For a parallel with Thomas Hobbes's thought, see *Leviathan*, ed. Richard Tuck (Cambridge, 1999), I, xi (70).

4   *Ibid.*, 244–5.

5   *Ibid.*, 63–8.

6   *Ibid.*, 144.

7   David Parker, *The Making of French Absolutism* (London, 1983), 24.

8   See Roland Mousnier, 'The Exponents and Critics of Absolutism', *The New Cambridge Modern History Vol. IV: The Decline of Spain and the Thirty Years War 1609–1648/59*, ed. J.P. Cooper (Cambridge, 1970), 121; Mousnier, 'The Development of Monarchical Institutions and Society in France', *Louis XIV and Absolutism*, ed. Hatton, 38–44; Victor-L. Tapié, *La France de Louis XIII et de Richelieu* (Paris, 1967); Parker, *Making of French Absolutism*, 81; Yves-Marie Bercé, *The Birth of Absolutism: A History of France, 1598–1661*, trans. Richard Rex (Basingstoke, 1992), 53.

9   See Claude de Seyssel, *The Monarchy of France*, ed. Donald R. Kelley and trans. J.H. Hexter (Yale, 1981), 51, 57–8; Jean Bodin, *Les six livres de la République*, ed. Gérard Mairet (Paris, 1993), I, viii (74–6).

10   Quentin Skinner, *The Foundations of Modern Political Thought. Volume II: The Age of Reformation* (Cambridge, 1978), 241–54.

11   See François Hotman: *Franco-Gallia: Or, an Account of the Ancient Free State of France, and Most other Parts of Europe, before the Loss of Their Liberties* (London, 1711), 6, 31, 65, 77–8; *Vindiciae contra tyrannos: Constitutionalism and Resistance in the Sixteenth Century: Three Treatises by Hotman, Beza and Mornay*, trans. J.H. Franklin (London, 1969).

12   Niccolò Machiavelli, *The Discourses*, trans. Leslie J. Walker, S.J., ed. Bernard Crick (London,

1983), I, 11 (141–2); Machiavelli separated the state from the prince by pointing to its perpetual institution beyond particular rulers. See Julian H. Franklin, *Jean Bodin and the Rise of Absolutist Theory* (Cambridge, 1973), 49.

13 See Quentin Skinner, *The Foundations of Modern Political Thought. Volume II: The Age of Reformation*, 349–58; Roland Mousnier, *Les institutions de la France sous la monarchie absolue 1589–1789: Société et Etat* (Paris, 1974), 499–500.

14 Louis XIV, *Mémoires*, 42. Paul W. Fox has stated that Louis's view of himself in the *Mémoires* as 'the universal proprietor of all property' and an emphasis on 'personal rule' separated him from all other French kings and exposed him as an 'autocrat' (tyrant). See Fox, 'Louis XIV and the Theories of Absolutism', 141–2.

15 Louis XIV, *Mémoires*, 154–5.

16 See Bodin, *Les six livres de la République*, I, viii and x; Hobbes, *Leviathan*, Books xvi, xvii, and xx. For a discussion on the influence of absolutist theory on Louis XIV's reign, see J.H. Burns, 'The Idea of Absolutism', *Absolutism in Seventeenth Century Europe*, ed. John Miller (London, 1993), 21.

17 Louis XIV, *Mémoires*, 82.

18 J.H. Shennan, *Philippe, Duke of Orléans. Regent of France 1715–1723* (London, 1979), 33.

19 *Ibid.*

20 Sturdy, *Louis XIV*, 44–5.

21 Louis XIV, *Mémoires*, 82.

22 *Ibid.*, 35.

23 See John A. Lynn, *The Wars of Louis XIV* (Harlow, 1999), 19; Colin Jones, *The Great Nation: France from Louis XV to Napoleon* (London, 2002), 11, 13–17.

24 See William Beik, *Absolutism and Society in Seventeenth-Century France: State Power and Provincial Aristocracy in Languedoc* (Cambridge, 1985), 31–3; Roger Mettam, 'The French Nobility, 1610–1715', *The European Nobilities in the Seventeenth and Eighteenth Centuries. Volume I: Western Europe*, ed. H.M. Scott (London, 1995), 127; Julian Swann, *Provincial Power and Absolute Monarchy: The Estates General of Burgundy, 1661–1790* (Cambridge, 2003), 9.

25 Parker, *Making of French Absolutism*, 138.

26 See Roger Mettam, *Power and Faction in Louis XIV's France* (Oxford, 1988), 36; Peter Robert Campbell, *The Ancien Régime in France* (Oxford, 1988), 54–5, 65; Albert N. Hamscher, 'Parlements and Litigants at the King's Councils during the Personal Rule of Louis XIV: The Example of Cassation', *Society and Institutions in Early Modern France*, ed. Mark P. Holt (Atlanta, 1991), 190; Emmanuel Le Roy Ladurie, *The Ancien Régime: A History of France 1610–1774*, trans. Mark Greengrass (Oxford, 1996), 146–51, 271–2; William Beik, *Louis XIV and Absolutism: A Brief Study with Documents* (Boston, 2000), 3–4.

27 Louis XIV, *Mémoires*, 40–3.

28 *Ibid.*, 137.

29 See Richard Bonney, *Political Change in France under Richelieu and Mazarin 1624–1661* (Oxford, 1978), 420; David J. Sturdy, *Louis XIV* (Basingstoke, 1998), 43.

30 Louis XIV, *Mémoires*, 130–1.

31 *Ibid.*, 196–7.

32 John J. Hurt, *Louis XIV and the Parlements: The Assertion of Royal Authority* (Manchester, 2002), 196.

33 Beik, *Absolutism and Society in Seventeenth-Century France*, 336–7; M-L. Legay, *Les états provinciaux dans le construction de l'état modern* (Geneva, 2001).

34 Roger Mettam, *Power and Faction in Louis XIV's France* 22, 44, 52–3, 203; Nicholas Henshall, *The Myth of Absolutism: Change and Continuity in Early Modern European Monarchy* (London, 1992), 51–2, 85; Mettam, 'French Nobility, 1610–1715', 127, 141. For a counter-position, see Guy Chaussinand-Nogaret, *The French Nobility in the Eighteenth Century: From Feudalism to Enlightenment*, trans. William Doyle (Cambridge, 1985), 12–13; Sharon Kettering, *Patrons, Brokers, and Clients in Seventeenth-Century France* (Oxford, 1986), 223, 232.

35 See Albert N. Hamscher, *The Parlement of Paris: After the Fronde 1653–1673* (London, 1976), 202; Mettam, *Power and Faction*, 15; Campbell, *The Ancien Régime in France*, 58; J. Russell Major,

From Renaissance Monarchy to Absolute Monarchy: French Kings, Nobles and Estates (Baltimore, 1994), xxi; Beik, *Louis XIV and Absolutism*, 219.

36 See Chapters 1 and 2.

37 In reference to Bossuet's defence of Louis XIV's rule, Raymond Scmittlein branded Bossuet 'a serf dazzled by his sovereign' who desired 'to legitimise the monstrous egoism and the indecent pride of Louis XIV' ('Introduction', *Politics Drawn from Holy Scripture*, ed. Patrick Riley (Cambridge, 1989), lxxiii).

38 The *Discours* was written in 1679 and published three years later. The first six books of the *Politique* were completed in the 1670s and the last four between 1700 and 1704 (Johann P. Sommerville, 'Early Modern Absolutism in Practice and Theory', *Monarchism and Absolutism in Early Modern Europe*, eds Cesare Cuttica and Glenn Burgess (London, 2012), 127).

39 Bossuet, *Discours sur l'Histoire Universelle*, Œuvres de Bossuet, ed. abbé B. Velat and Yvonne Champailler (Paris, 1961), 1015–16.

40 *Ibid.*, 667.

41 Bossuet, *Politique tirée des paroles de l'Écriture sainte*, ed. Jacques Le Brun (Geneva, 1967), book I, Article ii, 3 (p. 6).

42 *Ibid.*, I, i, 6 (10).

43 *Ibid.*, I, i, 5 (9).

44 *Ibid.*, I, ii, 3 (15–16). Bossuet viewed Cicero's application of a divine ordinance as common to all nations, and he appropriated Cicero's discussion of the 'love of one's country' (*caritas patriae*) from *De Officiis*, III, xxvii, 100 and *De legibus*, I, xv, 43.

45 *Politique*, I, iii, 2 (18). In the 'Introduction' to *Politics drawn from Holy Scripture* (*Politique*), Riley uses the term 'limited Hobbesianism' to show the prospective inspiration of Hobbes on Bossuet's view of the state of nature; see (lxii–lxiii). For a discussion of this influence, see S. Skalweit, 'Political Thought', *The New Cambridge Modern History Vol. IV: The Ascendancy of France 1648–88*, ed. F.L. Carsten (Cambridge, 1961), 100; J.P. Sommerville, 'Absolutism and Royalism', *Cambridge History of Political Thought Vol. III: The Cambridge History of Political Thought 1450–1700*, eds J.H. Burns and Mark Goldie (Cambridge, 1991), 363; Noel Malcolm, *Aspects of Hobbes* (Oxford, 2004), 506–7; Patrick Riley 'Social Contract Theory and Its Critics', *The Cambridge History of Political Thought Vol. IV: The Cambridge History of Eighteenth-Century Political Thought*, eds Mark Goldie and Robert Wokler (Cambridge, 2006), 354. Mark Hulliung has claimed that Bossuet's application of Hobbism brought a modernism through its personification of the state as person to his largely traditional descending view of sovereignty ('Patriarchalism and Its Early Enemies', *Political Theory*, 2, 4 (Nov. 1974), pp. 410–19 (412)).

46 *Politique*, I, ii, 6 (22).

47 Hobbes, *Leviathan*, xviii (120–1).

48 Riley, 'Introduction', *Politics drawn from Holy Scripture*, lix. For Riley this reveals Bossuet's appreciation of Hobbes's writing, although not his conclusions. Johann P. Sommerville argues that Bossuet's application of the Book of Samuel was part of a broader European dialogue concerning absolute sovereignty, both for and against ('Political Ideas in the Early Seventeenth Century: Revisionism and the Case of Absolutism', *Journal of British Studies*, 35, 2 (Apr. 1996), pp. 168–94 (178, 180–1, 190)).

49 Bossuet, *Politique*, II, i, 3 (46). It should be further noted that Bossuet's government did not follow Filmer's Adamite view of kingship. In Bossuet's opinion, kingship emerged as natural leaders arose within the family unit seizing the political authority granted to mankind, while Filmer saw kingship as a personal inheritance from God via Adam (*Patriarcha*, ed. Johann P. Sommerville (Cambridge, 1991), I, ii (6–10)). James Daly discounts any influence on Bossuet from Filmer (*Sir Robert Filmer and English Political Thought* (London, 1979), 159). See Chapter 1 in this book.

50 Bossuet, *Politique*, I, iv, 2 (23): 'les choses divines et humaines, publiques et particulières'.

51 *Ibid.*, III, ii, 3 (69). Bossuet cites Tertullian's belief (*Apology*, ch. 32) that the king was God's chosen governor.

52 Bossuet, *Politique*, III, iii, 8–14 (80–90).

53 *Ibid.*, IV, I, 9 (105).

54 *Ibid.*, IV, I, 8 (104).

55 *Ibid.*, VIII, ii, 1–4 (291–7). On the distinction between French absolute and arbitrary sovereign power, see Paul W. Fox, 'Louis XIV and the Theories of Absolutism and Divine Right', 134–5; Roland Mousnier, 'The Exponents and Critics of Absolutism', *The New Cambridge Modern History Vol. IV: The Decline of Spain and the Thirty Years War 1609–48/59*, ed. J.P. Cooper (Cambridge, 1970), 119–21; Cesare Cuttica, 'A Thing or Two about Absolutism and Its Historiography', *History of European Ideas*, 39, 2 (2013), pp. 287–300 (294–6).

56 *Politique*, V, iv, 1 (177–78).

57 *Ibid.*, V, i, 1 (116): '[t]ant d'humeurs, tant d'intérêts, tant d'artifices, tant de passions'.

58 *Ibid.*, VI, ii, 1 (192–3).

59 *Ibid.*, VI, ii, 4 (196).

60 Bossuet, *Discours*, 991–2.

61 *Ibid.*, 1012–13, 1022. See J.G.A. Pocock, *Barbarism and Religion Volume Three: The First Decline and Fall*, 5 vols (Cambridge, 1999–), 328–31.

62 Bossuet, *Discours* 948–52.

63 Bossuet, *Politique*, VII, vi, 4 (275–6); VIII, ii, 1 (291–3). On Bossuet's moral absolutism, see Roger Mettam, 'France', *Absolutism in Seventeenth Century Europe*, 50; Keohane, *Philosophy and the State*, 260; for Bossuet's preconceived notions of history and providence, see J.P Sommerville, 'Absolutism and Royalism', 352.

64 Bossuet, *l'Histoire Universelle*, 822–3, 948–9.

65 Bossuet, *Politique*, VII, ii, 4 (217–18).

66 Louis XIV, *Mémoires*, 54–7.

67 See Andrew Lossky, 'The General European Crisis of the 1680s', *European History Quarterly*, 10 (1980), 177, 195–6; K.H.D. Haley, 'The Dutch, the Invasion of England, and the Alliance of 1689', *The Revolution of 1688–89: Changing Perspectives*, ed. Lois G. Schwoerer (Cambridge, 1992), 25; J.F. Bosher, 'The Franco-Catholic Danger, 1660–1715', *History*, 79, 255 (Feb. 1994), pp. 5–30.

68 Jones, *Great Nation*, 34–5.

69 Louis XIV, *Mémoires*, 216, 231–2, 260.

70 *Ibid.*, 151–2. For the cultivation of Louis XIV's image, see Peter Burke, *The Fabrication of Louis XIV* (Yale, 1992), 2, 5, 6–7, 152, 158 .

71 See Bossuet, *Politique*, X, I, 1 (379–81) on luxury; and IX, I, 1–5 (317–19) on war.

72 Bossuet, *Discours*, 999–1002.

73 Duc de Saint-Simon, *The Memoirs of the Duke of Saint-Simon on the Reign of Louis XIV and the Regency*, 4 vols in 2, trans. Bayle St. John (New York, 1936), III, 16 (217–18), 21 (224).

74 In the opinion of Saint-Simon and many subsequent historians, the king was famously manipulated by his unofficial second wife Madame de Maintenon. Saint-Simon was unable to gain access to her cabal and therefore lacked influence with the king (Charlotte Haldane, *Madame de Maintenon: Uncrowned Queen of France* (London, 1970), 198).

75 Saint-Simon, II, 1 (6).

76 *Ibid.*, II, 8 (95–7). Saint-Simon disdainfully describes an incident in which the king was suddenly struck by scruples concerning the financial burden of the war. After consulting with the Sorbonne, who informed the king that his subjects' wealth was his, his conscience over the hardship of the war immediately cleared (II, 27).

77 Saint-Simon, II, 8 (95–7).

78 Of the Circle members, only Fénelon's pedagogical works were published during his lifetime and a number of Saint-Pierre's *Projets* were published outside of France. The remainder of the works remained secret, probably as they were active plans to reform France at the end of Louis XIV's life and they did not wish to cause offence to the king or suffer punishment. As will be discussed in this and the following chapter, there were essentially three groups within the Circle: Bourgogne and Saint-Simon; Fénelon and Bourgogne's other early educators, and a periphery, which included Saint-Pierre.

79 [Vauban], *Projet d'une Dixme Royale* ([Paris], 1707), 2.

80 *Ibid.*, 9.

81 *Ibid.*, 203.
82 *Ibid.*, 12–15.
83 *Ibid.*, 21–3.
84 *Ibid.*, 106–7.
85 *Ibid.*, 198.
86 Keohane, *Philosophy and the State*, 331.
87 Saint-Simon, III, 1 (6–11).
88 *Ibid.*, II, 15 (194–96).
89 See Roland Mousnier, *The Institutions of France under the Absolute Monarchy 1589–1789: Society and the State*, trans. Brian Pearce (Chicago, 1979), 17–19; Emanuel Le Roy Ladurie, *Saint-Simon ou le système de la Cour* (Paris, 1997), 183–4. Ladurie points to three cabals at court: one around the Dauphin, one around Bourgogne, and one around the king, which centred on Madame de Maintenon. The Burgundy Circle was known as the 'Minister's Cabal', because of its connection to the Colbert family, as well as including a number of ministers such as the controller general Desmartes (215–18).
90 Saint-Simon, III, 1 (6–11).
91 *Ibid.*, III, 13 (192–3).
92 Duc de Saint-Simon, *Projets de Gouvernement du Duc de Bourgogne Dauphin*, ed. M.P. Mesnard (Paris, 1860), 2.
93 *Ibid.*, 4.
94 *Ibid.*, 5–9.
95 *Ibid.*, 12.
96 *Ibid.*, 13–14.
97 *Ibid.*, 16.
98 *Ibid.*, 55–6.
99 *Ibid.*, 9–10.
100 *Ibid.*, 64.
101 *Ibid.*, 49–50.
102 *Ibid.*, 98–9.
103 *Ibid.*, 44.
104 *Ibid.*, 36–9.
105 Ladurie, *Saint-Simon ou le système de la Cour*, 414–15.
106 Sanford B. Kanter, 'Archbishop Fénelon's Political Activity: The Focal Point of Power in Dynasticism', *French Historical Studies*, 4, 3 (spring 1966), pp. 320–34 (329, 332).
107 Saint-Simon describes the death of Bourgogne, his wife and their eldest some in the *Mémoires* (III, 3). He also dismisses the notion that Orléans had poisoned them, an accusation made possible by Saint-Simon's forged reconciliation between the two men.
108 Saint-Simon, III, 13 (192).
109 *Ibid.*, IV, 11 (139–41).
110 *Ibid.*, IV, 27 (327).
111 *Ibid.*, IV, 31 (393).
112 See the end of the following chapter for a more comprehensive conclusion for the two chapters.

5

Confronting the legacy of Louis XIV: government reform and Britain

Despite his premature death, men attached to the Circle strove to encourage their reforming projects during the *Régence* (1715–23), notably the abbé de Saint-Pierre. Inspired by Fénelon and others, Saint-Pierre endeavoured to rescue the expansion of government through polysynody as the *Régence* moved back towards Louis XIV's sovereignty. This tenet of the Burgundy Circle met with mixed success as the polysynody quickly disappeared, although the innovation impacted on a new wave of political theorists. In this chapter the stultification of the Circle's plans will be charted, revealing France's explicit pursuit of absolutism after 1718. The emergence of new notions regarding monarchical government in Britain, however, began to have an impact from the 1720s, markedly in the early works of Montesquieu and Voltaire. Following the previous chapter, this chapter will outline the development of ideas concerning the French monarchy and the influence that British politics and theory had on these significant philosophies.

The abbé de Saint-Pierre's *Perpetual Peace* and *Polysynody*

Another member of the Burgundy Circle who became disillusioned with the lost promise of Orléans's rule during the *Régence* was the abbé Charles-Irénée Castel de Saint-Pierre (1658–1743). Influenced by Descartes, Saint-Pierre spent the years between 1680 and 1700 associating with scientists at the *Académie des Sciences*, adapting the Cartesian method of doubt to his own projects. During this period he lived in a household of 'ideas' with the renowned writer Bernard Le Bouyer de Fontenelle (1657–1757), the mathematician Pierre Varignon (1654–1722), plus the historian the abbé Vertot (1655–1735).[1] Saint-Pierre's interest in government and economics began in the early 1690s. He was strongly inspired by both Boisguilbert and Vauban fostering a belief in utility, free trade, and peace. To gain further experience he attended the *conseil dépêches* from 1702, and by 1708 he was consulted by Louis XIV in the *conseil d'état*.[2] This background provided him with a strong appreciation of the apparatus of state. Guided by Fénelon, he incorporated a number of works (including *Télémaque*) into his ideas on perpetual peace and the polysynody, which advocated a move away from Louis XIV's absolutism. Over the next five decades Saint-Pierre wrote prodigiously, forming projects to promote the increase of public happiness and the effectiveness of government. His views were equally mocked and respected, but his work went on to motivate Voltaire, Jeremy Bentham, Jean-Jacques Rousseau, and Immanuel Kant.[3] But his aggressive campaign for the worth of government councils and attack on Louis XIV's reign in his *Discours sur la Polysnodie* (1718) affronted Orléans, and he was expelled from the *Académie française* in that year.

Saint-Pierre's most celebrated work was the *Projet pour rendre la paix perpétuelle en Europe* (1712).[4] It was born of the public disaffection with the reign of Louis XIV and economic concerns for France from 1710 due to the protracted war. Saint-Pierre claimed that the incentive for the work was the extreme misery of the people as well as a desire to terminate future conflicts without war, while achieving lasting stability.[5] This belief in peace had been formed over a period of twenty years, particularly taking shape during the War of the Spanish Succession.[6] His scientific approach developed into a form of proto-utilitarianism which aimed to provide happiness for the people by maximising the public good. Public utility would be created through reason and the restraint of the self-interested passions, leading to happiness in the people.[7] France's involvement in numerous wars under Louis XIV had produced wretchedness for many people across Europe, causing destruction and heavy taxation levied to pay for war. Saint-Pierre's resolution was to form a perpetual peace through a union based on the duc de Sully's *Grand Dessein* of Henri IV.[8] The *Grand Dessein* purported to reflect Henri IV's plans to create a European union that would counteract the aggrandising ambitions of the Habsburgs at the beginning of the seventeenth century.[9] To Saint-Pierre's mind, Henri IV had grasped that the disparity of power between sovereigns was the cause of war. So if a confederation could be maintained within a single European republic, war could be terminated.

A European union was necessary because of the abject failure in attempting to maintain a balance between the leading houses of Europe, specifically the Houses of France and Austria. Saint-Pierre rejected Fénelon's attempt to craft a similar peace union through the reliance upon a balance of power between the European states. For the abbé, such a balance had been repeatedly proven not to work, as was evident from the historical behaviour of the two royal houses. Sovereigns by their nature sought more power via territorial aggrandisement, so the continual contravention of truces by princes who strived to further their ambitions at the slightest opportunity by engaging in war could only be terminated by a prohibitive confederacy.[10] Hobbes's influence on Saint-Pierre has been documented, and his *Projet* could be seen as an international Leviathan, perceiving as he did the cause of aggression between states to derive from fear and competition.[11] Consequently, large empires overextended their power and this led to collapse and ruination, as was the case with the Roman Empire. This could either be resolved through war (state of war) or through law. Treaties failed as they were not subject to a higher authority and security was lost. The answer for Saint-Pierre was to harness law by tying all states to a Leviathan-like peace union in which they were protected, possessed rights, and could enjoy prosperity. Saint-Pierre spurned the idea of a universal monarchy potentially led by France, due to its natural power and current strength as doomed to failure. He believed that only a cooperative union would provide a cessation to Europe's obsession with war. A union that would actually apply Henri IV's restriction of power by neutralising French aggrandisement, while still requiring active French participation for its success after its ambitions and boundaries had been voluntarily checked.

Saint-Pierre's model for success was based on an erroneous under-standing of the Germanic League, taken from Sully, which offered an example of a cooperative state union.[12] He felt it was conceivable to create a European union that ensured the independence of each state while effectively warranting peace.[13] As with Sully's plan, a permanent Senate would be established where all states would submit to the treaty of union. Utrecht was selected by Saint-Pierre for the Senate. Holland was viewed to be tolerant and peaceable, not monar-chical (thus assuaging fears of aggrandisement), a commercial centre, and its Northern climate would be conducive to hard work.[14] States would contribute to the running of the Senate in accordance with their size, and the number of seats within the Senate would be apportioned likewise. Laws would be estab-lished against war that would maintain peace and harmonise Europe through its cooperative confederacy. Territorial boundaries would be set with no possibility of further aggrandisement within Europe to prevent conflict. Finally, Saint-Pierre felt that it would take several generations for the peace union's efficacy to be fully appreciated. For royalty would only abandon aspirations of territorial expansion and the reliance upon war in disputes after several generations. The reimbursements from war's termination and protection of the king's internal position, matched by a fear that no participation in a European union would lead to ostracism for that state, would guarantee its success.

Saint-Pierre's desire for 'perpetual peace' was not only governed by a neces-sity for a cessation to constant European war. He realised that if a state was not preoccupied with war its taxation and the time it expended on fighting could be more productively spent. Not only could the arts and sciences be greatly enhanced, but commerce would flourish. This could be exploited as the greatest vehicle to harness the energies of the people for enriching the state.[15] Saint-Pierre undermined Louis XIV's policy of war, stating that it had manifestly detracted from French trade, especially foreign trade, which accounted for one-third of the total income of France. He followed (his friend) Pierre Nicole, Boisguilbert, and Fénelon in rejecting the ideas of Montchrétien and Colbert's mercantilism.[16] War provided an obvious barrier to trade, and a further consequence was a lack of future trust between states which effected state interaction. Crucially, war pulled subjects away from commerce and reduced the capacity for agriculture and trade while depleting the number of subjects within a kingdom. Saint-Pierre wanted the state to move away from the mercantile notion that France was required by other states as the breadbasket of Europe, supreme as a producer of goods and able to exist through autarchy. He considered this confidence to be fallacious and damaging, trusting that France would be considerably supplemented through foreign trade.[17] Saint-Pierre asseverated the benefits of trade to champion a confederacy that would provoke much greater prosperity through commerce, and which offered utility to both the state and the public (good).[18]

In an approach redolent of Nicholas Barbon's *A Discourse on Trade* (1690) and subsequently Bernard Mandeville's *Fable of the Bees* (1714), Saint-Pierre embraced this belief that free trade would engender much greater profit for the state. Understanding how the growing importance of commercial ventures could be to the expansion of the eighteenth-century state,[19] an enterprise that could be further maximised by permitting the pursuit of luxury. This view appreciated the potential profits enjoyed by the Dutch and English,[20] driven by a public appetite for superfluous goods regardless of the moral questions thrown up by their pursuit. A European union would be able to guarantee free trade between its states. In turn, encouraging and increasing commerce while enriching subjects financially and subsequently the sovereign through taxation.[21] The overall benefit to the Union and its constituent partners was immeasurable. Saint-Pierre was left to lament the failure of the plan under Henri IV as he believed Europe could have been four times richer in his own time.[22] In accepting luxury as a driving force for commercial reform, Saint-Pierre followed one of the two predominant paths that came to direct eighteenth-century European thought on political economy. He shunned Fénelon's conservative agrarian-based commercial activity which later preoccupied the Physiocrats. Instead he adopted a position that welcomed the possible advantage to society of the wealth created by luxury, which was to be later comprehended by Hume and Smith.[23] Saint-Pierre's early eighteenth-century scientific vision contained in numerous *Projets* grasped the universal value of peace to commercial endeavour and human association. This has led to his portrayal as a precursor of utilitarianism,[24] internationalism, and an early precursor of free trade.

Saint-Pierre applied this scientific approach to his promotion of government councils during the *Régence* in the *Discours sur la Polysynodie*. Orléans had introduced the polysynody within the first few weeks of his regency (16 September

1715).The formation of the polysynody was used by Orléans to win over the *parlements* when his position was questioned by the will of Louis XIV. The deceased king had stipulated that the regent's authority and the care of the young Louis XV should be mitigated by a number of protectors; notably Louis XIV's legitimised bastard the duc de Maine (1670–1736) who was charged with the king's education. Orléans managed to void the will quickly by appealing to the *parlement* of Paris who declared it illegal. As an act of reciprocity he encouraged the appearance of reinstituting the ancient branches of government and provided the *parlements* with more influence, and created the polysynody. This appeared to shadow the plans created by Fénelon, Saint-Simon and the Burgundy Circle for a France under Bourgogne: all of whom were associated with Orléans. However, the polysynody did not introduce any modifications to Louis XIV's system, and it is questionable whether the conciliar system diminished or assisted the regent's authority.[25] While the regent agreed to abide by the majority verdict of the regency council, this was not much of an encumbrance as those on the council were dependent upon him for their positions and were inclined to his will. Orléans also retained many of the key offices and privileges of his position, and many of the older councils endured. Personnel did change, but the seven new specialised councils of the polysynody – foreign affairs, war, marine (which include the administration of the colonies), finance, the interior, religion, and commerce – did not form part of the official royal council. They did not possess the authority to issue decrees and the regent was not present at their meetings, undermining their significance. Essentially the polysynody was used to prepare material and advice for the regency council.[26] By 1718 Orléans embraced the absolute authority permitted as the king's regent became unassailable and the polysynody fell into disuse.

This lost opportunity of the polysynody inspired Saint-Pierre to publish his work in an attempt to salvage the concept. He claimed that his desire to reform France through the expansion of government had existed for some time. Publication of his project had been deferred due to fears concerning the reaction of Louis XIV and state censors.[27] Saint-Pierre believed that a polysynody was essential to remove the threat of the realm returning to the domination of one or two key ministers. In such circumstances a single '*Grand visir*' (Richelieu) or two '*Demi-visirs*' (Colbert and Louvois) controlled the king for their own ends and power. This had been demonstrated during the reign of Louis XIV. His poor upbringing and aversion to the details of government had led to the outlandish behaviour of Louvois who had directed France towards excessive wars.[28] To prevent such behaviour, government must be enlarged so that it became more inclusive while employing the unused nobility to head the ministry.

What is noteworthy about Saint-Pierre's version of the polysynody is its greater ambition than either Fénelon or Saint-Simon's projects. While the system would utilise the external ranking system of the *robe* nobility, membership of the polysynody would be dependent upon merit and industry, so would therefore be meritocratic and open. This more inclusive organisation would subsume private interest as the councils and administrators of state were encouraged to work together for the public good.[29] The reliance on talent would generate a Mandevillian environment of emulation and competition. As posts were circulated within the system, competition between departments and individuals would increase productivity and standards as the ministers monitored their own work and that of others. Circulation of positions would familiarise ministers and administrators with all aspects of government including the provinces of the kingdom as they were moved around.[30] Saint-Pierre's aim was to drive up the efficiency, knowledge, and professionalism of the government to elevate the public good which had been absent under Louis XIV. In developing Fénelon's idea of the use of councils, Saint-Pierre argued that the government should elect its own representative or president every three years. The president, or head of the council, would evolve from the regency council after the king's minority and manage the business of administration for him, while directed by the king.[31] The enhancement of the polysynody would protect the king from usurpation or revolution, as the most politically talented members of the nobility or wider populace were engaged within the system.[32] The distraction of the role and rewards it would bring for the individual within the polysynody would remove ideas of resistance to the king, and foster an ethos of service to the public good.

It has been asserted that Saint-Pierre's two works were an early attempt to engender enlightened despotism in France several decades before such rulers governed continental Europe.[33] According to this view Saint-Pierre preferred 'consultative despotism' to a polity limited by reason and administrators. His *Polysynodie* did not want to expand government along the traditional lines current within the Burgundy Circle; rather, the objective was to depersonalise the absolute monarch by focusing on the machine and primacy of law. Saint-Pierre rejected Boulainvilliers's belief in a 'group of seigneurs' delivering reform to France, although he did promote an 'aristo-monarchie' through polysynody which would force a top-down revival of society.[34] This top-down revival of France was one of the key principles that held together what was in reality a Burgundy Circle that was a disparate group.[35] The other key principles were the expansion of government and the use of councils (polysynody).

Significantly, Saint-Pierre's vision of the polysynody undermined the sovereign authority of the king by effectively advocating a mixed form of government. Regardless of the benefits to the king (or Orléans), this new scheme not only greatly enlarged government it promoted its leadership under a president. Over time the king's power would necessarily have been eroded and divorced him (to an unknown extent) from the processes of administration. The members of the Burgundy Circle may not have believed in a British constitutionalism

model, yet both Fénelon and Saint-Pierre's views would have extended participation in government to a level that would have significantly undermined French
absolutism as a concept.[36] The notion that the Burgundy Circle did not wish to
assail the absolute system in which they operated only pertained to Saint-Simon.
In all probability, this would have been the form of administration enacted had
Bourgogne lived. The *Tables* of Fénelon went further. Fénelon realised that the
king was also responsible for the damaging policies of his state, not just his
ministers. The monarchy that existed under Louis XIV had to be overhauled
in order to mollify and restrain future kings for the public good. Saint-Pierre
went further still. His view was one that recognised the deficiencies of Louis
XIV's reign and applied a scientific methodology to reconfigure government
to promote utility and happiness through a quasi-modern state that predated
Emmanuel Sieyès.

Persia, Rome, and England in Montesquieu

The censure experienced by Saint-Pierre due to his guarded criticism of Louis
XIV's reign was shrewdly subverted by Charles de Secondat, Baron de Montesquieu's use of satire in the *Lettres persanes* (1721). Montesquieu (1689–1755)
knew Saint-Pierre, Bolingbroke, and Ramsay through his brief membership of
the *Club de l'Entresol*.[37] The *Lettres persanes* exploited satire as a means to critique
French society, applying a 'double optic of cultural relativism'. The epistolary
accounts of two Persian noblemen, Usbek and Rica, provided a long lens from
which to consider society, its mores, and government in a manner that was
'both problematic and amusing'. Montesquieu's criticisms of political life, Louis
XIV, the *Régence* and a corrupted culture were made safer under 'the pretext of
condemning Persian usages'.[38] Indeed Usbek's troublesome seraglio was itself a
conceit, which examined the idea of kingship and oriental despotism but was
in fact deliberating on French absolutism. The unsuccessful struggle by Usbek
(the king) to govern his wives (people) through fear via his eunuchs (ministers),
ultimately led to a loss of control over the seraglio (France). Absolute monarchy's
reliance on fear rather than love was a less successful method of government
than the institution of law and beneficent rule.[39] France required a new method
of administration to address the legacy of Louis XIV's reign and its problems
during the *Régence*.

The picture created of France in the *Lettres persanes* was often far from
flattering. Louis XIV's reign was depicted as paradoxical. He was a monarch of
greatness and France was wealthy and powerful; yet Louis was a deficient leader,
whose exaggerated trust in flatterers contradicted his power over them and
ability to command.[40] He was consumed by an obsession with glory and war,

which were paid for by the artificial manipulation of France's finances through venality.[41] The success of France had the appearance of artifice or display, when underneath the surface was a society riven by distrust and animosity. The three privileged orders – Church, *epée*, and *robe*[42] – despised one another, while the nobility were separated by extremes in wealth of whom the majority sat idle.[43] Rica discovers in his conversations with the French, that France had declined since its peak in the 1680s. During the 1680s it was possible for the favoured to become wealthier, and the Church had been satisfied by the Revocation of the Edict of Nantes.[44] Since that time France had lost its lustre.

Montesquieu's sardonic observations belied a condemnation of the damage sustained by France due to the religious intolerance exhibited under Louis XIV. In Montesquieu's opinion it was not a multiplicity of religions that led to war and internal division, it was intolerance that was dangerous. Intolerance was a violation of natural justice and eternal law, because states actually benefited from a multiplicity of religions through shared knowledge and skills.[45] Moreover, the ideological motivation of the Revocation and its effects had borne no fruit for the nation. It was not possible to make someone recant their religious convictions against their will (conscience), and Montesquieu desired to extinguish both state and religious prejudice.[46] Likewise, through the analogous Persian expulsion of the Armenians under Suleiman I (r. 1666–94), Usbek paralleled the politico-economic damage caused by the loss of the Huguenots. As had occurred with the Armenians, Louis XIV's desire to forge social and religious unity in France had led to the mass emigration of the Huguenots, many of whom were important merchants and artisans. The loss of Huguenot wealth and skills to Britain and the Dutch Republic injured the French economy and industry.[47] Persia's expulsion of the Armenians should have been viewed as a recent (historical) warning to France, as it brought down the Persian Empire.

The French political and economic difficulties revealed by Usbek and Rica afforded Montesquieu an opportunity to assess certain influential solutions to such negative practices. His parable of the Troglodytes provided an evaluation of Fénelon's virtuous kingship within the simple Fénelonian agrarian realm of Bétique. In the allegory the rapacious Troglodyte society had broken down into a state of nature due to its selfishness, corruption, and the loss of morality.[48] The ensuing war and sickness that occurred among them reflected a Hobbesian state of war, in which equity and justice were removed as government was annihilated by the self-interest of the people. The two remaining families appreciate that they must reject such Hobbesian passion-driven behaviour in order to survive. By ascending above their selfish individual needs, society can begin to flourish through cooperation and common interest. Choosing to live without the former domination of a king,[49] the Troglodytes thrived through simple living, industry, justice, the avoidance of luxury, and the development of virtue through religion.

Such an existence not only represented a Fénelonian frugality but also reflected a belief shared by the third Earl of Shaftesbury (1671–1713) that people retained an inherent moral sense of what was right and wrong.[50] Reason allowed the individual to discern that what benefited society profited them; public utility and community were preferable to egotistic vice.[51] The happiness and internal harmony of the Troglodytes led their curious neighbours to their shores in order to raid them. Despite their simplicity and the general avoidance of aggression, their military virtue expressed through the militia enabled a stout defence and protection of internal peace.[52] Over several generations, however, the expansion of the population and its growing sophistication as a society created a demand from the people for the election of a king regardless of their virtue, freedom, and communal way of life. As the king reluctantly received the crown he wept for the perceived reoccurrence of their past tribulations:

> O Troglodytes: your virtue is beginning to weigh you down: in your present state where you have no leader, you must be virtuous in spite of yourselves, otherwise you could not exist, and you would fall into your forefathers' misfortune. But this yoke is too hard, you prefer to be subjected to a prince, and to obey his laws which would be less rigid so you can acquire your wealth, and languish in a lax pleasure, and as long as you avoid falling into great crimes, you do not need virtue.[53]

Fénelon's appraisal of virtuous living and kingship was very significant to Montesquieu's early political works.[54] *Télémaque* did have an important impact on the political thought during the *Régence*. Indeed, not long after the success of the *Lettres persanes* the *Club de l'Entresol* frequently grappled with Fénelon's legacy during its weekly discussion of political topics and the works of its members.[55] Montesquieu's Troglodytes subverted Fénelon's civilisation through their rejection of a simpler virtuous existence in favour of kingship. Monarchy allowed the state to embrace its population increase and the capacity to generate greater wealth. All states eventually became corrupt in Montesquieu's opinion, law replaced virtue to enable riches and ambition while restraining morality and crime. He accepted Mandeville's conviction in the *Fable of the Bees* that a state could not be powerful, prosperous and industrious if it was blessed by a golden age of innocence and virtue.[56] Montesquieu further believed that civilisation and the arts had not enervated humanity but had actually allowed it to thrive. Despite the abundance of luxury goods and trades in Paris, Paris had continued to grow and enrich itself. Superfluities made kingdoms powerful and affluent because they created an exchange of services. This bound society together and crucially augmented the population, as it prospered under commercial activity, as had been the case with Rome.[57] Moreover, a strong population generated affluence and attracted foreigners to engage in trade to produce more wealth. A large population and a trade in superfluities reflected a sophisticated state which was designed to promote prosperity and the improved living standards of its people.

The proclivity for such affluence to flourish in republics like Switzerland and Holland was the result of equality among citizens. This frequently avoided the poverty and starvation found under the tyranny of absolute societies, as republics embraced a freedom that recommended commercial endeavour while absolute states stultified this enterprise through controls.[58] The solution for a thriving commercial culture was found in a republican concept of political economy as highlighted by Mandeville for example, rather than Fénelon's austerity. The introduction of kingship in Troglodyte society allowed the laws of a 'rational monarchy' to bear the heavy burden for the individual's behaviour in a modernising world. The 'language of the real world' revealed that the ideal of virtue was not compatible with a world that had begun to embrace ideas of wealth, justice, and liberty as defined by law rather than virtue.[59] While the end of this virtuous society was welcomed, Montesquieu did have faith in Fénelon's (French) aristocratic view of honour and duty; i.e. self-imposed limitations on a person's own power for the interests of the common good. This support of the public good meant that Montesquieu disapproved of John Law's promotion of self-interested financial speculation during the *Régence*.[60] The effects of this speculation had proved calamitous in the Mississippi Scheme of 1720, which saw the collapse of shares in the colony of Louisiana.[61] For Montesquieu, the entire episode had revealed the corrupted morals of the entire nation at all levels, and the ethical bankruptcy of the nation had witnessed an obsession with Mammon and greed.[62] The Mississippi Scheme's failure happened in the same year as the South Sea Bubble in Britain, and it revealed a concurrent attempt in both states to reconcile (independently) with the new commercial age. For Montesquieu, altruism was a form of political virtue that rose above the egotism accentuated by the Mississippi Scheme, and sacrificed individual consideration to the public good. This should be applied within monarchical societies to restrain both king and subjects alike. Montesquieu believed that Fénelon's *Télémaque* promulgated a realm more applicable to a 'small Greek city' rather than a large state (France).[63] A simple agrarian society devoid of luxury was not fitting for a large state like France. While the British looked to Parliament and the aristocracy to tackle these issues (as seen in *Cato's Letters*), the French continued to invest much hope in a powerful monarchy.

Yet the solution to this quandary did not lie in absolutism either, as unlimited authority in a king or his ministers was not conducive to good governance. Montesquieu therefore approved of the polysynody: where the harmful 'unlimited authority of the preceding ministers' had been divided to create 'six or seven councils' so that 'this ministry perhaps ruled France with more sense'. Unfortunately its 'duration was short', as was 'the good it produced'.[64] This stilted experiment of the *Régence* had been motivated by a desire to realise the public good through reason. It had not been allowed the time to exist before it was subsumed by the previous method of ruling. Good government did not need to be severe or punitive, as England and Holland were no less principled in matters of justice and equity than Persia, Turkey, or France. Revolutions could occur in any state: the motivation for anarchical behaviour in the masses was the disdain they held towards the government.[65] The love of liberty and hatred of kings expressed in republicanism – which began in Greece moved to the Roman Republic and spread into European tribes – was not an inherently unstable or weak system.[66] While Montesquieu admired classical republicanism, the picture he painted of British liberty in the *Lettres* was not flattering, as he judged it to be too turbulent. The crucial difference between the French monarchy and that of the British republican monarchy, was that the latter possessed the liberty to hold its rulers to account if they did not pursue the people's interests.[67] This was not necessarily conducive to the equilibrium of the state.

Between writing the *Lettres persanes* and the *Considérations sur les causes de la grandeur des Romains et de leur décadence* (1734), Montesquieu spent two years living in England (1729–31). While there he observed Parliament, read widely, was elected to the Royal Academy, and mixed in high society, meeting King George II and Queen Caroline. Politically, Montesquieu was especially intrigued by Britain's balanced constitution and obsession with the 'spirit of liberty'. To this end, the *Craftsman* proved to be very important in shaping his conceptions of liberty, corruption in government, the use of Machiavelli, and analogies between Britain and Rome.[68] His intellectual progress revealed itself in the *Considérations*, which strengthened Montesquieu's examination of republican liberty by comparing the Roman Republic and contemporary Europe. As for Machiavelli, such a comparison provided a 'complete' historical record of government through Rome, which afforded a comparative tool in relation to modern Europe.[69]

Liberty was particularly targeted by Montesquieu, as Rome offered an intriguing historical example of its life and decline. He claimed that in the Roman Republic the patricians had infused the plebeians with such an antipathy towards their monarchs after the deposal of Lucius Tarquinius Superbus (r. 535–509 BCE), that it led to 'an immoderate desire for liberty'.[70] The plebeians used this position to gain greater concessions from the patricians, which fashioned increasing tensions between the two groups. Unlike Bossuet who had assumed that the dissension between the two groups had led to the collapse of the Republic, Montesquieu followed the view of Machiavelli by asserting that discord had been necessary for its greatness.[71] The Republic had required conflict and turmoil to fend off decadence and decline. Bossuet's unity through absolutism removed the vigour of the state; cooperation despite disagreement provided true harmony in a state according for Montesquieu. Roman dissonance had increased as the Republic expanded geographically and became more powerful, leading to collaboration between the two tumultuous groups. Despite losing sight of what it meant to be a good citizen as wealth and luxury corrupted the Romans, its 'heroic valour' and allegiance to war meant that it continued to remain successful amidst the riches, violence, and sensual pleasures.[72] Rome was therefore built on perpetual conflict:

> Roman citizens regarded commerce and the arts as the occupations of slaves; they did not practice them … [I]n general, they were acquainted with only the art of war, which was the only route to magistrates and honours. So the warlike virtues remained after all others were lost.[73]

Rome had been obsessed with war; it had expanded through war and its victories had sated the people during their conflicts with the patricians.[74] It was the loss of its military prowess, its ability to control states through bribery, and the absence of military virtue that saw its decline.[75] As its citizen militia was replaced by a professional army made up of slaves whose morals and civic virtue became corrupted.[76] The 'art of war' plus its 'love of glory and country' had been replaced by weakness and degeneracy that caused its collapse.

Unlike the commercial empire of Carthage, Rome used war to enrich itself through booty. Its endless campaigning had prevented the collapse of the Republic because it had been successful. The modern state that Montesquieu likened to this once great civilisation was not France but England. He believed that France actually mirrored the Roman Empire under the Caesars; corrupt and immersed in pleasures. Such a regime led to the sequestering of its ruler from the people as they became immured in their palaces, trusting on the information from a 'few confidants' to rule his domains.[77] England, on the other hand, echoed the great Republic. The Republic and England both used their magistracy and law to control the liberty and disorders of their people. The 'spirit of the people' and the strength of the government meant that the constitution was adaptable, able to be corrected when the state required it. While Rome had no more liberty than Carthage, Athens or the Italian republics, it was able to sustain it through the successful management of the internal tensions within the state (plus military success). This ability was also evident in the British constitution, although for Montesquieu the government of England was:

> wiser, because there is a body that continually examines and continually examines itself; and such are its mistakes that are never long, and are often useful for the spirit of attention they give the nation.
>
> In a word, a free government – that is to say, always agitated – cannot last long if not capable of corrected itself by its own laws.[78]

The mixed constitutions of Rome and Britain despite fractious agitations, worked through balance and the constant maintenance of the law. The ability to amend the law, constitution, and government created a free government, which France did not possess.

The belief expressed in *Cato's Letters* and the *Craftsman* that Britain's balance was threatened by the executive's corruption was not an experience shared in France, where absolutism prohibited a free press and stifled debate on change or accountability. There was recognition by Montesquieu that an executive could unbalance a government through bribery to expand its power,[79] but in his opinion England was not tyrannical.[80] Unlike the Empire and France, Britain's valuable dissension maintained its liberty, and its mixed constitution retained contact between the executive and the wider populace. Via liberalism Britain had moved away from the idea of submission and obedience, shunning the autocratic model of government that dominated France.[81] The greatest threat to Britain was its status as a commercial nation. Commercial nations were not only subject to the perils of wealth and corruption, the example of Carthage had revealed the emergence of such empires burned brightly before quickly fading. Their prominence was of fleeting duration because other nations appreciated their greatness and sought to deprive them of their advantage.[82] Moreover, as illustrious nations like Rome (or Carthage) rose, they naturally declined. Over time all nations lost sight of the founding principles that had maintained them, and their inherent virtue was lost to weakness and corruption.[83] This made them inevitably open to defeat.

Liberty, toleration, and unity: Voltaire

Another Frenchman living in England during this period (1726–29) was Voltaire. François-Marie d'Arouet (1694–1778), better known by his pen name Voltaire, was the son of a prosperous public official and his aristocratic wife.[84] Under the instruction of the Jesuits he received an excellent education at the esteemed *Collège Louis-le-Grand* in Paris, and through his father's connections he began to mix in intellectual circles. In the early 1720s Voltaire became friends with Bolingbroke and often visited him at *La Source*, the exiled politician's estate. This proved to be an extremely fruitful relationship. Not only was Voltaire influenced by Bolingbroke's political thought and his ideas of natural philosophy, he also mixed within his circle. When Voltaire was forced to flee Paris accused by the duc de Rohan of defamation, he left for Britain. His move to Britain was driven by a pre-existing interest a thriving society of culture, science, and arts, plus a desire to publish a luxurious volume of his play *La Henriade* (1723).[85] While mixing in wide circles, his friendship with Bolingbroke remained important and he continued to visit him at a time when he had begun the *Craftsman*. Bolingbroke introduced Voltaire to Jonathan Swift, Alexander Pope, and John Gay when they were experimenting with 'literary forms', and creating a 'new kind of critical public politics'.[86] Britain provided Voltaire with an opportunity to immerse his polymathic interests, while being educated about British political thought and a range of other subjects.

Voltaire did not share the British or Montesquieu's view that Britain had become a new political Rome, although he did concede that its financial power was comparable to Roman supremacy.[87] For Voltaire this wealth generated by commerce had endowed the British with a freedom, that had in turn enlarged commercial activity allowing the nation to become great, but politically it was different.[88] While British MPs may have seen themselves as 'ancient Romans', except for their corruption in government there was 'nothing in common'.[89] The reason for the difference between the two states, in Voltaire's opinion, was war. Importantly civil war had produced dissimilar outcomes for the two states, and the Romans had not been troubled by wars of religion. Fuelled by religious conviction and a mission to overthrow the potential slavery of arbitrary government, the English Civil Wars had spawned greater liberty; conversely the Roman Republic's destruction had created the opportunity for slavery under the Caesars. Religious harmony in Rome and its control by the state meant that the destruction of the Republic was political, and witnessed a transfer of power from a bicameral system of patricians and plebeians to a single emperor (Augustus). The Romans had efficaciously distracted and restrained their people during this transmission of power by letting them loose on their neighbours like 'wild beast(s)', enabling them to possess the world.[90] This political transfer had been averted in England, and it had become the only nation in the world that had managed to control the power of its kings by resisting them. Kings had been prevented from this evil because of the mixed nature of its constitution, which had rebelled to safeguard the nation. Its representative organs, in which the people shared in government 'without confusion', had been sufficiently roused to restrain the ambitions of tyrannical rulers. Crucially, the aristocracy which was 'great without arrogance and vassals', played an integral and altruistic role that was lacking in their French counterparts. Britain did not possess the multiplicity of nobles seen in France, and from the time of Henry VII (r. 1485–1509) their key role had been to work cooperatively with others in the service of the state. In stark contrast to the largely redundant French aristocracy the British nobility not only assisted the government, but also paid tax and engaged in trade; endeavours that further benefited Britain.[91]

In promoting the power of Parliament, Voltaire's *Letters* moved beyond propaganda to delineate an accurate version of the British constitution for a French audience.[92] While the French believed that the English government was as stormy as the seas due to its reliance on a popular element within government, historically it only became 'tempestuous' if the king provoked confrontation.[93] French history had been far bloodier during the sixteenth and seventeenth centuries, as they assassinated a number of kings and the English had only killed Charles I. The evolution of liberty from slavery by the English had been made possible due to the inclusion of Parliament (the Commons) in politics over successive centuries. Magna Carta (1215) was not the turning point however, for although King John decreed rights for his barons and freemen, the vast majority of the populace remained slaves due to the lack of a Parliament. Following Bolingbroke, Voltaire believed that the reign of Queen Elizabeth had transformed England. In a golden era that brought law, unity, and happiness, public liberty was able to thrive in England as earlier political and religious discords were assuaged through unity.[94] Liberty had even been increased by the multiplicity of Protestant sects that had emerged after the Reformation, which meant an Englishman to 'whom liberty [was] natural', went 'to heaven his own way'.[95] This religious freedom astounded Voltaire and regardless of Anglican High Church zealousness in attacking nonconformists, he alleged that the plurality engendered peace. Voltaire claimed that if there had only been one religion in England it would be 'possibly become arbitrary', if two the people would 'cut one another's throats', but a multitude had created peace and happiness.[96]

This remark was a furtive denunciation of both French history and contemporary experience, in which France had become ostensibly unified through Catholicism under an absolute monarchy. During the sixteenth and seventeenth centuries France had seen Catholicism and Protestantism (under the Huguenots) fractiously exist together until the Revocation of the Edict of Nantes.[97] The *Henriade* depicted the enmity of the Wars of Religion, as the Catholic League headed by the Guises engaged in a bloodthirsty quest for political power under the banner of religion.[98] The internecine civil war between the Catholics (Guises, Papacy, and Spain) and the Huguenots (Navarre, Coligny, and Condé) saw Henri III's France divided and weakened.[99] Political anarchy abounded as the French elite nearly destroyed France following the assassination of Henri I, the duc de Guise in 1588 which led to the regicide of Henri III in 1589.[100] France was plunged into a conflagration of war as religious hatred drove hostilities between the royal houses. When the Huguenot Navarre succeeds to the throne as Henri IV (r. 1589–1610), and following bloody victory he recants to Catholicism as a method for achieving unity in France. In so doing, Henri presented a Fénelonian exemplar of kingship: one who sacrificed himself and his interests for the public good.[101] Indeed the play may be seen as a lyrical 'mirror-for-princes'; one following the lessons of *Télémaque* as Henri, led by a wise adviser (Mornay du Plessis) and the protection of Saint Louis IX (r. 1226–70), became a great king. Voltaire's Henri provided a historical example of a virtuous patriotic king, terminating the destructive murder of 'brothers',[102] while choosing unity and harmony over the right of vengeance and glory.[103]

Like Fénelon and Montesquieu, Voltaire perceived the lack of freedom and public harmony in a suffering France. For Montesquieu and Voltaire, Britain offered some answers to the ills of French government as they examined Fénelon's notion of 'virtuous rule'.[104] In Voltaire's case, Henri IV's appeal to Queen Elizabeth for English aid was suggestive of a need to look across the Channel for (ideological) assistance.[105] Britain's development of religious toleration and the representative institutions of government had provided it with liberty and unity. In France neither of these developments had occurred. Despite contractualist behaviour in the representative organs of French government during the Wars of Religion by the *parlements* and burgesses of the Parisian Sixteen, these elements were too weak for it to be sustained.[106] Instead, French history had been drenched in the bloodshed of discord, persecution, assassination, and absolutism. The 'Large Strides' towards 'Despotick Power' following the death of Henri IV under Richelieu and Mazarin had led to negative government.[107] This evolution of the French state had been cemented under Louis XIV, whose pursuit of glory had led to fear and praise but his reign had made his subjects 'Slaves'.[108] Voltaire believed that this despotism would have ended under Fénelon's former pupil Bourgogne, where:

> Plenty and Peace had been his sov'reign Care,
> Like Children, He his People wou'd have lov'd
> And counted by his Benefits, his Days.[109]

Bourgogne's death had left France in uncertainty, but Voltaire was hopeful that Fénelon's former friend Cardinal Fleury (1653–1743) would be able to guide the nation to 'Peace and Order' as the young Louis XV's First Minister.[110] His call for the spirit of Henri IV was an appeal for a strong king under which unity, freedom, toleration, and the public good could thrive. Like Bossuet before him, he believed that civilisation flourished under a 'protective monarchy';[111] but unlike him Voltaire assumed this could be bolstered through the support of wider government. British inspiration for both Montesquieu and Voltaire was the notion that a mixed constitution not only aided a monarch, it transported a state beyond despotism towards prosperity, greater tolerance, and liberty.

Concluding remarks

Louis XIV's yearning to shape the state using the constitution's emergency powers (prerogatives) enabled France to be moved towards absolute sovereignty. As revisionists have shown, in real terms France was not absolute. Instead, it was a cooperative state made up of central, provincial and local institutions and corporations that worked flexibly through cooperation. Yet, in theoretical terms, the opinion of the high aristocracy (*épée*) and foreign nations, France achieved a verisimilitude of absolute kingship under Louis XIV. Louis's persona, his wars, his mark on European geopolitics, his Versailles, and his state projected a monarch in absolute control of his kingdom and its administration. Many of those theorists who realised that this was not the case (some connected to the court) looked for ways to assist the king through reform. They recognised that the political and financial ills of France had not only been caused by Louis but an ineffective wider bureaucracy. From the 1690s it was understood that the king required help and the government system needed restructuring to prevent France from falling off a financial precipice. While France financially survived the death of Louis XIV it continued to underachieve economically into the eighteenth century. But the ideas that emerged at the end of the seventeenth century and the cautious optimism during the *Régence* gave rise to new ideas of how the French state could evolve.

Fénelon's use of classical and neo-classical republican texts to espouse liberty and mixed constitution saw the promotion of an expanded government to mitigate the (tyrannical) behaviour of Louis XIV. In an effort to provide liberty to the people and ease their suffering, Fénelon advocated a focus on the public good to encourage the welfare of the entire nation over the king's (personal) will. These views were generated independently of the British republican tradition, but found appreciation in that country. His ideas also stimulated debate in France in two ways. As discussed in the previous chapter, the first was his direct influence on his former pupil Bourgogne. Fénelon's desire to create a virtuous (republican) monarch who sacrificed himself to the public good, did work to an extent. The *Mémoires* and *Projets* of Saint-Simon show a new potential direction for France, akin to Louis XIV's model but which would reawaken the representative elements of government to generate the public good. While this future France was the most probable of the Burgundy Circle plans it did not have the ambition of Fénelon, and certainly did not possess the forward-thinking reforms of Saint-Pierre. It would have stepped away from Louis XIV's personalised state absolutism to reinvigorate the state through the high aristocracy and polysynody. Due to Bourgogne's death this alternative France was curtailed, but the brief lifespan of the polysynody offered a glimpse to some of a French monarchy beyond Louis XIV's sovereignty.

As shown in this chapter, the second point of influence was the impact that Fénelon's espousal of liberty had on later thinkers who emerged during the *Régence*. Disappointed by the lost opportunity under Orléans, thinkers such as Montesquieu and Voltaire turned to Britain as a working model of liberty, toleration, and mixed constitution in antagonism to tyrannical monarchy. The attraction of a mixed constitution under a monarch had a profound impact on the two men, and their thoughts (and others') helped to shape eighteenth-century French political theory. Country ideology espoused by Bolingbroke and others, and the visits to Britain by Montesquieu and Voltaire, were hugely significant for the appreciation of alternative political forms to the stultification of absolutism. A form of sovereignty that had seen the degeneration of France from the later seventeenth century, and which had not fully come to terms with a commercial age in the eighteenth century. Britain was important for French thought because it was the realisation of a state that had successfully rejected tyranny in favour of liberty and a mixed constitution. Its commercial society may have been at threat from eventual collapse, but in the early 1730s it was flourishing and alive with toleration, religious pluralism, an open public sphere, and freedom. This prospect was particularly attractive to some French thinkers after decades of Louis XIV's rule, and the apparent return of his form of sovereignty under Louis XV.

Notes

1   Merle L. Perkins, 'Late Seventeenth-Century Scientific Circles and the Abbé de Saint-Pierre', *Proceedings of the American Philosophical Society*, 102, 4 (27 Aug. 1958), pp. 404–12 (404).

2   Merle L. Perkins, 'The Abbé de Saint-Pierre and the Seventeenth-Century Intellectual Background', *Proceedings of the American Philosophical Society*, 97, 1 (14 Feb. 1953), pp. 69–76 (73–4).

3   See Nannerl O. Keohane, *Philosophy and the State in France : The Renaissance to the Enlightenment* (Princeton, 1980), 363–4, ch. 13; Peter van den Dungen, 'The Abbé de Saint-Pierre and the English "Irenists" of the 18th Century (Penn, Bellers, and Bentham)', *International Journal on World Peace*, 18, 2 (Jun. 2000), p. 18; Armand Mattelart, *Histoire de l'utopie planétaire: De la cité prophétique à la société globale* (Paris, 2009); Carole Dornier and Claudine Poulouin, *Projets de l'abbé Castel de Saint Pierre (1658–1743): Pour le plus grand bonheur du plus grand nombre* (Caen, 2011).

4   The work was first published in 1712, but Saint-Pierre completed a 2–volume edition in 1713, another edition in 1717, and an *abrégé* in 1729, as he attempted to perfect his *Projet*.

5   Saint-Pierre, *Projet pour rendre la paix perpétuelle en Europe, Tome I* (Utrecht, 1713), i–ii.

6   See Joseph Drouet, *L'Abbé de Saint-Pierre: L'Homme et L'Œuvre* (Paris, 1912), 108; Perkins, 'The Abbé de Saint-Pierre and the Seventeenth-Century Intellectual Background', 74.

7   See Keohane, *Philosophy and the State*, 365–6; Thomas E. Kaiser, 'The Abbe de Saint-Pierre, Public Opinion, and the Reconstitution of the French Monarchy', *Journal of Modern History*, 55, 4 (Dec. 1983), pp. 618–43 (623–4, 627–8).

8   Saint-Pierre, *Projet*, 123–5.

9   See Sully, *Memoirs of Maximilian de Bethune, Duke of Sully, Prime Minister of Henry the Great, Volume V*, trans. M. De L'Ecluse (Edinburgh, 1773). The *Grand Dessein* is contained within Volume XXX of the work as the *Grand Design*. Two folios of the work were published in 1638 and a further two posthumously in 1662. Saint-Pierre based his *Projet* on it, and from Saint-Pierre the perpetual peace plans of Rousseau and Kant stem. It has been argued that the *Dessein* is Sully's own work (inspired by earlier pacific plans) as no historical record can be found of Henri's involvement (Souleyman, *The Vision of World Peace in Seventeenth and Eighteenth-Century France* (New York, 1972), 28–9); Miriam Eliav-Feldon, 'Grand Designs: The Peace Plans of the Late Renaissance', *Vivarium*, 27, 1 (1989), 66; Andrew Mansfield, 'Emeric Crucé's *Nouveau Cynée* (1623), universal peace and free trade', *Journal of Interdisciplinary History of Ideas*, 2, 4 (2013), pp. 2–23 (5).

10   Saint-Pierre, *Projet*, 35–7.

11   Merle L. Perkins, 'The *Leviathan* and Saint-Pierre's *Projet de Paix Perpétuelle*', *Proceedings of the American Philosophical Society*, 99, 4 (30 Aug. 1955), 259–67; Richard Tuck, *The Rights of War*

and Peace: Political Thought and the International Order from Grotius to Kant (Oxford, 1999), 141; Céline Spector, 'Who Is the Author of the Abstract of Monsieur l'Abbé de Saint-Pierre's "Plan for Perpetual Peace"? From Saint-Pierre to Rousseau', *History of European Ideas*, 39, 3 (2013), pp. 371–93 (382).

12 Patrick Riley, 'The Abbé de Saint-Pierre and Voltaire on Perpetual Peace in Europe', *World Affairs*, 137, 3 (winter 1974–75), pp. 186–94 (187–8).

13 Saint-Pierre, *Projet Tome I*, 192.

14 *Ibid.*, 359–64.

15 *Ibid.*, 239.

16 See Chapter 3, for a discussion of debate on Colbertism.

17 Saint-Pierre, *Projet*, 260.

18 Kaiser, 'The Abbe de Saint-Pierre, Public Opinion, and the Reconstitution of the French Monarchy', 627–8.

19 J.G.A. Pocock, 'The political limits to premodern economies', *The Economic Limits to Modern Politics*, ed. John Dunn (Cambridge, 1990), 127; Michael Sonenscher, 'Fashion's Empire: Trade and Power in Early Eighteenth-Century France', *Luxury Trades and Consumerism in Ancien Régime Paris: Studies in the History of the Skilled Workforce*, eds R. Fox and A. Turner (Aldershot, 1998), 265; Istvan Hont, 'The Early Enlightenment Debate on Commerce and Luxury', *The Cambridge History of Eighteenth-Century Political Thought, Vol. 1*, eds Mark Goldie and Robert Wokler (Cambridge, 2006), 379–83.

20 Saint-Pierre, *Projet Tome I*, 192.

21 *Ibid.*, 321–6.

22 *Ibid.*, 50–3.

23 Fénelon, *Télémaque*, ed. Jacques Le Brun (Paris, 1997), livres III, VII, X, and XVII. For David Hume on free trade, see 'Of the Balance of Trade', *Essays, Moral, Political and Literary*, ed. Eugene F. Miller (Indianapolis, 1987), II, v, 35; for Adam Smith, see *An Enquiry into the Nature and the Wealth of Nations Volume I*, ed. Edwin Cannan (Indianapolis, 1994), IV, viii, 1 (455–81).

24 See Bernard Delmas, 'La Réforme fiscal cœur du "Perfectionnement de l'État" chez Castel de Saint-Pierre', 125–43; Robert F. Hébert, 'Économie, utopisme et l'abbé de Saint-Pierre', *Projets de l'abbé Castel de Saint Pierre (1658–1743): Pour le plus grand bonheur du plus grand nombre*, 224–6.

25 Shennan, J.H., Philippe, *Duke of Orléans: Regent of France 1715–1723* (London, 1979), 35.

26 *Ibid.*, 36–7; Ladurie, *Saint-Simon ou le système de la Cour*, 418–19.

27 Abbé de Saint-Pierre, *Discours sur la Polysynodie* (Londres, 1718), v.

28 *Ibid.*, 44–8.

29 *Ibid.*, 19–20.

30 *Ibid.*, 18–19, 24–7.

31 *Ibid.*, 30–3.

32 *Ibid.*, 38–41.

33 Kaiser, 'The Abbe de Saint-Pierre, Public Opinion, and the Reconstitution of the French Monarchy', 639–40; a view opposed by Keohane, *Philosophy and the State*, 370–1; Spector, 'Who Is the Author of the Abstract of Monsieur l'Abbé de Saint-Pierre's "Plan for Perpetual Peace"?', 391–2.

34 Kaiser, 'Abbe de Saint-Pierre, Public Opinion', 637–8.

35 See Claude Fleury, *The History of the Origin of the French Laws* (London, 1724), 99–100; Henri de Boulainvilliers, *Etat de la France, Tome Seconde* (London, 1727), 1, vi–vii. Much has been recently written on Boulainvilliers's ideas regarding aristocratic-led reform, but his membership of the Burgundy Circle was rather tenuous (hence his exclusion here); for example see Harold A. Ellis, *Boulainvilliers and the French Monarchy: Aristocratic Politics in Early Eighteenth-Century France* (Cornell, 1988); Jonathan Israel, *Radical Enlightenment: Philosophy and the Making of Modernity 1650–1750* (Oxford, 2001), 74–7, 565–74; Rachel Hammersely, *The English Republican Tradition and Eighteenth-Century France: Between the Ancients and the Moderns* (Manchester, 2010). As argued here, Ellis also believes that the Burgundy Circle worked independently of each other and lacked a coordinated approach (60).

36 See Sanford B. Kanter, 'Archbishop Fénelon's Political Activity: The Focal Point of Power in Dynasticism', *French Historical Studies*, 4, 3 (spring 1966), pp. 320–4 (330, 332); Roger Mettam, *Power and Faction in Louis XIV's France* (Oxford, 1988), 50, 78, 91, 316; Emmanuel La Roy Ladurie avec la collaboration de Jean-François Fitou, *Saint-Simon ou le système de la Cour* (Paris, 1997), 414–15, 420–2. For a conviction that the Burgundy Circle did not want to undermine French absolutism, see Keohane, *Philosophy and the State*, 345–6; Ellis, *Boulainvilliers and the French Monarchy*, 63–4.

37 Robert Shackleton, *Montesquieu: A Critical Biography* (Oxford, 1961), 12–13, 64, 65.

38 Melvin Richter, 'Introduction', *The Political Theory of Montesquieu* (Cambridge, 1977), 31, 34–5.

39 Montesquieu, *Lettres persanes*, Œuvres Complètes de Montesquieu, I, eds Jean Ehrard and Catherine Volpilhac-Auger (Oxford, 2004), see Lettres 2, 9, for example. See Mark Hulliung, *Montesquieu and the Old Regime* (Berkeley, 1976), 138; Judith N. Shklar, *Montesquieu* (Oxford, 1987), 30–2.

40 Montesquieu, Lettre 35 (229–30).

41 *Ibid.*, Lettre 27 (210–11).

42 *Ibid.*, Lettre 42 (243).

43 *Ibid.*, Lettre 74 (338–9).

44 *Ibid.*, Lettre 57 (269–70).

45 Sylvani Tomaselli, 'The Spirit of Nations', *Cambridge History of Eighteenth-Century Political Thought*, eds Mark Goldie and Robert Wokler (Cambridge, 2006), 16.

46 Montesquieu, Lettre 83 (365–8). For Montesquieu's attempt to destroy prejudice, see Shackleton, *Montesquieu*, 41.

47 Lettre 83 (367).

48 Lettre 11 (161–4).

49 Lettre 12 (165–8).

50 Third Earl of Shaftesbury, *An Essay on the Freedom of Wit and Humour*, *Characteristicks* (London, 1711), 88. Anthony Ashley Cooper, the Third of Shaftesbury (1671–1713), Whig politician and philosopher of great renown and influence in the early eighteenth century. He was the grandson of the First Earl who helped to shape the Whig party – see Chapter 1 in the present book.

51 Shaftesbury, *Ibid.*, 89–92; *An Enquiry Concerning Virtue*, *Characteristicks*, 56; Fénelon, *Télémaque*, Œuvres II, ed. Le Brun (Paris, 1997), 288–9; Richter, 'Introduction', *Political Theory of Montesquieu*, 38.

52 Montesquieu, Lettre 13 (169–70).

53 Lettre 14 (171): 'Ô Troglodites: votre vertu commence à vous peser: dans l'état où vous êtes, n'ayant point de Chef, il faut que vous soyez verteux malgré vous; sans cela vous ne sçauriez subsister, & [sic] vous tomberiez dans le malheur de vos premier Peres: mais ce joug partoît trop dur, vous aimez mieux être soumis à un Prince, & obéïr à ses Loix moins rigides que vos aquerir des richesses, & languir dans une lâche volupté; & que pourvû que vous évitiez de tomber dans les grands crimes, vous n'aurez pas besoin de la Vertu.'

54 Michael Sonescher, *Before the Deluge: Public Debt, Inequality, and the Intellectual Origins of the French Revolution* (Princeton, 2007), 95.

55 Nick Childs, *A Political Academy in Paris 1724–1731: The Entresol and Its Members* (Oxford, 2000), 147–8.

56 Bernard Mandeville, *The Fable of the Bees*, ed. Kaye (Oxford, 1924), Remarks L (119), Q (184–5, 191–3), Y (250–1). See Richter on Montesquieu's consideration of Mandeville's views ('Introduction', *Political Theory of Montesquieu*, 43–4; on Mandeville's rejection of Shaftesbury's sanguine simplicity and virtue, see Hector Monro, *The Ambivalence of Bernard Mandeville* (Oxford, 1975), 180–5. Istvan Hont claimed that in the *Grumbling Hive*, Mandeville attacked Fénelon's Salente ('Eutopia') for depicting a commercially successful and virtuous state stripped of luxury and vice. For Mandeville (and Montesquieu) luxury was part of a modern prosperous society (Hont, 'The Early Enlightenment Debate on Commerce and Luxury', *Cambridge History of Eighteenth-Century Political Thought*, vol. I, eds Mark Goldie & Robert Wokler (Cambridge, 2006), 388).

57 Montesquieu, Lettre 115. Montesquieu believed that the earth had become depopulated since ancient times, providing detailed examples explaining why (Lettres 108–18).

58 *Ibid.*, Lettre 118 (461–2).

59 See Richard B. Sher, 'From Troglodytes to Americans: Montesquieu and the Scottish Enlightenment on Liberty, Virtue, and Commerce', *Republicanism, Liberty, and Commercial Society, 1649–1776*, ed. David Wootton (Stanford, 1994), 374; Henry J. Merry, *Montesquieu's System of Natural Government* (Purdue, 1970), 205, 233.

60 Montesquieu, Lettres 126 (481–3), 129 (489–91), 136 (514–17). In Lettre 136, Law is famously depicted as the son of Aeolus (the king of the winds) and a Caledonian nymph, deceptively selling captured wind in bags.

61 See Richard Bonney, 'France and the First Paper Money Experiment', *French History* (2001), 15, 3, pp. 254–72 (257–60); Antoin E. Murphy, *John Law: Economiste et homme d'État* (Brussels, 2007).

62 Lettre 138 (528–9).

63 Richter, 'Introduction', *Political Theory of Montesquieu*, 44–5.

64 Montesquieu, Lettre 132 (498–9): abbreviated from 's'étoit mal trouvé de l'autorité sans bornes des Ministres précedons; on la voulut partager: on créa pour cet effet six ou sept Conseils: & ce Ministere est peut-être celui de tous qui a gouverné la France avec plus de sens: la durée en fut courte aussi bien qu'il produisit'.

65 *Ibid.*, Lettre 78 (352–4).

66 *Ibid.*, Lettre 125 (478–80).

67 *Ibid.*, Lettre 101 (415). For Montesquieu's earlier view of English liberty, see C.P. Courtney, 'Montesquieu and English Liberty', *Montesquieu's Science of Politics: Essays on The Spirit of the Laws*, eds David W. Carrithers, Michael A. Mosher, and Paul A. Rahe (Oxford, 2001), 274–8.

68 Shackleton, *Montesquieu*, 127. Rachel Hammersley has underlined Bolingbroke's role as an intellectual conduit between Britain and France after his time in France (*English Republican Tradition and Eighteenth-Century France*, 54–5). Bolingbroke's relationship with Montesquieu is uncertain, and it would appear that the men met in the *Entresol* but a friendship or correspondence did not truly develop (Shackleton, *Montesquieu*, 55–6, 126). Yet Hammersley's contention that Montesquieu was influenced directly by Britain is correct, and this includes theoretical trends found in Bolingbroke's thought and extant in the *Craftsman*. Hammersley does understate the shared classical and neo-classical heritage of the English Republican (Commonwealth) ideology, as well as the influence of sixteenth-century contractualists such as François Hotman on the British. Views expressed in Britain, however, did impact on Montesquieu's political theory and therefore affected eighteenth century French thought (*English Republican Tradition and Eighteenth-Century France*, 66–9, 74, 78). The membership of Bolingbroke and Ramsay in the *Entresol* was important. It enabled a pre-existing French fascination with the British constitution to be explored, while French thought permeated its British members (*ibid.*, 72–3); see also Chapter 2 in this book.

69 Richter, 'Introduction', *Political Theory of Montesquieu*, 51; Shklar, *Montesquieu*, 50.

70 Montesquieu, *Considérations sur les Causes de la Grandeur des Romains et de leur Décadence*, Œuvres complètes, ed. Roger Caillois (Paris, 1951), 111.

71 *Ibid.*, 118–19; Machiavelli, *Discourses*, I, 6. For a discussion on this conflict (and the introduction of the agrarian laws by the Gracchi as a solution), see J.G.A. Pocock, *The Machiavellian Moment: Florentine Political Thought and the Atlantic Republican Tradition* (Princeton, 1975), 211; J.G.A. Pocock, *Barbarism and Religion* (Cambridge, 1999), vol. III, *The First Decline and Fall*, 32–60; Eric Nelson, *The Greek Tradition in Republican Thought* (Cambridge, 2004), 52–78. For an examination of the different historiographical and philosophical approaches of Montesquieu and Bossuet, see Paul Schuurman, 'Determinism and Causal Feedback Loops in Montesquieu's Explanation for the Military Rise and Fall of Rome', *British Journal for the History of Philosophy*, 21, 3 (2013), pp. 507–28 (520–2).

72 Montesquieu, *Considérations*, 119–20. This view again opposes Bossuet who believed the Republic collapsed due to its corruption from luxury and effeminacy.

73 *Ibid.*, 122: 'Les citoyens romains regardoient le commerce et les arts comme des occupations

d'esclave; ils ne exerçoient point … en general, ils ne connoissoient que l'art de la guerre, qui étoit la seule voie pour aller aux magistratures et aux honneurs. Ainsi les vertus guerrières restèrent, après qu'on eut perdu tout les autres.'

74 *Ibid.*, 72–4. For Montesquieu's adaptation of Machiavelli regarding Roman expansion, see Hulliung, *Montesquieu and the Old Regime*, 155–7.

75 *Ibid.*, 171–5.

76 Georg Cavallar, '"La société générale du genre humain": Rousseau on cosmopolitanism, international relations, and republican patriotism', *From Republican Polity to National Community. Reconsiderations of Enlightenment Political Thought*, ed. Paschalis M. Kitromilides (Oxford, 2003), 92.

77 Montesquieu, *Considérations*, 165.

78 *Ibid.*, 116: 'Plus sage, parce qu'il y a un corps qui l'examine continuellement, et qui s'examine continuellement lui-même; et telles sont ses erreurs, qu'elles ne sont jamais longues, et que, par l'esprit d'attention qu'elles donnent à la nation, ells sont souvent utiles. En un mot, un gouvernement libre, c'est-à-dire toujours agité, ne saroit se maintenir, s'il n'est, par ses propres lois, capable de correction'.

79 *Ibid.*, 138–9. Montesquieu believed the Emperor Augustus (63 BCE–14 CE) had introduced this practice into government.

80 *Ibid.*, 146.

81 Hulliung, 'Patriarchalism and Its Early Enemies', 417.

82 Montesquieu, *Considerations*, 87.

83 *Ibid.*, 174.

84 In his *Mémoires*, Saint-Simon points out that the (now) famous Voltaire's father was a notary who had worked for him (*The Memoirs of the Duke of Saint-Simon on the Reign of Louis XIV and the Regency*, 4 vols in 2, trans. Bayle St John (New York, 1936), III, 25 (332)).

85 Leonard Tancock, 'Introduction', *Letters on England* (London, 1980), 9–10.

86 J.B. Shank, 'Voltaire', *The Stanford Encyclopedia of Philosophy* (summer 2010 Edition), ed. Edward N. Zalta: http://plato.stanford.edu/archives/sum2010/entries/voltaire

87 According to Peter Gay, Montesquieu did not like Voltaire (*Voltaire's Politics: The Poet and Realist* (Princeton, 1959), 185).

88 Voltaire, *Letters Concerning the English Nation* (London, 1733), Letter X (71). I have used the English editions of Voltaire's works in this section as they were also targeted at an English audience.

89 *Ibid.*, VIII (51).

90 *Ibid.*, VIII (54). Voltaire claimed that the British did not make war for conquest but rather to restrain the ambitions of its neighbours, notably Louis XIV.

91 *Ibid.*, IX (64, 66–8), X (71–2).

92 Gay, *Voltaire's Politics*, 58–9.

93 Voltaire, *Letters Concerning the English Nation*, VIII (56).

94 Voltaire, *Henriade: An Epick Poem* (London, 1732), 18–20. The expanded English edition of the *Henriade* was dedicated to Queen Caroline in celebration of English liberty and kingship (iv).

95 *Letters*, V (34). Voltaire famously spent time with Quakers, and the first four letters reveal his fascination with their (religious) views and customs.

96 *Ibid.*, VI (45).

97 In *The History of the Civil Wars of France, upon which the HENRIADE is grounded* (London, 1728), Voltaire claimed that the Revocation had led to a cruel and unfair persecution of Huguenots (15).

98 Voltaire: *Henriade*, III (53–4); *History of the Civil Wars of France*, 6–7.

99 Voltaire: *Henriade*, III (64), IV (82–3); *History of the Civil Wars of France*, 11, 19–21.

100 Voltaire, *Henriade*, V (100–2).

101 *Ibid.*, X (222–3).

102 *Ibid.*, VIII (172).

103 *Ibid.*, X (229).

104 Sonenscher, *Before the Deluge*, 102.

105 Voltaire, *Henriade*, I (8).
106 See *Ibid.*, IV (91–7); *History of the Civil Wars of France*, 25–7. In the *History* Voltaire writes that: 'These States resemble the Parliament of *Great Britain* in their Convocation but are very different from it in their Operations; as they are seldom call'd, they have no Rules to guide them, they are generally made up of Men who having never been in any regular Meeting, know not how to behave themselves, and 'tis rather a Confusion than an Assembly (23).'
107 Voltaire, *Henriade*, VII (154).
108 *Ibid.*, VII (155).
109 *Ibid.*, VII (158).
110 *Ibid.*, VII (159).
111 J.G.A. Pocock, *Barbarism and Religion*, vol. IV: *Barbarians, Savages and Empires*, 61.

6

Ramsay and his associations

Intellectual formation

Andrew Michael Ramsay was born in 1686 to an Episcopalian mother (Susanna) and a Presbyterian father (Andrew).[1] His birthplace was Ayr in Scotland, but Ramsay's parents fled due to the religious and political unrest of 1684 in which his father had become involved.[2] Returning to Ayr as a child, Ramsay grew up in a modest background: his father was a baker.[3] Despite this, Ramsay claimed descent from the Earls of Dalhousie on his father's side and the Lairds of Dun on his mother's, although no clear connection can be found. He added Michael to his name to mask his humble origins, as Scots very rarely had middle names unless they were of noble birth.[4] His claims of noble ancestry were later useful for opening doors on his travels and in allaying fears, particularly in France, that he was an adventurer or a chancer.

In his autobiography, *Anecdotes de la vie de Messire André Michel de Ramsay ... dictés par lui meme peu de jours avant sa mort par le instances reiterées de son Epouze*[5] Ramsay described an early interest in mathematics and the sciences. Perhaps unsurprisingly given his background, he was also drawn towards religion. The environment in which Ramsay grew up was riven by religious unrest – both intellectual and physical – augmented by the growth of deism. Ramsay stated in the *Anecdotes* that he had earlier adhered to deism following the advice of his mother to eschew the Calvinistic dogma of predestination,[6] and the deism present in the universities of Scotland took Ramsay to Edinburgh and Aberdeen.[7] While deism proved unsatisfying for Ramsay, he was introduced to the mysticism of St Francis de Sales (1567–1622), Archbishop Fénelon, and a range of other Catholic contemplative writers.[8] Ramsay began to avoid the prevailing forms of organised Christianity by 1708 and sought truth in the idea of a mystical union with a loving God.[9] He formed an attachment with the Garden Circle led by George and James Garden, who encouraged him to be critical of religion and to espouse toleration.[10] The Circle included George Garden (1649–1733), Scottish

Episcopal clergyman and controversialist; James Garden (1645–1726), minister and author of *Comparative Theology* (1700); George Cheyne (1671/2–1743), physician and natural philosopher; Robert Keith (1681–1757), Scottish Episcopalian Bishop and historian; Alexander Forbes, Lord Pitsligo (1678–1762), philosopher and Jacobite army officer; and the Jacobite James Ogilvy, Lord Deskford (1663–1730).[11] These men introduced him into Jacobite spheres and aided Ramsay in his spiritual journey, importantly becoming the means of introduction to a wider world of contacts in London and on the continent.[12] Many of these men Ramsay corresponded with for many years, connected through an interest in natural philosophy, religion, and toleration, as well as their dedication to Fénelon and Madame Guyon.

After moving to London at the end of 1708 as tutor of the Earl of Wemyss's children he became involved with the Philadelphian Society, a Protestant sect that rejected the constraints of the church. Ramsay's involvement with the Philadelphians allowed him to explore his attraction to mysticism. With the aid of George Garden, Ramsay left London and travelled to Rijnsburg, Holland in the spring of 1710 to visit Pierre Poiret (1646–1719).[13] Poiret was a French mystic and philosopher who exerted a strong influence on the Garden Circle, frequently corresponding with them. In his work *La Paix des âmes dans tous les partis du Christianisme* (1687), Poiret had disregarded religious creeds, asking Christians to move beyond the restriction of church membership to an inner communion between like-minded souls. Poiret's theological views led him to seek out a correspondence with the Catholic mystic Archbishop Fénelon, whom he believed may be sympathetic to his own Protestant form of mysticism.[14] Through correspondence the two men discussed the possibility of whether Catholics could be contemplatives and not actively part of the Church. Fénelon – also in correspondence with the Garden Circle – argued that Protestantism was a damaging schism to Christianity; while Poiret countered by claiming that the true message of Christianity was located in all of its branches.[15] For Poiret, religious understanding was achieved by elevating oneself above organised religion, which has lost its way through its use of priests and ceremony. Such an outlook had drawn Poiret towards the Catholic mystic Madame Guyon (1648–1717), a distant relation of Fénelon's who had instigated the Quietism Affair that had led to the Archbishop's exile to Cambrai. Poiret corresponded closely with Guyon over a number of years, attracted by her openness to religious doctrine, a lack of focus on an established Church, and desire to pursue a personal path to pure love and God.

Poiret proved to be a strong influence on Ramsay in his spiritual quest, and it was via Poiret that Ramsay travelled to Fénelon at Cambrai in August 1710.[16] During his time with Fénelon, Ramsay was converted to Catholicism by the Archbishop through a combination of spiritual discourse and confession over a period of about six months.[17] His time with Fénelon and its duration is of some debate, but he appears to have lived in Fénelon's household for a period of about three years, leaving in 1714. A letter dated 20 March 1714 reveals Ramsay to be already established in Blois and living with Madame Guyon, another of Poiret's correspondents.[18] The problem of Ramsay's stay at Cambrai arises from the uncertainty of his departure which may indeed be before 1714. It was assumed by many biographers of Fénelon that he lived with the Archbishop until shortly before his death on 7 January 1715, an assumption Ramsay appears to have cultivated in his *L'Histoire de la Vie de Fénelon* (1723) through a vivid description of Fénelon's death as if present. While at Blois, Ramsay acted as Madame Guyon's secretary, translating her correspondence from English into French and vice versa. At this point Ramsay still maintained a healthy correspondence of his own with the Garden Circle, who claimed devotion to Guyon: their 'NM' (*Notre mère*).[19] Ramsay left Guyon's service towards the end of 1716 to become the governor for the son of the Comte Ismidon-René de Sassenage (1670–1730), a soldier,[20] but returned to be by Guyon's side at her death on 9 June 1717.

At some point between the deaths of Fénelon and Madame Guyon in 1716 Ramsay wrote the *Discours de la Poesie Epique, de l'Excellence du Poeme de Télémaque* (*A Discourse upon Epick Poetry, and the Excellence of the Poem Telemachus*). In it Ramsay described the Archbishop's poetical genius and the humanity of *Télémaque*, combined with its application of ancient and modern erudition.[21] Its poetry not only entertained the reader, it eloquently instructed them in the beauty of virtue.[22] A virtue that ascended beyond the negative philosophical conceptions of humanity found in Machiavelli and Hobbes, while surpassing Grotius and Pufendorf's reliance on pagan ideals by infusing them with Christian love.[23] The work was well liked by the Archbishop's great-nephew, the Marquis de Fénelon (1688–1746), who employed Ramsay as the editor of his uncle's papers. Aided by another of Fénelon's nephews, the abbé de Fénelon, Ramsay began to edit *Télémaque* and by 1717 an extended and corrected two-volume edition was published containing Ramsay's *Discours* and a *Preface* by him.[24] In the following year Ramsay and the abbé de Fénelon went on to publish a further six works including the *Dialogues des Morts*. Ramsay then wrote the *Essay de Politique* (1719), which was expanded into a second edition *Essay philosophique sur les gouvernement civil* (1721). The latter edition was translated into English in 1722 by Nathaniel Hooke (1664–1738), a member of the Garden Circle who translated a number of works including Ramsay's *Vie de Fénelon* and *Les Voyage de Cyrus*.[25] Ramsay used his role and association with Fénelon to claim that the *Essay* was based on the principles of *Télémaque*,[26] a potentially advantageous marketing strategy regarding the incomplete nature of Fénelon's political work.[27] Ramsay's association with Fénelon was strengthened by the publication of the *Vie de Fénelon*,[28] in which Ramsay depicted a strong bond between the two men. The work is rather curious, and Fénelon features as an almost peripheral figure: a *Life* containing little of Fénelon's life. Instead it focuses on Ramsay's own conversion by Fénelon, the plight of Madame Guyon, the Quietism Affair, and the promotion of James Stuart's Jacobite cause. Importantly, Ramsay's inclusion of James Stuart in the *Vie* used the biography to link James to Fénelon with the *Essay*, thereby exploiting the supposed political principles of Fénelon to assert his claim to the British throne.

Ramsay's intervention in the Jacobite cause provided him with his next opportunity of employment when his work with the Comte de Sassenage ended in September 1722.[29] The following year his role as editor was terminated by the Marquis de Fénelon, who was incensed by the absence of the dead archbishop's real character in the *Vie*. Ramsay's Jacobite friends arranged a pension from the abbé de Signy, and he was appointed a Chevalier of the Jacobite *ordre de Saint-Lazare* on 20 May 1723. Ramsay's title was elevated to that of baronet in 1735 through his marriage to the under-secretary to James Stuart, Sir David Nairne's daughter Marie. The award of the earlier title was partly made possible by John Erskine the Earl of Mar (1675–1732), who allowed Ramsay to claim descent from his family. This acquaintance and that with the politician and writer George Granville, Lord Lansdowne the Jacobite Duke of Albermarle (1666–1735), proved to be fruitful when in December 1723 Ramsay was awarded the role of tutor to the young prince Charles Edward Stuart (1720–88) in Rome. As will be discussed below, this proved to be an extremely unhappy period for Ramsay who left in early 1724 never to return to the Jacobite court.

Ramsay followed his Jacobite disappointments by embarking upon a literary career and he became a member of the *Club de l'Entresol*. The *Entresol* contained members such as Montesquieu (1689–1755), the abbé de Saint-Pierre (1658–1743), and Viscount Bolingbroke (1678–1751), and was committed to the idea of reforming French absolutism, at times taking its inspiration from Fénelon.[30] While a member of the *Entresol*, Ramsay published *Les voyages de Cyrus* (1727) which was dedicated to his new patron the duc de Sully and translated into English by Hooke. The work proved to be hugely successful across Europe. It had to be quickly republished with amendments in 1728, however, due to accusations of plagiarism made in *Entretiens sur les voyages de Cyrus*.[31] This work made a series of allegations about Ramsay and his *Cyrus*, ranging from the more serious of plagiarism and his modest understanding of the classics and Latin, to a disgust at his poor writing style. As had been noted by a number of commentators, *Cyrus* bore a striking resemblance in style, method, content, and tone to Fénelon. Voltaire later wrote that:

> Ramsay, who after having been a Presbyterian in his native Scotland, an Anglican in London, then a Quaker, and who finally persuaded Fénelon that he was a Catholic and even pretended a penchant for celestial love – Ramsay, I say, compiled the 'Travels of Cyrus', because his master made his Telemachus travel. So far he only

imitated ... On conducting Cyrus into Egypt, in describing that singular country, he employs the same expressions as Bossuet, whom he copies word for word without citing; this is plagiarism complete. One of my friends reproached him with this one day; Ramsay replied that he was not aware of it, and that it was not surprising he should think like Fénelon and write like Bossuet. This was making out the adage, 'Proud as a Scotsman'.[32]

Yet for the author of the *Supplement* it was more egregious: 'While we were at *Tyre*, a Book fell into my Hands, intitled, *The Adventures of Telemachus*, where I met with that fine Discourse almost Word for Word.'[33] Ramsay was also censured for using passages from Ralph Cudworth's *Intellectual System of the Universe* (1678). More surprising for contemporaries, he was shown to have plagiarised over fourteen consecutive pages verbatim of Bossuet's *Discours sur l'Histoire Univer-selle* (1681):[34] 'he has such a veneration, that he has thought fit to fill fourteen pages of his Book with one of the finest passages in that History, almost without Variation'.[35] While the accusations meant that the offending pages were excised from subsequent editions they did little to diminish its success or the fame of its author. In 1729 Ramsay was elected a Fellow of the Royal Society in London, and in the following year he became a member of the Gentleman's Society at Spalding (which had Newton and Alexander Pope as members), and on 10 April 1730 he went to Oxford to receive a degree of Doctor of Civil Law from (the Jacobite) William King, largely through the success of *Cyrus*.

In Ramsay's later years he remained the tutor to the duc de Sully's family and lived with them at Andresy and then Pontoise.[36] He corresponded widely with figures such as Montesquieu, Swift and Hume and continued to publish, writing the *Histoire du vicomte de Turenne* in 1735 on the illustrious ancestor of his employer's family.[37] Like other Jacobites in France he became an active freemason in the Lodge of St Thomas – much of his reputation is as a freemason – and wrote *A Discourse Pronounced at the Reception of Freemasons* (1737). After his marriage to Marie Nairne in 1735 he moved to St Germain-en-Laye where he died on 6 May 1743 and was buried in its parish church. On his deathbed he dictated the *Anecdotes* to his wife, but left his great opus *The Philosophical Principles of Natural and Revealed Religion* unpublished. This work reflected Ramsay's primary interest in natural philosophy, and was eventually published by the Foulis Brothers of Glasgow (1748–9). It expanded many of the ideas within *Cyrus* while attempting to reconcile Newton's ideas with his own philosophy, revealing his deep interest in the nature of religion.[38]

Ramsay's association with Fénelon

While Ramsay's association with Fénelon began in August 1710 at Cambrai, the death of Madame Guyon revealed a passion in Ramsay that had a profound effect on Fénelon's legacy. Despite receiving the role of editor of *Télémaque* in June 1716,[39] the real target of Ramsay's attentions appears to have been Guyon. In his struggle with Poiret to write the biography of Guyon, Ramsay zealously and jealously guarded the very fresh legacy of Madame Guyon while apparently working on Fénelon's. A number of letters to the Garden Circle from Ramsay inform them of her death as a witness to her passing, likening it to '*Jesus crucifié*' ('Jesus crucified').[40] From the time of her death, Ramsay went to extraordinary lengths to prevent Poiret from being successful in the publication of his work. These endeavours were discussed by the Garden Circle, and Dr James Keith made his discomfort known in a letter to Lord Deskford:

> This last period brings to my mind what perhaps your Lop has not yet heard of, namely the very strong opposition that is made by A.R. [Ramsay] with all the other friends in Fr[ance] against Mr P's [Poiret] printing and publishing that most valuable Life at this time, and in order to hinder him from doing it, they have represented the copy wch he has as defective and imperfect, and therefore have desir'd him to return it to them to be corrected by one wch they call more perfect. R[amsay] has written several letters (by their order as he says) to Mr P[oiret] himself, to D.G. [George Garden] and to us here, to this purpose, wch is highly suprising to us all, and the more that he himself transcrib'd that very copy wch Mr P. has, and sent it to him by N.M'.s [Madame Guyon] express order (having first carefully revis'd and corrected it herself) to be published after her death. But the good old man refuses to give it up and resolves to be faithful to the trust reposed in him. They on the other hand have they say strong reasons for delaying it, but do not say what they are.[41]

Ramsay's vigorous attempts to stall and disrupt Poiret proved to be unsuccessful, and Poiret published his biography of Guyon's life with some of her unpublished works in that year. Overcoming his disappointment, Ramsay rapidly turned his focus away from Madame Guyon and back to Fénelon. By 1718 he and the abbé de Fénelon had worked on the publication of six works, followed by an announcement of his intention to publish the *Essay de Politique* in the *Nouvelles Littéraires*, viii.[42]

Ramsay's description of Fénelon has been described as hagiographical,[43] a tone set in the *Discours* and evident in his eulogy to Lord Deskford:

> This was the greatest and the smallest of men. What the world admired in him was only a veil to conceal from the eyes of men. All that pious condemnation in him was the effect of the purest abnegation. It was both secular and devout but there was much more from him. At present I feel as if I have lost a father on

earth but have won a protector in heaven. Senses and imagination have lost their purpose, but my heart is found in our common centre.[44]

Ramsay's adoration of Fénelon does appear to have been genuinely felt, and he may well have been awestruck by the prince of the Church that converted him and the great author of *Télémaque*. Chancellor d'Aguesseau said of Fénelon's character that: 'He was a man who always appeared to have just as much mind as the persons he might be conversing with; he stooped to their level, but without appearing to do it; this put them at their ease, and excited in them a lively sentiment of delight, so that they could neither quit him, nor, when absent, help returning to his company.'[45] In the *Anecdotes* Ramsay intimated a closeness with the Archbishop that may have been one-sided. Fénelon did not mention Ramsay in any of his own voluminous correspondence which included an expansive range of people.[46] Whatever their relationship, Ramsay seems to have developed an ardent protectiveness over the inheritance of the Archbishop (as he did with Guyon), and his editorial responsibilities and feelings for Fénelon combined to create his own version of the prelate.

His eulogy of Fénelon in the *Vie* had important consequences for Ramsay and the legacy of Fénelon.[47] As has been argued this may have been an overenthusiastic hero-worship of his subject or a desire for Fénelon to think in the same manner that he did.[48] Either way, it enabled Ramsay to insert himself into the legacy of Fénelon. There was also a sense that Ramsay used the reputation of Fénelon for his own personal gain. Not only did Ramsay feature prominently in the *Vie*, the (*Essay* and) biography's support of James Stuart aided his growing rise among the Jacobites.[49] James's fondness for Fénelon had led to his visit to Cambrai in 1709.[50] An episode vividly recounted by Ramsay in the *Vie* which depicted Fénelon's ostensible approval of James's plight and cause. Yet it was an episode that Ramsay could not have witnessed, as he did not arrive at Cambrai until the following year. This highlights the problem of Ramsay's involvement in the legacy of Fénelon and his intentions towards that heritage. For while there is much ambiguity, there also appears to have been duplicity. The ambiguity of intent is possibly best summed up by Ramsay himself: 'I shall make use, as far as I am able, of his own Words, and shall only perfect what he has written, by what I have had from his own Mouth. 'Tis no improper Digression to relate his Way of thinking, while I am writing the History of his Life.'[51]

An interesting corollary to Ramsay's relationship with Fénelon's legacy is provided through his dismissal by the Marquis de Fénelon as the editor of the Archbishop's papers. The Marquis was apparently outraged at the depiction of his uncle in the work, a depiction he found to be removed from the reality of the man.[52] There was further dissatisfaction at Ramsay's role in the *Vie* itself. The Fénelon family commissioned the historian and biographer Prosper Marchand in 1734 to write an accurate biography of the Archbishop using all of his papers, something Ramsay had lacked. Yet, as Cherel pointed out it was too late: the depiction of Fénelon promulgated by Ramsay had already become the accepted version.[53] With the exception of Cardinal Bausset, who also had access to all of Fénelon's papers, nearly all other biographers until Paul Janet in 1892 repeated Ramsay's view of Fénelon.[54] Ramsay had therefore managed to create an interpretation of *his* Fénelon that was subsequently used by a succession of biographers for over 150 years, and accepted predominantly without question due to his association with him. The result was a misconception of Fénelon's political thought, as Ramsay's works gave an inaccurate account of Fénelon's principles – as will be seen in the next chapter.

Ramsay and the Jacobites

Ramsay's association with the Jacobites dated back to his time among the Garden Circle in Aberdeen. Like the beginning of his fateful relationship with Fénelon's works, his Jacobite affiliations became more pronounced after the death of Madame Guyon as he mixed with the Parisian Jacobites. Ramsay had already made a number of Jacobite contacts such as Alexander Forbes, Lord Pitsligo in the Garden Circle, but from 1717 he began to associate with leading figures within the movement. Ramsay was particularly friendly with the Earl of Mar, and it is known that Mar was in Paris during October of 1717. Mar rather indiscreetly discussed with Jacobite sympathisers the potential of a Spanish-aided uprising in 1719.[55] One can only conjecture regarding Ramsay's knowledge of this information, but it is possible to speculate that an impending uprising may have been the catalyst for his *Essay de Politique*, announced within a few months and published in 1719. At this time Ramsay was befriended by an English Benedictine Thomas Southcott (1678–1748), and Father Lewis Innes (1651–1738) from the Scots College. It has been convincingly argued that as an acolyte of Fénelon, Southcott deliberately sought out Ramsay.[56] There was an express intention to connect James Stuart to the Archbishop's legacy to endorse Jacobitism in Britain. Together with Southcott, Ramsay managed to muster up support in France to attack a British tax imposed on Catholics. Ramsay successfully lobbied the Bishop of Fréjus, a friend of Fénelon and later Cardinal Fleury (1653–1743), to protest against Walpole's excessive taxation of Catholics. Ramsay's zeal and ability to make contacts impressed the Jacobite court. In a letter to James Stuart, Southcott wrote that Ramsay had 'a great deal of merit' and it would be a pity if 'he should not continue to improve his talents' for the benefit of the Jacobites.[57] Through his ability to network, his connection with Fénelon, and his efforts for the Jacobite cause, Ramsay obtained an audience with James in 1724.[58] Both the second edition of the *Essay* and the *Vie* were dedicated to James, in which

Ramsay pledged his loyalty to the true king of Britain.[59] Consequently, the use of Fénelon for Jacobite means and his relationship with the Archbishop appear to have ensured that Ramsay was received by James at Saint Germain-en-Laye.

After his dismissal as the editor of the works and papers of Fénelon in 1723, Ramsay was taken into the bosom of the Jacobite court. He received his peerage plus a pension, and was offered the role of tutor to the young prince Charles at Rome. This proved to be an unfortunate experience for Ramsay. He had already nurtured his 'most significant rapport' with Mar,[60] and had also become strongly attached to Lord Lansdowne and General Dillon. These three men had formed 'The Triumvirate' around James in the Jacobite leadership, but by the time Ramsay arrived in Rome they lacked influence, and men such as James Murray (1690–1770) and John Hay (1691–1740) had become pivotal figures at court. Mar was in fact viewed as a dangerous buffoon at court, and both Hay and Murray aggressively replaced him as James's chief minister. Mar, the former Tory minister had joined the Jacobites in 1715 after George I rejected his advances and refused to receive his loyal address. His botched leadership of the '15 uprising had 'proceeded to waste both his master's money and every opportunity for success in the most deplorable fashion'.[61] His tepid involvement in the uprisings of 1719 and 1721 were considered deeply suspicious, with some justification. For, while Mar's visit to Paris in 1717 was to ostensibly drum up funds and support for the Jacobite cause, he actually met with Lord Stair (1673–1747), the former soldier and diplomat, in an attempt at his own reconciliation with the British government.[62] Indeed, during the period between 1717 and 1724 Mar was working as a double agent for the British government.[63] So, while apparently working on behalf of the Jacobites, Mar was in fact negotiating his return to Britain by informing on their activities.

The involvement of Mar in the Jacobite court was seen as a reflection of James's poor Stuart judgement and a general ineptitude of the Jacobite's organisation. By the time that Ramsay arrived in Rome the court was a hotbed of intrigue and in-fighting. Pitsligo depicted the court as shambolic and toxic, filled with 'Quarrels and Humours'.[64] The court was made up of a disunited band of people headed by a vacillating leader who 'saw the finger of fate ... against him', and who was '(with somewhat excessive resignation) inclined to abandon all hope'.[65] The court consisted of a few loyal old (noble) families but many such as Mar, Murray, and even Bolingbroke had become Jacobites through disaffection.[66] In their cases, their political careers had ended with the Hanoverian accession (1714), and much of their involvement in the Jacobite cause was self-serving. Many of those who joined the Jacobites held either anti-English or British sympathies or, to be more exact, held anti-Whig sympathies. Jacobitism gave people with opposing views a figurehead with which to attack Whig supremacy and the sweeping reforms enacted throughout Britain. Yet despite this crucible of disaffection Pitsligo reveals the unrealistic optimism of the court and James's hopes when he wrote in 1719 to Mar, that 'much of the expectations of ... happiness after his restoration'.[67] The machinations of Murray and Hay in their fight for control over James, plus the direction of the court were played out against a backdrop of a delusional court separated from its home and the reality of their plight. Individuals continued to advise James that he would one day return to his rightful throne for their own gain and advancement, while any opportunity of this success had long since died.

It was into this cauldron in Rome that Ramsay as a known associate of Mar entered to tutor the young prince. Before he had arrived at the court some courtiers were already deeply suspicious of his appointment, notably Murray. Murray appeared to have passed on these doubts to James, for James wrote in a letter to Hay, that he had 'stopped literal Ramsay's journey till further order'. Stating that there was something 'odd' about the affair, which he would 'see clear through before [he] engage[d] him', though he would 'be sorry if [he] could not make a pedagogue of him', for he 'knew not where to find another'.[68] In a return letter Hay soothed James's fears by claiming that Ramsay's connection to Mar could have little effect as the prince was only 3 years old, and the prince required a first-class tutor. His recommendation as a tutor stems from his relationship with Fénelon who tutored the grandsons of Louis XIV, and Ramsay's work with the Sassenage family. Unfortunately, the suspicions of his connection with Mar appear to have been well founded and it was 'abundantly clear that Ramsay acted the part of Mar's "eyes and ears"'.[69] Within a few months of his arrival Ramsay was encircled at Rome.

His situation became untenable after an argument with a Scots Jacobite, Forster. The resultant fight saw Forster first stab Ramsay with an *épée* before Ramsay disarmed Forster and was then prevented from running his assailant through by Hay and others. James was apparently scandalised by the incident and it had to be covered up.[70] In juxtaposition with Atterbury's attacks on Mar in Paris and information passed to Hay by Atterbury, Ramsay the 'spy' was no longer required in Rome.[71] Ramsay asked James's permission to leave Rome and while James was initially reticent, a deluge of negative information from members of the court persuaded him to allow Ramsay to leave with 100 guineas. After nine months at the court he returned to Paris in the following February amid accusations that he had been dismissed. This provoked Ramsay to write to James requesting a return; however, the prince found this to be impertinent. James wrote to Fleury that Ramsay was 'a bothersome and superficial spirit', possessing no 'solid principles or maxims of true moral good policy'.[72] Later in a more circumspect frame of mind he wrote that Ramsay was 'an odd body', who had 'exposed himself strangely' to the Jacobite court, but the prince would 'be charitable enough to think him a madd man'.[73]

Ramsay experienced mixed fortunes as a Jacobite. His endeavours for the cause led to titles, a pension, and a brief period among the court at Rome, but he quickly became *persona non grata* after his duel added to questions over his talents as a political theorist. James wrote that, 'Ramsay [was] not to be anyways concerned in writing or politics', as he knew how to better able 'employ him according to his talents'.[74] After his devastating time in Rome, Ramsay experienced great acclaim and recognition as the author of *Les Voyages de Cyrus*, and his failure as a Jacobite may have aided this later success. In recognition of the achievements of Cyrus and his position as a man of letters Ramsay received his honorary DCL from Oxford. In celebration of this achievement the *Essay upon Civil Government* was republished in 1732, so that it could be included in the University's renewed *pro* and *con* debates with other works perceived to refute Locke.[75] The republication of Ramsay's *Essay* as a work deemed unthreatening to the Hanoverian regime only a decade after its original release, perhaps underlines its failure as Jacobite propaganda. Yet as will be shown in Chapters 7 and 8 Ramsay's political works were much more than Jacobite propaganda. *Cyrus* intervened in the growing market for literary classical works as the novel became an emergent form during the 1720s. Furthermore, the *Essay* was an attempt to provide a universal theory of civil government that could be employed to remove the perceived ills of contemporary society. While initially appearing anachronistic in his Jacobite assault on the 1688 Revolution, his intervention belied a shrewd understanding of the political ideology and his application of theory from both Britain and France.

Notes

1 For an account of the life of Ramsay, see Albert Cherel's *Un Aventurier Religieux au XVIIIe siècle: André-Michel Ramsay* (Paris, 1926); G.D. Henderson's *Chevalier Ramsay* (Edinburgh, 1953); Scott Mandelbrote, 'Ramsay, Andrew Michael [The Jacobite Sir Andrew Michael, Baronet] (1686–1743), Philosopher and Jacobite Sympathiser', *Oxford Dictionary of National Biography*; Georg Eckert, *'True, Noble, Christian Freethinking': Leben und Werk Andrew Michael Ramsay (1686–1743)* (Münster, 2009). Henderson's work provides the most comprehensive background of Ramsay's life in what is an admittedly small market, as detailed biographical material is sparse: there are few papers and letters but no portrait of him. Some information was left by Ramsay in his *Anecdotes* (below), but much of this is on his theoretical ideas. Ramsay is largely a hidden figure outside of his works.

2 The troubles in Ayr at this time were related to the Scottish Covenanters. With beginnings in the sixteenth century, the Covenanters signed a National Covenant in 1638 against the interference of the Stuart monarchs with the Presbyterian Church in Scotland. During the Civil Wars the desire to implement Calvinism across the three kingdoms led to a breach with their former English parliamentary allies. After an attempted re-establishment of Charles II in Scotland (1650), the Covenanters were defeated by Cromwell's army. The eventual restoration of Charles II in 1660 saw the return of Episcopalianism in Scotland, which created prolonged unrest and culminated in the Covenanters' defeat to government troops under Lord Claverhouse (1679). In 1684 disorder mounted as a number of Covenanters were summoned to court in Ayr for their political activities. At the accession of James II (1685), Covenanting was declared treasonous and Covenanters were persecuted, and it was at this point that Ramsay's family left for Ireland before subsequently returning to Ayr.

3 F.J. McLynn, *Charles Edward Stuart: A Tragedy in Many Acts* (London, 1988), 12.

4 Henderson, *Chevalier Ramsay*, 5–7.

5 Andrew Michael Ramsay, *Anecdotes de la vie de Messire André Michel de Ramsay … dictés par lui meme peu de jours avant sa mort par le instances reiterées de son Epouze* (Aix-en-Provence), 2.

6 *Ibid.*, 4.

7 *Ibid.*, 5.

8 *Ibid.*, 7–8.

9 *Ibid.*, 6–7.

10 *Ibid.*, 6.

11 For a discussion and brief biography of the Circle's members, see Henderson, *The Mystics of the North-East* (Aberdeen, 1934).

12 Ramsay, *Anecdotes*, 9–10.

13 *Ibid.*, 10.

14 Henderson, *Chevalier Ramsay*, 25.

15 *Ibid.*

16 In the *L'Histoire de la Vie de Fénelon* (The Hague, 1723), Ramsay recorded the beginning of his stay at Cambrai as 1710 (110), and Jacques Le Brun places it in August (*Chronologie*, Œuvres I (Paris, 1983)). I can find no record in Fénelon's extensive correspondence of any introduction to Ramsay by Poiret or the Garden Circle. Indeed, Fénelon does not mention Ramsay in any of his correspondence.

17 Ramsay, *L'Histoire de la Vie de Fénelon*, 145–6.

18 Henderson, *Mystics of the North-East*, 53.

19 Ramsay to Lord Deskford (13 Mar. 1715) (*ibid.*, 96).

20 Ramsay, *Anecdotes*, 14–16.

21 Andrew Michael Ramsay, *Discours de la Poesie Epique, de l'Excellence du Poeme de Telemaque, Les Avantures de Telemaque, fils d'Ulysse* (Paris, 1717), vii–viii, xli–xliii.

22 *Ibid.*, viii–ix.

23 *Ibid.*, xxxi–xxxii.

24 There are portions added to the 1717 edition that do not exist in Fénelon's original manuscript (in the Royal Library) or in the subsequent editions until 1717, and Book XII has six consecutive pages added in a different hand from the rest of the copy (Cardinal Louis François de Bausset, *Histoire de Fénelon, Tome Troisième* (Paris, 1850), 60–5). All subsequent editions of *Télémaque* have been derived from the 1717 edition.

25 Patrick Campbell of Monzie to Lord Deskford (15 May 1722), *Mystics of the North-East*, 177–8. For a brief discussion of Hooke as the translator of Ramsay's work – and nephew of the Maréchal Nathaniel Hooke, a Jacobite who served with distinction in the French army – see Thomas O'Connor, *An Irish Theologian in Enlightenment France: Luke Joseph Hooke 1714–96* (Dublin, 1995).

26 Ramsay, *Anecdotes*, 17.

27 Albert Cherel, *Fénelon au XVIIIe Siècle en France (1715–1820): Son Prestige – Son Influence* (Paris, 1917), 23.

28 The *Vie de Fénelon* was translated by Hooke into English (*The Life of Fénelon*) in the same year and published in London.

29 Ramsay, *Anecdotes*, 16.

30 Nick Childs, *A Political Academy in Paris, 1724–1731* (Oxford, 2000), 147–8.

31 The *Suite de la Nouvelle Ciropédie* and *Entretiens sur les voyages de Cyrus* were translated into English in 1729 as *A Supplement to the New Cyropaedia*. J-M Quérard's *La France Littéraire, ou Dictionnaire Bibliographique, Volume VII* (449) attributed the work to P. F. Guyot Desfontaines and F. Granet.

32 Voltaire, *The Works of Voltaire*, vol. VI, trans. William F. Flemming (New York, 1901), 274. The art historian and man of letters Horace Walpole later wrote in *Walpoliana* that, '[t]he Travels of Cyrus had their vogue, though a feeble imitation of Telemaque; and nothing [could] be more insipid or foreign to such a book, than the distilled nonsense concerning the trinity' (*Walpoliana* (London, 1799), vol. I, 136).

33 [anonymous], *A Supplement to the New Cyropaedia* (London, 1729), 111.

34 See appendix to the above *Supplement*. Bossuet, the Bishop of Meaux, became the nemesis of Fénelon, although the latter began as Bossuet's protégé and then his friend. They were eventually estranged due to Fénelon's involvement in mysticism and their confrontation over doctrinal matters during the Quietism Affair (1696–99). For Bossuet the friendship turned to enmity, and he appears to have focused his energies on ruining Fénelon and his position in the Church. The result of the Affair was Fénelon's effective banishment to Cambrai, which was a less severe punishment than Bossuet had hoped for.

35 *A Supplement to the New Cyropaedia*, pt II, 82.

36 Ramsay, *Anecdotes*, 19.

37 *Ibid.*, 20.

38 Michael Sonenscher states that the work found an audience because Ramsay held a 'literal interpretation of God's general will to save everyone', arguing that God loved all his creatures and people of all religions (*Sans-Culottes: An Eighteenth-Century Emblem in the French Revolution* (Princeton, 2008), 236). As will be argued below, Ramsay's deism never left him despite his conversion to Catholicism by Fénelon.

39 Marquis de Fénelon to Lord Deskford (3 Jun. 1716), *Mystics of the North-East*, 126. Ramsay personally wrote to Lord Deskford on 1 January 1717 to inform him of this honour, and that he would also write the *Preface* to the work (*Mystics*, 136–7). In the latter part of 1716 Ramsay sent Lord Deskford some of Fénelon's manuscripts (on the Church), but by July of 1717 he had still not sent the Garden Circle, the promised manuscripts of *Télémaque* via (the Jacobite) James Forbes.

40 Dr James Keith to Lord Deskford (2 Jul. 1717), *Mystics of the North-East*, 145 (Keith quoting Ramsay).

41 Dr James Keith to Lord Deskford (10 Sept. 1717), *Mystics of the North-East*, 149. In a letter from Keith to Deskford in May 1723 Keith discloses his displeasure at Ramsay's desire to include a letter in the *Vie de Fénelon* attacking Poiret as a false biographer of Guyon (*ibid.*, 189–90).

42 See Albert Cherel, *Fénelon au XVIIIe Siècle*, 631. I have been unable to locate this notification elsewhere.

43 See Paul Janet, *Fénelon: His Life and Works*, trans. Victor Leuliette (London, 1914), 194; Henderson, *Chevalier Ramsay*, 29.

44 Andrew-Michael Ramsay to Lord Deskford (13 Mar. 1715), *Mystics of the North-East*, 96: 'C'étoit le plus grand et le plus petit des hommes. Tout ce que le monde admiroit en luy n'étoit qu'un voile pour le cacher des yeux des hommes. Tout ce que les âmes pieuses condamnoient en luy étoit l'éffet de la plus pure abnegation. De manière qu'il étoit également caché et des profanes et des dévots, et encore plus de luy-même. Je sens à present que pour un père que j'ay perdu sur terre j'ay gagné un protecteur dans le ciel. Les sens et l'imagination ont perdu leur objet, mais mon coeur le trouve dans notre centre commun.'

45 Cardinal Bausset, *Histoire de Fénelon, Tome I*, 165–6. This view expressed by the Chancellor of France, Henri François d'Aguesseau (1668–1751), was countered in Saint-Simon's *Memoirs*. Saint-Simon portrayed Fénelon as an intelligent man who was manipulative, hugely ambitious, and able to use his piety for self-promotion (*The Memoirs of the Duke of Saint-Simon*, trans. Bayle St John (New York, 1936), I, 8 (95)).

46 Ramsay, *Anecdotes*, 11–17.

47 This view of Ramsay's hagiographical depiction of Fénelon can also be found in Paul Janet, *Fénelon: His Life and Work*, 150; Henderson, *Chevalier Ramsay*, 82.

48 Henderson, *Chevalier Ramsay*, 82.

49 This revised edition was written shortly before the *Vie*.

50 Letters written at this time in 1709 by Fénelon do not express overt support for Jacobitism; rather, they reveal a sympathy for James Stuart, whom Fénelon liked personally. He also mentions the failure of the 1708 invasion of Scotland (*Correspondance de Fénelon, Tome XIV*, eds. Jean Orcibal, Jacques Le Brun and Irénée Noye (Genève, 1992), 127, 136–7).

51 Ramsay: *Life of Fénelon* (London, 1723), 249; *Histoire de la vie de Fénelon*, 147.

52 Henderson, *Chevalier Ramsay*, 67. This claim is supported by the production of Prosper March-and's biography in 1734 for the Fénelon family, released in Britain in 1747 in a collection of works entitled, *Proper Heads of Self-Examination for a King. Drawn up for Use for the late Dauphin of France, Father to his present Majesty K. Lewis XV, whilst Duke of Burgundy. By M. De Fénelon, Archbishop and Duke of Cambray. Together with the Author's Life, A complete Catalogue of His Works, And Memoirs of his Family. Translated from the French* (London, 1747).

53 Cherel, *Fénelon au XVIIIe Siècle en France (1715–1820)*, 31.

54 Most early biographies on Fénelon simply replicated Ramsay's *Vie*, such as: d'Alembert and William Henry Melmoth (London, 1770), John Kendall (London, 1797), Charles Butler (Baltimore, 1810); Henrietta Louisa Lear (London, 1877).

55 *The Jacobite Court at Rome in 1719: From Original Documents at Fettercairn House and at Windsor Castle*, ed. Henrietta Tayler (Edinburgh, 1938), 9. The work includes a brief introduction by Tayler, but is predominantly a collection of Jacobite letters and a manuscript (memoir) written by Pitsligo on the Jacobite court in Rome and dated 16 September 1720.

56 Gabriel Glickman, *The English Catholic Community 1688–1745: Politics, Culture and Ideology* (Woodbridge, 2009), 227–8.

57 Southcott to James (16 Nov. 1722), Pauline McLynn 'Factionalism among the Exiles in France: The Case of the Chevalier Ramsay and Bishop Atterbury' (Huntingdon), 3.

58 See Henderson, *Chevalier Ramsay*, 87; Glickman, *The English Catholic Community 1688–1745*, 228–30. According to Henderson, attempts had been made as early as 1720 by Lord Lansdowne to introduce Ramsay to James. The dating of the first meeting between Ramsay and the Prince obviously contradicts his claim to have been present during the latter's meeting with Fénelon in 1709.

59 Ramsay, *Essay philosophique sur le gouvernement civil*, Preface (i).

60 McLynn, 'Factionalism among the Exiles in France', 2.

61 Pitsligo, *Manuscript, Jacobite Court at Rome in 1719*, 10.

62 On Mar's activities see E. Gregg, 'The Jacobite Career of John, Earl of Mar', *Ideology and Conspiracy: Aspects of Jacobitism, 1689–1759*, ed. E. Cruickshanks (Edinburgh, 1982), 179–200.

63 Christoph v. Ehrenstein, 'Erskine, John, styled twenty-second or sixth earl of Mar and Jacobite duke of Mar (*bap.* 1675, *d.* 1732)', *Oxford Dictionary of National Biography* online: www.oxforddnb.com.ezproxy.sussex.ac.uk/view/article/8868?docPos=5.

64 Pitsligo, *Manuscript*, 89.

65 *Ibid.*, 9.

66 For a discussion of the Jacobite supporters, see Chapter 2.

67 Pitsligo to Mar (1 Apr. 1719), *The Jacobite Court at Rome in 1719*, 167.

68 James to Hay (4 Oct. 1724), 'Factionalism among the Exiles in France', 3.

69 McLynn, *Ibid.*, 4.

70 'Factionalism among the Exiles in France', 6 (PRO. SP Italian States (85) is f.99): report by Philip Stosch a British spy codenamed 'Walton' in which only Forster's surname is provided (6 May 1724).

71 McLynn, 'Factionalism among the Exiles in France', 12–13.

72 James to Fréjus (25 Mar. 1725), RA Stuart 81/ 26, 'Factionalism among the Exiles in France', 7.

73 James to Murray (July 1725), *The Jacobite Court at Rome in 1719*, 135.

74 James to Murray (3 April 1724), *The Jacobite Court at Rome in 1719*, 229.

75 For a discussion of the *pro* and *con* debates at Oxford and the relaxation of censorship for unthreatening works by the Whig government, see J.C.D. Clark's *English Society, 1688–1832* (Cambridge, 1985) 152–3; Paul Kleber Monod's *Jacobitism and the English People, 1688–1799* (Cambridge, 1989).

7

A mythical conversation:
an *Essay* and a *Vie*[1]

The advancement of a mixed constitution to stimulate public liberty and erode absolute power in a single sovereign was addressed rather differently in the first phase of Ramsay's political works. While the application of Fénelon may have implied a continuation of this trend, Ramsay adapted Fénelon to further the Jacobite cause as he reversed the expansion of government. In linking the author of *Télémaque* to Jacobitism in the *Essay de Politique* (1719), the *Essay philosophique sur le gouvernement civil* (1721), and the *Histoire de la Vie de Fénelon* (1723), Ramsay assailed revolution and the British Parliament. His claim that he was inspired by his time with Fénelon was given credence by the *Vie de Fénelon*, in which Ramsay fondly recounted his time at Cambrai. This included a conversation between the prelate and James Stuart on civil government; a conversation that Ramsay duplicitously declared to have witnessed. A consequence of the deception was a repeated confusion (into the twentieth century) over the exact influence exerted by Fénelon on the *Essay*. Ramsay's maxims to tackle the '*maladies*' of civil government – namely an excess of political liberty in the people stemming from the development of popular government – were believed to be Fénelonian in essence.[2] His association with Fénelon as a former house guest, role as the editor of the Archbishop's papers and first biographer, provided Ramsay's work with unchallenged veracity.[3] By unpacking the theory of the *Essay* and its extended second edition, it will be possible to reveal a substantial discrepancy between the two men's political principles. In attempting to propose a solution to the ills of contemporary government, Ramsay's work not only exhibited a far greater engagement with (French and British) political ideology than Fénelon's, he employed surprising sources to undermine the 1688 Revolution. Wedded to this discussion will be an examination of the *Vie*, and Ramsay's attempt to portray Fénelon inaccurately as religiously tolerant for the Jacobite cause.

The Essay de Politique (1719)

The *Essay de Politique, où l'on traite de la nécessité, de l'Origine, des Droits, des Bornes, et des différentes formes de la Souveraineté. Selon les Principes de l'Auteur de Télémaque* (1719) claimed to propound the political principles of Fénelon's phenomenally successful *Télémaque*. Yet following Bossuet's interpretation of history, Ramsay began the *Essay* by asserting that in the history of empires and republics there were two causes of revolution: the 'love of limitless authority in those who governed, and that of independence in the people'.[4] Revolutions were instigated by a continual conflict between a sovereign and the people in which the sovereign was jealous for power and desired to possess more, while subjects were fearful of their liberty and wished to enhance it.[5] Ramsay's ambition for the work was to 'form a plan of government' producing a theory forceful enough to form good subjects, who were 'lovers of their country & their sovereigns, subject to order', but 'without being slaves'.[6] Two diametrically opposed positions suggested this possibility. The first viewed society as one of equality and independence, where self-love and particular interest directed the behaviour of men under a government formed from the sovereignty of the people. In Ramsay's second favoured position, the people were dependent and unequal. Society was shaped by a love of order and public good, and no contract existed between the people as sovereign authority was passed directly to the monarch from God.[7]

Society, according to Ramsay, was natural and found its genesis in man's sociable nature gifted by God to create union, drawing mankind together through the 'indigence of man', 'the admirable order of generation', and 'a love of country'.[8] The inherent inequality that existed between men in terms of 'wisdom, virtue, and valour' was required to create an order of minds and dependence natural to men, thereby conserving the 'order of generation'.[9] And in which children learned to obey their fathers and develop duties of tenderness together with acknowledgements of love and submission. Through this relationship the order of generation was nurtured as individuals realised that they were not equal in society and the predominance of others – fathers and social superiors – created subordination. While supreme sovereign authority was direct from God, it manifested itself originally in the government of the family in tribes as patriarchy formed the basis of civil society. Pagan society and the Biblical example of Noah's family revealed that tribes were led by fathers, who ruled through paternal rights and subordinated their children.[10] Kingship arose from this relationship. It sustained society, order and the natural ranks that originated in an unequal society essential by preserving the public good and averting the chaos of equality. For Ramsay, equality signalled the individual's pursuit of their passions through an unrestrained self-love and craving for power rather than wider care for the common good.[11] According to the laws of nature, government was necessary to prevent equality, which enabled the multitude to tyrannise government and destroy virtue by descending society into anarchy and savage liberty.[12] To resist this behaviour sovereignty must always be 'absolute' and hereditary. Absolute government allowed society to uphold rank and thwart the hegemony of the multitude's 'despotic will'.[13] While the king's authority was not arbitrary and was regulated by more than the bridle of his own will, the king did possess the capacity to judge in the *dernier ressort* ('last resort') and make the final decision as head of government. The extent of the king's prerogative empowered the sovereign to control the legislative power, the ability to make war and peace, and control taxation. Prerogative allowed the sovereign to claim rights over the actions, persons and goods of all subjects if it was judged to be in the public good.[14] Such prerogatives therefore authorised Ramsay's sovereign to sacrifice the rights of the people to their own will. Critically, it proscribed the people's capability to rebel against a tyrant, sanctioning the monarch to act in an arbitrary manner.[15]

Difficulties subsequently arise in Ramsay's claim to be adhering to the political principles of Fénelon's *Télémaque*, and four fundamental reasons emerge that contradict this contention. First, Fénelon did not expound a system of government that was reliant on natural law for its foundations. Instead, Fénelon suggested a view that provided examples of good and bad kingship, but did not delineate the origins of society and government.[16] Second, when examining the first of Fénelon's two grievances of government[17] we can see that Ramsay created a *'plan de gouvernement'* that was absolute and possessed great potential to become despotic. Fénelon vociferously argued against such kingship,[18] claiming that a king should be moderate in his behaviour;[19] sacrificing himself to the public good and liberty of his subjects.[20] Absolutism undermined these endeavours and confirmed a weak monarch whose subjects became a slave to his will.[21] This leads to a third point, in which Fénelon stated that the result of absolutism was revolution or assassination. Such power should be eschewed by a king or he (deservedly) faced the consequences of negative rule and the abandonment of the public good.[22] Lastly, Ramsay's claim to employ Fénelon's thought in the *Essay* was difficult to maintain due to the conspicuous absence of an analysis of the problems of luxury and that of war.[23] Instead, the *Essay* focused predominantly on providing a natural law argument for government's existence to subjugate the people while commerce and (the context of) war were ignored. Fénelon's promulgation of liberty for the people was replaced by Ramsay's patriarchal monarchy necessary to control the subjects who should be feared. The distinction in the two men's perspective on kingship was that Ramsay believed the people were there to serve the king, while Fénelon strongly argued that the king should serve the people. Such a dichotomy was evident in the difference between Fénelon's views and those expressed by Bossuet and Louis XIV.[24]

The often confusing nature of Ramsay application of Fénelon's political ideas is evident in the final chapter of the *Essay*. In chapters three, four and five of the second part of the work Ramsay set out the destructive nature of popular government on sovereignty. Ramsay included the historical examples of Sparta, Carthage, and Rome to demonstrate how the augmentation of 'popular power' exposed the decline of each state as they inevitably collapsed.[25] For Ramsay this decline was visibly active in the history of English government. Popular power in England had progressively risen from the signing of Magna Carta by King John in 1215 through to the inception of Parliament under Henry III in 1265.[26] Ramsay believed the progress of popular power was the result of numerous monarchs eroding the authority of the nobility. This endeavour was notably successful under Henry VII. Prior to Voltaire, Ramsay stated that the Sale of Manors had allowed commoners with money to purchase land and status in return for obedience to the king, crushing the powerbase of the barons.[27] As a result, the nobility no longer provided a buffer between the monarch and the people, allowing the latter to gain more political power throughout the seventeenth century. This power had manifested itself in the form of a regicide and rebellion.[28]

This evolution of popular government had produced a multiplicity of laws in a corrupted government as the English replicated the paths of decline in Sparta, Carthage, and Rome.[29] To prevent collapse, the solution to this (historical) problem was a return to 'monarchy moderated by aristocracy' ('*Monarchie moderée par l'Aristocracie*'). An aristocratic senate under the power of a monarch would assist the king in counsel and occupy part of the legislative. This original form of sovereignty meant the crown and elite aristocratic senate followed a hereditary succession: the template of sovereignty in Rome, the 'Northern nations', and England.[30] Interestingly, given the absolutist proclivities of the work, the *Essay* used elements of country ideology to perpetuate the return to an original Gothic government. Employing Machiavelli's dictum of the restoration of first principles to combat government corruption, Ramsay used country principles to counter the legitimacy of the Revolution and Whig Ministry. His discussion of virtue to oppose decline, his lesson of the Roman Republic's corruption as an historical warning, his attack on the degeneracy of Parliament, its faction and the Whig Ministry, and an advocacy to return the an original Gothic constitution for the public good predate both *Cato's Letters* and Bolingbroke.[31] Ramsay's inverted country perspective is an early Hanoverian example of opposition to a corrupted British constitution, emphasised by the reiteration of history.

In Ramsay's opinion 'Monarchy moderated by Aristocracy' possessed a number of advantages for achieving the public good. It produced the social cohesion required by the laws of nature through the subordination and order of ranks, guaranteeing unity in the people rather than disparate self-interested individuals. It reflected the natural inequality inherent in a monarchy where the king sat atop of society's apex. In this original society, the king would naturally rely on the counsel of his noble children, in a manner redolent of a tribal 'Grand father' seeking advice from his fellow tribal leaders. Such counsel was essential for a king, who required assistance in the legislature as this could not be left entirely as an exercise of the king's absolute will.[32] Furthermore, the nobility formed a barrier between the king and his people, while preventing the king's capacity to tyrannise the people; although a king should be aware of the nobility's potentially negative behaviour towards the people. While the multitude was not to be entirely excluded from politics for fear of arousing its jealousy, Ramsay did not elaborate how this would work.[33] Instead he tacitly advocated the French mechanism of potential involvement when levying extraordinary taxes, but never advanced the idea of how they would be consulted. Ultimately, he believed that the people must be excluded from government. They were to be occupied in continual labour to prevent an interest in politics, thereby ensuring an elite government of the monarch and his aristocratic senate in the legislature.[34]

A lack of detailed communication concerning extraordinary taxation was rather symptomatic of the issues surrounding Ramsay's 'plan' to extirpate the House of Commons. For a large part of the work, Ramsay promoted a sovereignty that was absolute before potentially undermining it with an aristocratic senate. Through Ramsay's approval of Charles II's sovereignty, however, it is perhaps possible to reconcile an absolutism that relied on a limited aristocratic senate. When Charles II was restored to the throne he was imbued with nearly all of the powers of his father prior to the Civil War.[35] These powers and extensive prerogatives enabled the king to act without much interference from a Parliament that was rarely called during his reign. As Charles II's authority resembled that of James I and Charles I,[36] the king's absolutism could coexist within a mixed system of government as it was hypothetically mitigated by Parliament. The exercise of prerogative gave the king the potential to be absolute or 'limitless' during extraordinary circumstances:[37] a tactic employed by Louis XIV to limit the representative institutions during his reign. Ramsay's mixture of absolutism with an aristocratic senate would thereby be permissible, as the king's absolute power coalesced within a mixed constitution. The senate would exchange two representative houses for one, restricting the number of aristocrats involved in the process of government, and removing any direct representation of the freeholders. In real terms, it would undo the gains in authority made by the ministry and Parliament since 1688, removing it from the executive.

Yet Ramsay's extreme endeavour to expunge the House of Commons in favour of an aristocratic senate could have been a misdirected attempt to follow Scotland's government during the reign of the Stuarts in the seventeenth century. When James I ascended to the English throne in 1603, to rule effectively over the larger kingdom he moved to London. Over the course of the century his heirs became increasingly distant from day-to-day Scottish politics. The leading Scottish nobles (magnates) began to advise them on important issues while successfully ruling in their stead. The Scottish model of Parliament boasted a single chamber dominated by these magnates, other leading aristocrats, Lords of the Articles and the Church, with the people essentially absent from Parliament.[38] Ramsay cites the recognition in Scotland of Charles II's authority as absolute, plus the crown's ability in the 1680s to extend its freedom of action by gaining greater financial independence from Parliament.[39] Ramsay therefore possessed ostensible historical precedents for his favoured absolute monarchy moderated by aristocracy. What is fascinating is his desire to mix sovereignty by completely excluding the popular element and applying it to the English Parliament, for it would garner no support due to the entrenched tradition of the Commons in England.[40] While the aristocracy played a pivotal role in England prior to and after the 1688 Revolution, in Scotland there was a strong (theoretical) custom underlining their role as arbiters. Prior to the seventeenth century, the nobility's role had been one that limited the power of the king and maintained the independence of the nation; but from the reign of James VI of Scotland and I of England (r.1567–1625), a shift occurred which favoured a policy of absolutism to limit the power of the aristocracy. Regardless of this shift, the nobility and clan chiefs were often portrayed as virtuous men in Scotland who protected relations between the people and the king.[41] This latter tack was often followed by Scottish Jacobites attacking 1689 and the Act of Union (1707). While English Jacobites and Nonjurors had a proclivity to favour restoration it was not at the expense of the Commons, which was seen as an integral (if troublesome) part of the constitution. Ramsay's 'plan' was therefore not one that could be realistically supported by eighteenth-century Jacobites under James Stuart.

While the removal of Parliament would maintain the subordination of rank and dispossess the people of any political power and the means to revolt, it would be too extreme for Britain. When one includes the French influence on Ramsay's thought there is no direct correlation, and even Louis XIV did not remove the representative institutions from the constitution. For the arch-absolutist Bossuet, the nobility occupied a special place within society and government as advisers and ministers, but this would have altered very little concerning the sovereignty of Louis XIV.[42] The desire to use the nobility, however, did perversely imitate Fénelon's call for the nobility to assist the king, and Ramsay cited *Télémaque* to support his claim. While the quotation employed by Ramsay was not present in *Télémaque*,[43] Fénelon's belief in the use of the revitalised nobility under Bourgogne's kingship was true, although Ramsay's inclusion of the nobility in government was quite different.[44] He essentially inverted the Burgundy Circle's approach of aristocrat-led reform by using it to exclude and restrict government rather than expand it. His aristocratic senate witnessed the centralisation and limitation of government to the few as a means to suppress popular government and prevent rebellion. Conversely, for Fénelon, the nobility were a vehicle for reform and the potential expansion of government through the Estates and the decentralisation of monarchical power.[45] Ramsay was offering a 'plan' that was rather singular in its nature, and had greater affinity with Louis XIV's model of government than current British or French thought. His move towards absolute monarchy, restrained by a limited senate, offered a much older vision of monarchy that gave the king a pre-eminence that contemporary theorists (in Britain and France) were beginning to eschew. The established role of the Parliament in government and the English psyche made such a manoeuvre by Ramsay destined to failure and unpopularity.

The *Essay philosophique sur le gouvernement civil* (1721)

Published in London in 1721 under the title the *Essay philosophique sur le gouvernement civil*, the second edition was a revised, corrected, and expanded version of the *Essay de Politique*. Its dedication made the edition's Jacobite allegiance clear from the beginning, despite the fact that much of the work was the same as the first edition.[46] Many of the revisions found in the second edition were designed to provide a more trenchant endorsement of Jacobitism on ideological grounds. Again, this espousal of Jacobitism within the *Essay* was promulgated under the alleged auspices of Fénelon. What the reader experiences is a belated intervention by Ramsay into the Leslie–Hoadly debate. The extensions in the second edition were designed to sharpen the attack on 'the lovers of Independency' (*'les Amateurs de l'Indépendance'*): those like Hoadly who championed popular government and defended the doctrines of the 1688 Revolution.[47] The noun 'Independency', evident in both editions of the *Essay*, was frequently applied by Hoadly to promote the rights and liberty of the individual. It was used by Hoadly to advocate the notions of contract and resistance as a means to attack Leslie's reliance on dependent patriarchal monarchy. Ramsay's employment of a new structure immediately brought to the fore this attack upon the lovers of 'Independency', as he promulgated a theory closely resembling Leslie's patriarchal absolutism which denied popular power and attempted to eradicate the possibility of resistance.

The most perceptible difference between the first and second editions of the *Essay* was the amendment of the title. While the title of the first edition had credited an adherence to the author of *Télémaque*, the second edition title attributed its maxims to Fénelon by name. This modification was made for two important reasons, and the first reason signalled Ramsay's growing involvement with the Jacobite movement in Paris. The alteration implied that the *Essay* was based upon his principles, forging a link between Fénelon and James Stuart, the former apparently endorsing Jacobite doctrines on sovereignty. This method facilitated Ramsay's professed reliance upon Fénelon's (European) renown, while depicting James Stuart as a contemporary Telemachus. Ramsay dedicated the second edition to the prince, the 'king of Great Britain', which James believed to be a reference to his own plight as a king outside of his rightful lands.[48] Ramsay likened James's suffering to that experienced by other 'heroes' and great kings, such as Robert I (of Scotland) and Charles II (of England and Scotland). It was a torment produced by James's removal from his own lands and throne, 'exiled in a foreign country'.[49] Yet it was a pain borne with 'moderation' and the knowledge that James was the 'true father of the people', and Ramsay claimed that he had undertaken the work to support the rightful king's rights.[50]

The second reason for the adjustment of the title was Ramsay's desire to convey a broadening in scope of Fénelon's philosophy for his *Essay* by not restricting them to *Télémaque*. From its original publication in 1699 to 1721, there had been six editions of *Télémaque* including Ramsay's own edition, so the work was readily accessible to the public. By stating that the work was in 'accordance' with Fénelon's principles Ramsay could imply the inclusion of a private, perhaps hitherto unknown knowledge of the Archbishop's political ideas. This implication was stated in the expanded *Preface*: 'The only merit of the author is to have been nurtured for years under the light and sentiments of the late François Salignac de la Mothe-Fenelon, Archbishop of Cambrai ...[taking his] instructions from this illustrious prelate, to write this essay'.[51] His time with Fénelon had immersed him in the Archbishop's political thought, and the *Essay* would move beyond the first edition's use of *Télémaque* to something 'philosophically' new in the second.

Ramsay's '*philosophique*' approach to his new edition on civil government was exerted in the extended *Preface*. The new *Preface* had a dual function. It claimed to anchor the *Essay* firmly in the political principles of Fénelon, and, in so doing, attached Fénelon to the work's principle of 'divine philosophy' and its 'ideas of justice, truth, and virtue'.[52] Ramsay set out a political system dependent upon divine philosophy (natural law) to uphold the notion that God had instituted an '*ordre*' in which society and government were determined and fixed by God, not man. Accordingly, as the father of mankind God had created man as part of a whole, so the happiness of the people and God relied on the subsumption of the individual into the whole, for the public good superseded private interest. The individual merged with his fellows to produce 'unity' and provide the foundations for law and the state.[53] Through providence, God had shaped the unity of man and society to inhibit individualistic interests from violating the most sacred rights. Ramsay's 'plan' to correct the maladies of civil government was founded on this notion of divine law to prevent revolution. His approach to controlling the 'excess of liberty' in both the people and princes was to appeal to the rigidity of God's will in the creation of a state that once established could not be changed: a system that regarded rebellion as an attack on providence.[54] Ramsay's 'philosophie' extended the Essay de Politique's aim to delineate how English popular government led to revolution and had exiled the rightful king of Britain.

If one departs from Ramsay's claim in the title and preface to have based his 'divine philosophy' on Fénelon's instructions, the new preface and other additions reveal considerable overlap with Bossuet's political thought.[55] Fénelon did not use theology to underpin a cohesive political system: it was applied to forge the moral character of a prince (Bourgogne). Ramsay instead turned to Bossuet in his endeavour to entwine religion and politics, as his theology linked with the ancient philosophy through scripture to reveal the origins of government. Justifying its rigid social hierarchy and the demands made upon people's behaviour. Indeed the Essay's premise of the conflict between the ruler and his people of the Essay was appropriated from Bossuet as Ramsay plagiarised elements of his work.[56] In abjuring Machiavelli's positive interpretation of the conflict between the two groups, he followed Bossuet's opinion in the Politics that a monarch must dominate his people through absolute sovereignty to preclude the opportunity of revolution. 'Divine philosophy' provided maxims from the laws of nature that created good subjects who loved their country and pursued virtue over self-interest, stultifying their desire to revolt. Respect for the natural law bound society together supplying the foundation of government and law. Justice, truth, and virtue would flourish in society if it pursued this eternal law; a belief discernible in the ancients who grounded their own law upon divinity. While customs differed between states, the law of nature was eternal, alike for the ancients and the moderns as God governed the law and generated all society.[57] The basis of the law of nature was dependent upon love. Not only did God's universal love permeate the law of nature, it permitted all human virtue to flow from this binding of society and man together. Six forms of love provided this social attachment: a love of God; a love of God's creatures; a love of mankind; a love of country; a love of one's parents, and a love of self (preservation).[58] The natural order for this love was for the individual to place the least emphasis on self-love, favouring a love for their families, then their country, their fellow man, and, most importantly, God.

Man's innate sociability obliged him to live together under law, maintaining the principles of union and society. The social bonds of God's laws exclude any possibility that man had ever existed in an independent condition or lived in fear, avarice, and ambition.[59] The commonality of this universal edict meant that humanity effectively occupied the world as brothers, forming 'one city'.[60] This union was made necessary and strengthened by man's intrinsic weakness that ensured the reliance on one's fellows and led to happiness through community. Driven by mutual wants and the individual's sense of obligation to their parents (paternal power), community was generated by the 'Order of Generation'.[61] An order secured by the experience that children had of their fathers, whom they freely learned to obey, thereby transmitting the values of inequality and dependence to the individual who became accustomed to obeying someone of superior status (rank).[62] Kingship arose from the rule of the father as head of the family, which progressed to the leadership of a tribe: a collection of connected fathers counselling and obeisant to a 'Grand father'.[63] This channel to sovereign authority was fed by inequality, which reflected the natural superiority of a few leaders who were able to display their right to rule through 'wisdom, virtue and courage'.[64] The 'order of Providence' dictated that most were born for subordination and obedience, guaranteeing that the order of society was sustained as God decreed.[65] To attempt to violate this subordination was treason against heaven, exposing the individual's pursuit of the passions and private interest in their craving for equality and selfish liberty.[66] Such behaviour tyrannised society as well as its leaders, and equality demonstrated a lust for power in which the laws of nature were subverted. Virtue became subsumed by immoderate self-love as avarice spread through the multitude to create a 'savage liberty'.[67] Tyranny, chaos, and self-love were averted by a society based upon the rank and order that mirrored God's supreme authority.[68] Obligations to parents revealed the acceptance of the law of nature while augmenting a love of country, to which the individual owed their 'birth, preservation and education'.[69] The 'Order of Generation' established a man's country, bound society, preserved unity, while engendering law and virtue.

Ramsay's application of natural law and of patriarchal kingship arose from the development of the family to engender a 'love of country' and unity that were extant in Bossuet's *Politique*. Within Bossuet's political system a strong emphasis was placed upon the need to utilise the absolute power of the king to create a robust platform for sovereign authority to withstand faction and resistance in the state. It was this political vision of kingly power that Ramsay depended upon to underpin his own politics, rather than the Bishop's reliance on scripture as a foundation of politics. Ramsay extracted the evolution of civil government through the family – from God's Providence – to establish a government that was wedded to natural law and the promotion of a patriarchal king. This genesis of civil government underscores a difference between Bossuet and Hobbes that is important for discussing his influence on Ramsay. While Hobbes relied on original contract to end the state of nature, Ramsay denied either the possibility of such a state's existence and the use of contract as the foundation of government. Like Bossuet's alternative path, Ramsay's government did not follow Sir Robert Filmer's (or Leslie's) Adamite view of kingship as a personal inheritance from God (*Patriarcha*).[70] For Ramsay, kingship arose as natural leaders emerged within the family unit seizing the political authority granted to mankind. Instead of an application of Fénelon's principles, what the reader actually encounters is a mélange of French and British patriarchal absolutism to restrain popular power and preclude revolution. Bossuet's principles provide an underlying platform from which Ramsay champions an absolute monarch who was in essence limited by an elite aristocracy. Yet for most of the *Essay* the monarch was not restrained, and much was made of the king's power over the people as he engaged in a struggle to contain their grasping liberty.

Ramsay's 'plan' echoes Leslie's attitude towards the British populace, who were to be completely extricated from politics to prevent social and political anarchy.[71] Using Bossuet's natural law as its foundation and his absolutism to restrain the people, Leslie's rhetoric was applied by Ramsay to attack the development of popular power. Other publications and his long-running opposition to Hoadly and the Whigs as displayed in the *Answer* debate were emulated by Ramsay. Regardless of Leslie's Adamite patriarchy, Ramsay followed the Nonjuring Jacobite in using patriarchy with absolutism to savage popular power in support of complete subordination and obedience.[72] Leslie had argued that patriarchy ensured that the people did not possess natural liberty, and that their birth right had made them subject to their fathers and king.[73] Public liberty was a Commonwealth principle and an affront to God, as the multitude's arbitrary nature and raging passions had to be controlled by a divinely instituted monarch.[74] The multitude was to be feared, as its behaviour, if unchecked, led to destruction and revolution. The solution was strong: robust kingship in which the people were controlled and the possibility of resistance or revolution was suppressed.[75] Ramsay shadowed Leslie's assault on those (Whigs) that propounded popular government, resistance, and supported the 1688 Revolution. His frequent references to 'Independency' and the closeness of his thoughts on the multitude and revolution, reveal a belated engagement in the *Answer* debate, to underline the pernicious effects of the British people on kingship.

Moving beyond the covert theoretical discussion in the first edition, the extended *Preface* reflected a sharpening of this attack on the 1688 Revolution for the second edition. He maintained that the alteration of the second edition for his 'enterprise' was defined by the 'imperfect' nature of the first edition. The method for the second edition was 'changed in several places in order to gauge every truth in its place, and give it new strength by this arrangement'.[76] Ramsay had no real need to alter the work greatly as the first edition espoused much of the same content. Part of the original *Essay*'s imperfection was its structure as a two-part work: the first explained the origins of sovereign government, and the second described the extent, origins, and forms of sovereign authority.[77] The second edition removed this division and relied on a single linear discussion of sovereignty as a progressive argument; from the origins of government to justifications and historical examples of the internecine danger of popular sovereignty to a solution.

Within this new structure there was a modification of certain chapters. Two chapters were fundamentally unchanged but had their titles amended in the second edition. The '*Introduction*' became '*Des différens Systèmes de Politique*', and the '*Du Roi de Providence*' switched to '*Du Roi de Fait & de Droit*'. These alterations swiftly established that Ramsay's *Essay* was in diametric opposition to supporters of '*Les Amateurs de l'indépendance*', and the belief that the monarchical succession in England could be corrected. The renaming of the '*Introduction*', which comprised the same content, achieved this.[78] Ramsay's viewpoint of order, inequality, dependence, and rejection of a contract in the foundation of government attempted to rebuff 'lovers of independency' and their belief in a pursuit of the individual and their passions. This led to insecurity and anarchy in civil government.[79] Ramsay's altered first chapter title effectively expounded his theoretical position in the new edition, generating an immediate tension between the two opposing theories on the origins of government. From this point onward he marshalled a sustained assault against those like Hoadly who believed in the idea of an original contract. Such support led to a conviction that the people were included in sovereign authority, and thereby empowered them to subvert the law through rights of property, power, and authority which could be defended by rebellion if necessary.[80]

The adjustment of the 1719 chapter '*Du Roi de Providence*' to '*Du Roi de Fait & de Droit*' was another example in which both chapters remained the same but were renamed. The chapter discussed 'Subordination' and the notion that the individual should submit to all that God permits.[81] Subordination must be stressed at all times to sustain the peace within a state and avoid anarchy. Ramsay discussed the obedience due to a king, and cited the example of Christ's obedience to the Emperors of Rome. Ramsay's submission to monarchy exhibited a need to support its existence as the frequently chosen form of government fixed in perpetuity.[82] This broadened to the people's acceptance of both tyrants and usurpers to ensure peace. There could be no rebellion, even against a usurper, as it created anarchy. 'It is certain', wrote Ramsay, 'that acts of jurisdiction exercised by a usurper who is in possession, have the power to oblige, not by virtue of his right, because he has none, but because he acts with the right of government'.[83] A usurper must be obeyed as the de facto head of state, even though the usurped king remained true sovereign (de jure). Through the new title of the chapter, Ramsay confirmed that he had more overtly entered into the debate previously discussed on de facto and de jure ownership of property and the throne of England in 1719.[84] It stressed a greater emphasis on the situation of James Stuart and situated Ramsay in opposition with contract theorists.

Ramsay's use of 'King de facto' and 'de jure' asserted James Stuart's position while condemning the illegality of James's exile.

As a piece of Jacobite propaganda, the difficulty with this intervention was that it came too late. The theory espoused by Ramsay and his attempts to undermine the position of contractualists like Hoadly, was that this debate had ended in 1714 when the great fear of Jacobitism began to subside after George I's accession. The threat had certainly ended by 1716 (after the '15), and so did this reliance on divine right, patriarchy, hereditary right, non-resistance, providence, and the legality of the Revolution. The events of 1714 ended the need to argue over such (religious) tenets because the Act of Settlement had come to pass under George I, and was truly established by 1719. This had been recognised by a new wave of Jacobite propagandists such as *Mist's Weekly Journal*, which employed new tactics in opposition to the new regime.[85] The impact of French thought and his time in France may have potentially clouded his intervention into British political propaganda, making it appear dated.

The anachronistic theoretical intervention aside, the opportunity to mount a more sustained attack on those who philosophically opposed the Revolution witnessed a very contemporary engagement with the ancients and moderns debate. In the second edition Ramsay excised the chapter '*Du Gouvernement de Sparte & de Carthage*', to permit a direct comparison between the chapters on ancient Rome and contemporary England. This comparison reiterated Bossuet's contention that popular power had let to the destruction of the once great Empire of Rome. By implication this was the fate that awaited England, as the unfettered increase in the authority of the people (Parliament) had engendered an excess of liberty. As historical lessons divulged – in Machiavelli and Bossuet – there were consequences for excessive liberty in government. Ramsay's use of comparison reveals him to be one of the early proponents in the eighteenth century of classical history to illuminate the path of contemporary states.[86] He inverted Machiavelli's view, but in so doing he pre-dated *Cato's Letters*, the *Craftsman*, and Montesquieu. After Ramsay's solution to this problem of a '*Monarchie modérée par l'Aristocratie*' (ch. XV), two new chapters were added at the end of the new edition: '*Du Gouvernement purement Populaire*' and '*Du Gouvernement où les Loix seules président*'. The chapters reiterate Ramsay's attack upon '*les Amateurs de l'indépendance*' and their belief that government was founded upon a free contract.[87] Government was not a free contract according to Ramsay.[88] It originated from God's divine plan in order to control the wicked, selfish passions of men;[89] and once established it was fixed permanently and could not be distorted through rebellion.[90] Sovereign power was visible and living, yet its unity and order did not reside in the people but in the sovereign, and by implication Britain's de jure sovereign was James Stuart (James III). These sentiments in the work were underlined by scriptural proof provided in the final chapter '*Des idées* que l'Ecriture Sainte nous donne de la politique', moved from the end of the first part in the first edition to add scriptural weight to the overall veracity of the second edition's argument.

Ramsay's 'revised, corrected, and expanded' version altered little of the original edition's theory on civil government, and simply presented a more precise and sustained attack upon '*les Amateurs de l'Indépendance*'. By restructuring his 'imperfect' critique on popular sovereignty and the right to rebel, Ramsay was able to offer his own 'plan' as a stark contrast to the turmoil of the excessive liberty of the people and the position of the apologists for 1688. While Ramsay's position would not have been out of place in the court of Charles II as a Court Tory, the views contained in the *Essay* were not far from those advocated by Nonjurors and High Church Tories into the second decade of the eighteenth century. Problematically, his application of the religious tenets that had formerly defended the power of monarchy had been shaped by Ramsay to create a monarch that could potentially act arbitrarily (tyrannically). His amalgamation of Bossuet's robust absolutism was designed to rebuff the Revolution that removed James III from the succession in favour of a return to an older (Stuart) form of monarchy. The combination of absolutism in a mixed (aristocratic) system would have been unpalatable to many in Britain before 1688, but nearly all after 1716. The work should therefore be viewed as a failed piece of Jacobite propaganda. It contains no cohesive plan of how to enact change and is at times actually rather vague. What the *Essay* is, however, is an attempt to create a (universal) political theory to remedy the ills of all governments. Ramsay's intervention was applied to a British context for the Jacobite cause but much of its content had larger aspirations. Linking French with British ideas of governance, Ramsay aimed to reverse the progress of popular sovereignty, targeting in particular the supporters of the 1688 Revolution.

Ramsay's *Vie de Fénelon* (1723)

Ramsay's attempt to promote the cause of James Stuart in the two editions of the *Essay*, made a surprising reappearance in *L'Histoire de la Vie de Fénelon*. The *Vie*'s concentration on Madame Guyon, Ramsay's conversion to Catholicism, and the conversation between Fénelon and James Stuart created an odd biography. But it was through this political conversation that Ramsay tied Fénelon to the plight of James Stuart, and began over two centuries of confusion regarding the origin of the political principles of the *Essay*. By binding the *Vie* retrospectively to the *Essay* Ramsay was able to substantiate his earlier claim that the *Essay* reproduced the political beliefs of Fénelon. These maxims were purportedly taken from a meeting which occurred between the Archbishop and the prince in 1709.

They were recounted by Ramsay, who admitted that he would 'use as much of [Fénelon's] own words' as he could, but it would not be perfect as he was writing about 'things he said' to him.[91] The discernible problem with Ramsay's account of this meeting was that he did not arrive in Cambrai until 1710 and did not meet James until 1724.[92] Ramsay explained, however, that he would provide a 'general idea of his political principles, prevalent throughout *Télémaque* and the *Dialogues des Morts* discussed with the young prince during his stay at Cambrai'.[93]

According to the conversation, Fénelon 'maintained the same political language as Mentor in *Télémaque*, and he made him see the benefits he might derive from the form of government in his country, and that he should have a senate'.[94] The scheme of government set out by Fénelon to the prince at Cambrai declared that all nations originated from many different families under God who was the common father, and consequently 'paternal authority was the first model of government'.[95] The natural and universal law which governed each family ensured that the public good was pursued over the private interest of the individual. Accordingly, 'the love of the people, the public good', and 'the general interest of the country' reflected 'therefore the immutable law & universal sovereign'.[96] A law that pre-dated all contracts and from which all other laws stem. This law was guaranteed by the government's supreme authority and ability to act in the 'last resort' (*'dernier ressort'*), which was the foundation of political unity and civil order. Those that governed must protect this order by serving the public good and could do anything to ensure it, including arbitrary action.[97] As in the *Essay*, the happiness of subjects was dependent on their 'subordination' and the observance of tradition. For 'liberty without order was a profligacy that attracted despotism', and 'order without liberty was a slavery lost to anarchy'.[98] Princes 'jealous of their authority would always want to extend it', while the 'people passionate about their liberty always wanted to augment it'.[99] The answer was to walk a middle path which avoided the chaos and tumult of revolution caused by this battle for supremacy between a king and his subjects. It was the duty of every wise King, to desire only to be 'the executor of the laws, and to possess a supreme council to moderate his authority'.[100] Ramsay concluded Fénelon's political lesson by stating:

> With these maxims, which are convenient for all states, the sage Mentor [claimed] that the happiness of the nation maintaining the subordination of ranks, reconciling the people's freedom with obedience to the sovereign, rendering men together as good citizens and faithful subjects without being slaves, free without being unrestrained. The pure love of order is the source of all political virtues as well as all divine virtues. This existed in all his sentiments.[101]

In addition to the political sentiments expressed in the *Vie*, Ramsay further portrayed Fénelon as an advocate of religious toleration.[102] He stated that Fénelon believed a prince should:

Never force subjects to change their religion. No human power can force, he told him, the impenetrable corner of freedom in the heart. Force can never persuade men that they are hypocrites. When Kings interfere with religion rather than protect it, they place it under constraint. Grant to all, therefore, civil tolerance.[103]

Ramsay cited this quote from Book XXIII of *Télémaque* (1717), and it was employed in both editions of the *Essay* to inspire religious toleration for the subjects of a king.[104] It has been convincingly argued that Ramsay was embraced by the Jacobite court to render James Stuart less threatening to the Protestant British.[105] Fénelon's elevation of liberty in his assault on tyranny was extended by Ramsay to nurture an image of the Archbishop as religiously tolerant. By implication, as a former protégé of Fénelon's, James Stuart was also tolerant and believed in a freedom of conscience, rather than Catholic bigotry like his father (James II). This use of *Télémaque* was contextually inaccurate, as the original text considered the need for a king to remove himself from matters of faith:

> Remember that Kings must submit to religion, and they should never undertake to adjust it; religion comes from God, and is above the King. If Kings attempt to interfere with religion rather than protect it, they place it in under constraint. Kings are so powerful, and men are so weak that everything is in peril of being altered through the indiscretion of Kings, if they concern themselves with things sacred. So leave the decision freely to the friends of the gods, and confine yourself to punish those who do not obey your judgment once it has been pronounced.[106]

Fénelon's meaning in *Télémaque* was quite different from that set out in the *Vie*. In *Télémaque*, Fénelon discussed the necessity of a king to resist the temptation to subjugate religion and the Church under his temporal power. Men must possess full liberty to pursue God via Catholicism, unless they contravened the laws of the state in which case they should be controlled. Such desires were later expressed in the *Tables de Chaulnes* (1711). In this work, Fénelon advocated a 'reciprocal independence of the two powers' spiritual and temporal.[107] Fénelon wanted to free both institutions from interference by the other, as they knew better how to run their own affairs; albeit with a great deal of cooperation and mutual assistance.[108] An important part of Fénelon's Church was its attack on sects and his insistence that it formulated a 'plan to eradicate Jansenism'.[109] Fénelon believed in one faith and that people must be returned to Catholicism. This had been his role as a young priest when educating Huguenot girls under Bossuet.[110] He wanted to root out Jansenism at all levels of the Church to avoid any possibility of schism. To achieve this he wanted the Benedictines to impose doctrinal rule.[111] Indeed, Fénelon was preoccupied by the danger that Jansenists and Huguenots posed in France in the final years of his life.[112] The significance of this view was that it countered Ramsay's depiction in the *Vie* of Fénelon as a bastion of religious toleration.[113] A principle promulgated by Ramsay that did not exist in his political works, just as he promoted an absolutism that Fénelon criticised in *Télémaque*.

Adding to the confusion of Ramsay's depiction of Fénelon's toleration is his account of the process by which he was converted to Catholicism by Fénelon and their discussions on natural religion. Such dialogues underline the Archbishop's commitment to the Catholic Church. For example, Fénelon compared Catholicism and deism with Ramsay, stating that in order for the individual to comprehend God's law they must be Catholic. Full understanding was attained through the idea of tradition; a tradition that Catholicism had transmitted from the beginning of history through the Jews, Christ, and the Apostles to the present time.[114] Catholicism was the keeper of the word and laws of God. Through a continued chain of tradition the Catholic Church had empowered humanity to discover the greatness of God's capacity and knowledge. Religious truth, like 'the certainty of our ideas depends on their universality, and the immutability of the accompanying evidence: even the certainty of the facts depends on the universality of the immutability of the tradition that affirms them'.[115] Time had been the testament to this truth and had been revealed in law through the Bible, as Catholic, luminous and filled with mystery.[116] To break with the Church was to lose sight of this message for the individual was no longer within the sanctity of the true faith.

Deism lacked this understanding, and Ramsay's spiritual quest was therefore found to be wanting through his adherence to deism and a belief in Christian plurality.[117] Tradition was lost in deism as it was in other Christian sects ('Hérétiques'), and under Mahomet and paganism because the true message became adulterated and broken.[118] Furthermore, Deism lacked the understanding of what it meant to sacrifice oneself to God, thereby precluding the deist from a real knowledge of God. According to Fénelon, 'to love purely' and 'humbly believe' in the 'Catholic religion' there were two articles of faith: 'the love of an invisible God' and 'obedience to the Church's living oracle'.[119] Catholicism over all other religions taught the spiritual poverty essential for pure love: a disinterested sacrifice of the self through a total love of God.[120] To believe absolutely in God and to comprehend the magnificence of faith one must be Catholic. Thus claimed Ramsay, the Archbishop told him that you 'cannot be a wise deist without becoming a Christian, nor philosophically Christian without becoming Catholic'.[121] Ramsay's conversion to Catholicism by Fénelon and their discourses on natural religion further underline the Archbishop's unequivocal loyalty to the Catholic Church. From Fénelon's early career as a priest to his deathbed letter to Louis XIV, the Archbishop did not tolerate schismatic sects. Ramsay's development of Fénelon's toleration may have stemmed from a misunderstanding of his discourse with Protestants and mystics such as the Garden Circle,[122] but it became an expedient tool to imply that his toleration had been absorbed in lessons by James Stuart. Such an image of a religiously tolerant Catholic king was one that the Jacobites had struggled to transmit to a Protestant

British public fearful of the memory of his Catholic father James II.[123] Members of the Jacobite court believed that if it could be communicated to the British it may appear more acceptable to restore James Stuart to the throne as James III.

Ramsay's claim to have harnessed the political principles of Fénelon as the foundation of his theory on government does not stand up to scrutiny. His efficacious personal association with Fénelon made it expedient for Ramsay to claim a use of the Archbishop's ideas as he endeavoured to generate an image of James Stuart that might be British. This notion was extended over the three works here discussed, including Fénelon's biography. The inclusion of the conversation in which Fénelon instilled sound principles of government and religious toleration was designed to promote James Stuart as a good king of sound convictions. Yet when one looks beneath the surface it quickly becomes evident that Ramsay was not employing the same approach to kingship as Fénelon. Instead of a concentration on the people's liberty and the public good, Ramsay promulgated a king that would restrain the liberty of the people as something to be feared, not nurtured. The example of Rome (and Carthage) had revealed that an excessive liberty in the people led to revolution, and the recent experience of England appeared to follow this path. Ramsay's solution was to squash public liberty, beginning with the extirpation of the British Parliament. Its replacement with an aristocratic (hereditary) senate would further the king's authority while re-establishing the ancient power of the nobility in Britain. Yet this was a power that did not need to be re-established in Britain, as the aristocracy had remained central to the behaviour of government from the seventeenth century.

Ramsay's attempt to graft French desires into British politics observed an idiosyncratic (and presumably) unpopular appeal to a sovereignty, that Fénelon was endeavouring to move beyond for wider government. Ramsay's theory of civil government offered eccentric innovation that wedded a 1670s Court (Tory) monarchy under Charles II as exemplified by Bossuet's Louis XIV, to a French desire to reinvigorate the aristocracy while juxtaposing it with British country ideology. At best, this merger of absolutism with limited aristocracy was a misguided replication of seventeenth-century Scotland; at worst, an outsider's lack of appreciation for the workings of the eighteenth-century British system. Either way, in rejecting the burgeoning theoretical trends in Britain and France towards greater liberty and the prominence of Parliament, Ramsay introduced an outdated 'plan of government' that did not suit the purposes of James Stuart and the Jacobites. Nor did it reveal contemporary trends in Jacobite propaganda, as this had jettisoned Leslie's Nonjuror religious tenets to embrace a wider understanding of country ideology that required a representative component.

Notes

1 The basis for this chapter began as 'Fénelon's Cuckoo: Andrew Michael Ramsay and Archbishop Fénelon', in *Fénelon in the Enlightenment: Traditions, Adaptations, and Variations*, eds Christoph Schmitt-Maaß, Stefanie Stockhorst, and Doohwan Ahn (New York and Amsterdam, 2014).

2 See Cardinal Louis François de Bausset, *Histoire de Fénelon, Tome Troisième* (Paris, 1850), 616; Paul Janet, *Fénelon: His Life and Works*, trans. Victor Leuliette (London, 1914), 280; Françoise Gallouédec-Genuys, *Le Prince selon Fénelon*, 290. Moreover, earlier editions of Fénelon's Œuvres contained the *Essay* either as a work of Fénelon's or an expression of his thought; such as the Œuvres de Fénelon, Archevêque de Cambrai, Publiées d'après les manuscrits originaux et les éditions les plus correctes, avec un grand nombre de pièces inédites, Tome XXII, ed. J-A Lebel (Paris,1824).

3 See Jean-Baptiste le Rond d'Alembert *Eulogy of Fénelon* (London, 1770); Jean François La Harpe, Éloge de François de la Mothe Fénelon (Paris, 1810); E.K. Sanders, *Fénelon: His Friends and Enemies, 1651–1715* (London, 1901); Chanoine Moïse Cagnac, *Fénelon: Politique tirée de l'Evangile* (Paris, 1912); Ely Carcassone, *Fénelon: l'Homme et l'Œuvre* (Paris, 1946); Françoise Gallouédec-Genuys, *Le Prince selon Fénelon* (Paris, 1963); James Herbert Davis Jr., *Fénelon* (Boston, 1978). For a period of over 150 years after Fénelon's death, many biographers relied upon Ramsay's *Vie de Fénelon* as the blueprint for their own biographies.

4 Andrew Michael Ramsay, *Essay de Politique* (The Hague, 1719), i: '*L'Amour de l'Autorité sans bornes dans ceux qui gouvernement, & [sic] celui de l'indépendance dans le peuple*'.

5 Bossuet, *Discours sur l'Histoire Universelle*, Œuvres de Bossuet, ed. abbé B. Velat and Yvonne Champailler (Paris, 1961), 1012–13. Bossuet rejected Machiavelli's positive reading of the tension between the two factions, believing that it led to the downfall of Rome. Such a tension should therefore be restrained by the absolute power of the monarch (see Chapter 4). Discussions of such internecine state conflicts between groups can be found in: Xenophon *Cyropaedia*, VIII; Plato, *Statesman*, 292–3; Plato, *Republic*, VIII; Aristotle, *Politics*, V, viii; Polybius, *Histories*, VI; *Histories*, vi. The specific conflict in Rome between the people and senate can be located in Livy and also in Machiavelli, *Discourses*, I, 40; Bossuet, *Discours sur l'Histoire Universelle*. These classical ideas were particularly influential on his political system as expressed in *Le Voyages de Cyrus*, which will be discussed in the following chapter. Fénelon does mention the two extremes of absolutism and anarchy in the *Examen de conscience* (977–8), but not to attack the people.

6 Ramsay, *Essay*, ii–iii: '*Amateurs de leur Patrie & leurs Souverains, soûmis à l'ordre, sans être Esclaves*'.

7 *Ibid.*, 1–3.

8 *Ibid.*, 18–21: 'indigence de l'homme', the 'ordre admirable de la Propagation', and 'par l'amour de la Patrie'.

9 *Ibid.*, 23.

10 *Ibid.*, 43–6.

11 *Ibid.*, 27–9.

12 *Ibid.*, 29–31. Ramsay's application of the laws of nature, were juxtaposed with a traditional Tory vision of society.

13 *Ibid.*, 31–2. Baldi has noted the similarities between Bossuet's views on absolute sovereignty but believes their application of natural law to be different (*Philosophie et politique chez Andrew Michael Ramsay* (Paris, 2008), 68–72).

14 *Ibid.*, 114–15.

15 *Ibid.*, 86.

16 Fénelon, *Télémaque*, Œuvres II, ed. Jacques Le Brun (Paris, 1997), 16 and 68–9.

17 *Ibid.*, 290.

18 *Ibid.*, 168–9.

19 *Ibid.*, 214.

20 *Ibid.*, 72.

21 *Ibid.*, 168.

22 *Ibid.*, 290–1.

23 See livres III, VII, X, and XVII on commerce, and livre II and IX on war.

24 See Chapter 4.

25 Ramsay, *Essay de Politique*, 145.

26 *Ibid.*, 150–2.

27 *Ibid.*, 161–2.

28 *Ibid.*, 170.

29 *Ibid.*, 184.

30 *Ibid.*, 200–1.

31 *Ibid.*, 177, 200. See Quentin Skinner, 'The Principles and Practice of Opposition: The Case of Bolingbroke versus Walpole', *Historical Perspectives: Studies in English Thought and Society, in Honour of J.H. Plumb*, 95–7 and 123–7; J.G.A. Pocock, *The Ancient Constitution and the Feudal Law: A Study of English historical thought in the seventeenth century. A Reissue with a Retrospect* (Cambridge, 1987), 369–70; E.J. Hundert, *The Enlightenment's Fable: Bernard Mandeville and the Discovery of Society* (Cambridge, 1994), 12; Mark Goldie, 'The English System of Liberty', *Cambridge History of Eighteenth Century Political Thought*, eds Goldie and Wokler, 64–70. As will be discussed in the following chapter Ramsay's ideas pre-date those of Bolingbroke, whom he knew through the *Entresol* after the publication of both editions of the *Essay*. Skinner and Pocock both discuss the attempt by Bolingbroke to employ the 'country' platform in the *Craftsman* (1726–52) to offer opposition to Walpole's Oligarchy. Bolingbroke's *Fragments* (or *Essays*) bear a striking resemblance in their treatment of the development of government to Ramsay, although they have different end points in their type of government sovereignty.

32 *Ibid.*, 189.

33 *Ibid.*, 190, 203–4.

34 *Ibid.*, 192–4.

35 See Chapter 1.

36 See J.G.A. Pocock, 'Machiavelli, Harrington and English Political Ideologies in the Eighteenth Century', *Politics, Language and Time, Essays on Political Thought and History* (London, 1972), 131; J.G.A. Pocock, *The Machiavellian Moment: Florentine Political Thought and the Atlantic Republican Tradition* (Princeton, 1975), 406–7; H.T. Dickinson, 'The Eighteenth-Century Debate on the Sovereignty of Parliament', *Transactions of the Royal Historical Society*, 5th series, 26 (1976), 190–1.

37 See David Wootton, 'Introduction', *Divine Right and Democracy: An Anthology of Political Writing in Stuart England*, ed. David Wootton (London, 1986), 29–30; Nicholas Henshall, 'The Myth of Absolutism', *History Today*, 42, 6 (Jun. 1992), pp. 40–7 (40, 47); Henshall, *The Myth of Absolutism: Change and Continuity in Early Modern European Monarchy* (London, 1992), 3, 128–9; Glenn Burgess, *Absolute Monarchy and the Stuart Constitution* (Yale, 1996), 142–50.

38 See Bruce Lenman, *The Jacobite Risings in Britain 1689–1746*, 12–17, 32; Bruce Lenman, *The Jacobite Cause* (Glasgow, 1986), 11–15; Geoffrey Holmes, *The Making of a Great Power: Late Stuart and early Georgian Britain 1660–1722*, 21–3; Colin Kidd, *Subverting Scotland's Past: Scottish Whig Historians and the Creation of an Anglo-British Identity, 1689–c. 1830* (Cambridge, 1993), 70–1, 131–2.

39 *Essay*, 172–3; Tim Harris, *Politics under the Late Stuarts: Party Conflict in a Divided Society 1660–1715* (London, 1993), 34–5.

40 One can speculate that James Stuart's belief Ramsay was not suited to politics (Chapter 6) stemmed from this proposal. Not even the Jacobite court would advocate Parliament's destruction, no matter how desirable. There are no figures regarding how many copies of the *Essay* were published or sold, so its (un)popularity is not known, although it ran to three French editions and two English.

41 Kidd, *Subverting Scotland's Past*, 20–1, 35, 137–40, 165–9.

42 Bossuet, *Politique tirée des paroles de l'Ecriture sainte*, ed. Jacques Le Brun (Geneva, 1967), V, ii, 3–7 (149–61); V, iii, 2 (175–7); X, ii, 2–7 (396–400), X, iii, I (409–11).

43 Ramsay, *Essay*, 198. The citation falsely claims to be taken from p. 466 of *Télémaque* (livre 12).

44 Fénelon, *Examen de conscience sur les devoirs de la royauté*, Œuvres II, 989–90; *Tables de Chaulnes*, Œuvres II, 1098–9; *Mémoires sur les mesures à prendre après la mort du Duc de Bourgogne*, Œuvres II, III, 1119–23.

45 See Fénelon: Œuvres II: *Télémaque* (64); *Examen de conscience sur les devoirs de la royauté* (984–5); *Tables de Chaulnes* (1089–91).

46 The dedication eventually led a number of commentators to connect the second edition with Ramsay's support for Jacobitism. See Cherel, *Fénelon au XVIIIe Siècle en France (1715–1820): Son Prestige – Son Influence*, 98; Jean Molino, "L'Essai philosophique sur le gouvernement civil": Ramsay ou Fénelon?', *La Régence*, ed. Henri Coulet (Paris, 1970), 282. In *Chevalier Ramsay*, Henderson discussed the promotion of the Jacobite cause in the *Essay* (87–89). He also revealed that a letter by Fénelon (74) present in the original French edition of the *Vie de Fénelon* (188–90) had been omitted from the English edition at the behest of the British government due to its apparent support of James Stuart. The letter dated 15 November 1709, seemingly endorsed James Stuart due to his acceptance of Fénelon's lessons from *Télémaque*. As will be discussed below, the letter led Ramsay to claim James Stuart's acceptance of Fénelon's political lessons simply detailed the character of '*le roi d'Angleterre*' – his title within the French court. A full version of this letter to the duc de Bourgogne can be found in the *Correspondance de Fénelon, Tome XIV*, ed. Jacques Le Brun and Irénée Noye, 165–6.

47 See Benjamin Hoadly, *The Original and Institutions of Civil Government, Discussed, The Works of Benjamin Hoadly*, vol. II (London, 1773), 266; Chapter 1 in the present book (for a discussion of the Hoadly–Leslie debate. Contemporaneously, the Third Earl of Shaftesbury used the phrase 'Lovers of Mankind' to endorse the importance of the people and public good against those who despised the multitude (*An Essay on the Freedom of Wit and Humour, Charachteristicks* (London, 1711), 76, 106–12).

48 This dedication is only present in the 1721 French second edition as it was withdrawn from subsequent editions: the third French edition (reprint) of 1721, plus the two English translations of 1722 and 1732. According to Henderson (*Chevalier Ramsay*, 74) it was removed at the request of the British government due to its censorship of works displaying any Jacobite sympathies.

49 Ramsay, *Essay philosophique sur le gouvernement civil*, Dedication. Robert I of Scotland (1274–1329), known as Robert the Bruce was an ancestor of James Stuart and leader of the Scots fight for independence against the English.

50 Ramsay, *Essay*, Dedication. His dedication stated: 'Je n'ai entrepris cet Ouvrage, SIRE, que pour soûtenir vos Droits. Daignez l'agréer comme un Tribut de ma fidelité, comme une marque de mon homage, & comme un gage du très-profond respect avec leque j'ai l'honneur d'être, SIRE, DE VOTRE MAJESTE', and was (pseudo-anonymously) signed 'les très humble, très-fidele & très-obéissant serviteur & Sujet, SAYMAR'.

51 Andrew Michael Ramsay, *Essay philosophique sur le gouvernement civil* (London, 1721), vi: 'Le seul mérite de l'Auteur est d'avoir été nourri pendant plusiers années de lumieres, & des sentimens de feu Messire François de Salignac de la Mothe-Fenelon, Archevêque de Cambray ... des instructions de cet illustre Prélat, pour écrire cet Essai.'

52 *Ibid.*, v.

53 *Ibid.*

54 *Ibid.*, 92–4.

55 See Chapter 4, for a breakdown of Bossuet's political thought.

56 The most direct example of plagiarism was in Bossuet's delineation of the creation of military tribunes. Bossuet wrote: 'La loi pour les y admettre est proposée. Plutôt que de rabaisser le consultant, les Pères consentent à la création de trois nouveaux magistrats qui auraient l'autorité des consuls sous le nom de tribunes militaires, et le peuple est admis à cet honneur' (*Discours sur l'Histoire Universelle*, Œuvres de Bossuet, ed. abbé B. Velat, 1016). This became in Ramsay: 'La Loi pour les y admettre est proposée. Plutôt que de rabaisser la Dignité Consulaire, les Pères consentent à la création de trois nouveaux Magistrats, qui auroient l'autorité de Consuls, sous le nom de Tribuns Militaires, & le Peuple est admis à cet Honneur' (*Essay philosophique sur le gouvernement civil* (London, 1721), 133). This plagiarism of Bossuet by Ramsay has not been previously noted in relation to the *Essay*. As stated in the previous chapter, it was noted by an anonymous author in reading *Les Voyages de Cyrus* (*A Supplement to the New Cyropaedia: or, The Reflections of Cyrus Upon his Travels* (London, 1729)); Voltaire, 'Plagiarism',

A *Philosophical Dictionary*, *The Works of Voltaire*, VI, ii, 204; Doohwan Ahn, 'From Greece to Babylon: The Political Thought of Andrew Michael Ramsay (1686–1743)', *History of European Ideas*, 37, 4 (2011).

57 Ramsay, *Essay*, iv. Ramsay later cited Cicero's *De Natura Deorum*, I (19), Plato and Lycurgus (21).

58 *Essay*, 16–17; Bossuet, *Politique tirée des paroles de l'Ecriture sainte*, ed. Jacques Le Brun (Genève, Librarie Droz, 1967), I, i, 3 (7–8).

59 *Essay*, 26; Bossuet, *Politique tirée des paroles de l'Ecriture sainte*, I, ii, 3 (15–16).

60 *Ibid.*, 19–20, 208. For the notion of a 'world city' Ramsay cited Cicero, *De Legibus*, iv. This notion of brotherly love is present in Bossuet, *Ibid.*, I, i, 3 (15–16), and Fénelon, *Télémaque*, Œuvres II, XIII.

61 *Essay*, 22–3; Bossuet, *Politique tirée des paroles de l'Ecriture sainte*, I, iii, 6–8 (25–9).

62 *Essay*, 31–2.

63 *Essay*, 50–1; Bossuet, *Politique tirée des paroles de l'Ecriture sainte*, II, I, 3 (46–7). Ramsay linked this to Noah's sons, and in the final chapter of the *Essay* he expanded the link to the Patriarchs of the Old Testament (212–13).

64 *Essay*, 27–8. Ramsay later cited Tertullian's belief (*Apology*, ch. 32) that the king was God's chosen governor, which Bossuet had applied in the same context (*ibid.*, 225–7).

65 *Essay*, 40; Bossuet, *Politique tirée des paroles de l'Ecriture sainte*, VIII, ii, 1–3 (291–3).

66 *Essay*, 44; Bossuet, *Politique tirée des paroles de l'Ecriture sainte*, III, ii, 3 (68).

67 *Essay*, 35, 64; Bossuet, *Politique tirée des paroles de l'Ecriture sainte*, V, I, 1 (116–17).

68 *Essay*, 97–8.

69 *Essay*, 23–4; Bossuet, *Politique tirée des paroles de l'Ecriture sainte*, I, ii, 3 (15–16).

70 This view reveals the profound disagreement with many commentators on Ramsay's political thought concerning the influence of Hobbes and Filmer (see the Introduction this book).

71 See Chapter 1.

72 Charles Leslie: *The Best Answer Ever Made* (London, 1709), 13–15, 18; *The Finishing Stroke* (London, 1711), 6–7, 112. Ramsay was actually friends with Leslie's sons (Ian Higgins, 'Jonathan Swift and Charles Leslie', *Loyalty and Identity: Jacobites at Home and Abroad*, eds Paul Monod, Murray Pittock and Daniel Szechi (Basingstoke, 2010), 149–54).

73 Charles Leslie, *The New Association* (Dublin, 1714), 16–17.

74 Charles Leslie: *The New Association. Part II* (London, 1703), 6, 7, 27; *Best of All* (London, 1709), 29.

75 Leslie: *Best of All*, 19, 30; *The Finishing Stroke*, 102–3.

76 *Essay*, v: 'en a change l'ordre en plusieurs endroits, pour metre chaque vérité à sa place, & lui donner une nouvelle force par cet Arrangement'.

77 Ramsay, *Essay de Politique*, 109.

78 Ramsay, *Essay philosophique sur le gouvernement civil*, 1.

79 *Ibid.*, v.

80 *Ibid.*, 69–77. As discussed in Chapter 2, while adherence to (original) contract theory had been problematic since the 1688 Revolution due to a distaste for its implications of resistance to the government, after the Whig ascendancy its ideas had greater currency and resistance theory had become resurgent (J.P. Kenyon, 'The Revolution of 1688: Resistance and Contract', *Historical Perspectives: Studies in English Thought and Society, in Honour of J.H. Plumb*, ed. Neil McKendrick (London, 1974); H.T. Dickinson, 'The Eighteenth-Century Debate on the "Glorious Revolution"', *History*, 61, 201, pp. 28–45, Feb. 1976; J.C.D Clark, *English Society, 1688–1832* (Cambridge, 1985); Geoffrey Holmes, *British Politics in the Age of Anne* (London, 1987)).

81 Ramsay, *Essay philosophique sur le gouvernement civil*, 58.

82 *Ibid.*, 60. For a discussion on the importance of non-resistance to British and French thought, see Chapters 1, 2, and 4. Ramsay was reiterating non-resistance in the same manner as Bossuet in France, or Blackall, Leslie and Sacheverell in Britain. The origin of the doctrine (Catholic or Anglican) is biblical, which sees a common ground for theorists who expounded it in defence of monarchy throughout Europe for several centuries.

83 *Ibid.*, 59: 'que les actes de jurisdiction qu'exerce un usurpateur qui est en possession, ont le pouvoir d'obliger, non en vertu de son droit; car il n'en a aucun, mais parce que celui qui a le vrai droit sur l'Etat'.

84 *Essay de Politique*, Livre I, chapitre viii.

85 See Chapter 2.

86 This comparison is signalled in the English translation of the work: *An Essay upon Civil Government:Wherein is set forth,The Necessity, Origine, Rights, Boundaries, and different Forms of Sovereignty. With Observations on the Ancient Government of Rome and England. According to the Principles of the Late Archbishop of Cambray* (London, 1722).

87 Ramsay, *Essay philosophique sur le gouvernement civil*, 190–2.

88 *Ibid.*, 193–4.

89 *Ibid.*, 204.

90 *Ibid.*, 204–5.

91 Andrew Michael Ramsay, *Histoire de la vie de Fénelon* (The Hague, 1723), 147: 'Je me servirai autant que je pourrai de ses propres paroles. Je ne serai que perfectionner ce qu'il a écrit par ce qu'il m'a dit. Encore une fois je ne raisonne point, je ne fais que raconteur. Ce n'est pas sortir des bornes de ma narration que de faire l'histoire de l'Esprit de Mr. de Cambray en écrivant celle de sa vie.'

92 See Henderson, *Chevalier Ramsay*, 87; Glickman, *The English Catholic Community 1688–1745: Politics, Culture and Ideology* (Woodbridge, 2009), 228–30.

93 Andrew Michael Ramsay, *Histoire de la vie de Fénelon*, 182: 'idée générale de ses principes sur la Politique, répandus dans le Télémaque & dans ses Dialogues des Morts don't il entretenoit souvent ce jeune Prince pendant son sejour à Cambray'.

94 *Ibid.*, 181–2: 'tint, sur la Politique le même langage que Mentor tient à Télémaque, Il lui fit voir les avantages qu'il pouvoit tirer de la forme du Gouvernement de son Païs, & des égards qu'il devoit avoir pour son Sénat'.

95 *Ibid.*, 182.

96 *Ibid.*, 183: 'L'amour du Peuple, le bien public, l'Intérêt general de la Société est donc la Loi immutable & universelle des Souverains.'

97 *Ibid.*, 184.

98 *Ibid.*, 186: 'La Liberté sans ordre est un Libertinage qui attire le Despotisme. L'Ordre sans la liberté est un Esclavage qui se perd dans l'Anarchie.'

99 *Ibid.*, 185: 'jaloux leur autorité veulent toûjours l'étendre. Les peuples passionnez pour leur liberté veulent toûjours l'augmenter'.

100 *Ibid.*, 182: 'l'Executeur des Loix, & d'avoir un Conseil supreme qui modére son autorité'.

101 *Ibid.*, 187–8: 'C'est par ces maxims, qui conviennent également à tous les Etats, que le sage Mentor le Bonheur de la Patrie, en conservant la subordination des rangs, concilioit la liberté du peuple avec l'obéïssance aux Souverains, rendoit les hommes tout ensemble bons Citoyens, & fidelles Sujets, soûmis sans être esclaves, libres sans être effrenez. Le pur amour de l'Ordre est la source de toutes ses vertus politiques aussi bien que de toutes ses vertus divines. La meme règne dans tous ses sentimens.'

102 D.P. Walker, *'Mon cher Zorastre' or the Chevalier Ramsay* (London, 1972), 234–5.

103 Ramsay, *Vie*, 181: 'Jamais forcer ses sujets à changer leur Religion. Nulle puissance humaine ne peut forcer, lui dit-il, le retranchement impenetrable de la liberté du Coeur. La force ne peut jamais persuader les hommes; elle ne fait que deshypocrites. Quand les Rois se mêlent de Religion, au lieu de la protéger, Is la mettent en servitude. Accordez, donc, à tous la tolerance civile.'

104 See *Essay de Politique*, 113; *Essay philosophique sur le gouvernement civil*, 113.

105 Glickman, *English Catholic Community 1688–1745*, 230–4, 251.

106 Fénelon, *Les avantures de Télémaque, fils d'Ulysse*, Tome Seconde (Paris, 1717), 481: 'Souvenez-vous qu'un Roi doit être soûmis à la Religion, & qu'il ne doit jamais entreprendre de la regler; la Religion vient des Dieux, elle est au-dessus des Rois. Si les Rois se mêlent de la Religion, au lieu de la proteger, ils la mettent en servitude. Les Rois sont si puissans, & les autres hommes sont si foibles, que tout sera en peril d'être alteré au gré des Rois, si on les fait entrer dans les

questions qui regardent les choses sacrées. Laissez donc en pleine liberté la decision aux amis des Dieux, & bornez-vous à réprimer ceux qui n'obéiroient pas à leur jugement, quand il aura été pronounce.'

107   Fénelon, *Tables de Chaulnes, Œuvres II*, 1093.

108   See Fénelon, *Discours pronounce au sacre de l'Électeur de Cologne, Œuvres II*, 952–3.

109   *Ibid.*, 1099: 'plan pour déraciner jansénisme'.

110   See Bausset, *Histoire de Fénelon, Tome Premier*, 105, 112, 123, 129.

111   Fénelon, *Tables de Chaulnes, Œuvres II*, 1099.

112   Fénelon to Chevreuse (27 February 1712), *Selected Letters of Fénelon*, trans. and ed. John McEwen (London, 1964), 179.

113   Ramsay included Fénelon's final letter in the *Vie* (199), which avowed his lack of toleration towards Jansenism. Fénelon wrote the letter to Louis XIV on his deathbed (6 Jan. 1715), and asked that the king appoint a successor who was: 'bon & ferme contre le Jansenisme, lequel est prodigiusement accrédité sur cette frontiére'. Fénelon's concern of Jansenism was partly doctrinal, but also indicated the close proximity of his archdiocese of Cambrai – which included part of the Low Countries – to the origin of Jansenism (Leuven). Bausset incorporated details of a letter sent to the *Mercure* (9 Dec. 1780) in which an abbé de Fénelon, a relative, condemned the notion that Fénelon was '"tolerant" of all religions' (*Histoire de Fénelon, Tome Troisième*, 490–4). There is no evidence of Fénelon's toleration of Jansenism, and he willingly complied with the Unigenitus Bull of 1713 against the Jansenists (Agnès de la Gorce, *Le Vrai Visage de Fénelon* (Paris, 1958), 323; Ragnhild Hatton, *Europe in the Age of Louis XIV* (London, 1969), 186).

114   Ramsay, *L'Histoire de la Vie de Fénelon*, 128–9. Fénelon used Bossuet's *L'histoire universelle* (1781) as an exemplary example of a discussion of this historical relationship.

115   *Ibid.*, 138: 'la certitude de nos idées depend de l'univeralité, & de l'immutabilité del'évidence qui les accompagne: de meme la certitude des faits depend de l'universalité & de l'immutabilité de la Tradition qui les confirme'.

116   *Ibid.*, 139–40.

117   Ramsay, *Anecdotes*, 6. The Garden Circle had encouraged Ramsay to be critical of religion and to espouse toleration from his time at Aberdeen University. And, based on the evidence of his later works, it is debatable whether this instinct ever left him, and questionable whether he ever thoroughly embraced Catholicism. Ramsay was therefore not the Catholic portrayed by many commentators, as he never attempted to overcome his deism.

118   Ramsay, *Vie de Fénelon*, 132–7.

119   *Ibid.*, 142: 'l'amour d'un Dieu invisible, & l'obéissance à l'Eglise son Oracle vivant'.

120   *Ibid.*, 144. Ramsay recommended the two works he had edited to the reader for an exposition of Fénelon's natural religion (*l'Existence de Dieu* (Paris, 1718); *Lettres sur la Religion* (Paris, 1718)).

121   *Ibid.*, 145–6: 'que Mr. de Cambray me fit sentir, qu'on ne peut être sagement Déiste sans devenir Chrêtien ni philosophiquement Chrêtien sans devenir Catholique'.

122   See Henderson, *Chevalier Ramsay*, 29. Henderson believed that Ramsay's interpretation of Fénelon as a man of religious tolerance was a consequence either of a desire for him to have believed in toleration, or through a misunderstanding of the prelate's spiritual thought. Henderson further claimed that this misinterpretation was the basis for his bastardised view of Fénelon's political principles in the *Essay* (123–4).

123   Glickman, *English Catholic Community 1688–1745*, 251.

8

A mythical education:
Ramsay's *Cyrus* and *Plan*

After Ramsay's calamitous time in Rome (1725) he embarked upon the second phase of his political thought, which is contained in two works. The first was the hugely successful *Les Voyages de Cyrus* (1727), the second was *A Plan of Education for a Young Prince* (1732). Fundamentally, *Cyrus* echoed the theory of the *Essay* and it should be seen as a mature continuation of its political thought. It reiterated the dangers faced by governments from the two extremes of popular anarchy and monarchical despotism. Xenophon's *Cyropaedia* provided an exemplar of a virtuous king who could walk a middle path between these two dangers, while retaining Ramsay's own vision of a monarchy moderated by aristocracy. Driven by the peripatetic wanderings of Cyrus, his youthful adventures enabled Ramsay to muse on a number of topics, making the work broader in scope than the *Essay*. As a literary device, *Cyrus* was therefore much closer to *Télémaque*, and its content had far more in common with Fénelon than the *Essay*. Unencumbered by a necessity to promote James Stuart after his abortive experience in Rome, support for Jacobitism in the work was far more opaque, although it remained in a fascinating alternative future for Britain which would become the 'capital of the universe' under a Stuart monarch.[1] But in many ways, *Cyrus* should be viewed as a work of literature rather than political propaganda; and in using *Cyropaedia* Ramsay engaged directly in the 'mirror-for-princes' genre begun by Xenophon's work and which contained *Télémaque*. Ramsay further emulated Fénelon's approach to education in the *Plan*, which adopted the prelate's guidance to an older Bourgogne in offering pragmatic advice for a contemporary prince. Intriguingly this included a complete reversal from his earlier belief in Parliament's extirpation, as he now saw its elevation as a necessary to bridle the king's power to warrant public liberty.

A king's education

Xenophon's *Cyropaedia,* or *The Education of Cyrus* (*c.*380 BCE) presented an account of the education, military virtue and life of the Persian king Cyrus the Great (600 or 576–530 BCE). Founder of the Achaemenid Empire, Cyrus presided over a territory which stretched from the Indus River to Greece. Famed for his abilities as a military leader he conquered the Babylonians, Medians, and Lydians while shaping the largest empire in the ancient world at that time. Of great interest and praise was Cyrus's protection for the religions and customs of his conquered peoples. He enjoyed a reputation, particularly among the Jewish people whom he liberated from persecution, as a paragon of kingship and wisdom. His reliance on a civil service and satraps (governors of provinces) enabled cohesion within the conquered territories as all were governed by an effective centralised bureaucracy. Sitting between the East and West, Persia offered an important bridge between the two transferring ideas of religion, science, philosophy and culture. The reputation of Cyrus and the Achaemenid Empire later proved to be alluring to peoples in both spheres, influencing the ancient Athenians for example.

Xenophon (*c.*429–354 BCE) the historian, philosopher and acolyte of Socrates, fought in the expedition of the Persian Prince Cyrus the Younger (d. 401 BCE) against his older brother King II Artaxerxes (r. 404–358/59 BCE). The death of Cyrus meant that Xenophon and the other Greek mercenaries who had agreed to fight for the prince – known as the 'Ten Thousand' – had to fight their way back to Greece from deep in Persian territory. Elected as one of the generals of the 'Ten Thousand', Xenophon recalled the retreat in the *Anabasis*. Once he had returned to his native Athens he discovered that his 'revered master Socrates had been put to death' by his fellow Athenians, and left his homeland to join the Spartan King Agesilaus II (444–360 BCE).[2] In joining the Spartans, Xenophon fought for them during the conquest of the East, even fighting against the Athenians at Coronea (394 BCE). His resultant exile from Athens ensured that he remained in Spartan territory at Scillus, where he composed his works before dying at Corinth. Xenophon developed the history of Cyrus the Great to answer questions on government – how to rule and be ruled – set against the great military feats of the former king. The 'spirit of the book is Hellenic throughout', and Xenophon's Persians possess ideals and practices that were Spartan in genesis.[3] The chief purpose of the *Cyropaedia* was to delineate the ideal monarch within an ideal state. Cyrus's education, his development as a military leader, conqueror, lawgiver, and man, reflect the training and discipline necessary to generate the virtues required by such a monarch. For regardless of his inherent abilities, Xenophon's Cyrus strove to improve himself continuously as a leader though pedagogy, religion, and discipline to create an example for his people.[4]

The *Cyropaedia* proved to be a popular work with a number of figures from classical antiquity, notably Cicero, Cato, and Tacitus. It was rediscovered in the fifteenth century and published in Latin by Francis Philelfus (1476), followed by Giunta's Greek edition entitled the *Princeps* (1516).[5] Its recovery in Western Europe led to its reputation as a progenitor of the 'mirror-for-princes' genre, in which practical counsel was offered to princes through the 'ancient conceit of holding up a "mirror"'.[6] At a time of the emerging modern (monarchical) state, early modern (humanist) scholars were drawn by the mixture of antiquity, education, and their application to governance. The work served as a classical model for leadership, highlighting the significance of a prince's education in the nature of kingship. The consequence of such pedagogical training for a future monarch was grasped across Europe, and continued for several centuries. Moreover, flattering descriptions of Cyrus the Great in the Bible,[7] meant that Xenophon's work was not 'essentially at odds with Christian belief apart from his pagan origin'.[8] In England *Cyropaedia* was first translated into English by William Barker in 1552, who was secretary to the Duke of Norfolk and sometime tutor to his son.[9] It was republished in 1567, followed by Philemon Holland's *Cyrupaedia* dedicated to Charles I in 1632 (reprinted anonymously in 1654), and Francis Digby's *Kyrou Paideia (Education of Cyrus)* published in 1685. *Cyropaedia* was translated into English as a means of promoting the virtues of monarchy, and during the Civil War this interest waned as republican ideas of government became more prevalent. From that time and throughout the Restoration, Xenophon 'became the object of a tug-of-war' between Royalists and those who favoured the king's rule within Parliament.[10] This struggle re-emerged during the Exclusion Crisis as Filmer's defence of Stuart monarchy harnessed Xenophon, while Sidney stressed his Athenian background to promote republican liberty within Cyrus's princely government.

Importantly for Ramsay, Xenophon's *Cyropaedia* offered a multifaceted vehicle with which to promulgate his views on government. When one examines Xenophon's Cyrus he bore scant resemblance to the version portrayed by Ramsay. In Xenophon's work, while Cyrus may aim for virtue in kingship and the obedience of his subjects, this was earned by enshrining the public good. As his father Cambyses warned Cyrus: 'all those from whom you expect obedience to you will, on their part, expect you to take thought for them'.[11] His reorganisation of the state not only embraced the powerful nobility but also expanded government to create a bureaucratic system of civil servants in a government that relied on the wider populace.[12] Indeed, Cyrus's restructuring of the army elevated Persian commoners to parity with the nobility – in terms of arms and rights – to bolster the limited number of nobles.[13] Yet there are common elements; such as the desire to create virtue in the king, to portray the king as an example to his obedient people, to reorganise the state, and a perception of the gods' significance as a means to ensure success. Crucially much of Cyrus's historical achievements and behaviour were not overly relevant to Ramsay. Cyrus provided Ramsay with a vehicle to underline his own beliefs on government, while amalgamating classical views on politics, religion and economics for contemporary society. His intervention into the 'mirror-for-princes' genre blended classical and modern thought to encourage a contemporary king who could rebuff the advances of popular government through religiously inspired ancient virtue.

Fénelon and Bossuet

Two contributors to the 'mirror-for-princes' genre who had a great impact on Ramsay's *Les Voyages de Cyrus* were Bossuet and Fénelon. Through their respective works *Discours sur l'Histoire universelle* and *Télémaque*, both men (of the Church) had engaged ancient history and literature to create a model of kingly virtue through education. Regardless of the authors' divergent views on monarchy, these works were immediately influential and publicly popular. Ramsay's use of antiquity not only offered a medium for his ideal king, it also tapped into a public market for histories of antiquity. Internalising Bossuet's historical description with Fénelon's literary schema and moral pedagogy, he built on the two men's work as a platform for his own views on government. An approach and methodology that proved to be both very successful and rewarding for Ramsay, as *Cyrus* ran to many editions throughout the eighteenth century.

As stated in Chapter 6, it was immediately discovered that Ramsay had plagiarised Bossuet's *Discours* by the authors of *A Supplement to the New Cyropaedia*.[14] Ramsay's replication of the descriptive passages on ancient states – notably Egypt – in Bossuet's work to aid his description of Cyrus's adventures was so brazen it received public censure. Examples included Bossuet's description of the geographical setting of Egypt: 'Il pleut rarement en Egypte; mais ce fleuve, qui l'arrose toute par ses débordements règles', which in Ramsay became: 'Il pleut rarement dans l'Egypte; mais le Nil l'arrose par ses débordements règles.'[15] While Bossuet's discussion of hereditary kingship: 'Le royaume était héréditaire; mais le rois étaient obligés plus que tous les autres à vivre selon les lois', remained completely intact.[16] The list of examples is more extensive than can be appreciated here, but like the *Essay* Ramsay's proclivity for plagiarism led to a larger difficulty of him concealing the actual influences on his theory. As seen with the *Essay*, Ramsay would proclaim a devotion to Fénelon on the one hand, but essentially use the work of others to guide the principles that he espoused.[17]

This contradiction is less evident in *Cyrus*. While the view of government remained distinct there was greater appreciation of Fénelon's literary style,[18] plus more congruence with his moral principles. Indeed, Ramsay paid homage to *Télémaque* by using the Fénelonian figure of Amenophis, an Egyptian priestly court counsellor. Amenophis extolled the virtue of a simple rural existence that provided a 'place for happiness in the study of wisdom', while allowing the 'sweetest of occupations', agriculture and the liberal arts.[19] Voluptuousness brought corruption into the kingdom, overawing the 'purity of manners' to infect the state with an idleness that intoxicated the individual. While at first appearing to be little more than 'innocent amusements', once such pleasures had taken hold of society virtue was lost as people pursued their passions.[20] Echoing Fénelon, Cyrus discovered that kingship was a solitary occupation that enslaved a monarch as they sacrificed personal interest to preserve the public good.[21] Kingship was therefore a thankless task, as the monarch's individual liberty was little more than slavery regardless of command or grandeur. A slavery compounded by those surrounding the monarch, who would deceive him for their own gain at the expense of the state.[22] Virtue guarded both the king and the public good.

The solution for these kingly travails was offered to Cyrus by two historical holy men: the biblical Daniel and Persian Zoroaster. Both men proclaimed that duty and the pursuit of virtue were essential for a king to rule well. Such wisdom had been lost to men, who had fallen from a Golden Age that possessed the original knowledge of God to one in which (Augustinian) original sin abounded.[23] The Golden Age had been a time in which the passions were subject to reason, conforming to a 'love of order' that generated virtue in men. Its loss had been caused by the corruption and selfishness of man who had begotten the Flood, plus the inferior governments that followed. To recapture the 'philosophy' of the Golden Age it was necessitous to understand religion in a much broader context. As Cyrus was informed by Daniel (later his adviser), Jewish philosophy or theology were conformable to all other religions.[24] Religion, like history, was by its nature universal. Traces of the original principles of religion could be located in the mythology of all ancient religions, which possessed 'a notion of the supreme deity'.[25] Such an idea was evident in Bossuet's *Discours*, in which he stated that religion was history and universal truths could be located in all ancient religions. For Bossuet, religion revealed the progress of civilisation through history as it advanced towards the truth of Christ and Catholicism.[26] History and revolutions in particular, elucidated God's providence and offered lessons to humanity regarding its capacities and arrogance.[27] Ramsay absorbed aspects of this approach – although he did not see Catholic progress but rather the loss of earlier sagacity – to claim that the Persian, Egyptian, Greek, and Jewish understanding of the deity and science reflected aspects of this absent knowledge. The enrichment of the individual (king) through education recaptured this wisdom, and exposed Ramsay's desire to create a 'republic of sages'.[28]

The Persian prophet Zoroaster (d. 583 BCE), provided Ramsay with an opportunity to merge Eastern antiquity with his love of (Newtonian) science. Viewed in eighteenth century Europe as a mystic, magician and sage, Zoroaster allowed Ramsay to discourse on a broad range of subjects – theology, God's eternal love, anatomy, botany, zoology, meteorology, astronomy, and physics – that incorporated science and religion.[29] Zoroaster personified Ramsay's endeavour to merge his deistic view of society with a love of contemporary science. In so doing, he discouraged the ostensible atheism or notions of popular government extant in Spinozism that appeared to threaten modern society.[30] Embracing the science of Newton, Ramsay believed that the world and man's place in it could only be comprehended through the certainty of a Supreme Being beyond the restriction of any organised church.[31] The universal principles of religion formed the basis of society and government, and their loss had ended the Golden Age.[32] This had subsequently eroded the moral fabric of society and plagued governments through its degeneracy. The embrace of (classical) spiritual truth and moral virtue was an essential platform for any king to repel the evils of this corruption. The education of a prince necessarily shunned a modern appetite for Spinozist proclivities towards atheism and popular government. Such advances contravened the laws of nature and the divine apparatus that held a traditional order in place.

Fénelon had earlier opposed Spinoza's views, but had done so on theological grounds, rather than building a system of government from a religious foundation. In the educational works on which Ramsay claimed to rely, kingship was the only model of government available. Rather, Fénelon's religious beliefs shaped his understanding of human behaviour and morality. He believed that as good Christians people retained the ability to act altruistically ('disinterestedly') for the benefit of others: this was a virtue. Allied to classical views of civic virtue that shared divine notions of altruistic duty such as in Cicero,[33] Fénelon's prince was educated on how to act as a sovereign for the good of his people. This meant an expansion of government beyond Louis XIV's sovereignty, yet in the later works this included the domination of religion by politics in the temporal realm.[34] To interweave religion with politics in modern society Ramsay turned to Bossuet. Bossuet infused the two through natural law (and scripture) to produce a government that was built on the foundations of religion and maintained this relationship to affirm ordered society. This justified the suppression of the people under a king to counteract revolution for the maintenance of public safety.[35] Moreover, Ramsay's utilisation of Bossuet's universal history to understand 'human affairs' fitted his need to look 'higher'[36] for the origins of civil government, its preservation, solutions to its ills, and the promise of greater earthly progress knowledge. Elements all absent in Fénelon's political theory.

The two extremes of government

Ramsay's attack on Spinozist unorthodoxy and popular government witnessed his return to Bossuet's defence of monarchy offered in the *Essay*. *Cyrus* provided a literary forum in which he could employ his version of ancient history to continue challenging the advance of the people's involvement in government. A version of the *Essay's* dichotomy of government extremes was used to explain the cause of revolution that can be found in Xenophon's *Cyropaedia*. Cambyses warns his fellow Persian citizens and his son Cyrus that there would be little profit in eroding the other's position:

> Cyrus, if you on your part become puffed up by your present successes and attempt to govern the Persians as you do those other nations, with a view to self-aggrandizement, or if you, fellow-citizens, become jealous of his power and attempt to depose him from his sovereignty, be sure that you will hinder one another from receiving much good.[37]

Yet Xenophon's (Spartan) view of the Persian constitution placed the king among his fellow citizens rather than above them as a superior entity designed to control their rampaging desire for liberty. Here the relationship was reciprocal, and should be respected as such for the constitution to work effectively in propagating the public good. For Persia to continue flourishing it had to nurture the status quo so the king could not aggrandise his power over the people; in return, the people would not 'become jealous of his power' and threaten to subvert the constitution. Law ensured the constitution, the reciprocal relationship, and the balance between the king and his citizens. While Xenophon accentuated the requirement for obedience in the people – especially those of the wider empire – this was underscored by his own virtuous behaviour, the law and the public good; so reciprocity was crucial for Xenophon.[38] Ramsay's dichotomy was different and loaded the dice to place the emphasis on the need to restrain the marauding populace rather than an aggrandising king, whose tyranny would have to be tolerated.[39]

This view remained in *Cyrus*, where Ramsay assailed the danger posed by popular government through the discussion of three historical examples: Egypt, Athens, and Sparta. In the case of Egypt, the nefarious counsellor Amasis was able to usurp the power of King Apries by appealing to the populace for support as the new ruler. According to Ramsay, Amasis espoused the ideals of popular sovereignty. This included an original contract that rooted sovereignty in the people, the role of the people as 'absolute arbitrators' in matters or religion and royalty, the beliefs that all men were born equal, plus the idea that will alone specified political authority in the people.[40] By condescending to the multitude's level Amasis gained support for his usurpation, yet he began to distrust his supporters and ministers. Acting as a metaphor for the Commonwealth under Oliver Cromwell, Amasis had to combat the people's new strength by adopting the powers of the former king.[41] His ultimate demise was the result of Amasis's subversion of the laws of nature, which dictated that once a government's form had been established it could not be altered. Transferring (legislative) authority to the multitude simply led to 'eternal discord', as weak princes were replaced by republics and a perpetual struggle for power began.[42] Any inclusion of the people in civil government was always divisive, as the rapacious desires of the populace eroded the natural order, unity, and stability that underpinned society.

Cyrus learned from a number of sages that such a corruption would be counteracted by three principle laws of sovereignty: kingship, the polity, and civil justice. First, good kingship was hereditary, a position protected by the monarch's observance of the law. Inspired by the lessons of religion and aided by wise counsel, a king was watchful of his own faults and any transgressions of the law he may have carried out.[43] The second law of polity guaranteed that the 'subordination of ranks' was strictly maintained throughout society. Land was divided into three parts between the king, priests (counsellors), and military as the common people were divided into three classes: of labourers, farmers, and artisans. The order of generation meant that these classes (roles) were hereditary, underlining a ranked society in which the people were subordinated. Its purpose was to maintain the prosperity of the kingdom through the labours of the people, while checking their ambition to 'rise above' their natural place in society.[44] All members of society could take pride in contributing something to the whole regardless of lowly status, as labour preserved their natural subservience and diverted potential jealousy of superiors. This was safeguarded by the final law which claimed that a king must select a small group of judges (nobles) to form a 'supreme council', to assist in legislation and make sure the laws were observed.[45] Cyrus's lessons from the three laws of good kingship reiterated the view of government promulgated by Ramsay in the *Essay*. One in which a king was to act in accordance with the law as he sat astride a populace who were subordinated by law, custom, and an aristocratic senate to prevent the creation of their dangerous jealousies that could subvert traditional society.

The consequence of this jealousy was examined in the historical examples offered by Sparta and Athens: the first a mixed constitution and the second a pure democracy. The two states enabled Ramsay to produce a pincer attack on any mixed constitution that contained a popular element. In so doing, Ramsay was warning the British against the preservation of the House of Commons. Sparta was frequently admired in eighteenth-century British political thought as providing an example (alongside Venice) of the use of a balanced constitution to sustain government. While Sparta had declined due to an overextension of its empire and a deterioration of military virtue through the loss of arms, its balanced organisation had maintained internal peace via kings, an elective senate and legislature.[46] Sparta was preferred by the neo-Harringto-nian or country interest as an exemplar of citizenship that employed a third element of government to generate harmony and prevent internal faction.[47] Parliament offered that medium to the British, and counteracted an internecine struggle between two forces. While Machiavelli and later country proponents saw advantage to the conflict between rival factions, Parliament safeguarded the Polybian harmony potentially threatened by such tensions. For Ramsay, however, this was not enough and was inaccurate. He believed that original Gothic government only contained two elements, that of the king and high nobility who acted as counsel within the legislation. This mixed Gothic consti-tution had existed from ancient times and had survived the Norman Conquest only to be subverted by the Tudors. Henry VII's widening of property owner-ship through the Sale of Manors had been designed to weaken former aristo-cratic rivals, but instead enfeebled the entire nobility and monarchy by shifting power towards the Commons. As the people gained in influence, the House of Commons possessed a much greater role that triggered an adjustment in the balanced constitution from two elements to three.[48] This sparked an unruly dichotomy throughout the seventeenth century as the people constantly strove for greater authority (liberty) at the expense of the king.[49] The fear of pure democracy extant in both the seventeenth and eighteenth centuries, allowed Ramsay to parallel the British experience and contemporary government with the collapse of Athens.[50] Under pure democracy and an unrestrained multitude, Athens revealed historically what would happen to Britain if it did not resist popular government.

Sparta had formerly possessed an absolute model of kingship, in which parental love bound the state into one family.[51] Fathers had educated their children, who from gratitude and subordination bound society through familial obligation. Forming the 'original bond of society', kingship had arisen as the country was created through a union of many families, securing a 'love of one's country'.[52] The education of children nurtured these sentiments to generate loyal and obedient subjects. Yet this had been undermined by King Eurytion's surrender of parts of his authority to please the people.[53] Having relinquished 'elements of his prerogatives' the people embraced republican values, becoming more impudent in their desire for a greater share in power. The conflict that ensued between the kings' endeavour to regain their authority and the people's thirst for more endangered the Spartan state according to Ramsay. Lycurgus the Lawgiver's (c.820–730 BCE) intervention, however, posed somewhat of a problem for Ramsay (Cyrus). Ramsay recognised that the mixed constitution engendered by Lycurgus had relied on an elective senate to act as a medium between the two extremes, providing solace from the domestic divisions.

While his laws and the education of the people were praised, Ramsay found fault in the idea of breeding men purely for war. It terrorised the liberty and common security of neighbouring states. As all men were brothers, Lycurgus's Spartans became 'enemies' of Greek society who threatened a common union through a need for conquest.[54] Ramsay was thereby able to dismiss the success of a balanced tripartite Spartan constitution, implying it was underpinned by a need for external war rather like Rome.[55] Sparta's behaviour was a dangerous affront to justice and liberty, fuelled by an unnatural bellicosity that was not to be emulated.

A similar attack on regal power was revealed by Athens, where the people slowly began to accumulate authority in the state with the birth of the Archons (eight century BCE): magistrates who formed the executive of Athens. Over a period of several centuries faction and intrigue were introduced under the pretence of equality, destroying ranked society.[56] Perpetual disagreement led a tumultuous multitude corrupted by 'excessive liberty' to create disagreement at the slightest perceived umbrage:

> How unhappy is the lot of Mortals! By endeavouring to avoid the frightful evils of popular government, we risk falling into slavery. By flying the inconveniences of royalty [kingship], we become exposed little-by-little to anarchy. The political path is bordered by precipices.[57]

The selfishness, passion, and ambition of the people destroyed their love of country as they pursued egoistical aspirations over the common good of the state. It led to a number of problems for Ramsay that were evident in contemporary Britain. These included extreme riches and poverty, the poor education of children, an unlimited pursuit of pleasure, a multiplicity of laws to combat a corrupted state, and the excessive power of the people.[58] Returning to observations made on English history from the seventeenth century in the *Essay*, Ramsay claimed that the pure democracy of Athens had destroyed both the political system and the wider social fabric. The subordination, order of generation, paternal authority, ranked hereditary society, and inequality that were essential for a virtuous state were washed away by the rampant liberty of the people.[59] Such unbridled selfish power submerged (obedient) traditional society as the people thought little beyond their individual ends. Akin to the warnings of Charles Leslie, the self-absorbed multitude undermined good government, and although despised, absolutism was preferable to popular fury.[60] For Ramsay, Parliament generated a potential precipice for Britain that could only be remedied through a return to ancient monarchy moderated by aristocracy found in antiquity prior to the tribulations experienced by Sparta and Athens.

'Capital of the universe'

While Ramsay's view of republican politics was contemptuous he did admire elements of its commercial behaviour. In Book Seven of *Cyrus*, Ramsay introduced a number of novel ideas concerning the commercial development of Britain that not only married his belief in ancient wisdom with modern innovation, but also asseverated his amalgamation of spiritual and political principles. Following Fénelon's lead, Ramsay discussed the commercial prosperity of the Phoenicians at Tyre, who utilised their mastery of the seas and navigation to augment commerce while attracting foreigners to their ports through free trade.[61] Protected by wise laws commerce flourished, and Ramsay discerned that increased trade would enrich society and express its 'magnificence'.[62] Moving beyond Fénelon's conservative view of frugal Christian economics, Ramsay envisaged a future in which Tyre (Britain) became the '*Capitale de l'univers*' ('Capital of the universe').[63] A city in which the people of all the world's nations would be assembled together to buy and sell. Focusing on its maritime heritage and seafaring aptitudes, Britain would become the world's trading hub as it generated great wealth for the nation and its people.[64]

What Ramsay offered the reader was an alternate Jacobite future Britain in which James Stuart had 'ascended [to] the throne of his ancestors'.[65] Moving back in time, Ramsay used the retrieval of the kingdom of Tyre by Ecnibal (James Stuart) to erase the perceived damage and illegality of the usurper Itobal (William III). Expunging the ascensions of both Queen Anne and King George I muted any narrative requirement to dwell on the unsuccessful Jacobite endeavours of the previous two decades. It allowed Ramsay to proffer an alternative Britain that had not become burdened by destructive and expensive wars with the French. The Nine Years' War and the Wars of the Spanish Succession had debilitated trade and also seen Britain act contrary to its nature by becoming a warmonger.[66] To push his opposition to war with the French further, Ecnibal's restoration was only made possible by the military assistance of the Babylonian king Nebuchadnezzar II (Louis XIV) as part of a revolution.[67] By relying on the (historic) Jacobite necessity for French aid to achieve a victorious restoration, *Cyrus* acknowledged the need of Louis XIV to accomplish realisation. Moreover, Ramsay pushed aside wider apprehensions regarding the impact of French support and the potential influence of the French king by depicting Ecnibal as an entirely independent ruler of Tyre. Any concerns over Ecnibal's suitability to rule were also quashed. James Stuart's education away from his homeland had been further shaped by adversity and his removal from the court's corruption. These were made the foundations of his virtue by Ramsay. For such a king, who had suffered the isolation of separation from his homeland and people, would endeavour to protect and enshrine the public good.[68]

The virtuous Ecnibal is credited with the positive economic changes in the future Britain in which a role is created as the world's trading hub. Rejecting internecine wars with its neighbours (i.e. the French), plus the costly embargos and blockades practised by Itobal, Tyre focused on its mastery of the seas to stimulate economic recovery and prosperity.[69] To attract trade the ports were opened to foreigners, while the nation had been rebuilt by loans to artisans from merchants encouraging recovery. The economy was strengthened by fostering a wider basis of commercial activities. In Britain there would be a three-pronged approach that would see commercial centres thrive as agriculture and manufactures were developed to consolidate a solid economic foundation.[70] Workhouses and manufacturer's factories would ensure growth alongside the activity of merchants, as the removal of monopolies and excessive taxation would force down prices to hearten a competitive market. Ramsay wanted a 'booming trade economy' achieved through a 'well-managed system of money and credit' that would invigorate the economy, maintained by 'a cash-based consumer sector' as coin circulated among the people in a free trade economy.[71] The money generated from this activity would be used to remove the national debt, offset the expenses of war, and build an empire. Ramsay viewed this regulation of commercial behaviour as essential to the health (and wealth) of all nations, from small republics to large monarchies. Fostering a Mandevillian environment of (internal and external) competition through 'Emulation' markets would be catalysed, enabling the state and European economies to flourish.[72]

Ramsay's vision of Britain's future was one of commercial enterprise rather than conquest,[73] and his recognition of the need to inspire positive competition ('Emulation') for greater activity exposed a radical departure from Fénelon's view of trade. Progressing beyond Fénelon's Christian agrarianism or proto-communism, Ramsay's alternative vision of Tyre acknowledged the trade in superfluities to enrich the nation.[74] Ramsay's attitude to luxury may at times appear puzzling. While occasionally censuring the corrupting effects of 'voluptuousness' and luxury, his economic system relied upon valuable trade that included superfluities, which according to Fénelon's definition would necessitate luxury items. Ramsay therefore walked a line between Fénelon and Mandeville, which was much closer to the thought of the latter. Like Montesquieu before him,[75] his view did not embrace luxury and vice in the same vein as Mandeville, but he accepted its place to build a realistically prosperous economy and global expansion. Combined with his appreciation of the necessity for emulation to a state both internally and externally, Ramsay proposed a third economic way between the two thinkers.[76] A path that did not impose restrictions on the market to provide it with freedoms like Mandeville but which trusted in the possibility of virtue in such an environment. This belief in virtue is evident in the Athenian innovation Ramsay transposed into a Jacobite Britain. Impressed by the Athenian use of the naval fleet to trade and produce civic virtue, Ramsay wanted to create a seaborne commercial militia.[77] In which, sailors would be able to pursue their moneymaking interests for private gain and to boost the coffers of the state in revenue; yet in times of national emergency, it was incumbent upon these sailors to fight as a navy for the nation. This essentially advocated the use of a British militia at sea to generate commercial wealth for the state at home, while affording the protection of the island nation from foreign attack. Harnessing Britain's strength as a maritime nation safeguarded and protected its commercial interests while expanding globally. It additionally qualified it to act as a balance for its neighbours intervening in wars if required to ensure peace.

Ramsay's depiction of a virtuous Britain bringing commercial wealth and military security to its neighbours was part of a larger vision of a new Europe. As a seafaring nation Britain not only enjoyed a role as the world's trading hub, it was playing to its strength as part of a larger whole. Europe was depicted by Ramsay as a block of cooperative trading units (or states), containing bigger and smaller units. Each made their own contribution to the whole by playing on their strengths as either land-based or seafaring states, with Britain at its centre.[78] Using the ancient Greek leagues as a model – in which separate republics worked together to defend Greece as a unified whole when attacked[79] – Ramsay envisaged a collaborative Europe that concentrated on trading with each other.[80] Considering the geopolitical context in which he was writing this is an intriguing suggestion. It is clear from Ramsay's use of Louis XIV's aid to effect a Jacobite restoration in his alternative future Britain, and his attacks on William III's bellicose foreign policy, that he disagreed with antagonism towards the French. Possibly encouraged by the Quadruple Alliance (1718) of the British, French, Holy Roman Empire, and Dutch, Ramsay supposed it was possible for old enemies to work cooperatively together. During what J.G.A. Pocock has termed the 'post-Utrecht Enlightenment', the Treaty of Utrecht (1713) sparked a brief period in which the 'mutual emulation of commerce and manners' led to a time of greater communication between European states.[81] The ending of confessional wars of religion permitted states to emphasise their commercial interests as they rebuilt their financially weakened economies following the War of the Spanish Succession (1701–14). Seizing on this momentum, Ramsay's Europe was one that embraced the opportunity to state-build through supportive international relations. This was a bold suggestion, for, despite the peace treaty between the British and French being nearly a decade old in 1727, there was still a great deal of distrust between the two states. Yet this vision was broader than a simple focus on improved relations with France, and it was not an acceptance of the Gallican economic or foreign policy models.[82] Ramsay indubitably desired improved Anglo-French relations; but this would have been accommodated as part of enhanced European-wide interaction with all of Britain's neighbours.

As these nations recognised the rationality of improved economic links and progress, with Britain placed at the centre of change.

Two other factors should be mentioned here which acted as an impetus for this cooperative European trading plan. The first is Fénelon, who had discussed a similar notion regarding Europe in his *Supplément* to the *Examen de conscience sur les devoirs de la Royauté*. This work imagined a Europe tied together by bounds of commerce and love, in which a union of states would provide lasting peace. Fénelon's Christian conception of all men as 'brothers' can be found here,[83] informed by his fusion of Judaeo-Christian and classical ethics. Ramsay transplanted this factor of brotherhood into both the *Essay* and *Cyrus*, trusting on it as a foundation for the state to forge unity among its people. On a grander scale, he believed because all men were brothers the world was in essence 'one city'.[84] In his undertaking to recreate wisdom from the Golden Age in the present, Ramsay allied his belief in God's universal love of all people (and religions) to the idea of a shared morality or commonality (brotherhood). Promoting cooperation between peoples and states was a means to rediscover the ancient knowledge fragmented with the loss of the Golden Age.[85] Truth, justice, wisdom, and virtue could be recovered if the (souls of the) people scattered by the coming of the Iron Age were reunited. By searching ancient texts and religions for their wisdom, modern knowledge could be applied to uncover their truths restoring love and order to the universe.[86] Economic and political cooperation between states made steps towards the rediscovery of the lost truths of the Golden Age. It promoted the bonds of unity between people that extended beyond nations, and the interaction generated would initiate a plethora of perspectives to be shared.

Ramsay's bold plan underlines his ambiguity as a theorist. While espousing Fénelon's condemnation of voluptuousness in the people for its effeminising effects on the state and its moral character, like Mandeville he recognised that emulation and the trade in superfluities were essential to the prosperity of modern nations. Rejecting Fénelonian simplicity, commercial investment and innovation became necessary elements of eighteenth-century political economy and state policy. Ramsay's employment of Fénelonian principles was restricted to the application of ancient wisdom and religion to propound moral leadership in an ordered society that nurtured unity. Many ideas surrounding this were blurred by a number of other influences, and Ramsay's desire to return to an ancient deistic knowledge of natural laws that had been lost. For Ramsay, this ancient knowledge was perfectly congruent with modern society, just as his theological views were compatible with the science of Newton. What was singular and perhaps odd when considered in light of his economic views, was his desire to extirpate a Parliament so enmeshed in the British political system. His understanding of English and classical history had created a picture that saw any form of popular involvement in government (republicanism) as a divisive threat to society and the state. In the *Essay* particularly, Ramsay's untenable solution encouraged the return and education of a king redolent of Charles II who was preserved by Bossuet's French absolutism. Grafted to this king was an amalgamation of French theories of an aristocratic-led reform to create a hereditary senate. This would fuse English country principles of an ancient Gothic balance to protect Britain from faction and exclude the Commons. While this robust form of monarchy remained in *Cyrus*, it was tempered by an acute appreciation of political economy's importance. Britain's (alternate) future greatness as the central world power and economic hub was therefore reliant on the direction of a strong monarch (James Stuart) to maintain civic virtue and build its economic pre-eminence.

Bolingbroke's society of order

Despite the less practical elements in Ramsay's theory, there were parts that may have appealed to his contemporaries and it is possible that Bolingbroke was among them. During this period Bolingbroke met and spent time with Ramsay in the *Club de l'Entresol*, at a time when Ramsay was reading parts of *Le Voyage de Cyrus* to its members.[87] Interestingly, Bolingbroke also advocated the juxtaposition of commerce with a focus on naval interests. Continuing his opposition to a standing army, Bolingbroke called for the British to move away from a land army towards a concentration on naval supremacy.[88] This would pull Britain from expensive and unreasonable European wars, enabling it to become a balance in future conflicts by acting as a naval power. This change in focus sanctioned Britain to play to its natural strengths as an island nation, while turning its focus inward to promote the internal health of the nation. The stimulation of commerce within Britain through trade would ease the burden of excessive taxation on the people and help to remove the public debt. Improved wealth under a Patriot King's commercial policy would enable greater investment in manufacture thereby driving up domestic productivity and profit, assisting trade abroad and with the colonies.[89] A Patriot King would direct his government to do all he could to augment trade and commerce for the benefit of the nation and ease of his people. Like Ramsay, the generation of commercial wealth through naval power was efficacious for an island nation's trade, defence, and virtue.

As discussed in Chapter 3, elements of Fénelon's *Télémaque* can be spied in Bolingbroke's *Patriot King*. He possessed the same preoccupations while embracing the people's liberty, enshrining the public good in government, using the king as a paragon of virtue for his people to emulate, and educating the king to rule effectively.[90] Aspects of this education of a prince were also contained in

Cyrus, and while Bolingbroke and Ramsay had different end points – the former to liberate government, the latter to restrain it – the natural law system they relied on to support their systems was very similar. Underpinning Bolingbroke's political principles was a view of natural law and philosophy formulated after his exile in France.[91] Both men's appreciation of French thought is central to understanding their interpretations of the genesis of civil government. Set out in the *Fragments or Minutes of Essays* and composed between 1727 and 1733, the work was sent to his friend Alexander Pope (1688–1744) the poet. Coalescing with seventeenth-century Tory (court) ideology seen in Blackall, Leslie, and others, Bolingbroke's natural law system spurned the Hobbesian idea of a state of nature in which individuality abounded through a contract.[92] Like Ramsay, scriptural revelation was rejected as the basis of the system and Bolingbroke claimed that society had always existed through the association of the family. The laws of nature dictated that society was directed by self-love, a combination of mutual dependence and sociability, held together under the paternal government of family which fortified the happiness of man.[93] From this primitive form of government civil society arose, as the demands of an expanding population required a more robust measure of paternal leadership in the shape of monarchy.[94] Bolingbroke disputed the notion that government would have been democratic – due to 'natural freedom and natural equality' – as the obvious form of government was kingship. This replicated the family, with a king (father) at its head, and the vast majority of the multitude comfortable in their subordination, familiar with paternal authority. Patriarchal civil society was a natural progression in an expanding world.[95] It maintained the unity of the people, while guaranteeing their liberty by precluding the chaos of democratic government produced through multiple leaders.[96] An 'absolute power' placed somewhere in government – lodged in any part of the constitution[97] – provided the facility to act in an unlimited capacity if required,[98] unifying the whole while embracing mutual dependence.

Bolingbroke claimed that government was one of consent from 'human institution, established by the people, and for the people', although this was not the consent of Whig ideology.[99] His idea of consent was an older conception, in which the good of the governed was not met through a contract but was generated from a paternalistic perception of authority where knowing what was best for the people implied consent. There was no literal compact between the people and its rulers, as the covenant was created between the head of the family unit and the prince when forming civil society, although government had been formed by men.[100] Bolingbroke's form of consent expressed a commitment to his belief in aristocratic society, governed by a rigid system of rank that prohibited freedom and equality. This was exposed by the social mobility facilitated through the Financial Revolution beginning under William III in the 1690s, which had started to undermine the social fabric and political order in the 1720s according to Bolingbroke. To counter this development, Bolingbroke attempted to ensure aristocratic prominence at the heart of society and government under the monarch. As discussed in Chapters 4 and 5, revitalisation of the aristocracy was a central consideration for those confronting the legacy of Louis XIV's reign, and for members of the *Entresol*. After eight years of the *Régence* under the duc de Orléans France once more possessed an absolute king, yet ideas for the reform of the monarchy spearheaded by the nobility continued. Bolingbroke harnessed this theoretical momentum to restore the original principle of government as he and Ramsay saw it. Both men believed that aristocracy was important to a revitalised mixed constitution headed by a dynamic and virtuous (patriotic) king.[101] What was fundamentally different, however, was Bolingbroke's adherence to Parliament and the protection of the spirit of public liberty to defend the British from the corruption of government and society by the executive.

Despite this variance, the two men systems were related through their overlapping use of natural law theory. Both relied upon self-love, love of country, unity, patriarchy, subordination, inequality, rank, and a belief that the genesis of government was located in the family. These tenets found in seventeenth- and early eighteenth-century British thought were applied to defend a traditional ordered society in which monarchy governed. What differed with British thought in the 1720s was the detailed treatment of Bossuet's natural philosophy that anchored civil government and man in a religiously conceived view of the universe. Allying religion with history provided an explanation and defence of a traditional society that eschewed the movement towards a popular government that corrupted modern society. While both men could be regarded as nostalgic in some ways,[102] they actually attempted to obtain lessons from the past to aid the present and future. Their observations on commerce, political corruption, and the education of the king to improve government were forward-looking, as was a willingness to use opposing ideology to synthesise solutions. The use of English and Roman history to comprehend the possible trajectory for the ills of British society informed their differing goals to stultify decline. The appeal to the country ideal of original (Gothic) government was designed to replace degeneracy with virtue.

A parliament for an educated prince

These sentiments were sustained in Ramsay's final political work, *A Plan of Education for a Young Prince* (1732). The work once more bid to encourage the advantage of educating a young prince in the arts of governance and morality to produce a moral and virtuous king. Understanding for the individual (prince) began with a clear and 'invincible Demonstration from the Idea of God and the Knowledge of [man's] own Nature' that he had fallen from his original purity.[103] Fortified and improved by a consideration of the rational sciences, the young prince's mind must search for the proofs of deity in material creation to consult with the 'Idea of Infinity'.[104] Following this path ensured that the prince developed his faculty of comprehension, increasing his attributes of 'Power, Wisdom, and Goodness'. Such comprehension would bolster the moral character of the prince as he eschewed evil to embrace a moral virtue founded upon religious truths. This education would allow all men to pursue truth and honesty in their dealings with others. The 'Love of Truth' engendered the 'Candour, Uprightness and Sincerity' that were essential for justice, goodness, and generosity in a king. It meant that a king would know how to appreciate men's talents and virtues, as well as their variations in 'Party, Country, and all the Differences in Religion and Politicks'.[105] From this divine source the 'great Maxims of Politicks and Government' flowed, ensuring that the public interest must always be paramount within a kingdom. A duty to the common good must always be placed above individual or private interest:

> God is the common Father and Prince, and every Kingdom [is] a particular Family of that universal Republick. Hence arises the eternal, immutable Law of Nature and Nations, antecedent to all fictitious, original Contracts betwixt King and People. This Law is, that in all Times, Places, and Circumstances, the Good of the Many is to be prefer'd to that of the Few, and publick to private Interest. We ought not to ruin our Families in order to gratify our own Passions, nor injure our Country to enrich our Family, nor invade the Rights and Privileges of Mankind to aggrandize our Country. Tho' Preservation of Self be our first Duty, yet it ought not to be our only Love.[106]

This highlighted the beginnings of an important change in tack by Ramsay concerning government. Still dismissing the notion of an original contract through a patriarchal 'Love of Order' in an unequal society, the people had to accept their place within the society. Acquiescence by the populace in the principle of order prevented an appeal to the 'Horror' for 'levelling' through the 'anarchical Principle' that created revolution.[107] As in the *Essay* and *Cyrus*, revolution was seen to unhinge government and society leading to a state of anarchy in which men acted like 'Savages'. Order and obedience ensured that the social and governmental status quo were protected, while reason and persuasion would do the rest.[108] Nature had decreed that there must always be a 'supreme, absolute, fix'd and visible Authority' that would defend wider society and the public good. However, Ramsay now argued that the 'Love of Order' and 'supreme' authority enabled the citizen to enjoy their 'Love of Liberty' too. Whether a government be 'lodg'd in one, in few, or in many' the harmony of the nation was paramount at all times. It was the duty of the prince and people to ensure the public good, so 'small Grievances' with lawful government could be accommodated by the multitude. It did not need to push them into a fury that may 'embroil a Nation in Civil Wars'. Yet in a complete volte-face, Ramsay now contended that:

> Kings and Princes may pass the Bounds of their Authority, reverse the End of all Government, and bring a Nation to Ruin by ther Tyranny and Oppression. They may, instead of being the living Images of the most High, become the Votaries and Viceregents of the Devil; to say there are no Bounds to be set to such Licentiousness, is to stake down Men's Minds to the vilest Slavery, and lose all Taste of true Liberty, the noblest Prerogative of our reasonable Natures. Here to teach the Parasitical Principles of an unbounded passive Obedience, is equally cruel to Monarchs, and to Mankind. Princes should be taught on the contrary, that to give their Will for a Rule, is to usurp the Rights of the Divinity, and invade the Privileges of human fraternity: That they have no Right to act against the eternal and immutable Law of universal Good; that Resistance and rebellion will be necessary Consequences of Oppression and Tyranny.[109]

Ramsay's modified theory now stated that hereditary right, which he claimed had never been strictly observed in England, should be concealed from a prince to prevent excessive ambition and potentially despotic behaviour. Instead, a king must obtain their title through the 'universal, free, unbrib'd Consent of the States of a Kingdom' as this was what truly gave the crown its true legitimacy. Freed from his early compunction to eradicate Parliament, Ramsay now reasoned that it was the greatest restraint against the 'two Extreams of Anarchical and Monarchical Frenzy'. The 'States of the Nation, assembled in Parliament ... [was] the best Bridle of the Multitude and of Kings'.[110] His paramount concern over the role of Parliament was its propensity to be corrupted by 'Bribery, Faction, and Prejudices' caused by the failings of weak human nature. The solution to these problems was to be found in Fénelon's own educational maxims located in *Télémaque*.[111] An appropriately rounded education would combine lessons in history, politics, religion, morality, natural philosophy, and mathematics to generate an understanding in the prince of the human condition. In Ramsay's opinion: 'By this Means he will never fall into the Absurdities of false Learning, the Whims of the superficial Virtuoso, not the Meanness of a Pedant, but acquire all the Accomplishments and Virtues of a true Christian, a good Patriot, and a fine Gentleman.'[112] Guided by a rounded education, therefore, a young prince could withstand the tribulations of governing and avoid his own personal defects which may harm the public good. Ramsay had moved from an extirpation of Parliament, a belief in passive obedience, indefeasible hereditary right, and the lack of need for popular legitimacy of an absolute sovereign to the reverse perspective in five years.

So how can Ramsay's dramatic reversal be explained? The first part of the answer is a weightier adoption of Fénelon's educational principles in the last

two political works. Beginning in *Cyrus*, Ramsay started to apply these principles to produce a virtuous and educated king who would be able to withstand
the maladies of civil government. In *Cyrus* these maladies were the same as the
Essay, and they originated in the dichotomy of extremes between the power of
the king and the liberty of the people. Yet what was important for the education of Cyrus was the amalgamation of politics and religion through ancient and
modern thought. This embraced universal truth, the knowledge of which could
withstand the defects of society. Both men relied on a combination of Judaeo-
Christian ethics with classical virtue and erudition. This methodology not only
belonged to Fénelon, it was located in Bossuet too. As a piece of Jacobite propaganda, pedagogy was not the purpose of the *Essay*; instead, it concentrated on
the prevention of revolution and a rejection of 1688. Ramsay targeted the tyrannical behaviour of the populace, drawing on Bossuet's interpretation of revolution to fiercely denounce 1688, the altered succession, and popular government.
The application of Bossuet's French absolutism, wedded to a figure like Charles
II, enabled Ramsay's bastardised view of the English constitution to promote a
return to an ancient Gothic form that eradicated the popular hazard.

Such condemnation subsumed the Fénelonian elements of his principles
as he provided a robust, absolute government that could withstand rebellious
behaviour by the people. In *Cyrus* a strict Jacobite commitment was submerged.
Ramsay was able to focus on the education of the king using a mixture of
Fénelon and Bossuet's principles to access ancient tenets of religion, pedagogical
techniques, as well as commandeering literary elements of their works. What
he provided were political maxims that drew on a religious or deistic understanding of the universe, connected through natural law. This led Ramsay to draw
up an ambitious economic vision of Britain's future under a Stuart monarch,
who headed a strong monarchical government rather than one corrupted by
Parliament: a future Britain which was at the centre of world-trading activity
and political relations, where a cooperative spirit of emulation shaped its global
expansion. His intervention in political economy at the time of the 'Utrecht
Enlightenment' is more reflective of his position as an original thinker, willing to
consider bold ideas for the advantage of the state. Just as he had countenanced
the extirpation of Parliament for the benefit of Britain, his call to stimulate the
British and European economies after decades of war was similarly designed for
the state's good. Never far away, however, was his spiritually infused ethics that
believed in the possibility of rekindling a Golden Age that would usher in a new
era of wisdom, truth, virtue, and justice for humanity.

The second part of the answer regarding his shift in thought is that in
between the publication of *Cyrus* in 1727 and the *Plan* in 1732 Ramsay had
visited Britain. After spending time in the object of his 'plan of government'
Ramsay would have been made truly aware that it was neither desirable nor

possible to extirpate either Parliament or public liberty. It may well be plausible to argue that ideas by theorists such as Bolingbroke, Montesquieu and others filtered into Ramsay's views on politics. The *Plan* certainly moved much closer towards the theoretical trends extant in Britain and France at the time which embraced public liberty, the reliance on a parliament (third estate) in a mixed constitution, and an advocacy of civic virtue over corruption. With the waning of Jacobite activities in the 1720s and Ramsay's own unsuccessful venture in Rome, his Jacobitism became less forceful in *Cyrus*, although he remained committed to the Stuarts. The later political works promulgated his deistic notions of government and history to emphasise the necessity of a good education to produce a strong king who possessed virtue and thwarted modern corruption. Like Montesquieu and Voltaire who visited England at a similar time, the prevalence of liberty and the centrality of Parliament (the Commons) must have impacted upon his political theory. Now under its second Hanoverian monarch (George II), it would have been very clear that much had changed since he left Britain in 1710 and also since the 1719 edition of the *Essay*. Despite an acceptance of Britain's government and the usefulness of Parliament as a bridle for the two extremes of government, it is plausible to maintain that the *Plan* sponsored the future restoration of Charles Edward Stuart. Under a Jacobite prince guided by a deistic education who embraced the settlements following the 1688 Revolution, monarchy would rule through Parliament and control a world-trading empire. This reveals Ramsay's ability to modify his philosophy when required: shifting from an earlier myopic Jacobite view to a sophisticated modern understanding of government that placed Britain at the centre of the 'universe' in a new commercial age.

Notes

1 The 1727 French edition of *Les Voyages de Cyrus* was dedicated to Ramsay's employer, the duc de Sully; the 1727 English edition to Ramsay's friend Lord Lansdowne. The work was not dedicated to Prince Charles Edward Stuart (1720–88), the son of James Stuart and Ramsay's former pupil.

2 Walter Miller, 'Introduction', *Cyropaedia*, trans. and ed. Walter Miller, 2 vols (London, 1960), vii–viii.

3 *Ibid.*, xi–xii. Miller argues that the *Cyropadia* brought together and summarised 'nearly all of Xenophon's literary activity', covering history, geography, custom, military behaviour, statesmanship, ethics, and philosophy. As such, the work straddles all three classifications of Xenophon's works: history, philosophy, and essays (viii).

4 Xenophon, *Cyropaedia*, vol. II, ed. Miller, VIII, 1, 21–42 (317–42). While advice on kingship permeates the work, the *Cyropaedia* is frequently broken down into constituent parts: Book One discusses the young Cyrus's education; Books Two to Seven reflect his military campaigns; and Book Eight reveals the organisation of Cyrus's government and his death.

5 Miller, 'Introduction', *Cyropaedia*, xv.

6 Quentin Skinner, *The Foundations of Modern Political Thought. Volume One: The Renaissance* (Cambridge, 1978), 118.

7 For examples see the Books of Ezra 4:1–6 and Isaiah 41:2–4.

8 Doohwan Ahn, 'From Greece to Babylon: The political thought of Andrew Michael Ramsay

(1686–1743)', *History of European Ideas*, 37, 4, 2011, pp. 421–37 (424).

9 Jane Grogan, 'Many Cyruses: Xenophon's *Cyropaedia* and English Renaissance Humanism', *Hermathena*, 183, Renaissance Greek (winter 2007), pp. 63–74 (63).

10 Ahn, 'From Greece to Babylon', (424). For further background on the use of Xenophon's *Cyropaedia* in the eighteenth century and its employment by Ramsay, see Doohwan Ahn, 'The Politics of Royal Education: Xenophon's *Education of Cyrus* in Early Eighteenth-Century Europe', *Leadership Quarterly*, 19 (2008), pp. 439–52.

11 Xenophon, *Cyropaedia*, Volume One, I, 6, 20–4, 41 (125).

12 *Ibid.*, Volume Two, VIII, 1, 6–8 (309), 1, 14–15 (313), 2, 26 (347).

13 *Ibid.*, Volume One, II, 1, 14–16 (143–5).

14 [P. F. Guyot Desfontaines and F. Granet], *A Supplement to the New Cyropaedia, Part II. The Second Criticism upon Mr. Ramsay's Cyropaedia* (London, 1929), 103–20. After the publication of the original French version of this work in 1728, Ramsay was forced to remove or amend the questioned sections. Another version of this work was published in the same year under the title *A Criticism upon Mr. Ramsay's Travels of Cyrus* (London, 1729). On the frontispiece the later work is attributed to Stephen Whately, who may be the translator of both editions. The works are the same except for the list of 'imitations', which is absent from the second 'Whately' version. Recently this plagiarism has been discussed by Ahn, 'From Greece to Babylon', 426

15 See Bossuet, *Discours sur l'Histoire Universelle*, Œuvres de Bossuet, ed. abbé B. Velat and Yvonne Champailler (Paris, 1961), 962; Andrew Michael Ramsay, *Les Voyages de Cyrus, avec un Discours sur la Mythologie*, Tome Premièr (Paris, 1727), 85; *Supplement*, 103–4: 'It seldom rains in Egypt, but this river which waters the whole through its overflowing'.

16 Bossuet, *Discours sur l'Histoire Universelle*, 959; Ramsay, *Les Voyages de Cyrus*, 93; *Supplement*, 111: 'the kingdom was hereditary, but the kings were obliged more than any other to observe the laws'.

17 See Chapters 6 and 7.

18 D.P. Walker, *'Mon cher Zoroastre' or the Chevalier Ramsay in 'The Ancient Theology'* (London, 1972), 240.

19 Chevalier Ramsay, *Les Voyages de Cyrus*, Tome Premier, Book III, 67; Fénelon, *Télémaque*, 159–60. This view reflects the ancient Greek illustration of such sentiments that proved an inspiration to Fénelon, who believed in the virtue of hard work and simple living. These attitudes are evident in Xenophon's *Cyropaedia* (Volume, I, 6, 2 (87); Volume II, V, 2, 16–19 (29–31), and VII, 5, 72–6 (293–5)).

20 Ramsay, *Voyages de Cyrus*, I, 14; Fénelon, *Télémaque*, 58, 140–7.

21 Ramsay, *Voyages de Cyrus*, II, 43; Fénelon, *Télémaque*, 237–8, 317.

22 Ramsay, *Voyages de Cyrus*, III, 66–79; Fénelon, *Télémaque*, 25, 171–8.

23 Ramsay, *Voyages de Cyrus*, Tome Deuxième, VIII, 87; Ramsay, *Discours sur la Mythologie*, 48.

24 Ramsay, *Voyages de Cyrus*, Tome Deuxième, VIII, 89.

25 *Ibid.*, 76; Ramsay, *A Discourse upon the Theology and Mythology of the Ancients*, 2.

26 Bossuet, *Discours sur l'Histoire Universelle*, 764.

27 *Ibid.*, 953.

28 Ramsay, *Cyrus*, Tome Deuxième, VIII, 76.

29 Ramsay, *Cyrus*, Tome Premier, II, 46–54.

30 Jonathan Israel, *Enlightenment Contested: Philosophy, Modernity, and the Emancipation of Man 1670–1752* (Oxford, 2006), 47.

31 This challenge was taken up by Ramsay in his (personal) magnum opus, *The Philosophical Principles of Natural and Revealed Religion: Unfolded in a Geometrical Order*, 2 vols (Glasgow, 1748). The work attempted to refute Spinoza's ethics (Volume I, 502), through a combination of Newtonian science and deism. In challenging Spinoza, Ramsay followed Fénelon who had attacked theological Spinozism in the *Démonstration de l'existence de Dieu* (Paris, 1718), for his undermining of religious orthodoxy (Part II, chapter ii, Œuvres II, 623–31).

32 Walker, *'Mon cher Zoroastre' or the Chevalier Ramsay in 'The Ancient Theology'*, 262–3.

33 See Cicero, *On the Commonwealth*, I, 2 (3), and *On the Laws*, ed. James E.G. Zetzel (Cambridge, 1999), I, 58 (126). Jay M. Smith has claimed that Ramsay used the model of French patriotism

embraced by Fénelon, in which ancient virtue and a commitment to one's country (especially in the nobility) were promoted for the public good (*Nobility Reimagined: The Patriotic Nation in Eighteenth-Century France* (Cornell, 2005), 109).

34 See Fénelon: *Discours pronouncé au Sacre de l'Électeur de Cologne*, Œuvres II, 949–50; *Tables de Chaulnes*, Œuvres II, 1093–4.

35 Bossuet, *Politique tirée des paroles de l'Ecriture sainte*, ed. Jacques Le Brun (Genève, 1967), V, i, 1 (116), VI, ii, 1 (192–3).

36 Bossuet, *Discours sur l'Histoire Universelle*, 953.

37 Xenophon, *Cyropaedia*, Volume Two, VIII, 5, 24 (407).

38 *Ibid.*, Volume One, I, 6, 20–4 (107–11).

39 Ramsay, *Essay de Politique* (The Hague, 1719), ii–iii, 31–2, 145, 184.

40 Ramsay, *Cyrus*, Tome Premier, III, 76.

41 *Ibid.*, 77–9.

42 *Ibid.*, IV, 137.

43 *Ibid.*, III, 93–4. This attitude was redolent of Fénelon (*Télémaque*, 15, 59, 149–52; *Examen de conscience sur les devoirs de la Royauté*, 975–8).

44 Ramsay, *Cyrus*, Tome Premier, III, 94.

45 *Ibid.*, 95; *Essay de Politique*, 177, 180, 190, 200.

46 See Polybius, *The Histories*, trans. Robin Waterfield and ed. Brian McGrig (Oxford, 2010), VI, 51 (406–7); J.G.A. Pocock, *Barbarism and Religion* (Cambridge, 1999–), vol. III, 209–10.

47 See Quentin Skinner, 'The Principles and Practice of Opposition: The Case of Bolingbroke versus Walpole', *Historical Perspectives: Studies in English Thought and Society, in Honour of J.H. Plumb*, ed. Neil McKendrick (London, 1974), 117; E.J. Hundert, *The Enlightenment's Fable* (Cambridge, 1994), 11.

48 Ahiro Fukuda, *Sovereignty and the Sword: Harrington, Hobbes and Mixed Government in the English Civil Wars* (Oxford, 1997), 15–16, 79–81.

49 Ramsay, *Essay de Politique*, 161–70.

50 See David Wootton, 'Introduction', *Divine Right and Democracy: An Anthology of Political Writing in Stuart England*, ed. David Wootton (London, 1986), 39; Quentin Skinner, *Liberty before Liberalism* (Cambridge, 1998), 30.

51 Ramsay, *Cyrus*, Tome Premier, IV, 115.

52 *Ibid.*, 119–20.

53 *Ibid.*, 115.

54 *Ibid.*, 127; see the 'Capital of the universe' section below.

55 Michael Sonenscher argues that for Ramsay, Rome combined Egypt's stable property regime, Athens' opportunity for individual merit to shine, and Sparta's fierce military patriotism (*Sans-Culottes: An Eighteenth-Century Emblem in the French Revolution* (Princeton, 2008), 246).

56 Ramsay, *Cyrus*, V, 144.

57 *Ibid.*, 154: 'Que le fort des mortels est malheureux: En évitant les maux affreux de gouverne-ment populaire, on court risque de tomber dans l'esclavage: En suyant les inconveniences de la Royauté, on s'expose peu-à-peu à l'Anarchie. De tout côté le chemin politique est bordé de precipices.'

58 *Ibid.*, 145–53.

59 *Ibid.*, 146–7, 148–9.

60 *Ibid.*, 156; Charles Leslie: *The New Association, Part II* (London, 1703), 6–7; *Best of All. Being the Student's Thanks to Mr. Hoadly* (London, 1709), 27–9.

61 *Ibid.*, Tome Deuxième, VII, 34–7. It should be stated that elements of Ramsay's description of Tyre are very similar to Fénelon's *Télémaque*, both stylistically and in terms of content (Fénelon, *Télémaque*, Œuvres II, Troisième livre (29–43)).

62 Ramsay, *Cyrus*, VII, 32–3.

63 *Ibid.*, 26.

64 *Ibid.*, 64.

65 *Ibid.*, 26: 'remonté le trône de ses Ancêstres'.

66 *Ibid.*, 34–5.

67 *Ibid.*, 27–9. Ramsay goes on to describe Nebuchadnezzar II ('Nabucodonosor') as a king who lost his former 'glory' and 'reason' in later years (33).

68 *Ibid.*, 31–2, 34.

69 *Ibid.*, 34.

70 *Ibid.*, 36, 38.

71 Sonenscher, *Sans-Culottes*, 247.

72 Ramsay, *Cyrus*, VII, 36–7. Sophus Reinert has argued that it became essential for states and kings during this period to control the material world and regulate economic relations through policy in order to shape their political destinies (*Translating Empire: Emulation and the Origins of Political Economy* (Harvard, 2011), 27).

73 Sonenscher, *Sans-Culottes*, 246.

74 Ramsay, *Cyrus*, Deuxième Tome, 37.

75 See Montesquieu's discussion of trade and the Troglodytes in Chapter 4.

76 For a comparative discussion on the economic views of Fénelon and Mandeville, see Istvan Hont, 'The Early Enlightenment Debate on Commerce and Luxury', *Cambridge History of Eighteenth-Century Political Thought, Volume I*, eds. Mark Goldie and Robert Wokler (Cambridge, 2006), 383, 387–90.

77 Ramsay, *Cyrus*, Tome Premier, 156–7.

78 *Cyrus*, Tome Deuxième, 37.

79 *Cyrus*, Tome Premier, 127–8.

80 Reinert makes clear that it was not simply the free trade model that was exalted during this period in which peace was promoted to engender greater commercial activity. There also existed a number of theorists who engaged in the 'Jealousy of Trade' idea, and encouraged aggressive competition between states to generate state power and wealth. Ramsay would tend towards the former model eschewing calls for universal monarchy in favour of peace, but he does not call for an end to war and he valued the importance of 'emulation' and competition (*Translating Empire*, 6, 7, 29–32; Istvan Hont, *Jealousy of Trade: International competition and the Nation State in Historical Perspective* (Harvard, 2005), 5–6). For Sonenscher, Ramsay modified the emulation of *Télémaque*'s ancient liberalism which lacked a 'proprietary spirit' towards a more ancient liberal view (*Sans-Culottes*, 236).

81 Reinert, *Translating Empire*, 37. See Pocock, *Barbarism and Religion*, vol. II, 189; Ahn, 'From Greece to Babylon', 430.

82 Ramsay was suggesting a new economic policy for Britain spearheaded by a Stuart king, rather than a seventeenth-century English embrace of Louis XIV's mercantilism (Steve Pincus, *1688: The First Modern Revolution* (Yale, 2009), 134–5).

83 See *Examen de conscience sur les devoirs de la Royauté*, Œuvres II, 1004–6. The *Examen* is more commonly known as *Two Essays on the Ballance of Europe* (London, 1720). It would be quite feasible to suggest that this English version of the work was either published at Ramsay's behest or someone connected to him. Fénelon always made a copy of the works he sent to the duc de Bourgogne and in 1730 Fénelon's copy of the *Supplément* was missing. The Marquis de Fénelon was given Bourgogne's copy of the work by the Beauvilliers family, which had been saved from Louis XIV's conflagration of the prince's papers after his death by Madame de Maintenon and secreted to the Beauvilliers. The *Ballance*'s publication in England while Ramsay was editor of the Archbishop's papers may suggest his involvement in its publication and the later absence of Fénelon's copy from his papers. The Fénelon family eventually published the *Supplément* as part of the *Examen de conscience sur les devoirs de la Royauté* as part of the *Proper Heads of Self-Examination for a King. Drawn up for Use for the late Dauphin of France, Father to his present Majesty K. Lewis XV, whilst Duke of Burgundy. By M. De Fénelon, Archbishop and Duke of Cambray. Together with the Author's Life, A complete Catalogue of His Works, And Memoirs of his Family. Translated from the French* (London, 1747).

84 See Ramsay, *Essay de Politique* (The Hague, 1719), 19–20; Chapter 7 in the present book.

85 Ramsay, *Cyrus*, Tome Deuxième, 8, 9–10.

86 *Ibid.*, 25–6.

87 On the 'circumstantial evidence' of the connection of Bolingbroke and *Les Voyage de Cyrus*, see

Ahn, 'From Greece to Babylon', 433–4. Ahn points to their mutual relationship with Jonathan Swift, and Bolingbroke's referencing of the virtuous King Cyrus. Following Ahn, there is no link to show a promotion of Jacobitism in Bolingbroke's contributions to the *Craftsman* or his later works, and it can be doubted that Cyrus was used to endorse Jacobitism by Ramsay with great vigour.

88 Viscount Bolingbroke, *The Idea of a Patriot King, Political Writings*, ed. David Armitage (Cambridge, 1997), 278–9.

89 *Ibid.*, 274–7.

90 *Ibid.*, 234–6, 280–2, 293–4.

91 There is a great deal of confusion surrounding the influences on Bolingbroke's natural law system. For earlier discussions, see Isaac Kramnick, *Bolingbroke and His Circle* (Harvard, 1968), 106–10; Harvey C. Mansfield, Jr., *Statesmanship and Party Government: A Study of Burke and Bolingbroke* (Chicago, 1965), 53–5; H.T. Dickinson, *Bolingbroke* (London, 1970), 170–1; Barry M. Burrows, 'Whig versus Tory – A Genuine Difference?', *Political Theory*, 4 (1976), pp. 455–69.

92 See Viscount Bolingbroke, *Fragments or Minutes of Essays: The Works of Lord Bolingbroke. Volume IV* (Philadelphia, 1841), 145, 182; Ramsay, *Essay philosophique sur le gouvernement civil* (London, 1721), 26. Burrows claims that this opposition to Hobbes reveals the potential influence of Shaftesbury's *Charactersiticks* on the formation of Bolingbroke's country 'Cosmic Toryism' (466–7). There are crucial discrepancies, however, notably Bolingbroke's (and Ramsay's) belief that sociability was generated by self-love, plus a trenchant application of patriarchal society to retain order, subordination, and prevent chaos among the multitude. Shaftesbury's confidence in natural affection and virtue led him to oppose Hobbes's negative conception of humanity, which expressed a wider contentment with the multitude's importance to society. Shaftesbury (and the 'Lovers of Mankind') thought it ridiculous to despise and fear the multitude as all government was for them, hence 'public good' (*An Essay on the Freedom of Wit and Humour, Charachteristicks* (London, 1711), 76, 88–92, 106–12).

93 Bolingbroke, *Fragments*, 146–7, 164; Ramsay, *Essay*, 10–11.

94 Bolingbroke, *Fragments*, 181, 202; Ramsay, *Essay*, 23, 31–2.

95 Andrew Mansfield, 'Aristocratic Reform and the Extirpation of Parliament in Early Georgian Britain: Andrew Michael Ramsay and French Ideas of Monarchy', *History of European Ideas*, 40, 2 (2014), pp. 185–203 (202).

96 Bolingbroke, *Fragments*, 190; Ramsay, *Essay*, 40.

97 Bolingbroke, *Fragments*, 193, 198; Ramsay, *Essay*, 36.

98 Bolingbroke, *The Idea of a Patriot King*, 231; Ramsay, *Essay*, 37.

99 Bolingbroke, *Fragments*, 194.

100 Kramnick, *Bolingbroke and His Circle*, 94, 99. Bolingbroke rejected Filmer's interpretation of the Adamite evolution of government, as did Ramsay and Bossuet (Ramsay, *Essay*, 40; Bossuet, *Politique*, II, i, 3 (46)).

101 Bolingbroke, *On the Spirit of Patriotism, Political Writings*, 195, 201.

102 Kramnick, *Bolingbroke and His Circle*, 5–6.

103 Chevalier Ramsay, *A Plan of Education for a Young Prince* (London, 1732), x. The work lacked a dedication, and at the time of writing the work he was employed by the Turenne family as tutor to Godefroy de La Tour d'Auvergne (1728–92), later duc de Bouillon. As the possessors of a principality the male children of the senior branch of the Auvergne family were styled princes (of Turenne), so it is conceivable that the work had his pupil in mind when framing the moral character of the student. Yet its inclusion of English government would favour the education of a British prince, so it is likely that the work was meant for his former pupil Prince Charles Edward Stuart (1720–88); or, less likely, one of George II's younger sons. The Turenne's were connected to the Jacobite court through marriage, as James Stuart's sister-in-law (Maria Karolina Sobieska) was the mother of Godefroy.

104 *Ibid.*, ix.

105 *Ibid.*, xi.

106 *Ibid.*, xi–xii.

107 *Ibid.*, xii.
108 *Ibid.*, xii–xiii.
109 *Ibid.*, xiii–xiv.
110 *Ibid.*, xiv.
111 This sentiment is not strictly accurate, as a number of Fénelon's works contained these pedagogical ideals; this includes the *Fables*, *Dialogues des Morts*, *Télémaque*, *Examen de conscience sur les devoirs de la Royauté*, and *Lettre à l'Académie*.
112 Ramsay, *Plan of Education for a Young Prince*, xvi.

Conclusion

Andrew Michael Ramsay's political works offer an intriguing synthesis of ancient and modern thought. Even though they were written at a time when classical ideas were adapted to inform contemporary society, Ramsay produced a distinctive response to contextual issues and theory. The solutions that Ramsay proposed for the ills of eighteenth century British government evolved dramatically over a relatively short period of time. Indeed, it would be fair to argue that his final work performed a volte-face in relation to his earlier principles. These changes were influenced by his personal circumstances, notably his connection to Jacobitism. His association with the Jacobites led Ramsay to use his earlier works as propaganda for the restoration to the British throne of James Stuart. As he became involved with members close to the dethroned prince, Ramsay's Jacobitism became more pronounced. Following the failure of his role as tutor to the young Prince Charles and swift retreat from the Jacobite court in Rome, Ramsay was freed to pursue his own intellectual interests and while remaining a Jacobite, this gave him a fresh perspective. This was evident in *Les Voyages de Cyrus*, which reflected a more overt desire to amalgamate politics and religion through education to recover lost virtue and knowledge for a modern king.[1] The political works accordingly fall into two distinct periods. The first found in the editions of the *Essay* and *Vie de Fénelon*, concentrated on the promotion of Jacobitism through a discourse on the origins of sovereignty in civil government. The second period, contained his pedagogical 'mirror-for-princes' works to educate princes. While the political principles did not shift radically until the *Plan of Education*, his incorporation of politics, religion and political economy to solve social maladies were prominent in *Cyrus* and the *Plan*.

Two important consequences emerge from Ramsay's works for the history of political thought. The first was his relationship with and impact on Fénelon's legacy as a political theorist. For many years, commentators on Fénelon supposed that Ramsay's work and biography replicated the Archbishop's political principles. This was not the case and their diametrically opposed views on the public good – that for Fénelon was focused on the people's needs, while for Ramsay it was for the profit of the king – emphasise divergent opinions on the *raison d'être* of government. While Albert Cherel and G.D. Henderson astutely perceived Ramsay's desire to alter Fénelon's political views to suit his own, the extent of his association with Jacobitism has not been fully appreciated.[2] The meeting and unrecorded conversation between the prelate and the prince was employed as a convenient vehicle by Ramsay for Fénelon's approval of James Stuart. Riding on the back of the immense popularity of *Télémaque*, Ramsay used his role as editor to portray Fénelon as a purveyor of divine right monarchy and religious toleration. Both of these claims were erroneous, but had a lasting effect on the legacy of the Archbishop.

Conversely, Fénelon was rather vociferous in his denunciation of religious schism and was particularly determined to eradicate Jansenism. Although religious attitudes reinforced Fénelon's convictions regarding moral character and virtue as a political pedagogue and adviser to the duc de Bourgogne, it underestimates his political acumen to derive his outlook solely from religious sentimentality. Unlike Ramsay's claims, the Archbishop did not develop a political system from religion. Rather his political works, especially the later *Mémoirs*, reveal a shrewd political pragmatist who made religion subservient to the king as he attempted to offer solutions to Louis XIV's sovereignty. As part of the Burgundy Circle, Fénelon's proposals may have been less realistic than Saint-Simon's and less ambitious than Saint-Pierre's, yet there was a genuine desire to alleviate the suffering of the people and shift government away from the negative politics of aggrandisement. The tendency to focus on *Télémaque* as the location for his political principles remains to this day. But it is in the latter reform works that the real political Fénelon can be found. As editor and biographer Ramsay neglected these works, instead he traded off *Télémaque*'s fame to propound the idea of James Stuart as a contemporary Telemachus.[3] The suppression of Fénelon's more radical desire to escape absolutism by reforming the French monarchy has mired his thought in *Télémaque*. While censorship may have precluded publication in France, Ramsay's concentration on the educational works has ensured that modern critiques of Fénelon's political philosophy are frequently restricted and unreflective of his actual ambitions.

The lack of a political system in Fénelon not only offered a source of attraction for the public when looking at the views in the *Essay*, it meant that Ramsay was inspired by other concealed sources. This stimulus came from Fénelon's nemesis, Bossuet. In Bossuet's works religiosity and politics were firmly entwined to produce a view of civil government and history that harnessed ancient wisdom. Ramsay's application of Bossuet (and Leslie) allowed him to reject the contract and resistance theory underpinning the Whig view of the 1688 Revolution, as well as the neo-Harringtonian country ideology that believed in the positive effects of Machiavellian discord. Instead, revolutions were portrayed as revealing the eternal struggle between two factions within society: a king's pursuit of power and the people's jealousy of the king as they desired greater liberty (political authority). Bossuet's reading of revolution formed the basis of the political theory in the *Essay*, *Vie*, and *Cyrus* as Ramsay railed against the growing power of the people, blaming them for the extreme behaviour within the dichotomy. Bossuet proved to be helpful to Ramsay's 'plan of government' in a second way, and that was his linkage of politics and the deity through natural law. By grounding politics in religion when explaining the genesis of society, Ramsay's presentation of patriarchal monarchy and divine right precluded the people from political power. Wedded to British notions of a traditional ordered and ranked patriarchal society, Ramsay used absolutism to eradicate the ability to revolt and thereby the legitimacy of 1688. This rejection of 1688 enabled Ramsay to advocate a return to his ancient Gothic form of a 'monarchy moderated by aristocracy,' in which the king was aided by an elite hereditary senate to control the people.

Ramsay has therefore been misunderstood and not fully appreciated by many of his commentators. He was far more ambitious than credited and instead of peddling anachronistic views Ramsay should be seen as idiosyncratically engaging with issues in Britain and France during the early Enlightenment. His application of these principles and certain solutions may have been misguided, but initially he struggled to preserve an older form of society and governance assailed by modernity. When he understood that his principles on Parliament were impractical, he shrewdly jettisoned them and adapted his theory to encompass contemporary ideas. This monograph has revealed the extent of his aspirations, as well as the depth of his engagement with contemporary ideology beyond his subjugation by theology. Furthermore, the common belief that religion controlled his political considerations is not accurate until the second period of his works. Frequent references by commentators to Ramsay's domination by religious concerns and his Catholicism are not borne out in the persistent political attack on 1688 for the restoration of James Stuart. Religion did permeate his political system throughout his works, but in the *Essay* the political context was the greater consideration as he posed a rebuttal of 1688. Even in *Cyrus* where the melding of religion and politics was very evident, both considerations were entwined and religion did not dominate his politics. For the *Essay* it was not desirable that religion would be the primary concern. Not only was this a potentially thorny issue due to James Stuart's Catholicism, the purpose of the work was to abjure the British revolutionary settlement. In truth, it could be strongly ventured that Ramsay was not ever truly Catholic, as his works reflect no desire to escape the deism that Fénelon attempted to cure him of through his conversion. Bossuet's thought was not adapted for an appreciation of its Catholic proclivities; rather he extrapolated the deistic implications of virtuous pagans to locate universal truths. It is erroneous to claim that his politics were always primarily concerned by religion or his Catholicism over political considerations.

While the influence of Bossuet continued in *Cyrus* and the *Plan*, a much greater appreciation of Fénelon was evident. In these works Fénelon's pedagogical principles have much greater use for Ramsay as he attempted to delineate the picture of a virtuous king atop a robust government that controlled its people. Both Bossuet and Fénelon's educational works and reliance on antiquity fitted with Ramsay's belief that humanity must search theology and mythology to locate lost universal truths absent since the disappearance of the Golden Age. *Cyrus* concatenated Bossuet and Fénelon's philosophies with a number of other (classical) sources for Ramsay to offer moral government. Bossuet's entwining of politics and religion from God's natural laws as the foundation and maintenance of civil government, plus the manifestation of the deity in history revealed these lost truths. Ramsay eschewed the Bishop's Catholicism to embrace a deistic model of education fuelled by a combination of pan-religious ancient knowledge and modern science. In a sense Bossuet was a kindred spirit. He too fused religion and politics to justify traditional monarchical society, while searching for the bigger questions regarding man's place in the universe. This combination was not to be found in Fénelon's political works, although in *Cyrus* the pedagogical lessons from *Télémaque* can be observed. Benefiting from his plagiarism of Bossuet's descriptions of ancient civilisations, Ramsay took the adventures and essence of *Télémaque* to educate a moral prince. Fénelon's reflections on human behaviour and confidence in humanity's inherent capacity to act beyond oneself through disinterested altruism reflected universal truths present in the ancients. Such lessons offered a path to virtue in the present, and mythology afforded a diverting and digestible medium for young pupils. Fénelon's views on pedagogy were more evident in *Cyrus* and the *Plan*, emphasising the importance of a rounded education for a prince to understand his government and his people. No longer driven by a requirement to promote the Jacobite cause, Ramsay was freed to pursue a greater interest in eclectic knowledge seeking. *Cyrus* was a tribute to Fénelonian principles fused with Bossuet's appreciation for universal truths revealed in history and mythology and added to his own philosophy.

The complex nature of Ramsay's political theory and its influences lead to the second consequence of Ramsay's political works: his role as a conduit between France and Britain. It would be too straightforward to dismiss large parts of his early works as obsolescent for Ramsay exposed a link between British and French political thought on monarchical reform in two instances. The first is through the application of Bossuet and absolutism in the *Essay*. Despite Bossuet's reliance on scripture to justify Louis XIV's system of government in France during the seventeenth century, he was also inspired by the secular ideas of

Hobbes. Bossuet and Louis XIV's engagement with Hobbes's negative use of liberty highlighted a long-standing relationship between the two states in which ideas were passed back and forth within a wider European context. The theory of absolutism for example spread throughout Europe, and Bodin's influence on James I and Hobbes meant that their ideas returned to France and were adapted. As a monarch, Louis XIV endeavoured to actualise the personification of Hobbes's *Leviathan*, offering an apparent model of absolute kingship that proved alluring to both Charles II and James II. Crucially, the seventeenth century witnessed shared experiences in England (Britain) and France, as both suffered from the disunity of religious and political civil wars. Charles II and Louis XIV simultaneously endeavoured to gain independence from the apparatus of government and the nobility to end discord through absolutism.

Values of strong independent monarchy permeated Europe at this time. But while Louis XIV's France provided the apotheosis of absolute monarchy, Britain remained the only large state to resist the ostensible implementation of absolutism. The evolution of parliamentary power from Tudor times provided an obstacle that Louis XIV did not have to contend with. France's constitutional organs had not developed to the extent that its English counterpart had, particularly after the sixteenth century. Oppositional country theory that emerged during the Exclusion Crisis presented a strong rebuttal of the Stuart desire throughout the seventeenth century to gain independence from the active function of Parliament in the legislation. Neo-Harringtonian and country applications of Italian republicanism (representation) and liberty to curb interference by the executive proved to be persistent. Importantly for the history of political thought, its usage to challenge government and social corruption during its Augustan incarnation in the eighteenth century was harnessed by Ramsay before it can be discovered in either *Cato's Letters* or Bolingbroke. Ramsay adapted the examination of Roman history found in Britain and Bossuet, to underline the corruption of the British government due to the prominence of popular power and Parliament. Investing the country ideology, Ramsay called for a return to Machiavellian first principles to reconstitute government according to its original foundation. For Ramsay, Gothic government was mixed, but only between the monarch and a small aristocratic senate. Again predating *Cato's Letters*, Bolingbroke, Montesquieu or Voltaire, Ramsay contended that if the degeneration was not halted the historical examples of Sparta, Athens, Carthage, and Rome would disclose Britain's fatal destiny. This makes Ramsay a pioneer of this historiographical approach as well as an important conduit of thought and methodology, notably through his membership of the *Entresol* and the success of *Cyrus*.

In Ramsay a true mélange of French and British political theory can be observed, and to an extent the two periods of his work mirror the ideology of the two centuries. In the first, his attack on the 1688 Revolution followed an absolutist tradition extant in both countries in the seventeenth century. This eagerly sought unity in sovereignty that had the authority to judge in the *dernier resort*. A model founded on a system that blended religion and politics infused with natural law and divine right theory to underpin the king's power and control of his subjects. His Stuart British monarch would enjoy the powers of Charles II (in Scotland) aided by the counsel of a senate: a bastardised employment of Fénelon's aristocratic-led reform to preserve the status quo. This engagement in Jacobite propaganda would appear to be unsuccessful. His belated intervention in the Leslie–Hoadly–Blackall *Answer* debate regarding the sovereignty of the monarch, attitudes towards the Revolutionary settlement and suspicion of the populace, were obsolete by 1719. The trifecta of the Treaty of Utrecht, George I's successful accession and the failure of the '15, had ended realistic Jacobite aspirations and made the Nonjuror tenets that attacked 1688 redundant.

Ramsay's desire to protect elite society through natural law and the prescription of country philosophy to reform a corrupted government, however, was shared by his associate Bolingbroke. When Ramsay's later reversal finally accepted Fénelon's views of liberty, republican monarchy and the public good after his visit to England, there was considerable overlap between the two men's political theories. While Bolingbroke has been rightly assigned the position of conduit between French and British thought, Ramsay also enjoyed that role and earlier. His membership of the *Entresol*, his contacts in two countries, the success of *Cyrus* and his accolades in England engendered great interest in his ideas. Furthermore, in influencing Bolingbroke's thought it is credible to suggest his impact on Montesquieu, Voltaire and later Enlightenment thinking concerning monarchical reform and kingship. After an initial reaction against the transformations of eighteenth century society and politics, he eventually incorporated these changes to produce a different philosophical outlook. One that searched for truths located in history, religion, (ancient) erudition, mythology, and modern science for the good of the nation. His application of lessons from classical history with country ideology provided very early opposition to the burgeoning Hanoverian Whig government, predating *Cato's Letters* and the *Craftsman*. Married to French ideas of kingship and aristocrat-led reform, Ramsay offered a bridge between the two state's political thought. A role previously inadequately appreciated. By the end of his second period, Ramsay's views of a king who ruled through Parliament at the head of a global trading empire were far closer to British contemporary thought. It principally shared many features with a number of French thinkers post-Louis XIV, who enshrined the need for strong monarchy in an expanded government. Yet it was Ramsay's vision of a cooperative Europe bound by the competition of trade with Britain at its centre that was particularly striking. This grasp of Britain's potential destiny exposes Ramsay to have ultimately been a forward-thinking man in the early Enlightenment.

Notes

1 It should be noted that Ramsay did spend much of his adult life as a tutor to the high aristocracy.

2 See Cherel, *Fénelon au XVIIIe Siècle en France (1715–1820): Son Prestige – Son Influence*, 98; Henderson, *Chevalier Ramsay*, 87–9; Jean Molino, '"L'Essai philosophique sur le gouvernement civil": Ramsay ou Fénelon?', 282.

3 Andrew Michael Ramsay, *Essay philosophique sur le gouvernement civil*, Dedication.

Select bibliography

Ramsay's works

Discours de la Poésie Épique, de l'Excellence du Poème de Télémaque in Les Aventures de Télémaque, fils d'Ulysse (Paris, 1717).

Essai Sur le Gouvernement Civil, Où l'on traité De la Nécessité, de l'Origine, des Droits, des Bornes, & des différentes formes de la Souveraineté; Selon les Principes De feu M. François de Salignac de la Mothe-Fénelon, Archevêque Duc de Cambray, Troisième Edition, Revûë, corrigée, & augmentée (London, 1722).

Essay de politique, où l'on traite de la nécessité, de l'Origine, des Droits, des Bornes, et des différentes formes de la Souveraineté. Selon les Principes de l'Auteur de Télémaque (The Hague, 1719).

Essay philosophique Sur le Gouvernement Civil, Où l'on traite De la Nécessité, de l'Origine, des Droits, des Bornes, & des différentes formes de la Souveraineté; Selon les Principes De feu M. François de Salignac de la Mothe-Fénelon, Archevêque Duc de Cambray, Seconde Edition, Revûë, corrigée, & augmentée (London, 1721).

An Essay upon Civil Government, Wherein is set forth, the Necessity, the Origin, the Rights, the Titles, and the Different forms of Sovereignty. With Observations on the Ancient Government of Rome and England. According to the Principles of the late Archbishop of Cambray (London, 1722).

An Essay upon Civil Government, Wherein is set forth, the Necessity, the Origin, the Rights, the Titles, and the Different forms of Sovereignty. With Observations on the Ancient Government of Rome and England: According to the Principles of the late Archbishop of Cambray. Written Originally in French by the Chevalier Ramsay, Author of, The Travels of Cyrus (London, 1732).

Histoire de la vie de Mess. François de Salignac de la Motte-Fénelon, Archveque Duc de Cambrai (The Hague, 1723).

Histoire de la Vie et des Ouvrages de Messire François de Salignac de la Mothe-Fénelon, Archevêque Duc de Cambrai (Amsterdam, 1729).

Life of François Salignac De La Motte Fénelon, Archbishop and Duke of Cambray (London, 1723).

Maxims of Civil Government (Edinburgh, 1722).

A Plan of Education for a Young Prince (London, 1732).

The Philosophical Principles of Natural and Revealed Religion. Unfolded in a Geometrical Order, 2 vols (Glasgow, 1748).

Les Voyages de Cyrus, avec un Discours sur la Mythologie, 2 vols (Paris, 1727).

Manuscript

'Anecdotes de la vie de Messire André Michel de Ramsay … dictés par lui meme peu de jours avant sa mort pressé par les instances réiterées de son Epouze' (Aix-en-Provence, Méjanes Bibliothèque, MS. no. 1188).

Primary sources

[anonymous], *Vox populi, vox dei: Being the True Maxims of Government* (London, 1709).

Atterbury, Francis, *English Advice to the Freeholders of England* (London, 1714).

Barrington, John Shute, *A Dissuasive from Jacobitism* (London, 1713).

——, *The Revolution and Anti-Revolution*, 3rd edn (London, 1714).

——, *The Layman's Letter to the Bishop of Bangor* (London, 1716).

Blackall, Ofspring, *The Divine Institution of Magistracy, and the Gracious Design of Its Institution* (London, 1709).

——, *The Lord Bishop of Exeter's Answer to Mr. Hoadly's Letter* (London, 1709).

Bodin, Jean, *Les six livres de la République*, ed. Gérard Mairet (Paris, 1993).

Boisguilbert, Pierre le, *Le détail de la France; la cause de la diminution de ses biens et la facilité du remède* (Paris, 1696).

Bolingbroke, Viscount, *The Works of Lord Bolingbroke*, 4 vols (Philadelphia, 1841).

——, *Bolingbroke's Political Writings*, ed. David Armitage (Cambridge, 1997).

Bossuet, Jacques, *Œuvres de Bossuet*, ed. abbé B. Velat and Yvonne Champailler (Paris, 1961).

——, *Politique tirée des propres paroles de l'Écriture sainte*, ed. Jacques Le Brun (Genève, 1967).

Defoe, Daniel, *The Two Great Questions Consider'd* (London, 1701).

Fénelon, François, *Les avantures de Télémaque, fils d'Ulysse*, 2 vols (Paris, 1717).

——, *Proper Heads of Self-Examination for a King. Drawn up for Use for the late Dauphin of France, Father to his present Majesty K. Lewis XV, whilst Duke of Burgundy. By M. De Fénelon, Archbishop and Duke of Cambray. Together with the Author's Life, A complete Catalogue of His Works, And Memoirs of his Family. Translated from the French* (London, 1747).

——, *Œuvres de M. François de Salignac de la Mothe Fénelon, Précepteur des Enfants de France, Archevêque-duc de Cambrai* (Paris, 1792).

——, *Œuvres Complètes de François de Salignac de la Mothe Fénelon, Archvêque-duc de Cambrai, Prince du Saint-Empire; Nouvelle edition, mise dans un nouvelle ordre, revue et corrigée avec soin* (10 vols, Paris, 1810).

——, *Œuvres de Fénelon, Archvéque de Cambrai, Publiées d'aprés les manuscripts originaux et les editions les plus correctes Avec un grand nombre de pieces inédites*, ed. J.-A. Lebel (Paris, 1824).

——, *Correspondance de Fénelon*, 18 Tomes, Commentaire de Jean Orcibal avec la collaboration de Jacques Le Brun and Irénée Noye (Genève, 1976–99).

——, *Œuvres I*, ed. Jacques Le Brun (Paris, 1983).

——, *Telemachus*, trans. Patrick Riley (Cambridge, 1994).

——, *Œuvres II*, ed. Jacques Le Brun (Paris, 1997).

Filmer, Sir Robert, *Patriarcha and Other Writings*, ed. Johann P. Sommerville (Cambridge, 1991).

Fletcher of Saltoun, Andrew, *The Political Works of Andrew Fletcher Esq* (London, 1732).

[Harbin, George], *The Hereditary Right of the Crown of England Asserted* (London, 1713).

Harrington, James, *The Commonwealth of Oceana*, ed. J.G.A. Pocock (Cambridge, 1992).

[Hervey, John], *Observations on the Writings of the Craftsman* (London, 1730).

—— *Farther Observations On the Writings of the Craftsman* (London, 1730).

Hickes, George, *The Pretences of the Prince of Wales Examin'd, and Rejected* (London, 1701).

Hoadly, Benjamin, *The Measures of Submission to the Civil Magistrate Consider'd* (London, 1706).

——, *An Humble Reply to the Right Reverend the Lord Bishop of Exeter's Answer* (London, 1709).

——, *Some Considerations Humbly offered to the Right Reverend the Lord Bishop of Exeter* (London, 1709).

—— *The Original and Institutions of Civil Government, Discussed, The Works of Benjamin Hoadly, D. D.*, vol. II, ed. John Hoadly (London, 1773).

Hobbes, Thomas, *Leviathan*, ed. Richard Tuck (Cambridge, 1999).

Lawton, Charlwood, *The Jacobite Principles Vindicated. In Answer to a Letter sent to the Author* (London, 1693).

Leslie, Charles, *The New Association II* (London, 1703).

——, *Best of All: Being the Student's Thanks to Mr. Hoadly* (London, 1709).

——, *The Best Answer Ever Was Made. And to which no Answer Ever will be Made* (London, 1709).

——, *The Finishing Stroke* (London, 1711).

——, *The New Association* (Dublin, 1714).

Locke, John, *Two Treatises of Government*, ed. Peter Laslett (Cambridge, 1999).

Louis XIV, *Mémoires for the Instruction of the Dauphin*, trans. Paul Sonnino (New York, 1970).

Machiavelli, Niccolò, *The Discourses*, trans. Leslie J. Walker, S.J., ed. Bernard Crick (London, 1983).

Mandeville, Bernard, *The Fable of the Bees: Or, Private Vices, Publick Benefits*, ed. F.B. Kaye (Oxford, 1924).

[Marvell, Andrew], *An Account of the Growth of Popery, and Arbitrary Government in England* (Amsterdam, 1677).

Mist, Nathaniel, *A Collection of Miscellany Letters, Selected out of Mist's Weekly Journal*, 2 vols (London, 1722).

Montchrétien, Antoine de, *Traicté de l'oeconomie politique*, ed. Th. Funck-Brentano (Paris, 1889).

Montesquieu, Charles Secondat (Baron de), *Considérations sur les Causes de la Grandeur des Romains et de leur Décadence, Œuvres complètes*, ed. Roger Caillois (Paris, 1951).

——, *Lettres persanes, Œuvres Complètes de Montesquieu, I*, eds Jean Ehrard and Catherine Volpilhac-Auger (Oxford, 2004).

Neville, Henry, *Plato Redivivus, or Dialogues concerning Government*, 3rd edn (London, 1745).

Sacheverell, Henry, *The Perils of False Brethren, both in Church, and State* (London, 1709).

Saint-Pierre, Charles Irénée, *Projet pour rendre la paix perpétuelle en Europe*, 2 vols (Utrecht, 1713).

——, *Discours sur le Polysynodie* (London, 1718).

Saint-Simon, Louis, *Projets de Gouvernement du duc de Bourgogne*, ed. M.P. Mesnard (Paris, 1860).

——, *The Memoirs of the Duke of Saint-Simon on the Reign of Louis XIV and the Regency*, 4 vols in 2, trans. Bayle St John (New York, 1936).

Sidney, Algernon, *Discourses concerning Government*, ed. Thomas G. West (Indiana, 1990).

Shaftesbury, Anthony-Ashley (Third Earl of), *Characteristicks* (London, 1711).

Toland, John, *Anglia Libera* (London, 1701).

Trenchard, John, and Gordon, Thomas, *Cato's Letters or Essays on Liberty, Civil and Religious, and Other Important Subjects*, 4 vols in 2, ed. Ronald Hamowy (Indianapolis, 1995).

Tyrrell, James, *Patriarcha non Monarcha* (London, 1681).

[Vauban], *Projet d'une Dixme Royale* ([Paris], 1707).

Voltaire (François-Marie d'Arouet), *La Henriade de Mr. de Voltaire* (London, 1728).

——, *The History of the Civil Wars of France, Upon which the HENRIADE is grounded* (London, 1728).

——, *Henriade. An Epick Poem* (London, 1732).

——, *Letters Concerning the English Nation* (London, 1733).

——, *Lettres Philosophiques par M. de V**** (Amsterdam, 1734).

Xenophon, *Cyropaedia*, ed. and trans. Walter Miller, 2 vols (London, 1960).

Secondary sources

[anonymous/Whately, Stephen], *A Criticism Upon Mr. Ramsay's Travels of Cyrus, Wherein the Character of CYRUS is clear'd up, and the Many Absurdities, Inconsistencies, Trifling Sentiments, Affected Expressions, Obscurities, Injudicious Reflections, False Quotations, and Notorious Plagiarisms of Mr. Ramsay, are Expos'd and Rectify'd* (London, 1729).

[anonymous], *A Supplement to the New Cyropaedia: or, The Reflections of Cyrus Upon his Travels. In Six Evening Conversations betwixt that prince and his Prime Minister. Being a Criticism on Mr. Ramsay's Cyropaedia. To which is added, Another criticism upon the same Performance. In Four Conversations, betwixt the Marchioness de **** and Two gentlemen of Distinction in France*, translated into English for J. Pemberton (London, 1729).

Ahn, Doohwan, 'From Greece to Babylon: The Political Thought of Andrew Michael Ramsay (1686–1743)', *History of European Ideas*, 37, 4, 2011, pp. 421–37.

Baldi, Marialuisa, *Philosophie et politique chez Andrew Michael Ramsay* (Paris, 2008).

Bausset, Cardinal Louis François de, *Histoire de Fénelon*, 4 vols (Paris, 1850).

Beik, William, *Absolutism and Society in Seventeenth-Century France: State Power and Provincial Aristocracy in Languedoc* (Cambridge, 1985).

—— *Louis XIV and Absolutism: A Brief Study with Documents* (Boston, 2000).

Black, Jeremy, *The Hanoverians: The History of a Dynasty* (London, 2004).

Bonney, Richard, *Political Change in France under Richelieu and Mazarin, 1624–1661* (Oxford, 1978).

Browning, Reed, *Political and Constitutional Ideas of the Court Whigs* (Baton Rouge, 1982).

Burgess, Glenn, *The Politics of the Ancient Constitution: An Introduction to English Political Thought, 1603–1642* (Basingstoke, 1992).

—— *Absolute Monarchy and the Stuart Constitution* (Yale, 1996).

Cagnac, Chanoine Moïse, *Fénelon: Politique tirée de l'Evangile* (Paris, 1912).

Campbell, Peter R., *Power and Politics in Old Regime France 1720–1745* (London, Routledge, 1996).

Cannon, John, *Aristocratic Century: The Peerage of Eighteenth-Century England* (Cambridge, 1984).

Carcassonne, Ely, *Fénelon: l'Homme et l'Œuvre* (Paris, 1946).

Chaussinand-Nogaret, *Guy, La noblesse au XVIIIe siècle. De la Féodalité aux Lumières* (Paris, 1976).

Cherel, Albert, *Fénelon au XVIIIe Siècle en France (1715–1820): Son Prestige – Son Influence* (Paris, 1917).

——, *Un Aventurier Religieux au XVIIIe siècle: André-Michel Ramsay* (Paris, 1926).

Childs, Nick, *A Political Academy in Paris 1724–1731: The Entresol and Its Members* (Oxford, 2000).

Clark, J.C.D., 'A General Theory of Party, Opposition and Government, 1688–1832', *Historical Journal*, 23, 2 (1980), pp. 295–325.

——, *English Society 1688–1832: Ideology, Social Structure and Political Practice during the Ancien Regime* (Cambridge, 1985).

——, *Revolution and Rebellion: State and Society in England in the Seventeenth and Eighteenth Centuries* (Cambridge, 1986).

Cruickshanks, Eveline (ed.), *Ideology and Conspiracy: Aspects of Jacobitism 1689–1759* (Edinburgh, 1982).

—— and Corp, Edward, *The Stuart Court in Exile and the Jacobites* (London, 1995).

Cuche, F. and Le Brun, J. (eds), *Fénelon: Mystique et Politique (1699–1999). Actes du colloque international de Strasbourg pour le troisième centenaire de la publication de Télémaque et de la condamnation des Maximes des Saints* (Paris, 2004).

Cuttica, Cesare, *Sir Robert Filmer (1588–1653) and the Patriotic Monarch: Patriarchalism in Seventeenth-Century Political Thought* (Manchester, 2012).

Cuttica, Cesare and Burgess, Glenn (eds), *Monarchism and Absolutism in Early Modern Europe* (London, 2012).

Daly, James, 'The Idea of Absolute Monarchy in Seventeenth-Century England', *Historical Journal*, 21, 2 (Jun. 1978), pp. 227–50.

—— *Sir Robert Filmer and English Political Thought* (Toronto, 1979).

Devine, T.M., *The Scottish Nation 1700–2000* (London, 1999).

Dornier, Carole and Poulouin, Claudine (eds), *Projets de l'abbé Castel de Saint Pierre (1658–1743): Pour le plus grand bonheur du plus grand nombre* (Caen, 2011).

Drouet, Joseph, *L'Abbé de Saint-Pierre. L'Homme et L'Œuvre* (Paris, 1912).

Eckert, Georg, *'True, Noble, Christian Freethinking': Leben und Werk Andrew Michael Ramsay (1686–1743)* (Münster, 2009).

Ellis, Harold A., *Boulainvilliers and the French Monarchy. Aristocratic Politics in Early Eighteenth-Century France* (Cornell, 1988).

Figgis, J.N., *The Divine Right of Kings* (New York, 1965).

Fukuda, Arihiro, *Sovereignty and the Sword: Harrington, Hobbes and Mixed Government in the English Civil Wars* (Oxford, 1997).

van Gelderen, Martin and Skinner, Quentin, *Republicanism: A Shared European Heritage. Volume II: The Values of Republicanism in Early Modern Europe* (Cambridge, 2002).

Glickman, Gabriel, *The English Catholic Community 1688–1745: Politics, Culture and Ideology* (Woodbridge, 2009).

Goldie, Mark, 'The Roots of True Whiggism 1688–94', *History of Political Thought*, 1, 2 (Jun. 1980).

—, 'John Locke and Anglican Royalism', *Political Studies*, 31 (1983), pp. 61–85.

—, 'The English System of Liberty', *Cambridge History of Eighteenth-Century Political Thought*, eds Mark Goldie and Robert Wokler (Cambridge, 2006).

Goldsmith, M.M., *Private Vices, Public Benefits. Bernard Mandeville's Social and Political Thought* (Cambridge, 1985).

Goré, Jeanne-Lydie, *L'Itinéraire de Fénelon: humanisme et spiritualité*, 2 vols (Paris, 1957).

Habermas, Jürgen, *The Structural Transformation of the Public Sphere: An Inquiry into a Category of Bourgeois Society*, trans. Thomas Burger and Frederick Lawrence (Cambridge, 2002).

Hammersley, Rachel, *The English Republican Tradition and Eighteenth-Century France: Between the Ancients and the Moderns* (Manchester, 2010).

Harris, Tim, *Politics under the Later Stuarts: Party Conflict in a Divided Society 1660–1715* (London, 1993).

Hatton, Ragnhild (ed.), *Louis XIV and Absolutism* (London, 1976).

—, *George I. Elector and King* (London, 1978).

Henderson, G.D., *The Mystics of the North-East* (Aberdeen, 1934).

—, *Chevalier Ramsay* (Edinburgh, 1952).

Henshall, Nicholas, *The Myth of Absolutism: Change and Continuity in Early Modern European Monarchy* (London, 1992).

Holmes, Geoffrey, *British Politics in the Age of Anne*, rev. edn (London, 1987).

—, *The Making of a Great Power: Late Stuart and early Georgian Britain 1660–1722* (London, 1993).

Hoppit, Julian, *A Land of Liberty? England 1689–1727* (Oxford, 2000).

Houston, Alan and Pincus, Steve (eds), *A Nation Transformed: England after the Restoration* (Cambridge, 2001).

Hulliung, Mark, *Montesquieu and the Old Regime* (Berkeley, 1976).

Hundert, E.J., *The Enlightenment's Fable: Bernard Mandeville and the Discovery of Society* (Cambridge, 1994).

Israel, Jonathan, *Radical Enlightenment: Philosophy and the Making of Modernity 1650–1750* (Oxford, 2001).

—, *Enlightenment Contested: Philosophy, Modernity, and the Emancipation of Man 1670–1752* (Oxford, 2006).

Janet, Paul, *Fénelon: His Life and Works*, trans. Victor Leuliette (London, 1914).

Jones, Colin, *The Great Nation: France from Louis XV to Napoleon* (London, 2002).

Jones, J.R., *The First Whigs: The Politics of the Exclusion Crisis 1678–1683* (London, 1963).

Kaiser, Thomas E., 'The Abbe de Saint-Pierre, Public Opinion, and the Reconstitution of the French Monarchy', *Journal of Modern History*, 55, 4 (Dec. 1983), pp. 618–43.

Kanter, Sanford B., 'Archbishop Fénelon's Political Activity: The Focal Point of Power in Dynasticism', *French Historical Studies*, 4, 3 (spring 1966), pp. 320–34.

Kenyon, J.P., *Revolution Principles: The Politics of Party, 1689–1720* (Cambridge, 1977).

—, (ed.), *The Stuart Constitution 1603–1688: Documents and Commentary*, 2nd edn (Cambridge, 1986).

Keohane, Nannerl. O., *Philosophy and the State in France: The Renaissance to the Enlightenment* (Princeton, 1980).

Kidd, Colin, *Subverting Scotland's Past: Scottish Whig Historians and the Creation of an Anglo-British identity, 1689– c.1830* (Cambridge, 1993).

Knights, Mark, *Politics and Opinion in Crisis, 1678–81* (Cambridge, 1994).

Kramnick, Isaac, *Bolingbroke and His Circle: The Politics of Nostalgia in the Age of Walpole* (Harvard, 1968).

Ladurie, Emmanuel Le Roy, *The Ancien Régime: A History of France 1610–1714*, trans. Mark Greengrass (Oxford, 1996).

—, *Saint-Simon ou le système de la Cour* (Paris, 1997).

Lake, Peter and Pincus, Steve (eds), *The Politics of the Public Sphere in Early Modern England* (Manchester, 2007).

Lamoine, Georges, 'Introduction', Andrew Michael Ramsay, *Essais de Politique*, ed. Georges Lamoine (Paris, 2009).

Legay, M.-L., *Les états provinciaux dans le construction de l'état modern* (Geneva, 2001).

Lenman, Bruce, *The Jacobite Risings in Britain 1689–1746* (London, 1980).

McKendrick, Neil (ed.), *Historical Perspectives: Studies in English Thought and Society, in Honour of J.H. Plumb* (London, 1974).

McLynn, Pauline, 'Factionalism among the Exiles in France: The Case of the Chevalier Ramsay and Bishop Atterbury' (Huntingdon, Royal Stuart Society, 1989, Royal Stuart Papers 33).

Mansfield, Andrew, 'Émeric Crucé's *Nouveau Cynée* (1623), Universal Peace and Free Trade', *Journal of Interdisciplinary History of Ideas*, 2, 4 (2013), pp. 2–23.

—, 'Aristocratic Reform and the Extirpation of Parliament in Early Georgian Britain: Andrew Michael Ramsay and French Ideas of Monarchy', *History of European Ideas*, 40, 2 (2014), pp. 185–203.

—, 'Fénelon's Cuckoo: Andrew Michael Ramsay and Archbishop Fénelon', *Fénelon in the Enlightenment: Traditions, Adaptations, and Variations*, eds Christoph Schmitt-Maaß, Stefanie Stockhorst, and Doohwan Ahn (Amsterdam and New York, 2014).

Miller, John, 'The Potential for Absolutism in Later Stuart England', *History*, 69, 226 (Jan. 1984).

Mettam, Roger, *Power and faction in Louis XIV's France* (Oxford, 1988).

Molino, Jean, '"L'Essai philosophique sur le gouvernement civil": Ramsay ou Fénelon?', *La Régence*, ed. Henri Coulet (Paris, 1970).

Monod, Paul Kleber, 'Jacobitism and Country Principles in the Reign of William III', *Historical Journal*, 30, 2 (Jun. 1987), pp. 289–310.

—, *Jacobitism and the English People, 1688–1788* (Cambridge, 1989).

Mousnier, Roland, 'The Exponents and Critics of Absolutism', *The New Cambridge Modern History Vol. IV: The Decline of Spain and the Thirty Years War 1609–48/59*, ed. J.P. Cooper (Cambridge, 1970).

——, *Les institutions de la France sous la monarchie absolue 1589–1789: Société et Etat* (Paris, 1974).

Parker, David, *The Making of French Absolutism* (London, 1983).

Perkins, Merle L. 'The Abbé de Saint-Pierre and the Seventeenth-Century Intellectual Background', *Proceedings of the American Philosophical Society*, 97, 1 (Feb. 1953), pp. 69–76.

——, 'Late Seventeenth-Century Scientific Circles and the Abbé de Saint-Pierre', *Proceedings of the American Philosophical Society*, 102, 4 (Aug. 1958), pp. 404–12.

Pincus, Steve, *1688: The First Modern Revolution* (Yale, 2009).

Pittock, Murray G.H., *The Invention of Scotland: The Stuart Myth and the Scottish Identity, 1638 to the Present* (London, 1991).

Plumb, J.H., *The Growth of Political Stability in England 1675–1725* (London, 1967).

Pocock, J.G.A., 'Machiavelli, Harrington, and English Political Ideologies in the Eighteenth Century', *William and Mary Quarterly*, 3rd series, 22, 4 (Oct. 1965), pp. 549–83.

——, *The Machiavellian Moment. Florentine Political Thought and the Atlantic Republican Tradition* (Princeton, 1975).

——, (ed.), *Three British Revolutions: 1641, 1688, 1776* (Princeton, 1980).

——, *The Ancient Constitution and the Feudal Law: A Study of English Historical Thought in the Seventeenth Century. A Reissue with a Retrospect* (Cambridge, 1987).

——, *Barbarism and Religion Vol. III: The First Decline and Fall*, 5 vols (Cambridge, 1999–).

Pocock, J.G.A., with Schochet, Gordon J., and Schwoerer, Lois G., *The Varieties of Political Thought, 1500–1800* (Cambridge, 1993).

Reinert, Sophus A., *Translating Empire: Emulation and the Origins of Political Economy* (Harvard, 2011).

Richter, Melvin, 'Introduction', *The Political Theory of Montesquieu* (Cambridge, 1977).

Robbins, Caroline, *The Eighteenth-Century Commonwealthman. Studies in the Transmission, Development and Circumstance of English Liberal Thought from the Restoration of Charles II until the War with the Thirteen Colonies* (Harvard, 1961).

Rothkrug, Lionel, *Opposition to Louis XIV: The Political and Social Origins of the French Enlightenment* (Princeton, 1965).

Russell, Major, J., *From Renaissance Monarchy to Absolute Monarchy: French Kings, Nobles and Estates* (Baltimore, 1994).

Schochet, Gordon J., 'Politics and Mass Attitudes in Stuart England', *Historical Journal*, 12, 3 (1969), pp. 413–41.

——, *Patriarchalism in Political Thought: The Authoritarian Family and Political Speculation and Attitudes Especially in Seventeenth-Century England* (Oxford, 1975).

Schuurman, Paul, 'Fénelon on Luxury, War and Trade in the Telemachus', *History of European Ideas*, 38 (2012), pp. 179–99.

Scott, David, *Leviathan: The Rise of Britain as a World Power* (London, 2013).

Scott, Jonathan, *Algernon Sidney and the English Republic, 1623–1677* (Cambridge, 1988).

——, 'Radicalism and Restoration', *Historical Journal*, 31, 2 (1988), pp. 453–67 (458–9).

Shackleton, Robert, *Montesquieu: A Critical Biography* (Oxford, 1961).

Shennan, J.H., Philippe, *Duke of Orléans: Regent of France 1715–1723* (London, 1979).

Shklar, Judith N., *Montesquieu* (Oxford, 1987).

Skinner, Quentin, *The Foundations of Modern Political Thought*. 2 volumes (Cambridge, 1978).

—, *Liberty before Liberalism* (Cambridge, 1998).

Sommerville, J., *Politics and Ideology in England, 1603–1640* (London, 1986).

—, 'Political Ideas in the Early Seventeenth Century: Revisionism and the Case of Absolutism', *Journal of British Studies*, 35, 2, *Revisionisms* (Apr. 1996), pp. 168–94.

Sonenscher, Michael, *Before the Deluge: Public Debt, Inequality, and the Intellectual Origins of the French Revolution* (New Jersey, 2007).

— *Sans-Culottes: An Eighteenth-Century Emblem in the French Revolution* (Princeton, 2008).

Swann, Julian, *Provincial Power and Absolute Monarchy: The Estates General of Burgundy, 1661–1790* (Cambridge, 2003).

Szechi, Daniel, *Jacobitism and Tory Politics, 1710–14* (Edinburgh, 1984).

—, *The Jacobites, Britain and Europe 1688–1788* (Manchester, 1994).

Tapié, Victor-L., *La France de Louis XIII et de Richelieu* (Paris, 1967).

Tayler, Henrietta (ed.), *The Jacobite Court at Rome in 1719: From Original Documents at Fettercairn House and at Windsor Castle* (Edinburgh, 1938).

Tuck, Richard, *The Rights of War and Peace: Political Thought and the International Order from Grotius to Kant* (Oxford, 1999).

Vallance, Edward, *The Glorious Revolution. 1688: Britain's Fight for Liberty* (London, 2007).

Walker, D.P., *'Mon cher Zorastre' or the Chevalier Ramsay* (London, 1972).

Western, J.R., *Monarchy and Revolution: The English State in the 1680s* (London, 1972).

Wootton, David (ed.), 'Introduction', *Divine Right and Democracy: An Anthology of Political Writing in Stuart England* (London, 1986).

—, (ed.), *Republicanism, Liberty, and Commercial Society, 1649–1776* (Stanford, 1994).

Doctoral theses

Ahn, Doohwan, 'British strategy, economic discourse, & the idea of a patriot king 1702–1738' (Cambridge, 2012).

Chapman, P.M., 'Jacobite political argument in England, 1714–66' (Cambridge, 1983).

Index